Domestic Abuse and the Family Justice System

Law and Practice

Domestic Abuse and the Family Justice System

Law and Practice

Professor Jo Delahunty KC,
4 Paper Buildings

Ian McArdle
LLB (Hons), LLM, Solicitor (Non-Practising) and Barrister

Michelle Heeley KC,
No 5 Chambers

Chloë Ashley,
BA (Hons), Pg Dip (Law), Barrister

Bloomsbury Professional

LONDON • DUBLIN • EDINBURGH • NEW YORK • NEW DELHI • SYDNEY

BLOOMSBURY PROFESSIONAL

Bloomsbury Publishing Plc
50 Bedford Square, London, WC1B 3DP, UK
1385 Broadway, New York, 10018, USA

Bloomsbury Publishing Ireland Ltd
29 Earlsfort Terrace, Dublin 2, D02 AY28, Ireland

First published in Great Britain 2026

2

Printed 2026, Reprinted 2026

British Library Cataloguing-in-Publication Data

A catalogue record for this book is available from the British Library.

ISBN: PB: 978 1 52652 771 4
Epdf: 978 1 52652 818 6
Epub: 978 1 52652 772 1

Typeset by Evolution Design & Digital (Kent)
Printed and bound by TJ Books, Padstow

MIX
Paper | Supporting responsible forestry
FSC® C013056

Dedicated to the professionals who work so tirelessly for so little recognition trying to patch up a broken and underfunded system – and to the public who deserve better from it.

Jo Delahunty

To my wife and boys, Lyndsey, Zac, Harry, Oscar and Thomas for your unwavering love, support and tolerance! Now and always. And to my late Grandad – the man I aspire to be. Always loved. Never forgotten. He'd be proud!

Ian McArdle

For Ron Heeley, for his never ending support and love.

Michelle Heeley

For my parents, Rachel and Steve Ashley, with love and thanks for your support and endless patience.

Chloë Ashley

Preface

It is extraordinary to reflect on the fact that *Re H-N & Ors* [2021] EWCA Civ 448 was only the second of two Court of Appeal cases specifically convened to consider how the family courts should address that most insidious form of abuse that infects the health of not just the victim but all those who live in the household – namely partner abuse. There had been more than a 20-year gap between the landmark cases of *Re L* [2000] EWCA Civ 194 and *Re H-N & Ors* yet in that time the Family Court had not seen any lessening of domestic abuse. Rather, it had risen and its forms became more subtle and invasive with the increased availability of the internet and the use of mobile phones as a weapon for coercion and control.

Domestic abuse is now understood to embrace so much more than the deployment of violence by the abuser – emotional and psychological scars of systemic abuse take longer to heal (if they ever do) than bruises after a physical attack. Back in 2021, in his address to the International Family Law Conference in Jersey, the President of the Family Division did not shy away from the harrowing situation we found ourselves in – addressing and dealing with domestic abuse was, he said, 'understandably at the very heart of the court's work'. But, roll on four years and it appears we still have lessons to learn that families have paid the cost of. Consider these examples. It had taken a vigorous campaign spearheaded by Claire Throssell whose two sons, Paul and Jack (aged 12 and 9), were murdered by their father during a contact visit despite known risks, for the government to pledge, on 22 October 2025, to legislate and rebalance 'the presumption in favour of contact' that many victims of violence had said placed them and their children at risk of harm.[1] In *Re M (Children: Contact In Prison)* [2024] EWCA Civ 1104, Peter Jackson LJ held that Lieven J had failed to address the seriousness of the father's conviction for the rape of the mother and the children's best interests – an oversight influenced, at least in part, by her reliance on the presumption of parental involvement.

Re L, V, M, H (Contact: Domestic Violence) [2000] EWCA Civ 1946 could not have given us a better start when, over 20 years ago, the Court of Appeal laid down guidelines for courts and professionals to follow in cases where allegations of domestic violence are made (these were later known as the '*Re L* guidelines').

This book offers its readers a guide as to how the Family Court should approach domestic abuse in light of the decision of *Re L*, right up to the present day up to and

1 Ministry of Justice, 'Government action to protect children from abusive parents' (Gov.uk, 22 October 2025) https://www.gov.uk/government/news/government-action-to-protect-children-from-abusive-parents.

beyond *Re H-N & Ors*. We now have an abundance of material to illuminate our understanding of how the Family Court should deal with allegations of coercive and/or controlling behaviour, psychological and physical abuse including rape and internet exploitation and so called 'parental alienation', now referred to as alienating behaviours.

The challenge for advocates and the judiciary is to seek out the learning and then to apply it in practice. Not all will do so and that's why appeals will continue to be made to higher courts. It would be foolish to assume the number of appeals heard represent anything other than the tip of the iceberg of cases where poor practice and ignorance as to the impact of domestic abuse have led to poor decision-making by the court.

No one thinking about domestic abuse should pigeonhole it as a private law issue. It is not. Domestic abuse is a disease that rots family life to its core. Children in the household become the victims of it and not just because they may get caught in the physical crossfire. It should not have taken until the coming into force of the Domestic Abuse Act 2021 for that to be properly recognised. Local authority 'child in need' files are littered with references to police calls outs for abuse. At the most extreme end, the children are left as victims of parental homicide when abuse reaches a fatal point. In other cases, domestic abuse is a pointer to things going wrong in the family home that put the child's safety directly at risk. Training on spotting domestic abuse, patterns of abuse, controlling and coercive behaviour and potential adult victims and children are essential skills required by all levels of the judiciary, legal and social care professionals.

Failure to spot and engage with the problem may warp the Court's approach to Children Act 1989, s 31 as much as Children Act 1989, s 1, not just because it may impact on the broad canvas of relevant evidence the Court reflects on but also on how the evidence is given by involved adults and the way in which the Court assesses that evidence. Mothers may have issues with recall on child protection issues because of the trauma they themselves have suffered as victims of domestic abuse. That reliability of account may be compounded by the trauma of being required to give evidence when their abuser is a co-respondent and they may still be in a relationship with them or 'tethered' to them by ingrained controlling behaviours. Be aware that, in private or public law cases, abuse and control within the adult relationship may persist in courtroom dynamics and can inhibit the proper exploration in court of the trigger for, and the perpetrator of, the child's injuries. It may also affect welfare options. If a non-perpetrator parent can be guided to understand that protection of the child from further abuse begins with them being separate from and protected from the abuser then adoption may not be inevitable, especially when considering welfare alternatives for older children for whom foster care is the only realistic option absent placement within family.

Thinking a victim can just 'leave the abuser' is simplistic when one considers it takes, on average, 17 attempts to leave an abusive relationship, around three years, six months, and the risk of extreme harm and homicide is greatest at the point of attempted separation.

In a powerful keynote address at The Family Law Week Conference, 'Reframing Private Children Law: Voice, Choice, and Protection in a Changing Landscape', held on 23 October 2025, the Domestic Abuse Commissioner, Dame Nicole Jacobs, urged attendees to drive meaningful change, noting that 'our systems were simply never set up with a full understanding of domestic abuse'.

Those working in the Family Court – whether as a judge, a lawyer, a social work professional or other professional – should not need a further resource on domestic abuse. A book like this should not be required. Yet, the frequency with which domestic abuse – and the Court's approach to it – triggers adverse commentary by campaign groups, the press and the public, and given the published appellate decisions, one cannot dismiss the suggestion that this book is exactly what is required. We have tried within these pages to identify relevant legal principles and then to align them with practical tips as to how to apply them to achieve a trauma-informed, competent practice. It is a book designed to be a trigger point for learning, reflection and discussion. It is not a substitute for self-directed research and updating oneself on the law.

The core message of this book is that 'we cannot be bystanders to poor practice'. Every practitioner has a duty to confront decision-makers, whether that be advocates, judges, social workers, CAFCASS or experts, when proper procedures and training are not being followed and they can only do that if they themselves are properly trained and informed as to what a vulnerable client and families are entitled to expect from them and from the Family Court.

Finally, a word on the structure of the book. We begin with an overview of the Family Court's increasing appreciation of the issues at play within domestic abuse but move on, in Chapter 2, to address the wide lens view through which domestic abuse must be analysed, namely controlling and coercive behaviour. Chapter 3 sets out the key parts of the Domestic Abuse Act 2021, a vital companion to the Children Act 1989, without an appreciation of which no practitioner should go to court. We next turn to our legal cousins in crime to set out how they approach cases which often replicate, in terms of fact, those we encounter in the Family Court. Whilst, of course, criminal legal concepts are not to be imposed into our division, it would be foolish not to lean into that system to extract learning points. It was, after all, crime that led the way in terms of how to best extract reliable evidence from vulnerable witnesses, specifically children; how to (and not to) cross-examine alleged victims of sex abuse; and it was crime that enforced specialist mandatory training for prosecutors in RASSO (rape and serious sexual offences) cases, whereas we have no such lower limit to bring such a case in the Family Court.

We are grateful to Michelle Heeley KC and Chloë Ashley for adding their insight, expertise and experience to this book. Chapters 5–8 then deal with specific aspects of controlling and coercive behaviours, whether that be financial abuse, serious sexual assault such as rape, the mis/use of intimate images and the controversial issue of alienation which is often raised as a rebuttal to domestic abuse allegations. The final chapters (9–15) take the reader through key stages of a family case, from injunctive relief through to fact-finding hearings and welfare disposal without losing sight of issues to be borne in mind at all times such as participation measures and evidence-gathering tools (including covert recording).

We hope readers will update and customise the ‘practice notes’ boxes they will find in each family chapter as their knowledge and practice base expands and that they will share their learning as generously and frankly with colleagues as we have tried to do in this publication.

Professor Jo Delahunty KC

Ian McArdle

5 November 2025

Guidance Note

As with any book which seeks to guide and explore an area of law, case law will feature throughout this book. It is important to note that not all case law is binding on other courts: decisions made by the Supreme Court (or, prior to 1 October 2009, the House of Lords) and the Court of Appeal are binding.

Whilst there may be some decisions made by circuit judges and district judges included in this book, it is important to note that such cases serve to illustrate how the law has been applied in practice: they are not intended to be cited as authority.

Readers and practitioners should have regard to the guidance issued by the President of the Family Division on 24 February 2025[1] which provides:

> '5. It follows that judgments at Circuit and District Judge level should not be cited unless they contain an express statement that the judge intends that the judgment should be citable (i.e. relied upon in the future in respect of that legal issue). Judgments that do not contain such an express statement will not be citable. These judgments can and should be published in the usual way to promote transparency but will not be capable of being referred to as primary authority.
>
> 6. It is not expected that the practice of including a statement as described above will become common. It will not apply to judgments where the judge has applied existing law and/or which provide examples of how the law operates in practice. An express statement that a judgment is intended to be citable should be reserved only for (probably very rare) cases where new ground is being broken. A judge who is considering including such a statement within a published judgment should only do so with the approval of the appropriate leadership judge.'

1 President of the Family Division, *Citation of Authorities: Judgments of Circuit Judges and District Judges* (24 February 2025) https://www.judiciary.uk/wp-content/uploads/2025/02/PFD-Guidance-citation-of-authorities-2025.pdf.

Contents

Table of Statutes

[All references are to paragraph numbers.]

Table of Statutory Instruments

[*All references are to paragraph numbers.*]

Table of Cases

[*All references are to paragraph numbers.*]

O

P

R

S

CHAPTER 1

What is Domestic Abuse?

> 'Domestic violence involves a very serious and significant failure in parenting – failure to protect the child's carer and failure to protect the child emotionally (and in some cases, physically) – which meets any definition of child abuse.'
>
> *Re L & Ors*[1]

INTRODUCTION

1.01 The concept of domestic abuse (DA) is one which the majority of the public *think* they have some understanding of, especially with the concepts of DA and domestic violence being used interchangeably (the evolution of these terms will be the subject of further discussion). The terms DA and domestic violence (DV) have now been part of society's lexicon for as long as most of us can remember. But do we really know what DA is? And do we – as a society – really have an understanding of the effects of DA and what can be done to prevent or manage it? Can we ever safely say that we recognise an abuser and victim in a dysfunctional relationship? These questions are important from a societal perspective but in the Family Court, they are brought into sharper focus and require all those working within the family justice system to grapple with them.

1.02 Whilst DA can be perpetrated by all sexes and genders, statistics consistently reveal that there is a higher prevalence, persistence, severity and impact of violence inflicted by men against female intimate partners.[2] Around 73.5 per cent of DA complaints in the year ending March 2023 were made by women.[3] The World Health Organization estimates that 25 per cent of women in Europe experience physical or sexual violence in the context of an intimate relationship.[4] Nonetheless, as our concept of a 'traditional' family composition

1 *Re L & Ors (Children)* [2000] EWCA Civ 194; [2000] 2 FLR 334.

2 Marianne Hester, 'Who does what to whom? Gender and domestic violence perpetrators in English police records' (2013) 10 European Journal of Criminology 623–37; Stephanie Holt, Helen Buckley and Sadhbh Whelan, 'The impact of exposure to domestic violence on children and young people: A review of the literature' (2008) 32 Child Abuse and Neglect 797–810; Andy Myhill, 'Measuring domestic violence: context is everything' (2017) 1(1) Journal of Gender-Based Violence 33–44; 'Domestic abuse in England and Wales: year ending March 2018' (Office for National Statistics, 2018) https://www.ons.gov.uk/peoplepopulationandcommunity/crimeandjustice/bulletins/domesticabuseinenglandandwales/yearendingmarch2018.

3 Peter Jones, 'DA victim characteristics, England and Wales: year ending March 2023' (Office for National Statistics, 24 November 2023) https://www.ons.gov.uk/peoplepopulationandcommunity/crimeandjustice/articles/domesticabusevictimcharacteristicsenglandandwales/yearendingmarch2023.

4 Ministry of Justice, *DA and Private Law Children Cases: A Literature Review* (Ministry of Justice Analytical Series, 2020).

expands as society diversifies, the traditional gender division of older research needs to be revisited. We have to take account of all forms of LGBTQi+ relationships, power dynamics in multi-generational households and the myriad of household compositions, some long-lasting, some more transient, that we now embrace in our society. It would be naive to suggest that DA does not feature in many different types of relationships. It would be foolhardy not to recognise that cultural, religion, social and sexual stigmas impact on reporting levels, especially to the police, in some marginalised sectors of our divided society.

1.03 The simple fact is that every allegation of DA and every enquiry into it must be fact driven and not assumption based.

1.04 In reality, the ways in which toxic power dynamics can be played out in a family home are infinite and evolve. 'Stalking' or tracking a victim via a location app (overt or covert) on a mobile phone or internet abuse through 'deep fake' porn would not have been imaginable a number of years ago but as technology and our access to it increases, so do the ways in which power can be exercised by an abuser over a victim. The law, and its application through case law and good practice, must not lag in technology's wake. The law relating to DA pervades civil and criminal law and is indiscriminate in the lives it affects. Where abuse exists in a home, it is a poison that infects the family with a legacy that can contaminate generations.

1.05 This book does not engage in gender nor cultural or religious debates or politics concerning the societal causes of DA, that would be a valid but different book. Our book seeks to drills down into the core concept of what the the law in England and Wales currently sees DA to be and how the Family Court does and should address it. The authors proceed on the basis that DA is a scourge on someone's life, however the parties identify themselves or whatever sector of society they come from. The protection of the law should be equally afforded to all who need and seek it.

1.06 DA is a very broad concept. It should be seen through the lens of coercive and controlling behaviour. We propose, in this chapter, to deal with the historical development of DA and its various forms and to devote, separately, a chapter to coercive and controlling behaviour because of its significance. The approach parallels the learning of the Family Court which transitioned from thinking of DA as DV, evolving and widening its understanding to appreciate the impact of abuse that transcends the purely physical such that we now see abuse as an issue to be framed within the wide parameters of controlling and coercive behaviour.

DA IS NOT A NEW CONCEPT

1.07 The problem of DA is not new and yet it persists despite increasing public and professional awareness and a growing political consensus of its toxicity. One view is that the use of the word 'domestic' in describing familial abuse has minimised and reduced this serious form of abuse to a day-to-day/banal/'it happens' type of acceptance of the unacceptable. It somehow minimised abuse that would be, if inflicted on a stranger, considered to be criminal behaviour. Commonplace excuses of old such as 'she asked for it', 'it was only a slap', 'I was teaching her a lesson' made light of an unacceptable form of abuse where society expected the victims to tolerate more than they ought ever to have been subjected to. DA is destructive and has both direct and indirect victims.

Ongoing judicial minimisation of domestic abuse still arises. Notably, *Re C (A Child: Appeal Fact Finding of Domestic Abuse)*[5] concerned the previous judge's approval of a recital that stated that there had been 'limited' abuse from the father.[6] This was despite the serious findings of fact in their judgment. The Court of Appeal decision in *Re M (Children: Contact In Prison)*[7] exposed a lack of appreciation by Lieven J of the seriousness of the father's conviction for the rape of the mother, its impact on her and the implications for the children's contact arrangements. We clearly have some way to go. We have few excuses for that.

1.08 The scourge of DA on our society has long been on the political radar. In 2012, the Labour Party published their policy on DV in which reference was made to the considerable criticism being made of the way in which DA was policed, with few perpetrators being arrested let alone prosecuted for domestically violent acts.[8] The government of the day responded by improving guidance to the police in Home Office Circular 1990/60 which stated that complaints of DV should be recorded and investigated in the same way as crimes committed by strangers. Then take, for example, the Conservative Government saying in 2019 that:

> '... DA destroys lives. It is a cruel and complex crime that can affect anyone, leaving physical and emotional scars that can last a lifetime. No one should have to suffer the pain of this abhorrent crime, particularly at the hands of those closest to them. Children should not have to witness violence and abuse in their own homes. We have a duty to support victims and prevent people from being hurt'.[9]

5 *Re C (A Child: Appeal Fact Finding of Domestic Abuse)* [2025] EWHC 1648 (Fam).

6 *Re C (A Child) (Appeal: Fact-finding: Domestic Abuse)* [2025] EWHC 1648 (Fam).

7 *Re M (Children: Contact In Prison)* [2024] EWCA Civ 1104.

8 Pat Strickland, *Labour Policy on Domestic Violence – 1999- 2010* (House of Commons Library Standard Note SN/HA/3989, 2012) https://researchbriefings.files.parliament.uk/documents/SN03989/SN03989.pdf.

9 Secretary of State for the Home Department, *Transforming the Response to DA: Consultation Response and Draft Bill* (Cm 15, ISBN 978-1-5286-0923-4, 2019), pp 1–3; following the publication of John Devaney, 'Research Review: The Impact of DA on Children' (2015) 12 Irish Probation Journal 79–94.

1.09 2025 saw the Labour Government launch a pilot programme called 'Raneem's Law'[10] which sought to embed DA specialists in 999 control rooms of five police forces[11] with the aim of identifying and providing better support to victims as part of a bid to overhaul emergency responses by the police to DA. The point being made by the selective examples above is that, despite all-party recognition, for the decades that DA has been seen to be a toxic issue that must be eradicated it has not been tackled effectively.

DOMESTIC VIOLENCE OR DOMESTIC ABUSE? WHAT'S IN A WORD? ANSWER? A LOT

1.10 The phrase 'DV' remains common parlance in the Family Court and amongst professionals who work in the family justice system. It is a phrase that all professionals are familiar with. That reductive approach to abuse must change. It came into being at a time when abuse was understood to mainly consist of acts of physical violence in intimate relationships; we now know it can be far more subtle and consist of a wide range of behaviours.

1.11 In recent years, DA has come to be understood as encompassing psychological, emotional and economic abuse, and more recently, coercive and controlling abuse, although these other forms of abuse had been recognised by those working with victim/survivors in the US since the 1970s and 1980s.[12]

1.12 The continued use of the phrase 'DV' undermines the full extent of domestically abusive behaviours which can result in horrendous experiences for direct and indirect victims. Whilst the harm suffered by an episode of physical assault might be obvious, the effects of coercive and controlling behaviour can be equally as devastating with long-lasting effects and a skewed perception of what a healthy relationship should look like.

1.13 The continued use of the term 'DV' perpetuates a trope that misinforms the public and leads, even now, to many a victim thinking that what they are experiencing does not amount to abuse if there are no bruises or broken bones to evidence it. Under reporting is still an issue. The use of 'DA' as a term is more reflective of the spectrum of abuse which lies behind it. We have lessons to hand from long established case law that we should have learned more from. Despite the simple summary in the citation – *Re L (Contact: Domestic Violence)*[13] – the

10 Raneem Oudeh, 22, was murdered along with her mother, Khaola Saleem, at the hands of Ms Oudeh's ex partner, Janbaz Tarin, in 2018. In November 2022 an inquest concluded mistakes made by West Midlands police 'materially contributed' to the women's deaths. On the night they were killed Ms Oudeh called the police four times to report concerns about her safety. The force had records of ten previous call-outs regarding DA incidents linked to violence by Tarin. The murder came about after multiple flags of controlling and obsessive stalking behaviours. See: Senior Coroner for Birmingham and Solihull, *Regulation 28 Report to Prevent Future Deaths* (Coroner's Report, 2022).

11 West Midlands, Northumbria, Northamptonshire, Bedfordshire and Humberside forces.

12 Evan Stark, *Coercive Control: How Men Entrap Women in Personal Life* (2nd edn, New York: Oxford University Press, 2023).

13 *Re L (Contact: Domestic Violence)* (2000) 2 FCR 404; (2000) 2 FLR 334.

Sturge/Glaser research in *Re L* that was so crucial to the court's analysis was far thinking, went wider than DV, and can still offer valuable insights to the careful reader who goes back to it as a source.

RE L & ORS TO *RE H-N & ORS*: AN EVOLUTION?

1.14 The laser-like legal focus of the Court of Appeal was directed towards the impact of DA on the arrangements for children following the separation of their parents in the important cases of *Re L (Contact: Domestic Violence); Re V (Contact: Domestic Violence); Re M (Contact: Domestic Violence); Re H (Contact: Domestic Violence)*. In *Re L & Ors,*[14] the Court of Appeal took the opportunity to undertake a wholesale review of how the Family Court should approach cases in which DV (as it was then referred to) was a feature. Four conjoined appeals were heard, with all four appeals arising out of contact applications where the father's applications for direct contact were refused against a background of DV between the spouses or partners.

1.15 Back in 2000, the Court of Appeal in *Re L & Ors* was assisted on a number of different fronts – far thinking for its time: the Children Act Sub-Committee of the Advisory Board on Family Law gave the Court of Appeal permission to look at their report on parental contact in DV cases and their recommendations.[15] Further, the Official Solicitor acted as Amicus to the Court, who instructed Dr Sturge and Dr Glaser to provide a joint report and to advise the court. Just pause to reflect on the fact that it was to take another 20 years for DA to receive the same level of attention, using the vehicle of four conjoined appeals with a number of interested parties and bodies joined and access to an agreed library of research to draw upon, including the seminal *Harm Report.*[16]

1.16 The Court of Appeal's approach in *Re L & Ors* resulted in the first comprehensive overview of how the Family Court should approach not only the issue of DV but also the interplay between DV and contact with children in cases where there has been – and is – DV.

1.17 Prior to the Court of Appeal considering the individual appeals, the Court made a number of general comments having considered the report from the Sub-Committee and the report of Dr Glaser and Dr Sturge. Those comments remain largely as relevant today as they were in 2000:

(a) Family judges and magistrates need to have a heightened awareness of the consequential impacts (some long-term) that exposure to DV between parents, or between a parent and a partner, can have on children.

14 *Re L & Ors* (n 1).

15 Advisory Board on Family Law: Children Act Sub-Committee, *A Report to the Lord Chancellor on the Question of Parental Contact in Cases where there is Domestic Violence* (HMSO, 2000).

16 Ministry of Justice, *Assessing Risk of Harm to Children and Parents in Private Law Children Cases* (Final Report, 2023).

(b) There has, perhaps, been a tendency in the past for courts not to tackle allegations of domestic violence and to leave them in the background on the premise that they were matters affecting the adults and not relevant to issues regarding the children.

(c) The general principle that contact with the non-resident parent is in the interests of the child may sometimes have discouraged sufficient attention being paid to the adverse effects on children living in the household where violence has occurred.[17]

(d) There is not, however, nor should there be, any presumption that, on proof of domestic violence, the offending parent has to surmount a prima facie barrier of no contact.[18] As a matter of principle, domestic violence of itself cannot constitute a bar to contact. It is one factor in the difficult and delicate balancing exercise of discretion.

(e) In cases of proved domestic violence, as in cases of other proved harm or risk of harm to the child, the court has the task of weighing in the balance the seriousness of the domestic violence, the risks involved and the impact on the child against the positive factors, (if any) of contact between the parent found to have been violent and the child. In this context, the ability of the offending parent to recognise his past conduct, be aware of the need to change and make genuine efforts to do so, will likely be an important consideration.

(f) A court hearing a contact application in which allegations of domestic violence are raised should consider the conduct of both parties towards each other and towards the children, the effect on the children and on the residential parent and the motivation of the parent seeking contact.[19]

(g) In cases of serious domestic violence, the ability of the offending parent to recognise his or her past conduct, to be aware of the need for change and to make genuine efforts to do so, will likely be an important consideration.

(h) On any application for interim contact, when the allegations of domestic violence have not yet been adjudicated upon, the court should give particular consideration to the likely risk of harm to the child, whether physical or emotional, if contact is granted or refused.

(i) The court should ensure, as far as it can, that any risk of harm to the child is minimised [and] the safety of the child and residential parent is secured before, during and after such contact.[20]

17 This remains an issue that had to be readdressed by the Family Justice Council Guidance and the CAFCASS Guidance of 2024/25. A 'pro contact' culture was found to have led to an underappreciation of harm and what protection the victims required (direct and indirect).

18 This facet may have influenced a 'pro contact culture' (as it has been termed). We explore the presumption of parental involvement in a **Chapter 15**.

19 Now encapsulated in Family Procedure Rules 2010 (SI 2010/2955), Practice Direction 12J (PD12J).

20 Consistent with the approach now enshrined in PD12J.

1.18 In dismissing most of the appeals before the Court, Waller LJ offered non-exhaustive key points:

> '1. The effect of children of being exposed to DV between their parents, or one parent as against the other, may up until now have been underestimated by judges and advisers alike;
>
> 2. It follows that alleged domestic violence is a matter that ought to be investigated, and on which findings of fact should be made because, if it is established, its effect on the children exposed to it, and the risk to the residential carer are highly relevant factors in considering orders for contact and their form;
>
> 3. In assessing the relevance of past domestic violence, it is likely to be highly material whether the perpetrator has shown an ability to recognise the wrong [they have] done, and the steps taken to correct the deficiency in the perpetrator's character;
>
> 4. There should, however, be no presumption against contact simply because domestic violence is alleged or proved; domestic violence is not to be elevated to some special category; it is one highly material factor amongst many which may offset the assumption in favour of contact when the difficult balancing exercise is carried out by the judge applying the welfare principle and the welfare check list, section 1(1) and (3) of the Children Act 1989.'

1.19 The Court of Appeal in *Re L & Ors* in 2000 endorsed a two-stage process when dealing with cases in which allegations of DA are made:

(a) a Finding of Fact Hearing is held to determine the truth of the allegations; and

(b) the Court then makes a welfare-based decision about child arrangements, incorporating and weighing up:

  (i) the proven facts concerning DA;

  (ii) the expert evidence concerning the effects of DA on children; and

  (iii) the other factors in the welfare checklist.[21]

RE L & ORS: WHAT CHANGED IN THE FAMILY 'JUSTICE' SYSTEM AS A RESULT OF THIS SEMINAL CASE? 'NOT ENOUGH' IS THE HONEST ANSWER

1.20 *Assessing Risk of Harm to Children and Parents in Private Law Children Cases*,[22] otherwise known as the *Harm Report* was commissioned by the Ministry of Justice in 2019 to achieve a better understanding of the experiences of those

21 *Re L & Ors* (n 1).
22 Ministry of Justice (n 16).

involved in private law children cases, to identify any systemic issues and build a more robust evidence base to inform improvements.

PRACTICE NOTE

The *Harm Report* was considered required reading for the President of the Family Division and the Court of Appeal in the conjoined appeal cases heard in *Re H-N & Ors* which we discuss below. If it was a key guide for the judges in the Court of Appeal, it is essential reading for practitioners involved in DA cases.

Its lessons (as suggested by Jo Delahunty KC and Ian McArdle) can be applied with force to public law as well as private law cases as DA in life does not recognise such neat legal distinctions as our litigation structures contemplate.

DA is often alleged by local authorities in furtherance of threshold criteria in the public law arena. As such, the law and practice relating to DA is as relevant to public law children lawyers as it is to private law children lawyers. Often, the only difference is the lead litigating body – in private law children proceedings, it is more often than not the alleged victim who will plead and pursue the allegations whereas in the public law arena, this task falls to local authorities.

1.21 Although it was conceded by the Harm Panel that there were limits to the evidence and it was not fully representative of all those in the system it represented, it was the most authoritative and comprehensive review of the issue in decades.[23] The *Harm Report* was able to provide an understanding of how effectively the family courts identify and respond to allegations of DA and other serious offences in cases involving disputes between parents about the arrangements for their children.

1.22 It is with some regret and a degree of frustration that we (Jo Delahunty KC and Ian McArdle) note that a number of the issues raised in the *Harm Report* are reminiscent of the difficulties which existed in the family justice system when the Court of Appeal heard the appeals in *Re L & Ors* 20 years past.

1.23 The *Harm Report* noted:

(a) Successive revisions of Practice Direction 12J (PD12J) might not have made much difference in practice, with concerns about resource constraints being particularly prominent. The inability to provide judicial continuity, the large number of litigants-in-person, courts having too little time for each case, the pro-contact culture, the adversarial process of fact finding and the

23 Ministry of Justice (n 16), p 14.

silo working of the Family Court also contribute to the ineffectiveness of PD12J.[24]

(b) The presumption of parental involvement puts a misplaced emphasis on the child's right to a relationship with both parents and the father's right to family life, above the child's welfare and right to be safe from abuse and its effects.[25]

(c) The structure of a Finding of Fact Hearing and the strategies courts have adopted to manage Finding of Fact Hearings within their limited resources are not well suited to determining allegations of DA, particularly long-term abuse, emotional abuse, coercive control, and child sexual abuse. Read more about Finding of Fact Hearings in **Chapter 14**.

(d) Evidence received by the Harm Panel suggests that the Family Court is not obtaining information about the facilities available locally (including local DA support services) to assist any party or the child.[26]

(e) Respondents to the Panel consider that CAFCASS officers are not sufficiently trained to assess risk, that not enough time is allowed to investigate the circumstances of the family, and that risk assessments in section 7 reports are too brief and superficial and do not adequately identify or respond to the effects of DA on the child and the non-abusive parent.[27]

(f) The objective of judicial continuity can be very difficult to achieve.[28]

(g) Cross-examination is often a distressing, humiliating and re-traumatising experience for victims of DA.[29]

(h) The adversarial system rests on an assumption of equality of arms. The reality in private law children proceedings is that many parties are either unequally armed (one party is legally represented and the other is not) or equally unarmed (both lack legal representation so skewed power, intimidation and control in the private relationship is not mitigated in the litigation dynamic).[30]

(i) In criminal proceedings where the allegation is rape, there are evidential provisions which prevent or restrict the questions that can be asked about the victim's sexual history; no such restrictions exist in the Family Court.

(j) PD12J does not define what constitutes an 'unmanageable risk of harm' which judicial participants described as 'the nub of the problem'.[31]

(k) The Family Court is often unwilling to order supervised contact on a long-term basis, despite the Court of Appeal having emphasised that there is no

24 Ministry of Justice (n 16), p 85.
25 Ministry of Justice (n 16), p 87.
26 Ministry of Justice (n 16), p 98.
27 Ministry of Justice (n 16), p 100.
28 Ministry of Justice (n 16).
29 Ministry of Justice (n 16), p 121.
30 Ministry of Justice (n 16).
31 Ministry of Justice (n 16), p 132.

general principle that direct contact should be ruled out if it would require long-term supervision in order to remain safe.[32]

(l) A major theme has emerged that the effect of court-ordered contact was to trap victims of DA in a relationship with their abuser until their children were old enough to be able to make their own decisions. Victims felt that perpetrators had found that they could use the court process to inflict further harm on their victims.[33]

(m) Many submissions from fathers complained that resident mothers exerted complete control over contact and breached contact orders with impunity, and that family courts were not sufficiently robust in enforcing contact orders.[34]

(n) There is a strong association between claims of alienation and DA allegations, with the weight of the research evidence and submission suggesting that accusations of parental alienation were often used to threaten and blame victims of DA who were attempting to protect their children and achieve safer contact arrangements.[35] This issue is discussed in more detail in **Chapter 8**.

(o) Children and resident parents should not be compelled to live with unsafe contact orders and resident parents should not be threatened, blamed or punished for not forcing children to have contact in these circumstances.[36]

(p) The presumption of parental involvement should not remain in its present form.[37]

(q) Orders pursuant to section 91(14) of the Children Act 1989 should not be considered exceptional.[38]

(r) The Child Arrangements Programme should incorporate a procedure for identifying abusive applications and managing them swiftly to a summary conclusion.[39]

(s) It is essential that proper resourcing is provided for Local Authority social workers undertaking work in private law children proceedings, to ensure that section 7 and section 37 reports are completed by experienced social workers who are well trained in DA.[40]

(t) DA Perpetrator Programmes should be more widely available and should be capable of self-referral.[41]

(u) There should be extensive training in the family justice system covering a large number of areas.[42]

32 Ministry of Justice (n 16), p 140; *Re S (A Child) (Child Arrangements Order: Effect of Long-Term Supervised Contact on Welfare)* [2015] EWCA Civ 689.
33 Ministry of Justice (n 16), p 153.
34 Ministry of Justice (n 16), p 158.
35 Ministry of Justice (n 16), p 159.
36 Ministry of Justice (n 16), p 170.
37 Ministry of Justice (n 16), p 174.
38 Ministry of Justice (n 16), p 178.
39 Ministry of Justice (n 16), p 178.
40 Ministry of Justice (n 16), p 182.
41 Ministry of Justice (n 16).
42 Ministry of Justice (n 16), p 184.

(v) Social workers undertaking assessments in private law children proceedings should undergo additional training and be accredited.[43]

(w) There should be ongoing monitoring and oversight of private law children's proceedings to ensure that they are operating effectively to protect all children and victims of DA.[44]

RE H-N & ORS – A SEMINAL CASE

1.24 Two decades after *Re L & Ors*, in January 2021, the Court of Appeal once again heard four conjoined appeals, each of which involved allegations of DA by one parent against the other. The well-known case of *Re H-N & Ors (Children) (DA: Finding of Fact Hearings)*[45] saw the Court of Appeal follow a similar approach as that followed in *Re L & Ors*: the Court of Appeal began their judgment with an overview of how DA had evolved in the Family Court and then offered 'more general guidance about matters which commonly arise in the Family Court and are of great importance'.[46] In addition to the oral and written submissions made on behalf of all four appellants and respondents, the Court of Appeal was assisted by the participation of a number of intervenors, each of whom played an active part in the appeal: Children and Family Court Advisory and Support Service (CAFCASS), Women's Aid, Women's Aid Wales, Rape Crisis, Rights of Women, Families Need Fathers and the Association of Lawyers for Children.[47]

1.25 The Court observed that approximately 22,000 cases come before the Family Court annually which require the Court to engage with the issue of DA. Further, the Court noted that in 2019/20, almost 30,000 applications were made for injunctive orders under the Family Law Act 1996, although there could be a degree of overlap as it is well known that often applications under the Family Law Act 1996 and the Children Act 1989 are linked.

1.26 The Court of Appeal further observed that:

> 'Those responsible for the delivery of Family Justice and for the training of the Family judiciary have for decades focussed on the importance of engaging the court's ability to deal appropriately and insightfully with cases where DA is raised as an issue. The most visible example of this endeavour is Family Proceedings Rule 2010: Practice Direction 12J – Child Arrangements and Contact Orders: DA and Harm ('PD12J') which was originally implemented in 2008'.[48]

43 Ministry of Justice (n 16), p 185.

44 Ministry of Justice (n 16).

45 *Re H-N & Ors (Children) (DA: Finding of Fact Hearings)* [2021] EWCA Civ 448.

46 *Re H-N & Ors* (n 45).

47 Declaration of interest – Professor Jo Delahunty KC acted in *Re T*, one of the successful appellant mothers in *Re H-N & Ors*. She led Chris Barnes and Adele Cameron-Douglas, instructed by Jenny Beck KC (Hons) of Beck Fitzgerald.

48 *Re H-N & Ors* (n 45), [9].

1.27 Emphasising the importance of PD12J, it was reiterated that, 'over the course of 40 detailed paragraphs, PD12J imposes a step-by-step template that courts are *required to follow* in such cases'.[49]

1.28 A number of other useful points were made by the Court of Appeal in *Re H-N & Ors*:

(a) In light of the binary nature of the burden and standard of proof, the responsibility placed upon each of those magistrates and judges in each one of those cases is a weighty one.

(b) Family judges and magistrates also have the responsibility at an earlier stage of proceedings in deciding whether or not it is necessary to conduct a fact-finding hearing and, if so, which of a range of allegations that may be before the court should be the focus of that exercise. Such 'case management' decisions may not be straightforward, yet they too may have a long-lasting impact on the outcome of the court case and the final orders that are, or are not, made.

(c) The task of engaging with and determining allegations of DA is at the very core of the everyday work of the Family Court; is it what family judges do.

(d) The Family Court is engaged in a continuing process aimed at developing and improving its procedures.

(e) The task of reviewing the approach to DA is a complicated one in respect of which the understanding of society, those who work with victims, and politicians and professionals, is developing all the time.

(f) It would be impossible and inappropriate for the Court of Appeal to lay down comprehensive guidance in this judgment aimed at resolving (or even identifying) the many difficulties that are said to exist and which are the very subject of these other more extensive endeavours.

(g) *'Obsolete'* is the approach often seen in the 1980s where, although DV had been established and an injunction granted, judges regarded violence as purely a matter between the adults and not as a factor that would ordinarily be relevant to determining questions about the welfare of children.

(h) PD12J is, and remains, fit for the purpose for which it was designed and properly reflects modern concepts and understanding of DA.

(i) Coercive and/or controlling behaviour should be given greater prominence in family proceedings and should be the primary issue for determination at a Finding of Fact Hearing.

(j) Scott schedules are of limited utility in the Finding of Fact process:

> '... by reducing and then further reducing its field of focus, the court is said to have robbed itself of a vantage point from which to view the quality of the alleged perpetrator's behaviour as a whole and, importantly,

49 *Re H-N & Ors* (n 45), [10] (emphasis added).

removed consideration of whether there was a pattern of coercive and controlling behaviour from its assessment'.[50]

(k) Serious thought is needed to develop a different way of summarising and organising the matters that are to be tried at a Finding of Fact Hearing so that the case a respondent has to meet is clearly spelled out. However, the process of organisation and summary must not so distort the focus of the court proceedings that the question of whether there has been a pattern of behaviour or a course of abusive conduct is not before the court.

(l) The overwhelming majority of DA (particularly abuse perpetrated by men against women) is underpinned by coercive control and it is the overarching issue that ought to be tried first by the court.

(m) The Court of Appeal is confident that the modern approach is already well understood and has become embedded through training and experience in the practice of the vast majority of judges and magistrates sitting in the Family Court.[51]

(n) In cases where an alleged pattern of coercive and/or controlling behaviour falls for determination, and the court has made that issue its primary focus, the need to determine a range of subsidiary date-specific factual allegations will cease to be 'necessary' (unless any particular factual allegation is so serious that it justifies determination irrespective of any alleged pattern of coercive and/or controlling behaviour).

(o) Family courts should avoid analysing evidence of behaviour by the direct application of the criminal law to determine whether an allegation is proved or not proved.

1.29 So far as PD12J is concerned, the Court of Appeal offered the following 'pointers':

(a) PD12J is focused upon 'DA' and 'harm' in the context of 'child arrangements and contact orders'; it does not establish a free-standing jurisdiction to determine DA allegations which are not relevant to the determination of the child welfare issues that are before the court.

(b) PD12J, para 16 is plain that a Finding of Fact Hearing on the issue of DA should be established when such a hearing is *'necessary'* in order to:

   (i) provide a factual basis for any welfare report or other assessment;

   (ii) provide a basis for an accurate assessment of risk;

   (iii) consider any final welfare-based order(s) in relation to child arrangements; or

   (iv) consider the need for a DA-related activity.

50 *Re H-N & Ors* (n 45), [45].

51 This is open to legitimate debate in the family law legal profession in the authors' (family practitioners') experience.

(c) Where a Finding of Fact Hearing is 'necessary', only those allegations which are 'necessary' to support the above processes should be listed for determination.

(d) In every case where DA is alleged, both parents should be asked to describe in short terms (either in written statement or orally at a preliminary hearing) the overall experience of being in a relationship with each other.

WHERE DO WE STAND NOW WITH THE FAMILY COURT AS AN EFFECTIVE FORUM FOR DECISION-MAKING?

1.30 Given that the *Harm Report* was published in June 2020, and *Re H-N & Ors* was heard in 2021 – 20 years after the handing down of judgment in *Re L & Ors* – two questions must be asked: how much has the family justice system *actually* learned in the intervening 20 years, and, as of 2026, a quarter of a century after *Re L & Ors*, how much of that learning has translated into effective practice?

1.31 In truth, (in the view of Jo Delahunty KC and Ian McArdle) the family 'justice' system did not do, and has not done, enough for as many victims as it should and could have done. There has been a lack of effective 'trickle down' of the crucial learning curves evident in *Re L & Ors*, the *Harm Report* and *Re H-N & Ors*. It is this lack of learning and consistent application of good practice by practitioners (whether that be social workers, CAFCASS, the National Youth Advocacy Service (NYAS), barristers or solicitors), the judiciary and magistrates' courts that motivated the commissioning and writing of this book.

THE IMPACT OF DA UPON VICTIMS – DIRECT AND INDIRECT

1.32 DA harms more than its targeted victim. Bystanders are caught up by its impact. Children are exposed and vulnerable. Old school minimisation of the impact of abuse on them must be discarded. Too many times, we still hear platitudes such as 'they were not in the room', 'they didn't hear anything', 'they were asleep'. As was observed in *Re H-N & Ors*, the courts historically regarded DA as purely a matter between adults and 'not as a factor that would ordinarily be relevant to determining questions about the welfare of their children'.[52] This did the children exposed to it a great disservice.

1.33 Jonathan Herring eloquently sets out the effects of DA on children:

> 'Children bear the scars of DA. Living with it infects their every moment, their attitudes, their beliefs and tragically, their future. Children are used by

52 *Re H-N & Ors* (n 45), [24].

abusers as powerful methods of coercive control. We have seen how court proceedings on child welfare have facilitated and enabled this ...'[53]

1.34 During a literature review commissioned by the Ministry of Justice, Dr Adrienne Barnett pointed out that there are a vast range of studies available on the physical, psychological, behavioural, developmental and emotional problems, disorders and traumas sustained by children experiencing DA, who 'may be the most distressed in the population'.[54]

1.35 At least 750,000 children witness DA annually in England and Wales,[55] and it is likely to manifest itself with children's physical, emotional, learning and behavioural development being compromised.[56]

1.36 The scars DA can leave on children were summarised by the London Safeguarding Children Procedures (LSCB) as long ago as 2016 in their report *Safeguarding Children Affected by DA and Violence:*

> 'Children who witness domestic violence suffer emotional and psychological maltreatment. They tend to have low self-esteem and experience increased levels of anxiety, depression, anger and fear, aggressive and violent behaviours, including bullying, lack of conflict resolution skills, lack of empathy for others and poor peer relationships, poor school performance, anti-social behaviour, pregnancy, alcohol and substance misuse, self-blame, hopelessness, shame and apathy, post-traumatic stress disorder – symptoms such as hyper-vigilance, nightmares and intrusive thoughts – images of violence, insomnia, enuresis and over protectiveness of their mother and/or siblings.'[57]

1.37 Following this through to its logical conclusion, children who witness DA should not be treated as witnesses but rather victims of DA in their own right. This assertion is supported by a number of pieces of research.[58] However, it is not

53 Jonathan Herring, *Domestic Abuse and Human Rights* (Cambridge University Press, 2021), 241.

54 Ministry of Justice (n 4).

55 Department of Health, *Secure Futures for Women: Making a Difference* (London, 2002).

56 Audrey Mullender, *Tackling Domestic Violence: Providing Support for Children Who Have Witnessed Domestic Violence* (London: Home Office, 2005).

57 London Safeguarding Children Procedures, 'Safeguarding Children Affected by DA and Violence' (2016) https://www.londonsafeguardingchildrenprocedures.co.uk/sg_ch_dom_abuse.html, [4.2].

58 Jane E M Callaghan, Joanne H Alexander, Judith Sixsmith and Lisa Chiara Fellin, 'Beyond "witnessing" children's experiences of coercive control in domestic violence and abuse' (2018) 33(10) Journal of Interpersonal Violence 1551–81; Danielle McLeod, *Coercive Control: Impacts on Children and Young People in the Family Environment* (Research in Practice, 2018) https://www.researchinpractice.org.uk/media/ybkc4pea/coercive_control_impacts_on_children_and_young_people_in_the_family_environment_literature_review_2018.pdf; Lauren Smith, *Children Experiencing Inter-Parental Coercive Control* (The Institute for Research and Innovation in Social Services (IRISS), 2018) https://www.iriss.org.uk/sites/default/files/2018-04/iriss-esss-outline-children-experiencing-interparental-coercive-control-2018-3-19.pdf; Nicky Stanley, *Children Experiencing Domestic Violence: A Research Review* (Research in Practice, 2011) https://www.researchinpractice.org.uk/media/zssp0cum/children_experiencing_domestic_violence_signpost_summary.pdf.

just experiencing it first-hand which can impact on a child's welfare, with research showing that, even if they are not present, they will be aware of the aftermath of incidents 'and the distorted inter-partner relationships, communications and behaviours' it represents.[59] It is the scars left behind by this exposure to the aftermath of incidents which can lead to the perpetuation of domestically abusive behaviours in generations to come.

1.38 It is for all of these reasons that the status of children as victims of DA now has a statutory footing with the coming into force of the Domestic Abuse Act 2021 (DAA 2021). Section 3 of the Act provides:

'3 **Children as victims of domestic abuse**

(1) This section applies where behaviour of a person ("A") towards another person ("B") is domestic abuse.

(2) Any reference in this Act to a victim of domestic abuse includes a reference to a child who—

(a) sees or hears, experiences the effects of, the abuse, and

(b) is related to A or B.

(3) A child is related to a person for the purposes of subsection (2) if—

(a) the person is a parent of, or has parental responsibility for, the child, or

(b) the child and the person are relatives

…'

1.39 In October 2025, two changes to the law were proposed which, upon implementation, would better respond to the impact of DA upon children. Firstly, the government announced plans to repeal the presumption of parental involvement.[60] This announcement follows years of campaigning from Claire Throssell, a mother whose children were killed by their father after the Court ordered that he should have unsupervised time with them despite Throssell's insistence that he was a danger to them. For what it is worth, we support the express removal of the presumption of parental involvement but regret the fact it has been made necessary – our view, based on case reports and experience, being that, had there been better informed and more consistently applied use of existing law, precedent and practice directions, we would not have needed the government to step in to remedy poor legal practice and psychological ignorance. The removal of the presumption of parental involvement will sharpen the Court's focus on its central duty, ie making arrangements that promote the welfare and best interests of the child unencumbered by any pressure to ensure

59 Claire Sturge, Danya Glaser, 'Contact and domestic violence – the experts' court report' (2000) 30 Family Law 615–29.

60 Ministry of Justice, 'Government action to protect children from abusive parents' (Press release, 22 October 2025) https://www.gov.uk/government/news/government-action-to-protect-children-from-abusive-parents.

ongoing involvement with parents merely because of their status as a parent. Contact is not a matter of rights.

1.40 The second amendment announced in October 2025 was that fathers whose child was born of their rape of the mother, and parents who are found to have committed serious sexual offences on other children, would have their parental responsibility automatically restricted.[61] This amendment is partly motivated by a recognition that the children of such individuals are at risk of harm. It will also protect the other parent who, under the current law, may have to have contact with, possibly co-parent or facilitate contact with their abuser.

TYPES OF DA

What follows is a short resumé of what might be encompassed within the term 'DA' but it is not exhaustive.

> PRACTICE NOTE
>
> Types of abuse can be as unique as the abuser and victim's partner history and individual psychological makeup. What follows below is the most basic of illustrations. By way of example, as same sex partners become less stigmatised by society and willing to seek the Court's protection, sexual preferences and practices that have been manipulated/misused to become part of an abusive control dynamic are now becoming the object of court attention having hitherto been hidden from 'straight' view.

Physical

1.41 One of the most easily understood – and tangible – forms of DA is physical abuse. Punching (closed fist or slap), pinching, biting, kicking, twisting limbs, pushing, being slammed into objects, etc. Physical abuse always comes with emotional and psychological abuse as its companion whereas the reverse may not (or need to) be so. It does not take a highly educated professional to be able to see the physical remnants of an assault and associate it with an incident of DA. Indeed, organisations and charities working with victims of DA have been known to use images of a woman with a blackened eye (arguably, perpetuating the stereotype).

1.42 We start by offering up an understanding of the basic categorisation of assaults available to the criminal courts as they may help practitioners understand

61 Ministry of Justice, 'Thousands of children protected from abuse under victim reforms' (Press release, 20 October 2025) https://www.gov.uk/government/news/thousands-of-children-protected-from-abuse-under-victim-reforms.

some distinctions that mark a scale of seriousness of each form of assault in that forum. These paragraphs are to be read as companions to the far more detailed and authoritative analysis by Michelle Heeley KC and Chloë Ashley in **Chapter 4**. By including this material in this book, we do not seek to import concepts of criminal law into the family field. We provide them for a fuller understanding of how family and criminal courts approach partner abuse. Criminal law showed us the way in which we might hear from very young children in court. It produced the forerunner of the Advocate Toolkits that are now of universal assistance and application when dealing with disability, vulnerability, religion, and culture in court. Looking directly to DA, crime led the way in critically scrutinising the purpose and necessity of permitting cross-examination of complainants on their previous sexual history. We suggest comparison with criminal practice may also help the family practitioner distil potentially important/distinguishing factual characteristics from a client's narrative that may be relevant to spotting aggravating features, identifying the right level of court for litigation and honing in on areas for further exploration/evidence gathering. In *F v M*,[62] Justice Hayden found that various sections of the Serious Crime Act 2015, and the statutory guidance surrounding it, were 'strikingly relevant' to our understanding of controlling and coercive behaviour.[63]

- **Battery/Common Assault**

  Section 39 of the Criminal Justice Act 1988

  Two separate criminal offences are encapsulated by Criminal Justice Act 1988 (CJA 1988), s 39. Common assault is an act during which a person intentionally or recklessly causes another to suffer or apprehend unlawful violence. *Note that this does not require the infliction of any force.* Battery is committed by the intentional and reckless application of unlawful force to another person. Offences contrary to CJA 1988, s 39 are summary only offences, which means that, generally, they can only be heard in the magistrates' court.[64]

- **Assault Occasioning Actual Bodily Harm**

  Section 47 of the Offences Against the Person Act 1861

  This offence builds upon the offence of battery. It requires more than unlawful violence: the battery must result in actual bodily harm. Such harm need not be permanent but must be more than transient and trifling.[65] The Crown Prosecution Service (CPS) provides the following examples of harm which would meet this threshold: damaged teeth or bones, extensive or severe

62 *F v M* [2021] EWFC 4.

63 *F v M* (n 62), [60].

64 The summary nature of the offences ordinarily means that the perpetrator must be charged within six months of the offence. However, CJA 1988, s 39A extends the time in which a prosecution for a domestically abusive offence can be prosecuted so criminal proceedings can be brought within two years from the date of the offence to which the proceedings relate.

65 *R v Donovan* [1934] 2 KB 498.

bruising, cuts requiring suturing and loss of consciousness.[66] This offence can be dealt with in either the magistrates' court or the Crown Court. In the magistrates' court, the maximum sentence which the court can impose is one of six months' imprisonment. In the Crown Court, the maximum sentence which the court can impose is one of five years' imprisonment.

- **Strangulation and Suffocation**

  Section 75A of the Serious Crime Act 2015

  According to the CPS, strangulation is the obstruction or compression of blood vessels and/or airways by external pressure to the neck.[67] Suffocation is the depriving of a person of air which affects their normal breathing. This offence can be dealt with in either the magistrates' court or the Crown Court. In the magistrates' court, the maximum sentence which the court can impose is one of six months' imprisonment. In the Crown Court, the maximum sentence which the court can impose is one of five years' imprisonment.

  Author's Note – we deal with attempted strangulation at **1.40** and following below. For the purposes of this list at this stage simply be aware DAA 2021, s 70 introduced a criminal offence of non-fatal strangulation or non-fatal suffocation, inserting it into the Serious Crime Act 2015 at s 75A.

- **Unlawful Wounding/Inflicting Grievous Bodily Harm**

  Section 20 of the Offences Against the Person Act 1861

  Grievous bodily harm means really serious harm, which requires a break in the continuity of the skin. According to the CPS, grievous bodily harm encompasses harm which has life threatening consequences and/or requires extensive medical treatment.[68] In order to be prosecuted for an offence contrary to Offences Against the Person Act 1861, s 20, the perpetrator must intend or foresee that the act might cause some harm.[69] This offence can be dealt with in either the magistrates court' or the Crown Court. In the magistrates' court, the maximum sentence which the court can impose is one of six months' imprisonment. In the Crown Court, the maximum sentence which the court can impose is one of five years' imprisonment.

- **Wounding/Causing Grievous Bodily Harm with Intent**

  Section 18 of the Offences Against the Person Act 1861

  Using the same definition of grievous bodily harm as above, this offence can only be committed where the grievous bodily harm or wound is intended.

66 Crown Prosecution Service, 'Offences Against the Person, Incorporating the Charging Standard' (last updated October 2024) https://www.cps.gov.uk/legal-guidance/offences-against-person-incorporating-charging-standard#:~:text=Examples%20where%20the%20injury%20is%20most%20likely,extensive%20or%20severe%20bruising.%20cuts%20requiring%20suturing.

67 CPS (n 66).

68 CPS (n 66).

69 *R v Savage; DPP v Parmenter* [1992] 1 AC 699.

This offence can only be heard in the Crown Court and carries a maximum sentence of life imprisonment.

Strangulation and attempted strangulation – the psychological impact on the victim

PRACTICE NOTE

Whilst the use of physical force is shocking in and of itself, the practitioner needs to remember that it need not be the repeated use of force that controls and intimidates the victim. Once force has been unleashed, it demonstrates how far the abuser is prepared to go – a boundary has been breached. Thereafter, the threat hangs in the air. The fear of violence is as controlling as the act itself in many instances – and therein lies a source of coercive and controlling behaviour (see below).

Parallels can be drawn between strangulation and attempted strangulation. An intent to kill through strangulation may not have been in the abuser's mind. Strangulation, pulling back just before or after the loss of consciousness but only stopping at the stage when the victim is terrified and fears for their life, is an act of severe psychological and physical abuse in itself. It is a weapon of control. It says, 'I have the power of life and death over you – don't push me'.

1.43 In recent years, there has been growing awareness about the use of attempted strangulation as a form of DA, albeit not wide enough. It was a form of abuse that was the subject of the successful appeal in the *Re T* case within the conjoined appeals in *Re H-N & Ors*.[70]

1.44 This particularly pernicious form of physical abuse traverses all forms of DA and the impact of it is incapable of overstatement – the physicality of it, the pain of it, the psychological impact of it (the 'not knowing how it will end' or 'if it will end'), the sheer terror of it, all of these reactions can be experienced at any stage, individually or cumulatively. As a form of control, non-fatal strangulation, whether in the family or criminal jurisdictions, represents a serious escalation of power abuse and can be a predictor for fatal abuse. Its seriousness goes to explain why DAA 2021, s 70 introduced a criminal offence of non-fatal strangulation or non-fatal suffocation, inserting it into the Serious Crime Act 2015 at s 75A:

'75A Strangulation or Suffocation

(1) A person ("A") commits an offence if—

(a) A intentionally strangles another person ("B"), or

(b) A does any other act to B that—

70 *Re H-N & Ors* (n 45).

(i) affects B's ability to breathe, and

(ii) constitutes battery of B.

(2) It is a defence to an offence under this section for A to show that B consented to the strangulation or other act.

(3) But subsection (2) does not apply if-

(a) B suffers serious harm as a result of the strangulation or other act, and

(b) A either–

(i) intended to cause B serious harm, or

(ii) was reckless as to whether B would suffer serious harm.

(4) A is to be taken to have shown the fact mentioned in subsection (2) if—

(a) sufficient evidence of the fact is adduced to raise an issue with respect to it, and

(b) the contrary is not proved beyond reasonable doubt.'

1.45 The statute defines serious harm by reference to harm caused in the commission of offences contrary to Offences Against the Person Act 1861, ss 18, 20 and 47 *(hence why it is useful to refer to the summary of the offences under Offences Against the Person Act 1861, ss 18, 20 and 47 above).*

Sexual

PRACTICE NOTE

Whilst we repeat again our warning that the Family Court must be careful not to import criminal *legal* concepts of sexual assault, such as rape, into its assessment of sexual abuse – a matter we address in more detail in **Chapter 6** – an awareness of how acts of abuse are seen in our sister profession is crucial knowledge for the family practitioner. This is especially true given that a Finding of Fact Hearing in a family case may be held concurrent with a pending criminal investigation on the same or similar allegations and heard well in advance of any criminal trial given the huge lags in listing in that jurisdiction.

Moving away from criminal gradations, we now turn to more commonly understood terms and types of abuse.

1.46 According to the United Nations,[71] sexual abuse involves forcing a partner to take part in a sex act when the partner does not consent. Again, it is

71 'What is Domestic Abuse?' (United Nations) https://www.un.org/en/coronavirus/what-is-domestic-abuse.

also physical, psychological and emotional abuse. Giving examples of when a victim may be in a sexually abusive relationship, the United Nations offers the following:

- If your partner accuses you of cheating or is often jealous of your outside relationships.
- If your partner wants you to dress in a sexual way.
- If your partner insults you in sexual ways or calls you sexual names.
- If your partner has ever forced or manipulated you into having sex or performing sexual acts.
- If your partner holds you down during sex.
- If your partner demands sex when you are sick, tired or after beating you.
- If your partner hurts you with weapons or objects during sex.
- If your partner involves other people in sexual activities with you.
- If your partner ignores your feelings regarding sex.

PRACTICE NOTE

The Family Court must also look to non-gendered types of sexual assault.

Within their practises, the authors have encountered allegations of sexual assault through forced artificial insemination, as well as the taking, storing and sharing of explicit images of a partner and the use of deep fake sex images.

Again, the only thing that limits the type or nature of sexual abuse is imagination – and the dark web can provide a library of images to emulate for those who wish to abuse or seek ever more sinister methods of control. As one of the most humiliating and dehumanising acts of abuse, sexual abuse can be the hardest to reveal and recount. *As we go on to discuss, that is one of the many reasons why a trauma-informed trial process is a vital part of a DA inquiry.*

As technology develops, so do the ways in which sexual abuse can be perpetrated. Yesterday's science-fiction (such as deep fake images or videos) can easily become today's reality. The law will need to evolve. Practitioners will be at the forefront of the court's ability to recognise and create appropriate protective measures from the legal frameworks available to us.

Emotional and psychological abuse

1.47 Emotional abuse has become more widely understood in recent years. Emotional abuse, also known as psychological abuse, is a form of abuse that involves using words and non-physical actions to manipulate, hurt, or frighten someone. It can cause significant psychological harm and should be considered just as damaging as physical abuse, if not more so. Whilst the physical scars left behind by a physical assault may heal in a matter of days or weeks, the wounds and scars left behind by emotional and psychological abuse can take many years to heal – if they ever heal at all. Acts such as undermining a person's sense of self-worth through constant criticism; belittling one's abilities; name-calling or other verbal abuse; damaging a partner's relationship with children; or not letting a partner see friends and family. As the example list below goes to indicate, the overlap with coercive and controlling behaviour is manifest.

- If your partner calls you names, insults you or continually criticises you.
- If your partner does not trust you and acts in a jealous or possessive manner.
- If your partner tries to isolate you from family or friends.
- If your partner monitors where you go, whom you call and with whom you spend your time.
- If your partner does not want you to work.
- If your partner controls finances or refuses to share money.
- If your partner punishes you by withholding affection.
- If your partner expects you to ask permission.
- If your partner threatens to hurt you, the children, your family or your pets.
- If your partner humiliates you in any way.

'Gaslighting'

1.48 Gaslighting is a form of emotional abuse where someone is manipulated to question their own sanity, memory and perception of reality. 'Gaslighting' is not necessarily a new concept. The concept can be traced back to at least the 1944 film 'Gaslight', where a husband manipulates his wife to believe she's losing her mind.[72] Gaslighting as a vehicle of abuse is a concept which has gained greater traction and understanding in recent years. This manipulation can involve denying reality, twisting words, and making the victim question their own experiences, leading to feelings of confusion, anxiety, and isolation.

1.49 Gaslighting received judicial recognition in the Family Court in the case of *Re B-B (DA: Fact-Finding)*[73] when it was observed by Cobb J (as he then was):

> 'I am satisfied on the evidence that the father did indeed repeatedly allege that the mother suffered from bipolar disorder; I further and significantly

72 'Gaslight' (1944) (Wikipedia https://en.wikipedia.org/wiki/Gaslight_(1944_film)).

73 *Re B-B (DA: Fact-Finding)* [2022] EWHC 108 (Fam).

> find that there was no clear medical evidence that she did suffer such a condition. Although there was a provisional diagnosis at one time (though unclear on what basis), the mother's GP explicitly reported that he did not consider that she had a bipolar disorder. On the evidence which I have seen, it seems to me likely that the mother did suffer from depression, anxiety, and mood swings; her mood was affected by excessive drinking and/or very occasional drug-taking and/or by the inconsistency of the father's relationship with her. In this state, at times she threatened to self-harm. I find that the father made this purported diagnosis in an attempt to characterise her to third parties as mentally unstable and/or unreliable; I find that it was immensely disparaging and undermining of the mother, damaging to the mother's self-confidence and self-esteem, and caused her to doubt her own mental health ("he made me believe that I was mentally unwell ... He convinced me that I had bipolar when I was never diagnosed with it ... He made me out to be mentally ill"). Dr. Proudman's use of the term "gaslighting" in the hearing to describe this conduct was in my judgment apposite; the father's conduct represented a form of insidious abuse designed to cause the mother to question her own mental well-being, indeed her sanity.[74]

Gaslighting is an incredibly powerful weapon in the hands of a perpetrator of DA.

PARTING COMMENTS

1.50 DA and controlling and coercive behaviour (CCB) (which we explore in the following chapter) are prevalent. DA and CCB are insidious. Their consequences are far-reaching and long-lasting. They leave scars which can take years to recover from. Society has come a long way in its understanding of DA and CCB but not far enough given the emergence of particularly misogynistic internet forums. Professionals must be alert to normalisation of abnormal and unacceptable behaviour. With increased awareness, comes an increased need to ensure that the professionals and the Court are fully conversant with the tools that can be deployed to ensure that victims (including children) are protected from the toxic effects of DA and CCB.

YOUR CLIENT, YOUR CAREER, YOUR RESPONSIBILITY: KEEP YOUR LEARNING AND PRACTICE UP TO DATE!

1.51 As you read this book, please bear in mind that case law has become our most direct and responsive library to direct our work. It will have produced other valuable commentary and guidance since we prepared this text. A case in point is that, just as this book reached final copy stage, CAFCASS released, on 6 January

74 *Re B-B* (n 73), [66] emphasis added.

2026, its updated *Domestic Abuse Practice Policy,*[75] which required a redraft of **Chapter 15**. There will be another update in June 2026. Equally, planned but not published at the time this goes to print, are two important documents: *President's Practice Guidance: Protective Orders under the Family Law Act 1996*; and the Family Justice Council, *Best Practice Guidance for Practitioners on making an application for a Protective Injunction.*

1.52 We have been told that the new *President's Practice Guidance* will entirely replace the 2023 guidance and that these materials will include two important new templates heralding a way to tackle local variance under the current scheme in relation to 'without notice' hearings:

- an example model witness statement in support of an application for protective injunction; and
- a model template injunction order (using plain, simple and non-legal language).

1.53 McFarlane P's new guidance will remind courts that, when deciding whether it is 'just and convenient' to make an order without notice, the Court's approach must be informed by a modern understanding of DA, referring to the modern definition set out at DAA 2021, s 1, with its specific reference to CCB and psychological, emotional or economic abuse. He announced 'a radical change' in that the new guidance must be followed in every court centre.

1.54 *Family law and practice does not stand still – you need to be eagle-eyed and up to date in your legal research, which is a non-delegable duty – especially not to AI. This book is not a substitute for your own development. It's just trying to offer a helping hand.*

75 CAFCASS, *Domestic Abuse Practice Policy* (January 2026), https://www.cafcass.gov.uk/domestic-abuse-practice-policy.

CHAPTER 2

Controlling and Coercive Behaviour (CCB)

INTRODUCTION

2.01 In recent years, there has been an increasing awareness and recognition of controlling and coercive behaviour (CCB) as a form of domestic abuse (DA) within the family justice system. The recognition of this form of abuse as insidious and harmful has not just been noted in the family jurisdiction: it is a criminal offence.

2.02 Whilst neither the Family Court nor CAFCASS collect or report data on cases involving DA, an ongoing barrier to the understanding of and effective response to DA in the family courts,[1] a recent report by the Domestic Abuse Commissioner found evidence of DA in 73 per cent of cases observed as a part of a study and in 87 per cent of case files which were examined as part of the same study.[2] Of the 87 per cent of case files examined, 35 per cent of those case files recorded allegations of CCB.

2.03 These figures, published in October 2025, serve to demonstrate the extent to which allegations of CCB are raised in the Family Court. The role that CCB can play in relationships and how the Family Court should approach such allegations was explored in the Court of Appeal decision in *Re H-N & Ors (Children) (Domestic Abuse: Finding of Fact Hearings)*.[3]

2.04 Whilst all forms of DA are harmful, CCB provides a lens through which all other forms of DA can and should be viewed. Only by viewing other behaviours through that lens can a proper understanding of the relationship be obtained and any risk properly evaluated. It is for that reason that this book devotes a chapter to CCB: to ensure that the lens it provides is prominent and is grounded in a solid understanding of what it is and the approach the Court should take.

1 Domestic Abuse Commission, *Everyday Business* (October 2025), p 12 https://www.gov.uk/government/publications/everyday-business-addressing-domestic-abuse-in-the-family-court/everyday-business-addressing-domestic-abuse-and-continuing-harm-through-a-family-court-review-and-reporting-mechanism.

2 Domestic Abuse Commission (n 1) p 13.

3 *Re H-N & Ors (Children) (Domestic Abuse: Finding of Fact Hearings)* [2021] EWCA Civ 448.

PRACTICE NOTE

CCB has caused the most 'excitement' in the family justice system in recent years and should no longer be an underappreciated concept. With hindsight it should never have been as overlooked as it has been by the family justice system. CCB is now, rightly we say, the lens through which DA should be seen. That is not to say that other forms of DA are not as serious or have an impact: they absolutely do. Acts of physical and sexual abuse which have been perpetrated as part and parcel of a controlling and coercive relationship will inevitably reinforce the victim's fear. But CCB may have already 'deadened' the victim's sense of injustice at the treatment meted out to them; it may have undermined their ability to recognise that they are worth more and are entitled to self-protection. Under a regime of CCB, a victim may 'adapt' to the abuser's demands, leading to a downward spiral of self-confidence and grip on what is or is not 'normal' behaviour as the victim adjusts their day-to-day life to conform to the abuser's demands.

2.05 CCB featured in the definition of DA as long ago as the Family Procedure Rules 2010 (SI 2010/2955), Practice Direction 12J (PD12J), and found a statutory basis in Serious Crime Act 2015, s 76 (which created a criminal offence of CCB), yet it had, in many ways not been fully addressed in the family courtroom or prepared for by practitioners. It had not been elevated to become the primary lens through which we viewed an alleged victim's experiences. That changed through a line of case heralded by Hayden J as approved in the Court of Appeal decisions in *Re H-N & Ors* where it was said that:

> '... it follows that consideration of whether the evidence establishes an abusive pattern of coercive and/or controlling behaviour is likely to be the primary question in many cases where there is an allegation of DA, irrespective of whether there are other more specific factual allegations to be determined.'[4]

2.06 The primacy to be afforded to allegations of CCB was reinforced by the Court of Appeal in *K v K* where it was stated that:

> 'In *Re H-N* at [50]-[59], the court explained the correct approach where an allegation of coercive or controlling behaviour is made. The message in those paragraphs was plain. Where coercive or controlling behaviour is alleged in this context, it is likely to be the primary matter requiring determination, provided that it is likely to be relevant to a live issue relating to a child's welfare. *Re H-N* at [56] made clear that the focus on coercive or controlling behaviour as the primary issue should make it generally unnecessary to determine other subsidiary date-specific factual allegations.'[5]

4 *Re H-N & Ors* (n 3), [55].
5 *K v K* [2022] EWCA Civ 468, [68].

2.07 It also stated that para [53] of *Re H-N & Ors* may inadvertently have been misunderstood. It read:

> ([53] of *Re H-N*):
>
> 'Where however an issue properly arises as to whether there has been a pattern of coercive and/or controlling abusive behaviour within a family, and the determination of that issue is likely to be relevant to the assessment of the risk of future harm, a judge who fails expressly to consider the issue may be held on appeal to have fallen into error.'
>
> *K v K:*
>
> 'That sentence is a requirement to consider an overarching issue of coercive or controlling behaviour, where to do so is necessary for the determination of a dispute relating to a child's welfare. It is not a requirement for the court to determine every single subsidiary allegation that may also be raised. The court only decides individual factual allegations where it is strictly necessary to do so in addition to determining the wider issue of coercive or controlling behaviour when that itself is necessary.[6]

With that in mind, the authorities identified below were prescient.

THE DEVELOPMENT OF CCB

2.08 In *SD v AFH (Appeal: Coercive and Controlling Behaviour: Inference or Speculation),*[7] a father sought permission to appeal against a decision with findings of fact that he had demonstrated CCB, undermining and assault of the mother. In respect to whether findings were made contrary to the literal 'definition' of 'coercive and/or controlling behaviour' from PD12J, Williams J made the following comments:

> 'The judge found that the coercive and controlling behaviour at the time of the agreement was at a lower level than that which emerged later. That finding is consistent with the picture which emerges from the text exchanges and from the evidence of each of the parties and from the obvious escalation which emerges from the audio and visual recordings.
>
> The dividing line between behaviour which can properly be characterised as coercive or controlling and within PD12J and behaviour which does not cross that threshold is not a bright line. The PD12J definition by its own terms makes clear that to amount to coercive or controlling behaviour the behaviour will be well outside that which is acceptable within a relationship. The evidence in this case plainly demonstrated that the father's behaviour was outside those fairly broad parameters of acceptable

6 *K v K* (n 5), [68]–[70].

7 *SD v AFH (Appeal: Coercive and Controlling Behaviour: Inference or Speculation)* [2019] EWHC 1513 (Fam).

> relationship based behaviour. In respect of the behaviour surrounding the reaching of the agreement in June it may have been towards the lower end of the spectrum of behaviour within PD12J but within it, it plainly was. By September it had progressed along the spectrum. There is no merit in the father's contention that his behaviour could not properly be characterised as controlling or coercive behaviour within the statutory definition'.[8]

Williams J ruled there was no merit in any of the grounds of appeal and permission to appeal was refused.

2.09 The decision in *R v P (Children: Similar Fact Evidence)* is a vital Court of Appeal decision, and one that should be kept in mind when clients bring evidence forwards and seek to adduce it to show a course of conduct amounting to CCB.[9] Notably this decision was the precursor to *F v M* which we address fully below.[10]

2.10 In *R v P (Children: Similar Fact Evidence),* the Court of Appeal considered relevant procedural rules, practice directions and case law (see para [19] onwards of the judgment). The court summarised some of the main principles from case law, and considered that the analysis which applies in civil cases also applies to family proceedings:

> '... There are two questions that the judge must address in a case where there is a dispute about the admission of evidence of this kind. Firstly, is the evidence relevant, as potentially making the matter requiring proof more or less probable? If so, it will be admissible. Secondly, is it in the interests of justice for the evidence to be admitted? This calls for a balancing of factors of the kind that Lord Bingham identifies at paragraphs 5 and 6 of *O'Brien v Chief Constable of South Wales Police* [2005] UKHL 26].'[11]

2.11 The Court of Appeal went on to consider the fact that, in this case, the similar factual evidence involved 'propensity' and the extent to which facts relating to the other occasions have to be proved for propensity to be established. It considered the Supreme Court criminal decision of *R v Mitchell*,[12] and summarised it as follows:

> 'Where the similar fact evidence comprises an alleged pattern of behaviour, the assertion is that the core allegation is more likely to be true because of the character of the person accused, as shown by conduct on other occasions. To what extent do the facts relating to the other occasions have to be proved for propensity to be established?

8 *SD v AFH (Appeal: Coercive and Controlling Behaviour: Inference or Speculation)* [2019] EWHC 1513 (Fam), [45]–[46].
9 *R v P (Children: Similar Fact Evidence)* [2020] EWCA Civ 1088.
10 *F v M* [2021] EWFC 4.
11 *R v P (Children: Similar Fact Evidence)* [(n 9), [24].
12 *R v Mitchell* [2016] UKSC 55.

> … In summary, the court must be satisfied on the basis of proven facts that propensity has been proven, in each case to the civil standard. The proven facts must form a sufficient basis to sustain a finding of propensity but each individual item of evidence does not have to be proved.'[13]

2.12 The appeal was allowed to set aside the judge's order; a necessary analysis concerning whether the disputed evidence should be admitted had not been carried out by the trial judge. It was noted by the Court of Appeal that it had no doubt the evidence from the Welsh reports, the evidence from Mr D and Mrs D's parents, and the second London local authority report were relevant, and therefore admissible, and that it should be admitted in the interests of justice. Whether propensity is established, and whether it is of probative value was, however, a matter for the trial judge.

2.13 Following *R v P (Children: Similar Fact Evidence)*, the Court of Appeal transferred the matter back to the High Court where it came before Hayden J for a ten-day Finding of Fact Hearing. The Court of Appeal reiterated what was required in understanding and identifying CCB, and recognised in particular its insidious scope and manner. Although often difficult for professionals to identify, there would sometimes be clues, hints, indicators and triggers as to what people reported which should stimulate forensic curiosity as opposed to superficial investigation.

2.14 The judgment provides important guidance in respect of (a) key guidance for identifying CCB; (b) approaching cases involving similar fact evidence, and the significance and importance of such evidence in cases of CCB (following on from the *R v P (Children: Similar Fact Evidence)* decision).

2.15 Hayden J, in his trial management and analysis of evidence in *F v M,* provided us with a masterclass in how to approach and understand the insidious nature of CCB which can be hidden in plain sight.[14] As Hayden J said, this was the, 'first time the Family Court, at High Court level, has been called upon to analyse allegations of controlling and coercive behaviour' in detail.[15]

2.16 Practitioners should take this case and Hayden J's approach to unpicking CCB within it, namely the, 'key to assessing abuse in the context of coercive control is recognising that the significance of individual acts may only be understood properly within the context of wider behaviour'[16] as their CCB touchstone. In other words, what may be seen as anodyne, inoffensive and 'normal' behaviour may not be indicative of CCB when viewed in isolation, yet when viewed in conjunction with other behaviours, a wholly different picture may be painted. It is for this reason that practitioners must explore the nature

13 *R v P (Children: Similar Fact Evidence)* (n 9), [25]–[26].
14 *F v M* (n 10).
15 *F v M* (n 10), [102].
16 *F v M* (n 10), [109].

of the relationships their clients are involved in to be able to properly and fully advise them.

2.17 In *F v M,* Hayden J referred to the definition in the Family Procedure Rules 2010 (SI 2010/2955) as providing some useful guidance when it is broken down:

> 'Coercive Behaviour:
>
> i. a pattern of acts;
>
> ii. such acts will be characterised by assault, threats, humiliation and intimidation but are not confined to this and may appear in other guises;
>
> iii. the objective of these acts is to harm, punish or frighten the victim.
>
> Controlling Behaviour:
>
> i. a pattern of acts;
>
> ii. designed to make a person *subordinate* and/or *dependent*;
>
> iii. achieved by isolating them from support, exploiting their resources and capacities for personal gain, depriving them of their means of independence, resistance and escape and regulating their everyday activities.'[17]

2.18 The approach adopted by Hayden J in *F v M* was expressly approved of by the Court of Appeal in *Re H-N & Ors.* The Lord and Lady Justices said:

> '… The arrival of Hayden J's judgment was timely. All parties commended it to the court for its comprehensive and lucid analysis, and for the plea contained within it urging greater prominence to be given to coercive and controlling behaviour in Family Court proceedings. The parties' endorsement of the judgment in *F v M* is, in our view, fully justified.
>
> … The judgment of Hayden J in *F v M (which should be essential reading for the Family judiciary)* is of value both because of the illustration that its facts provide of what is meant by coercive and controlling behaviour, but also because of the valuable exercise that the judge has undertaken in highlighting at paragraph 60 the statutory guidance published by the Home Office pursuant to Section 77(1) of the Serious Crime Act 2015 which identified paradigm behaviours of controlling and coercive behaviour …'[18]

2.19 Accordingly, due to its landmark importance it is necessary to hone in on the guidance in *F v M* in more detail.

(a) Having observed that, in the Family Court, 'coercive and controlling behaviour is given no legal definition', Hayden J went on to say:

17 *F v M* (n 10), [108] (emphasis added).
18 *Re H-N & Ors* (n 3), [29]–[30].

'In my judgement, it requires none. The term is unambiguous and needs no embellishment. Understanding the scope and ambit of the behaviour however, requires a recognition that "coercion" will usually involve a pattern of acts encompassing, for example, assault, intimidation, humiliation and threats. "Controlling behaviour" really involves a range of acts designed to render an individual subordinate and to corrode their sense of personal autonomy. Key to both behaviours is an appreciation of a "pattern" or "a series of acts", the impact of which must be assessed cumulatively and rarely in isolation. There has been very little reported case law in the Family Court considering coercive and controlling behaviour. I have taken the opportunity below, to highlight the insidious reach of this facet of domestic abuse. My strong impression, having heard the disturbing evidence in this case, is that it requires greater awareness and, I strongly suspect, more focused training for the relevant professionals.'[19]

(b) Understanding and identifying CCB required 'an evaluation of a pattern of behaviour in which the significance of isolated incidents could only be understood in the context of a much wider picture'.[20]

(c) The statutory guidance published pursuant to the Serious Crime Act 2015, Pt 5 s 77(1), identified paradigm behaviours: it is necessary to be vigilant to those. The behaviours identified by Hayden J in *A County Council v LW & Anor*[21] as apposite in the context of vulnerable adults were described as 'strikingly relevant here'[22] too:

'• Isolating a person from their friends and family
• Depriving them of their basic needs
• Monitoring their time
• Monitoring a person via online communication tools or using spyware
• Taking control over aspects of their everyday life, such as where they can go, who they can see, what to wear and when they can sleep
• Depriving them access to support services, such as specialist support or medical services
• Repeatedly putting them down such as telling them they are worthless
• Enforcing rules and activity which humiliate, degrade or dehumanise the victim
• Forcing the victim to take part in criminal activity such as shoplifting, neglect or abuse of children to encourage self-blame and prevent disclosure to authorities

19 *F v M* (n 10), [4].
20 *F v M* (n 10), [60].
21 *A County Council v LW & Anor* [2020] EWCOP 50.
22 *F v M* (n 10), [60].

- Financial abuse including control of finances, such as only allowing a person a punitive allowance
- Controlling ability to go to school or place of study
- Taking wages, benefits or allowances
- Threats to hurt or kill
- Threats to harm a child
- Threats to reveal or publish private information (e.g. threatening to "out" someone)
- Threats to hurt or physically harm a family pet
- Assault
- Criminal damage (such as destruction of household goods)
- Preventing a person from having access to transport or from working
- Preventing a person from being able to attend school, college or University
- Family "dishonour"
- Reputational damage
- Disclosure of sexual orientation
- Disclosure of HIV status or other medical condition without consent
- Limiting access to family, friends and finances.'[23]

(d) Hayden J also quoted with approval, however, the following from *A County Council v LW & Anor*:

> 'It is important to emphasise that this list is not exhaustive. It does not, for example, include controlling intake of food and nutrition, which was such a striking facet of the evidence here. Abusive behaviour of this kind will often be tailored to the individual circumstances of those involved. The above is no more than a checklist which should prompt questioning and enquiry, the responses to which should be carefully recorded so that the wider picture emerges. That which might, in isolation, appear innocuous or insignificant may in the context of a wider evidential picture be more accurately understood.'[24]

(e) Hayden J also said it was helpful to consider the guidance and assistance in Family Procedure Rules 2010 (SI 2010/2955), PD12J, and the offence of CCB in an intimate or family relationship as defined in Serious Crime Act 2015, s 76 whereby:

> '(1) A person (A) commits an offence if—

23 Ibid.
24 *A County Council v LW & Anor* (n 20) [22] as quoted in *F v M* (n 8) [61].

(a) A repeatedly or continuously engages in behaviour towards another person (B) that is controlling or coercive,

(b) at the time of the behaviour, A and B are personally connected,

(c) the behaviour has a serious effect on B, and

(d) A knows or ought to know that the behaviour will have a serious effect on B.

(2) A and B are "personally connected" if-

(a) A is in an intimate personal relationship with B, or

(b) A and B live together and-

(i) they are members of the same family, or

(ii) they have previously been in an intimate personal relationship with each other …'[25]

In relation to this legislation, Hayden J emphasised that:

> 'a tight, overly formulaic analysis may ultimately obfuscate rather than illuminate the behaviour … When Judges are called upon to resolve issues of fact, we do so by evaluating separate strands of evidence and then considering them in the context of the whole. Some features of the evidence will weigh more heavily than others and evidence which may not be significant, in isolation, may gain greater relevance when placed in the context of the wider evidential canvas.'[26]

(f) Hayden addressed and applied the definition in PD12J:

'Coercive Behaviour:

i. a pattern of acts;

ii. such acts will be characterised by assault, threats, humiliation and intimidation but are not confined to this and may appear in other guises;

iii. the objective of these acts is to harm, punish or frighten the victim.

Controlling Behaviour:

i. a pattern of acts;

ii. designed to make a person subordinate and/or dependent;

iii. achieved by isolating them from support, exploiting their resources and capacities for personal gain, depriving them of their means of independence, resistance and escape and regulating their everyday activities.'[27]

25 Serious Crime Act 2015 s76.
26 *F v M* (n 10), [108].
27 *F v M* (n 10).

(g) As he said, in assessing evidence of CCB, it was necessary to factor in a recognition of the behaviour's 'insidious scope and manner'.[28]

> 'The emphasis in Section 76 of the Serious Crime Act 2015, is on "repetition" and "continuous engagement" in patterns of behaviour which are controlling and coercive. Behaviour, it seems to me, requires, logically and by definition, more than a single act. The wording of FPD 2010 12J is therefore potentially misleading in so far as it appears to contemplate establishing behaviour by reference to "an act or a pattern of acts". Key to assessing abuse in the context of coercive control is recognising that the significance of individual acts may only be understood properly within the context of wider behaviour. I emphasise it is the behaviour and not simply the repetition of individual acts which reveals the real objectives of the perpetrator and thus the true nature of the abuse.'[29]

(h) The difficulty in spotting CCB was tackled head on with Hayden J acknowledging that it was often difficult for professionals to identify the behaviour, but nonetheless, he highlighted there would:

> 'frequently be clues, hints, indicators and triggers in which people reported that that might stimulate wider forensic curiosity and investigations of greater subtlety and nuance. Much of the evidence in this case for example showed how families, friends, work colleagues and neighbours knew what was happening to both the mother and the father's previous partner from an early stage. Broader professional education on the scope and ambit of CCB was likely to generate greater alertness to abuse of that type which all too frequently lies buried or only superficially investigated. Communication and sharing of information between police forces is imperative.'[30]

(i) Hayden J looked at the trajectory of the father's behaviour after the breakup between the parents as well as its pre-history and then history with her.[31] This proved highly relevant for soon after the mother left in September 2017, the father commenced a relationship with a woman in her 40s and moved in with her and her two young sons. Within a few weeks she had resigned from her teaching career and sold her car. She moved with the father and her sons to Wales without telling anyone. Her children's new school contacted their father and the boys were eventually transferred into his care in December 2018.

Considered by Hayden J in the context of the father's earlier relationship, the Court was easily able to identify a pattern of behaviour which was described as 'insidious, unsettling and controlled behaviour enacted in a virtually identical manner'. This approach – and Hayden J's exposition throughout

28 *F v M* (n 10), [109].
29 *F v M* (n 10).
30 *F v M* (n 10), [112].
31 *F v M* (n 10), [72]–[81].

this judgment not only makes crucial reading for any practitioner but provides us with a masterclass as to why patterns of behaviour are so crucial and why we must not be curtailed by courts seeking to limit allegations in both number and timespan.

(j) Hayden J found that the similar factual evidence concerning F's relationship with his other partner was relevant and admissible due to the striking parallels with both the father's relationship with the mother and J. When compared, the force of F's abuse came into greater focus, and the comparison served to better illustrate the corrosive and debilitating impact of that abuse.

> 'I have emphasised the extracts above to underscore that which is obvious. These descriptions could be inserted seamlessly into MGM's statement. They describe insidious, unsettling and controlling behaviour enacted in a virtually identical manner. Thus, two women who have never met, with entirely different experiences of life are describing how their daughters were coerced into a distorted relationship which gradually and relentlessly chipped away at their own sense of self and personal autonomy. It need hardly be said that these two accounts, strikingly similar as they are, each reinforce the other. It is also the case that when the two relationships are compared, it brings the force of the abuse, in each separate relationship, into greater focus and serves better to illustrate its corrosive and debilitating impact.'[32]

2023 GUIDANCE ON CCB

2.20 Such is the importance of CCB as an issue that, in 2023, the government published statutory guidance[33] on it with the intention of providing:

- 'Clear information on what constitutes controlling or coercive behaviour and how to identify the offence;
- Guidance to the police and other criminal justice agencies on circumstances where the offence applies and where other offences might be considered;
- Guidance to the police and criminal justice agencies on the different types of evidence that can support in identifying, evidencing and charging the offence, and how this should support prosecutions and sentencing;
- Information on reducing risks to the victim, including: using protection orders; supporting the victim; and responding to the perpetrator's behaviour.'[34]

32 *F v M* (n 10), [72].

33 *Controlling or Coercive Behaviour: Statutory Guidance Framework* (Home Office, 5 April 2023) https://assets.publishing.service.gov.uk/media/642d3f9e7de82b001231364d/Controlling_or_Coercive_Behaviour_Statutory_Guidance_-_final.pdf.

34 Home Office (n 33), p 5.

This guidance also addresses the importance of risk assessments, evidence gathering, and managing cases where victims withdraw their support.

2.21 The framework includes various annexes providing further details on related considerations, legal definitions and available support services for victims and perpetrators. A significant portion is dedicated to understanding perpetrator tactics and identifying CCB within various contexts. It is a highly educative document which can be cross-applied to cases that benefit from an illustrative template of behaviours from an authoritative source.

2.22 Whilst this statutory guidance is primarily aimed at police and criminal justice agencies in England and Wales involved in the investigation of criminal behaviour, it is of use to those who practise in the Family Court and should be important reading for all practitioners.

PRACTICE NOTE

A final point to note before leaving this introduction to CCB is that some forms of abuse used by the abuser to achieve and maintain control can be self-inflicted or self-directed – ie self-harm by cutting themselves or taking overdoses, threats of self-harm, threats to commit suicide (and so on) if the partner leaves them or threatens to report partner abuse.

If such self-harm or threats to self-harm are used as a means of controlling the victim by compelling them to stay in an abusive relationship that they wish to escape, then that is psychologically and emotionally abusive behaviour that may properly be seen as part of coercion and control.

Remember: The point to consider is the impact of that behaviour on the partner and how it fits within a pattern of behaviour they are exposed to by the alleged abuser.

CHAPTER 3

An Introductory Outline of the Domestic Abuse Act 2021

> 'Domestic abuse is an abhorrent crime perpetrated on victims and their families by those who should love and care for them. This landmark Bill will help transform the response to domestic abuse, helping to prevent offending, protect victims and ensure they have the support they need.'
>
> **Victoria Atkins MP, Minister for Safeguarding**[1]

3.01 The Domestic Abuse Act 2021 (DAA 2021) is a comprehensive piece of legislation aimed at tackling domestic abuse (DA) in England and Wales. It became law on 29 April 2021. This much needed and welcome piece of legislation highlights the importance society now attributes to the scourge of DA. This chapter is simply designed to flag its key headings to the reader by way of introduction. It was a groundbreaking, and long overdue, Act. As you follow this book through to its end, you will see its influence.

3.02 The government heralded the DAA 2021 as bringing the following issues to the fore; the Act would, it said:

- 'Create a statutory definition of domestic abuse, emphasising that DA is not just physical violence, but can also be emotional, controlling, coercive, and economic;
- Establish in law the office of Domestic Abuse Commissioner and set out the Commissioner's functions and powers;
- Provide for a new Domestic Abuse Protection Notice and Domestic Abuse Protection Order;
- Place a duty on local authorities in England to provide accommodation based support to victims of DA and their children in refuges and other safe accommodation;
- Prohibit perpetrators of abuse from cross-examining their victims in person in the civil and family courts in England and Wales;
- Create a statutory presumption that victims of domestic abuse are eligible for special measures in the criminal, civil and family courts;

1 'Domestic Abuse Act 2021: Overarching Factsheet' (Gov.uk) https://www.gov.uk/government/publications/domestic-abuse-bill-2020-factsheets/domestic-abuse-bill-2020-overarching-factsheet.

- Clarify the circumstances in which a court may make a barring order under section 91(14) of the Children Act 1989 to prevent family proceedings that can further traumatise victims;
- Extend the controlling or coercive behaviour offence to cover post-separation abuse;
- Extend the offence of disclosing private sexual photographs and films with intent to cause distress (known as the "revenge porn" offence) to cover threats to disclose such material;
- Create a new offence of non-fatal strangulation or suffocation of another person;
- Clarify by restating in statute law the general proposition that a person may not consent to the infliction of serious harm and, by extension, is unable to consent to their own death;
- Extend the extraterritorial jurisdiction of the criminal courts in England and Wales, Scotland and Northern Ireland to further violent and sexual offences;
- Provide for a statutory domestic abuse perpetrator strategy;
- Enable domestic abuse offenders to be subject to polygraph testing as a condition of their licence following their release from custody;
- Place the guidance supporting the Domestic Violence Disclosure Scheme ("Clare's law") on a statutory footing;
- Provide that all eligible homeless victims of domestic abuse automatically have 'priority need' for homelessness assistance;
- Ensure that where a local authority, for reasons connected with domestic abuse, grants a new secure tenancy to a social tenant who had or has a secure lifetime or assured tenancy (other than an assured shorthold tenancy) this must be a secure lifetime tenancy;
- Prohibit GPs and other health professionals in general practice from charging a victim of domestic abuse for a letter to support an application for legal aid; and
- Provide for a statutory code of practice relating to the processing of domestic abuse data for immigration purposes.'[2]

3.03 The question is how many of those measures are in force five years on, bearing in mind that the government professed an expectation that most would be in force by 2022.

3.04 The DAA 2021 has come into effect in stages.

The following sections came into force on 1 October 2021:

(a) s 1 (definition of 'domestic abuse');

(b) s 2 (definition of 'personally connected');

2 Gov.uk (n 1).

(c) s 3 (children as victims of domestic abuse) only for the purposes of s 63 (special measures in family proceedings: victims of domestic abuse) and Pt 4 (Local Authority support);

(d) s 63 (special measures in family proceedings: victims of domestic abuse); and

(e) Pt 4 (Local Authority support).

On 1 November 2021, the following sections entered into force:

(a) s 3 (children as victims of domestic abuse) only for the purposes of s 79 (grant of secure tenancies in cases of domestic abuse);

(b) Pt 2 on the domestic abuse commissioner;

(c) s 79 (grant of secure tenancies);

(d) s 84 (power of the Secretary of State to issue guidance about domestic abuse).

On 31 January 2022, the following sections entered into force: s 3 (children as victims of domestic abuse) so far as not already in force.

The provisions relating to the prohibition of cross-examination in person came into force on 21 July 2022.[3]

3.05 On the 8 of April 2024, the Domestic Abuse Protection Orders (County Court: Relevant Proceedings) Regulations 2024 (SI 2024/253) came into force as a necessary companion to DAA 2021, s 31(7). Both the person against whom the order is made, and the person being protected, must be parties to these proceedings. These regulations define what constitutes 'relevant proceedings' for this purpose. Note: the provisions to support Domestic Abuse Protection Orders (DAPOs) are not in place throughout the country at the time of writing.[4]

3.06 The most pertinent sections of the DAA 2021 will be discussed below as well as in later chapters in more detail. Whilst this means that there may be some duplication/overlap between chapters, there is a good reason for this: it is essential that every practitioner familiarises themselves with the Act as a whole as well as its component parts, for each section informs and underpins the others.

3 But the means to give effect to that through the use of funded Qualified Legal Representatives (QLRs) was lamentably slow.

4 As of April 2025, only the following courts had launched DAPOs: Bolton Magistrates and County Court; Bromley Magistrates and County Court; Caernarfon Justice Centre, Croydon Magistrates, County and Crown Courts, Llandudno Magistrates, Manchester Magistrates, Crown and Civil Justice Centre, Mold Justice Centre, Prestatyn Justice Centre, Stockport Magistrates and County Court, Teesside Combined Court and Justice Centre, Wigan County Court and Magistrates, Wrexham County Court and Magistrates. Note that police force areas in which the person must reside are currently limited to: Metropolitan Police South BCU, covering Bromley, Croydon and Sutton; Greater Manchester Police, covering Greater Manchester; Cleveland Police, covering Hartlepool, Middlesbrough, Redcar, Cleveland and Stockton-on-Tees; and, finally, North Wales Police, covering North Wales (Isle of Anglesey, Gwynedd), Conwy, Denbighshire, Flintshire and Wrexham.

WHEN WILL DIRECT CROSS-EXAMINATION OF THOSE ABUSED BY THE ALLEGED ABUSER BE PROHIBITED?

3.07 Section 65 of the DAA 2021, which came into force in May 2022, amended the Matrimonial and Family Proceedings Act 1984, adding ss 31Q onwards in relation to cross-examination. This section is designed for the purpose of making regulations.

3.08 These new sections automatically prohibit cross-examination where:

(a) a party has been convicted of, given a caution for, or charged with a 'specified offence'; or

(b) an on-notice protective injunction is in force between the parties; or

(c) where 'specified evidence' is adduced that a party has carried out DA.

3.09 'Specified offences' and 'specified evidence' will be defined in upcoming regulations. Based on previous drafts before Parliament, the former will likely include violent offences, sexual offences, offences of DA/coercive control and possibly harassment and/or breaches of DAPOs.

3.10 As well as the automatic prohibitions listed above, there is a provision which gives the Court discretionary power to prohibit a party from cross-examining even if none of the above applies. This might be relevant in cases of DA which do not meet the mandatory threshold listed above, and/or where a party/witness is vulnerable for some other reason. This discretionary power applies where:

(a) the quality of evidence given by the witness is likely to be diminished if the cross-examination is conducted by the party in person, and it would be likely to be improved if the prohibition was imposed; or

(b) the cross-examination by one party in person would be likely to cause significant distress to the witness or another party and that distress is likely to be more significant than if the cross-examination were conducted some other way.

3.11 We provide a more detailed exploration of this in **Chapter 13** where we look further at 'Participation in the Family Court'.

PRACTICE NOTE

The Court's familiarity with and use of Qualified Legal Representatives (QLRs) is steadily increasing. Invocation of this discretionary power is going to be influenced by how trained and 'trauma aware' practitioners are of the conflict points that can lie buried in the ordinary process of family litigation.

Practitioners can assist by addressing their minds to the potential need for QLRs at every stage in the proceedings.

It is very common for a represented party to become unrepresented when funds run out for privately paid legal representation and then the pressure is on for an order for the appointment of a QLR to be made and one sourced who can manage the trial dates.

Time will have to be factored in for the unrepresented party to first be given the chance to secure their QLR of choice, failing which the Court will request allocation. That builds in a time lag. So insert clear timescales for each step.

Time may also have to be factored in for the draft questions prepared by the QLR to be seen by any intermediary for a vulnerable party. Anticipate and plan for that.

The message here is to be proactive, not reactive, in thinking about barriers to keeping a fixture and anticipating solutions.

Delay is going to impact on memories and the quality of evidence heard (readers please familiarise yourselves with the section on weakness in oral evidence based on past traumatic events discussed further in **Chapter 13 Participation in the Family Court**).

3.12 This discretionary power can either be initiated by the judge or requested by the parties. In coming to their decision, the judge must consider:

(a) the views of the witness/proposed questioning party;

(b) the nature of the questions likely to be asked, having regard to the issues in the case;

(c) any behaviour findings in these or other proceedings against either the witness or proposed questioning party;

(d) any behaviour by the party at any stage of the case, both generally and in relation to the witness/party; and

(e) any relationship (of whatever nature) between the witness and the party.

PRACTICE NOTE

The DAA 2021 has not specifically addressed any limitation to cross-examination on sexual history in DA cases. Though this is something which the Court can limit and/or prevent by virtue of the discretionary power above, this does not go as far as the statutory restrictions imposed in the criminal courts. The practitioner, therefore, needs to keep abreast of how this aspect is evolving through case precedent. See, for example the case of *K & L & M* below.

3.13 The Court must consider, with the parties in advance, the remit of cross-examination.

PRACTICE NOTE

The represented parties must be ready to assist by turning their minds to the key issues in dispute and the scope of cross-examination needed to resolve them.

Matters put in cross-examination must be relevant and have probative value in contrast to being used as a weapon to humiliate, control or abuse through the court adversarial system (whether or not those questions are being put by an unrepresented litigant or advocate acting on a party's behalf).

That means advance trial preparation at all stages of the process (which is a heavy demand when the rates of pay for this type of work under legal aid are so low).

3.14 A case in point is Judd J in *K & L & M*.[5] This was an appeal following a fact-finding hearing as to allegations of rape and DA in the course of private law proceedings relating to a two-year-old. The mother had met the father whilst working as a 'cam girl', providing sexual services for payment. The father was a client. The mother gave up her work in favour of the personal relationship that developed between the adults. The relationship broke down. Allegations of rape and sexual abuse of M by F were made. The case management direction made no reference to Family Procedure Rules 2010 (SI 2010/2955), rule 3A and PD3AA, there was no application for participation directions, no Ground Rules Hearing.

3.15 It is important to note that this matter was heard under Covid-19 hybrid arrangements. Arrangements for the parties entering and being in court therefore arose not from consideration of special measures and participation issues but from Covid-19 case plan/court occupancy issues.

3.16 Mrs Justice Judd held that the provisions of rule 3A and PD3AA are mandatory (a 'must') and the obligation is on the Court to consider vulnerability and how best that person can participate in the hearing. Even if the advocates or parties themselves do not raise it, the duty exists since; such considerations are not just for the 'sake of the mother but for the integrity of the court process itself'.[6]

In paras [66] and [67], Judd J illustrated why it is necessary to engage with the rules regarding vulnerability and participation:

> 'It must be clear from the matters I have set out above that this was a case which cried out for participation directions and a ground rules hearing, not just for the sake of the mother, but for the integrity of the court process itself. The purpose of the rules and Practice Direction is to avoid the quality of the evidence being diminished. Here, the need for directions went beyond the

5 *K & L & M* [2021] EWHC 3225 (Fam).
6 *K & L & M* (n 5), [66].

need to consider whether the parties should not come into physical contact in the court room or building. Matters, such as whether the mother should be visually shielded from the father as she gave her evidence, and what topics should be covered in cross examination, were highly relevant.

It was inevitable that the mother would have to answer very personal questions, but the questioning should have been restricted to what was necessary for a fair trial. An example of the line of questions which may not have been necessary is apparent from the start of her cross examination. She was taken to explicit material from her days six years earlier as a 'cam girl' to demonstrate she knew the meaning of some swear words. There may have been a different way of achieving this goal.'[7]

3.17 When discussion arose about whether some sex videos should be admitted as evidence, Judd J was clear about the impact on the mother: 'It does not need much imagination to think this might have had a deleterious effect on someone who was a victim of intimidation and/or abuse.'[8] Counsel can and should benefit from a Ground Rules Hearing when contemplating cross-examination on such delicate issues. The failure to apply the procedural rules was fatal to the safety of the judge's findings in the lower court.

PRACTICE NOTE

This case provides a salutary lesson in how injustice can result when advocates and the Court fail to think through their cross-examination subject matters and to engage the Court in assessing their probative value and relevance (and any alternative means of making the points if relevant and probative) when agreement cannot be reached between the parties. The fact that rule 3A and PD3AA were entirely omitted from consideration in the lower court shows the depth to which all in court for the hearing had failed to engage with their duties. These Rules and Directions are not 'optional extras' – they are a core part of hearing preparation and trial management.

IF CROSS-EXAMINATION IS PROHIBITED, WHAT ARE THE ALTERNATIVES?

3.18 The Court must first consider whether there are satisfactory alternative means for the witness to be cross-examined or obtaining evidence that the witness might have given under cross-examination in the proceedings. If there are not satisfactory alternative means, the Court must invite the prohibited party to arrange, by a specified date, for a QLR to act for them for the purpose of cross-examining the witness. If no representative has been appointed by the party by

7 *K & L & M* (n 5), [66]–[67].
8 *K & L & M* (n 5).

the specified date, the Court itself must consider whether to appoint a QLR to represent the interests of the party.

3.19 If the QLR is appointed, their remit is limited to cross-examining the claimant party only. The extent of a QLR's role is explored fully in a later chapter. For the present, we mention only that liaison time is often limited to a telephone call prior to the trial followed by a face to face meeting at court. That places significant pressure on the QLR to get to grips with the nuances of the case that often comes from a wider read of the papers than the core bundle often sent for the sole task the QLR is appointed to undertake.

3.20 Whilst the appointment of a QLR avoids the problems associated with regard to judges undertaking questions, it does not solve all of the participation issues the Court will need to grapple with.[9] For example, it does nothing to lessen the client's vulnerability at other points of the hearing, which may also be significantly distressing. This may, however, be alleviated by special measures, depending on their efficacy.

SPECIAL MEASURES

3.21 Sections 62–64 of the DAA 2021 address the use of special measures in criminal, family and civil proceedings respectively. Section 63 (which came into force on 1 October 2021) pertains to family proceedings and creates a presumption where a party or witness is, or is at risk of, being a victim of DA from a member of their family or a witness or party in the proceedings, that the quality of their evidence and/or their participation as a party is likely to be diminished by reason of vulnerability. As explained above, PD3AA already caters for this; however, the key difference is that a presumption now applies – parties will no longer have to justify their eligibility.

3.22 A judge's failure to implement PD3AA, among other failures, was assessed in *Re A (Domestic Abuse: Incorrect Principles Applied).*[10] Although the mother was a potentially vulnerable witness as a complainant of DA, DDJ Watson failed to consider special measures at first instance. The mother cried during the father's cross-examination of her. On appeal, His Honour Judge Ahmed allowed the appeal and ordered that the fact-finding hearing be reheard by another judge. See also Judd J, cited above.[11]

9 Lucy R, 'Domestic Abuse Act 2021 – What does it mean for Family Courts and the people using them?' (*Transparency Project*, May 2021) http://www.transparencyproject.org.uk/domestic-abuse-act-2021-what-does-it-mean-for-family-courts-and-the-people-using-them/?fbclid=IwAR0rcNRMjwva-1ytqt7iCwfLCKdPiaDwRpDzi4GCPIBVcE98OlOpa7R7Xms.

10 *Re A (Domestic Abuse: Incorrect Principles Applied)* [2021] 6 WLUK 601.

11 *K & L & M* (n 5).

SECTION 67 OF THE DAA 2021 AND SECTION 91(14) CHILDREN ACT ORDERS

3.23 Section 91(14) of the Children Act 1989 allows the Court to prevent a parent making further applications without first obtaining permission from the Court to do so. These were often referred to, incorrectly, as 'barring orders'. They do not, and never did, 'bar' an application. They introduce a judicial filter to prevent unmeritorious claims being issued. Section 91(14) used to be referred to as a last resort option, typically where the respective parent had made repeated, vexatious or unmeritorious applications. Whilst this is no longer the case, old attitudes and presumptions regarding rarity can linger – be prepared to confront them.

3.24 Section 67 of the DAA 2021 adds s 91A to the Children Act 1989 to allow the Court to make an order pursuant to Children Act 1989, s 91(14) where it is satisfied that the making of an application would put the child or another 'relevant individual' at risk of harm. The Court will have in mind whether the application is part of a continued course of coercive and controlling behaviour as well as what welfare issues it raises for a child in terms of its content.

CONCLUDING REMARK

3.25 This chapter is but a very short overview of the Act. It is not a substitute for practitioners making themselves familiar with its purpose and component parts, including those which are in force and those which are not currently in force.[12]

3.26 The DAA 2021 represents significant progress in the way the law recognises the pernicious nature of DA and the harm it causes. It provides a legal framework for protective measures and creates important tools to equip the Court with a raft of measures designed to protect victims of DA. Case law complements that framework, as does an ever-growing awareness of what DA is. Both evolve and a practitioner must keep themselves abreast of developments in research and case law.

12 It should be noted that, at the time of writing, some sections of the Act are not currently in force. Furthermore, some aspects of it are in force for time-limited periods (for example, the provisions relating to the use of Domestic Abuse Protection Notices and Orders which are currently being trialled in some areas).

CHAPTER 4

Domestic Abuse in the Criminal Courts

Authors' note: As we said in **Chapter 1**, by including this chapter in this book we do not seek to import legal concepts of criminal law into the family field. Rather we have looked to Michelle Heeley KC and Chloë Ashley to guide us towards a fuller understanding of how family and criminal courts approach partner abuse so we can see and learn from overlap and distinctions. Family law is not an island. Criminal law showed us the way in which we might hear from very young children in court. It produced the forerunner of the Advocates Toolkits that are now of universal assistance and application when dealing with disability, vulnerability, religion and culture in court. Looking directly to domestic abuse, crime led the way in critically scrutinising the purpose and necessity of permitting cross-examination of complainants on their previous sexual history. The family and criminal courts preside over almost identical facts in multiple areas of practice, whether that be alleged non-accidental injury to a child, infant death, or as here, in matters concerning domestic and sexual abuse, controlling and coercive behaviour and attempted strangulation. We suggest comparison with criminal practice may also help the family practitioner distil potentially important/distinguishing factual characteristics from a client's narrative that may be relevant to spotting aggravating features, identifying the right level of court for litigation and honing in on areas for further exploration/evidence gathering.

INTRODUCTION

4.01 Over recent years, there has been a sea change in the approach of the police, the Crown Prosecution Service (CPS) and the courts as to how allegations of domestic abuse are dealt with. It was only in 1991 that the then House of Lords held that a husband could be guilty of a crime if he raped his wife. It took until the Sexual Offences Act of 2003 for that to be dealt with legislatively.

4.02 Until then, there had been a culture in the criminal courts that what happened between 'man and wife' was private, and it was not for the criminal courts to interfere. One only needs to listen to police officers talk about how they attended 'domestics' in the 1990s to understand that allegations of abuse within the family were not treated seriously.

4.03 A common approach was for the police to attend; speak to both parties and offer words of advice; however, parties were rarely arrested.

4.04 Throughout the 1990s, several groups began to encourage greater rights for women, with groups such as the Campaign Against Domestic Violence, founded in 1991, seeking to secure funding for women's refuges and helplines and also to develop a programme of awareness of the issues surrounding domestic violence so that relevant authorities such as the police, courts and legal staff would be trained in dealing with such allegations.

4.05 Cases were also making headlines around the country; Sara Thornton was accused of murder, having stabbed her abusive husband as he lay drunk on the sofa. She was convicted of murder in 1991 but was freed after a retrial in 1995 when the Court of Appeal ruled that she ought to have been allowed to adduce evidence of 'battered woman syndrome' which meant she had lost control and was thus guilty of manslaughter by reason of diminished responsibility as opposed to murder.

4.06 There have also been significant developments in our understanding of domestic abuse generally, and more specifically, our understanding of coercive control and its impact on individuals. No case highlights this better perhaps than that of Sally Challen. After decades of every aspect of her life being controlled by her husband and his constant humiliation of her, she killed him. At the time of her conviction, 'coercive control' was not a crime in England and Wales, only becoming recognised in law as a form of domestic abuse (DA) in 2015. Without the work of pivotal groups such as Justice for Women, who assisted Ms Challen in overturning her conviction, and others including Rape Crisis, Refuge and the Southall Black Sisters – who famously supported Kiranjit Ahluwalia – championing these issues, progress would likely have been even slower.

4.07 The seriousness with which this issue is now taken is reflected in the many ongoing consultations launched by the Home Office in recent years, including, in 2022, the consultation which sought to develop statutory guidance on controlling and coercive behaviour (CCB) and the government's publication of its Draft Victims' Bill in May 2022 as part of its ongoing commitment to improving support for victims in the criminal justice system. We also now have a Victims Commissioner, dedicated to promoting the interests of victims and witnesses. Dame Jacobs has famously campaigned for urgent reform for DA victims, including stronger accountability for criminal agencies to ensure victims receive an effective response.[1]

4.08 That aside, cases such as those noted above meant that domestic violence was thrust into the limelight. The police had always had the power to arrest for offences of assault, but they had generally chosen not to. The current position is reflected in CPS guidance, as per their website:

> 'DA cases are amongst the highest priority work dealt with in the criminal justice system. The safety of adult and child victims is imperative when prosecuting cases of DA. There is no specific offence of "domestic abuse".

1 Victims Commissioner, 'Domestic abuse victims are being failed by the criminal justice system at every stage' (22 January 2025), https://victimscommissioner.org.uk/news/domestic-abuse-victims-are-being-failed-by-the-criminal-justice-system-at-every-stage/.

It is a general term describing a range of behaviour and can be applied to a number of offences …

Support and safety needs for victims should be identified from the outset and continually considered throughout the life of a case. Improving a victim's safety is key. It may help to raise their confidence in the criminal justice system and facilitate their participation in the investigation and prosecution process.'

4.09 The CPS are also swift to highlight that the longer abuse continues, the more likely it is that the seriousness of it will escalate and, of course, that it does not discriminate: those of all ethnicities, genders, sexualities, ages, disabilities, immigration statuses, religions or beliefs, and socio-economic backgrounds can be victims or perpetrators.

4.10 Indeed, recently, there has been a greater acknowledgement of this, as reflected in the many so-called honour-based cases and child sex abuse cases which are now prosecuted thanks to campaigns spearheaded by advocates such as Nazir Afzal, a former Chief Crown Prosecutor who was critical in ensuring those responsible for the death of Banaz Mahmood were brought to justice.

4.11 Further, guidance to assist prosecutors in these cases is under almost constant review as we come to better understand the dynamics of domestic offences. As recently as April 2023, the CPS introduced new guidance to prosecutors concerned with CCB cases, which highlighted the phenomenon of 'love-bombing', a tactic used by suspects to confuse victims and gain more control. In summary, this is the varied, sophisticated and subtle ways victims are manipulated in the initial stages of a relationship, for example, by being sent gifts by their abusive partners as a means to later exert control over their lives.[2]

DOMESTIC ABUSE OFFENCES – ELEMENTS OF THE OFFENCES (INCLUDING HOW THEY MAY DIFFER FROM THOSE 'ALLEGATIONS' IN THE FAMILY COURT)

4.12 DA, of course, encompasses a wide range of offences. However, the majority of cases that appear before the courts relate to assaults, serious and sexual violence; we have, of course, already touched upon the latter.

4.13 The offences of assault occasioning actual bodily harm (ABH), contrary to Offences Against the Person Act 1861, s 47, and common assault, contrary to s 39 of the same Act, have existed for 150 years, but in the past, the police were not as committed to pursuing offences of that nature where they had occurred in a domestic setting.

2 The Crown Prosecution Service includes 'love-bombing' in guidance on abusive partners.

4.14 More recently, new offences have been introduced to address significant gaps in the legislation that previously permitted harmful activities to go unpunished, including the offence of non-fatal strangulation, as provided for in Domestic Abuse Act 2021, s 70.

4.15 As with all legal matters, we return to basic principles before analysing how they differ from 'allegations' in the Family Court. In respect of offences of violence, the common ones are as follows.

Common assault

4.16 Common assault: s 39 provides that an assault is committed when the defendant intentionally or recklessly causes another to apprehend immediate and unlawful violence.

4.17 This charge is typically used to address lower-level violence, including incidents that result in a single bruise or less. Potential defences include self-defence and defence of another.

4.18 On the one hand, it is a relatively easy offence to prove in that there does not need to be an actual strike or any resulting injury, just that someone fears that violence will be used; on the other hand, the sentencing powers of the court are limited to a maximum six months' imprisonment, and the offence is also summary only, meaning any summons must be laid within six months of the date of the alleged offence otherwise it will be time-barred.

4.19 For many women, the idea of reporting a single slap or threat of violence was unrealistic, and thus, very few common domestic assaults made their way to court. If the assault led to more serious injury, however, then ABH could be charged.

Assault occasioning actual bodily harm

4.20 ABH: s 47 is committed when a person intentionally or recklessly assaults another. It is necessary to prove that the assault caused the victim actual bodily harm. Bodily harm has its ordinary meaning and includes any hurt that interferes with the health or comfort of the victim: such hurt need not be permanent but must be more than transient.

4.21 This offence carries a maximum of five years' imprisonment and can be dealt with in either the Crown Court or the magistrates' court. Thus, it is not limited by the six-month requirement to bring charges.

Intentional strangulation

4.22 On 7 June 2022 a new offence of intentional strangulation came into force (Domestic Abuse Act 2021, s 70). Whilst strangulation can be an offence in any setting the CPS recognised that many offences of this nature often occur within a domestic setting.

4.23 The offence carries the same maximum sentence of ABH, namely five years, but reflects the fact that strangulation or suffocation could, on the face of it, only cause injuries analogous with a common assault. The Act is designed to rectify this lacuna, punishing the actions rather than the outcome.

4.24 In order to prove the offence one must show either strangulation, which means:

- A intentionally strangles another person ('B'), or
- A does any other act to B that –
  - affects B's ability to breathe, and
  - constitutes a battery of B,

it does not require proof of injury, or proof of consequence of the actions.

Or one can demonstrate suffocation – that is to deprive a person of air which affects their normal breathing.

4.25 It has been acknowledged that some people indulge in restriction of breathing as part of consensual sexual behaviour, therefore there is a defence of consent, however the defence does not apply if:

- B suffers serious harm as a result of the strangulation or other act, and
- A either –
  - intended to cause B serious harm, or
  - was reckless as to whether B would suffer serious harm.

Grievous bodily harm

4.26 The most serious offence, short of homicide, is grievous bodily harm (GBH). For GBH, under Offences Against the Person Act 1861, s 18, the prosecution must prove that, at the time of committing the offence, the defendant unlawfully and maliciously wounded another or otherwise inflicted a serious level of harm upon the victim. This offence usually requires proof of broken bones or a wound to the skin that requires at least stitches.

4.27 It is common practice in the criminal courts when charging s 18 to include an alternative of s 20 on the indictment. For a s 20 offence, the defendant must intentionally or recklessly wound or inflict grievous bodily harm on the victim. On the other hand, for an s 18 offence, only a clear intention to wound and inflict GBH is sufficient.

4.28 Police and Parliament have recognised that for many women (and some men), their lives are ones of constant but relatively low-level violence, a series of common assaults, or general bullying behaviour that does not necessarily involve an assault but nonetheless leads to a life of oppression. This recognition has led to the creation of two offences, one of controlling and coercive behaviour and one of offences contrary to the Domestic Abuse Act, which, when one reads the offences, reflects the type of abusive behaviour those who deal with domestic allegations in the Family Court are more used to dealing with.

THE DOMESTIC ABUSE ACT 2021 (DAA 2021)

'1 Definition of "domestic abuse"

(1) This section defines "domestic abuse" for the purposes of this Act.

(2) Behaviour of a person ("A") towards another person ("B") is "domestic abuse" if—

(a) A and B are each aged 16 or over and are personally connected to each other and

(b) the behaviour is abusive.

(3) Behaviour is "abusive" if it consists of any of the following—

(a) physical or sexual abuse;

(b) violent or threatening behaviour;

(c) controlling or coercive behaviour;

(d) economic abuse (see subsection (4));

(e) psychological, emotional or other abuse,

and it does not matter whether the behaviour consists of a single incident or a course of conduct.

(4) "Economic abuse" means any behaviour that has a substantial adverse effect on B's ability to—

(a) acquire, use or maintain money or other property, or

(b) obtain goods or services.

(5) For the purposes of this Act, A's behaviour may be behaviour "towards" B despite the fact that it consists of conduct directed at another person (for example, B's child).

(6) References in this Act to being abusive towards another person are to be read in accordance with this section.

(7) For the meaning of "personally connected", see section 2.

2 Definition of "personally connected"

(1) For the purposes of this Act, two people are "personally connected" to each other if any of the following applies—

(a) they are, or have been, married to each other;

(b) they are, or have been, civil partners of each other;

(c) they have agreed to marry one another (whether or not the agreement has been terminated);

(d) they have entered into a civil partnership agreement (whether or not the agreement has been terminated);

(e) they are, or have been, in an intimate personal relationship with each other;

(f) they each have, or there has been a time when they each have had, a parental relationship in relation to the same child (see subsection (2));

(g) they are relatives.

(2) For the purposes of subsection (1)(f) a person has a parental relationship in relation to a child if—

(a) the person is a parent of the child, or

(b) the person has parental responsibility for the child.

(3) In this section—

"child" means a person under the age of 18 years;

"civil partnership agreement" has the meaning given by section 73 of the Civil Partnership Act 2004;

"parental responsibility" has the same meaning as in the Children Act 1989 (see section 3 of that Act);

"relative" has the meaning given by section 63(1) of the Family Law Act 1996.'

4.29 The DAA 2021 uses the same definition of 'relative' as Family Law Act 1996, s 63. This is wider than the previous definition and means:

- the father, mother, stepfather, stepmother, son, daughter, stepson, stepdaughter, grandmother, grandfather, grandson, or granddaughter of that person or of that person's spouse, former spouse, civil partner, or former civil partner, or
- the brother, sister, uncle, aunt, niece, nephew or first cousin (whether of full blood or of half blood or by marriage or civil partnership) of that person or of that person's spouse, former spouse, civil partner, or former civil partner.

4.30 There is no requirement in the DAA 2021 for the victim and suspect to be cohabiting.

OFFENCE OF CONTROLLING AND COERCIVE BEHAVIOUR

4.31 Section 76 of the Serious Crime Act 2015 created a new offence of CCB in an intimate or family relationship. Prior to the introduction of this offence, case law indicated the difficulty in proving a pattern of behaviour amounting to harassment within an intimate relationship. The offence now formally recognises the harm which can be caused by coercion or control, the cumulative impact on the victim and that a repeated pattern of abuse can cause.

The offence is committed by an individual against a victim if (under s 76(1)(a)–(d)):

(a) they repeatedly or continuously engage in behaviour towards another person that is controlling or coercive;

(b) at the time of the behaviour, those two people are personally connected;

(c) the behaviour has a serious effect on the victim; and

(d) the perpetrator knows or ought to know that the behaviour will have a serious effect on the victim.

4.32 Although not an exhaustive list, behaviours commonly include:

(a) isolating a person from their friends and family;

(b) taking control over aspects of their everyday life, such as where they can go, who they can socialise with, what they can wear;

(c) withholding immigration documents, eg passports and visas;

(d) limiting access to finances, taking wages, benefits; or

(e) controlling their ability to go to school or place of study.

4.33 The purpose of the legislation has been to enable the type of abuse generally only seen in a domestic context to be properly punished. Behaviour that was traditionally not criminalised, such as isolating women from their friends and controlling what they wore and how they lived their lives, is now capable of being brought before the court.

4.34 The CPS has encouraged the use of these new powers, and there has been a noticeable increase in charges of CCB. The new powers, along with greater support for victims of DA, are ensuring that victims' voices are being heard within the criminal courts.

OFFENCES WHICH CAN BE COMMITTED IN A DOMESTICALLY ABUSIVE RELATIONSHIP (RAPE, SEXUAL OFFENCES, ETC)

4.35 As is our common experience, sexual offences can and do occur in a domestic setting. The offences are no different between man and wife or complete strangers. This chapter will not deal with the litany of sexual offences, ranging from rape to sexual assault, but it is worth touching upon some of the issues that can arise in a domestic context that perhaps do not arise elsewhere, and also to consider what protection there is for complainants of offences of this nature.

4.36 As noted above, until as recently as 1991, it was not illegal for a man to rape his wife. The House of Lords finally overturned centuries of common law, which meant women had no protection in the courts against a husband who wished to have sex with them.

4.37 It was not until the Sexual Offences Act 2003 that the common law position was put into statute and the Act applies equally to sexual assault between a man and wife. Juries are directed as to the legal definition of consent, whether the parties to an alleged rape are known to one another or not; thus, in a domestic context, a wife or girlfriend is still entitled to have a jury consider consent and whether that consent was reasonable.

4.38 However, it is important to note that, in respect of marital rape, the usual issue is consent, and in that respect, the *Bench Book*, used by Crown Court judges to direct juries, contains the following direction:

> 'It is agreed that D and W have had a long-term sexual relationship. This is relevant to the question of whether or not W consented to D [specify act] on this occasion. That is because the situation between two people who have/have had a long-term sexual relationship is different from a situation in which two people are strangers or have met one another only a few times. When two people have/have had such a relationship, there may be some give and take between them in relation to any number of things, including their sexual relationship. And sometimes, a partner who is not feeling enthusiastic may nevertheless reluctantly give consent to sex. However, when two people are/have been in a long-term sexual relationship, it is not the case that both of them will consent to any sexual activity which takes place. One person is fully entitled not to consent, regardless of their relationship. What you must decide in this case is whether W consented freely and by choice, even if reluctantly, to what took place or whether W did not consent but submitted to it. You must also decide whether D may have reasonably believed that W was consenting, taking into account all the evidence, including the nature of the [previous] relationship between W and D.'

4.39 This direction could be seen as watering down consent when the issue arises between those in a long-term relationship. Is a partner entitled to think his wife or girlfriend will consent because she has done so frequently in the past? It is questionable whether this direction should still be given in this day and age.

4.40 Complainants in these types of cases are still afforded the same protection in the way they give evidence as every other complainant in a rape or sexual case, namely their primary evidence is given by way of pre-recorded examination-in-chief, which is then played to the jury.

4.41 There are then other measures put in place to control cross-examination, ranging from who can conduct cross-examination to how that evidence is presented. We will first deal with who can cross-examine whom.

INABILITY OF DEFENDANT TO CROSS-EXAMINE IN PERSON (YOUTH JUSTICE AND CRIMINAL EVIDENCE ACT 1999, SS 34, 35 AND 36)

4.42 Most defendants benefit from legal representation; however, some defendants represent themselves. For some, this may be for financial reasons, for example, they earn too much to qualify for Legal Aid but cannot afford to pay privately for representation. Many have taken that course following the long-since decision made by a past government to refuse to reimburse legal fees if a defendant is acquitted. Others actively choose to represent themselves, believing that they can do better than qualified solicitors or barristers.

4.43 These defendants are known as unrepresented litigants (though sometimes still referred to as litigants-in-person (LIPs)). They conduct all litigation and advocacy in their own case, including cross-examining witnesses and making speeches. There has been a rise in the number of LIPs as restrictions on legal aid grow. However, the courts recognised that for offences of a certain nature, it would be inappropriate to allow LIPs to cross-examine particular witnesses. Hence, the court will appoint a suitably qualified advocate on their behalf.

4.44 The categories are broken down into three main areas:

- Youth Justice and Criminal Evidence Act 1999 (YJCEA 1999), s 34 prevents cross-examination of complainants in sexual offences;
- YJCEA 1999, s 35 protects child witnesses; and
- YJCEA 1999, s 36 is a wider section which is to be applied at the court's discretion.

4.45 In short, no defendant can cross-examine a complainant in a sex case, whether the complainant is a child or an adult. This applies equally in a domestic context.

4.46 Where the witness is a child that is under 18, under YJCEA 1999, s 35 they cannot be cross-examined by a defendant where the offence charged is one of the following

> '(a) any offence under—
>
> …
>
> (iva) any of sections 33 to 36 of the Sexual Offences Act 1956;
>
> (v) the Protection of Children Act 1978;
>
> (vi) Part 1 of the Sexual Offences Act 2003 …; or
>
> (vii) sections 1 and 2 of the Modern Slavery Act 2015;
>
> (b) kidnapping, false imprisonment or an offence under section 1 or 2 of the Child Abduction Act 1984;
>
> (c) any offence under section 1 of the Children and Young Persons Act 1933;

(d) any offence (not within any of the preceding paragraphs) which involves an assault on, or injury or a threat of injury to, any person.'

4.47 The child need not be a victim or complainant to be afforded the protection offered by this section and s 36 offers protection to any witness if:

'(a) the prosecutor makes an application for the court to give a direction under this section in relation to the witness or

(b) The court, of its own motion, raises the issue of whether such a direction should be given.

(2) If it appears to the court—

(a) that the quality of evidence given by the witness on cross-examination—

(i) is likely to be diminished if the cross-examination (or further cross-examination) is conducted by the accused in person, and

(ii) would be likely to be improved if a direction were given under this section, and

(b) that it would not be contrary to the interests of justice to give such a direction,

the court may give a direction prohibiting the accused from cross-examining (or further cross-examining) the witness in person.

(3) In determining whether subsection (2)(a) applies in the case of a witness, the court must have regard, in particular, to—

(a) any views expressed by the witness as to whether or not the witness is content to be cross-examined by the accused in person;

(b) the nature of the questions likely to be asked with regard to the issues in the proceedings and the defence case advanced so far (if any);

(c) any behaviour on the part of the accused at any stage of the proceedings, both generally and in relation to the witness;

(d) any relationship (of whatever nature) between the witness and the accused;

(e) whether any person (other than the accused) is or has at any time been charged in the proceedings with a sexual offence or an offence to which section 35 applies, and (if so) whether section 34 or 35 operates or would have operated to prevent that person from cross-examining the witness in person;

(f) any direction under section 19 that the court has given or proposes to give in relation to the witness.

(4) For the purposes of this section—

(a) "witness", in relation to an accused, does not include any other person who is charged with an offence in the proceedings; and

(b) any reference to the quality of a witness's evidence shall be construed in accordance with section 16(5).'

4.48 The purpose of the legislation is to protect vulnerable witnesses. The criminal courts have recognised that allowing some defendants to cross-examine witnesses or complainants, particularly in violent or sexual cases, can itself be a form of abuse perpetrated by a defendant. The legislation is deliberately wide-ranging so as to ensure that those witnesses in need of protection from the trauma of being cross-examined by a LIP are afforded it.

4.49 The parameters of the appointment of a suitably qualified advocate by the court were considered in the Court of Appeal case of *Abbas v CPS*, in which Hallett LJ stated that:

> '48. The role of a section 38 advocate is, undoubtedly, limited to the proper performance of their duty as a cross-examiner of a particular witness. Sections 36 and 38 are primarily concerned with protecting vulnerable witnesses from cross-examination by the accused. Therefore, it should not be thought that an advocate appointed under section 38 has a free-ranging remit to conduct the trial on the accused's behalf. The professional duty and their statutory duty would be to ensure that they are in a position properly to conduct the cross-examination. Their duties might include, therefore, applications to admit the bad character of the witness and or applications for disclosure of material relevant to the cross-examination. That is as far as one can go. All these matters must be entirely fact-specific. The important thing to note is that the section 38 advocate must ensure that s/he performs his/her duties in accordance with the words of the statute.
>
> 49. It also means that their appointment comes to an end, under section 38, at the conclusion of the cross-examination, unless the court otherwise determines. Technically, the lawyer no longer has a role in the proceedings thereafter. However, if the lawyer is prepared to stay and assist the defendant on a pro-bono basis, I see nothing in the act and no logical reason why the court should oblige them to leave. The advocate may well prove beneficial to the efficient and fair resolution of the proceedings.'[3]

4.50 In practical terms, the court or prosecutor will identify cases to which this legislation applies. Part 23 of the Criminal Procedure Rules 2025 (SI 2025/909) sets out the court's duties. It is not replicated here, but, in summary, it offers the following protection: the court allows a defendant to nominate an advocate, but if they do not select one, then the court will appoint an advocate. It is important to note that this advocate does not act on behalf of the defendant. Thus, their role is limited to cross-examination of specific witnesses as per the guidance above.

4.51 The court-appointed advocate can take instructions from the defendant as to what it is they challenge in a witness statement. The advocate can cross-examine on instruction; however, their role ends there. They are not permitted to deal with legal arguments that may arise and do not make a speech on behalf of the defendant unless they decide to continue acting on a pro bono basis.

3 *Abbas v CPS* [2015] EWHC 579 (Admin), [48]–[49].

4.52 It is rare that the courts must appoint such advocates, but it is reassuring to know that the powers exist.

4.53 This is not, however, the only way in which victims of DA and violent or sexual offences are protected in the criminal courts. There are a range of measures that can be adopted that dictate how the evidence is given.

SPECIAL MEASURES

4.54 By virtue of the YJCEA 1999, witnesses can apply for special measures as to how they deliver their evidence. For rape offences, it is standard procedure that the initial evidence will have been recorded, and this will stand as evidence-in-chief, known as an ABE – Achieving Best Evidence. A witness can then apply to be cross-examined from behind a screen, seen only by the judge, the advocates and the jury, or can ask that they give their evidence from another location via video link, meaning they are not in the courtroom at all, but the whole court can see them as they answer questions.

4.55 The use of ABEs used to be reserved for complainants in sexual offences, but DAA 2021, s 62 came into force in part on 19 May 2022 and ensures that all DA complainants are automatically eligible for special measures whenever it is alleged that behaviour falls within the DA definition. However, this does not currently apply to special measures available under YJCEA 1999, ss 27 and 28 (video recorded evidence-in-chief and video recorded cross-examination or re-examination). When this comes into force, the guidance will be updated, but it is clear that the courts are recognising the benefits of such special measures in cases beyond sexual offences.

4.56 There has been a greater increase in pre-recorded cross-examination, dealt with in more detail in at **4.61**. This means that rather than wait until trial, a witness's cross-examination takes place within months of the Plea and Trial Preparation Hearing (PTPH); it is recorded and then available for playback when the trial finally gets listed, which at present can be over three years from the alleged offence.

4.57 The CPS has taken great strides in dealing with alleged victims of DA, and a new policy has been created to ensure that complainants receive enhanced support. Prosecutors dealing with these type of offences are now required to adhere to the policy *Victims and Witnesses: CPS Public Policy Statement on the Delivery of Service to Victims – The Prosecutor's Pledge*.

4.58 Complainants in sexual offences have long been supported by Independent Sexual Violence Advisers (ISVAs). These are professionally trained support workers who talk complainants through the trial process, explain the different ways of giving evidence, and then support witnesses in court. The benefits of ISVAs have been recognised and support is now being rolled out in

DA cases too. Victims may be supported by an Independent Domestic Violence Adviser (IDVA) who provides similar levels of support to an ISVA.

4.59 For children, the special measures offered can be more subtle; alongside the standard procedure of pre-recorded evidence, there are also more practical measures, such as advocates and judges removing their wigs and gowns, to take some of the theatre away from the trial process, and make the parties seem more 'normal'.

4.60 There is no minimum age for someone to be a witness in the criminal courts. Therefore, the test that is applied is 'Can the witness understand the questions?' and 'Can they give answers that can be understood?' This has led to the use of intermediaries, who are now being used far more frequently, particularly at an early stage for children. An intermediary acts as a facilitator to ensure that a child understands the questions they are being asked, often by using props to explain concepts such as 'in' or 'on' – which can be crucial when it comes to framing an indictment in a sexual offence. They also use dolls, or body maps, to help a child explain which part of the body they are discussing, if relevant. The benefit of intermediaries has become invaluable when it comes to assisting children in giving evidence, but it has led to a far greater change in the way evidence is given.

INTRODUCTION OF VULNERABLE WITNESS ADVOCACY TRAINING AND A SEA CHANGE IN THE MANNER IN WHICH VULNERABLE WITNESSES ARE DEALT WITH

4.61 Operation Chalice was a case that hit the headlines for all the wrong reasons. The case is more commonly known as the Telford grooming case and dealt with allegations that four girls had been sexually assaulted and raped over the course of a number of years. The original trial began in 2011 and gained notoriety for the way in which the child victims were cross-examined, with one child being cross-examined for many days by different advocates covering the same topics repeatedly. One girl was asked whether she would 'repent on her sins' and was accused of consenting to sexual activity with older men.

4.62 This was just one example of aggressive cross-examination, and it led to the government commissioning a review, with Damien Green MP stating the following:

> 'On 30 June 2013, I announced a review that would look into ways to reduce the distress that some victims suffer during cross-examination in sexual violence cases, particularly where there are multiple defendants and barristers. In addition, the Government committed to consider the appointment of additional jurors in cases of child sexual exploitation and violence against women and girls. This would avoid victims being required to give evidence more than once by minimising the risk of disruption to trials. Both were actions in the Transforming the CJS Strategy and Action Plan.'

4.63 The report was published in March 2014. It is 27 pages long, but the key recommendations were as follows:

> '**(i) Strengthening and improving case management and the conduct of trials**
>
> 1.1 It is recommended that there should be consultation with the judiciary and prosecution and defence practitioners about whether the scope and use of Ground Rules Hearings (GRHs) could be widened to more/all sexual violence cases. Consideration should be given as to how to support this as a best practice approach with guidance and reference to GRHs in relevant case management materials.
>
> 2.1 It is recommended that consideration be given to the introduction of a trigger to ensure that all sexual violence cases are automatically identified for active and continuous case management to help ensure that the focus is clearly on the needs of the victim throughout.
>
> 3.1 It is recommended that the rules of professional conduct be reviewed to identify inconsistencies and propose ways to align them for the purposes of trials of sexual violence cases.
>
> **(ii) Specialisation of courts and/or those involved in sexual violence cases**
>
> 1.1 It is recommended that the bodies responsible for professional conduct and practitioners be encouraged and supported to develop an accreditation system for defence advocates that it is open and transparent.
>
> **(iii) Special measures and other arrangements for victims at court**
>
> 1.1 It is recommended that the potential benefits of expanding the role of intermediaries should be examined, including consideration of the feasibility of doing so within the current legislative framework or by amendment of it, and an assessment of cost implications. This work should also consider the respective roles of intermediaries, Independent Sexual Violence Advisors (ISVAs) and other "supporters" so that there is clarity on the role and purpose of each.
>
> 2.1 Pending the outcome of the pre-trial recording of the cross-examination pilot, it is recommended that further work be undertaken to raise awareness and encourage greater use of live links and other special measures that would enable victims and witnesses in sexual violence cases to give evidence and be cross-examined from outside of the court room.
>
> 3.1 It is recommended that the potential benefits of a further review should be considered once the outcomes of the pilot of pre-trial recorded cross-examination and other planned and ongoing programmes impacting on cases of sexual violence and /or child victims are known.
>
> **(iv) Codifying the appointment of "reserve" jurors for the opening stage of sexual violence trials in some circumstances**
>
> 1.1 It is recommended that there is a benefit in codifying the approach of appointing additional jurors for the opening stage so that judges have guidance about the steps to take, jurors can be informed, and jury managers can take a consistent approach in managing the jury pool. In addition, the

> rule changes should also provide that, in appropriate cases, jurors should be empanelled at the end of the day before the start of the trial.'[4]

The report specifically referred to Operation Chalice and the need for reform:

> 'The Crown Prosecution Service has reviewed a number of cases that involved multiple victims and/or defendants (such as Operation Retriever (Derbyshire), Operation Central (South Yorkshire), Operation Chalice (West Mercia), Operation Span (Greater Manchester), and Operation Bullfinch (Thames Valley)) using the case files maintained by prosecutors on which timings and details were recorded of the trial process. From this information it is evident that any distress and trauma that victims might endure in trials of sexual violence offences by virtue of the very nature of the allegations under consideration, would be exacerbated in trials where there are multiple defendants, when cross-examination is protracted (lasting many hours and sometimes days) and repetitive (with several counsel covering the same issues with victims) … A factor said to contribute to the trauma for victims is the manner in which cross-examination is conducted. In trials of sexual violence offences, victims are required to recount their ordeal and be challenged about personal and sensitive experiences and information. At present, section 41 of the Youth Justice and Criminal Evidence Act 1999 limits the potential to question a victim about their sexual behaviour outside of the specific incident. There have been examples of cases reported by the press and media where it is said that cross-examination was aggressive, with victims, for example, repeatedly being called a liar. However, although such cases appear infrequently, they receive a significant amount of coverage and commentary. There is no evidence to show that inappropriately aggressive cross-examination is a widespread issue in sexual violence trials involving multiple defendants or otherwise. Anecdotal evidence from practitioners and observers that we spoke to is that there are some examples of bad practice, but generally, practices are changing as experience, and learning is showing that cross-examination is most effective when done in a non-aggressive way.'[5]

4.64 This report has led to a sea change in the way in which advocates cross-examine vulnerable witnesses and also ensured that those who prosecute these cases are fully trained Rape and Serious Sexual Offences (RASSO) Counsel.

4.65 All counsel who prosecute cases involving vulnerable witnesses, whether those witnesses are the complainant or not, must now undertake Vulnerable Witness Advocacy Training. This course has been created and developed by the Inns of Court College of Advocacy, and it involves using the 20 principles of advocacy training.

4 Ministry of Justice, *Report on review of ways to reduce distress of victims in trials of sexual violence* (March 2014).

5 Ministry of Justice (n 4), para 14.

4.66 The course is delivered during a morning session but requires a great deal of preparation as advocates are given a hypothetical case and told to prepare a cross-examination for three witnesses, all of whom have different needs. The course is structured so that the first session involves the trainer assessing the questions submitted and pointing out those that do not comply with the 20 principles. Trainees then rewrite the questions, and there is a role play involving cross-examining a 'six-year-old child' to allow advocates to try out their new skills.

4.67 In practical terms, this means that those witnesses who are deemed to be vulnerable, such as children or persons suffering from some form of mental disability, must be cross-examined in line with the 20 principles. The cross-examination is in a form that is unrecognisable from the traditional style; leading questions are not permitted, and tag questions are forbidden. The whole process is designed to be as non-confrontational as possible.

4.68 The 20 principles are set out here:

Principles for preparation:

1. Ground Rules Hearing
2. Identify the key issues
3. Pre-draft

Principles for conduct

4. Rapport
5. Pace
6. Behaviour
7. Distress

Principles for questioning

8. Ask, don't talk
9. Chronology
10. Signposting
11. No repetition
12. Avoid statements put as questions
13. Avoid pronouns
14. Avoid 'remember' questions
15. Telling someone else (collusion)
16. Consider avoiding 'how' and 'why' questions
17. No 'tag' or 'directive leading' questions

18. No compound questions
19. Ask direct questions
20. No leading questions

4.69 A Ground Rules Hearing must be held to see what assistance the witness needs. Questions must be submitted ahead of the hearing so that the judge and intermediary can check that they comply with the 20 principles. Some of the principles are self-evident, such as removing leading questions, tag questions and a number of other ways in which advocates have been traditionally taught to cross-examine.

4.70 The idea is to shorten the time a witness is cross-examined, and make sure they are only asked about relevant material. For example, if a witness has given an account to a nurse and a different account to a police officer, the 20 principles would mean the differing accounts are not put to the complainant – instead, the differing accounts are adduced in another way by way of agreed facts, or through the officer in the case. The witness is not asked about the differing accounts, but the advocate is entitled to comment on it in their speeches. The rationale is the defence advocate can make the point they wish – that different accounts have been given – without the need to question the witness.

4.71 The witness is not challenged in the normal way; for example, in a rape case, a line of questioning may go as follows:

Q You initiated the kissing didn't you?

Q Then you undid his trousers?

Q You wanted to have sex with him, didn't you?

4.72 This style of questioning offends a number of the 20 principles, they are statements put as questions, with tag and leading questions used. To make the same point using the 20 principles, the advocate would have to start with a signpost, then ask questions, so 'I am going to ask you about how the sexual activity took place':

Q Did you kiss X?

Q Did you undo X's trousers?

Q Did you want to have sex with X?

4.73 One can see how the questions are different; the challenge is implicit rather than explicit and less confrontational.

4.74 Some advocates have found the change difficult to process, but all judges have been trained in the principles, and cases involving vulnerable witnesses are flagged to ensure that advocates follow the correct rubric. Challenges in the Court of Appeal have been unsuccessful, it was argued that the constraints placed on advocates were so unfair as to mean the trial process was in breach of Article 6 of the European Convention on Human Rights. In *Lubemba* the Court of Appeal disagreed.[6]

4.75 The principles have had the effect of reducing the length of time cross-examination takes; there is no repetition of topics, and in cases involving multiple defendants, one advocate takes the lead to ensure that there is no unnecessary cross-examination on matters which have already been covered.

4.76 The style of questioning has been particularly prominent in cases involving pre-recorded cross-examination. Criminal practitioners have long been familiar with a witness's account being recorded, the ABE interview. This is usually played to the jury, in edited form, as their examination-in-chief. What s 28 has introduced is cross-examination in the same format.

4.77 Cases where pre-recorded cross-examination may be appropriate are flagged by the CPS at the PTPH stage. If an application is made, a judge will likely grant pre-recorded cross-examination. The CPS must then truncate the normal timetable; all disclosure must be dealt with in order to ensure that a witness can be cross-examined ahead of the proposed trial date.

4.78 The idea is that it ensures cross-examination takes place far closer in time to the actual date of the allegation; further, as the criminal courts become busier and busier, trial dates are fixed months and sometimes years in advance. Pre-recording the cross-examination means a witness is not waiting months or years to be cross-examined.

4.79 In theory, this is a good idea; it reduces waiting time, which in turn can lower stress for witnesses; if there is a retrial, then the same recording can be used, meaning witnesses do not have to attend court as often.

4.80 In practical terms, it can be less effective. Witnesses are still having to wait for the trial to know the outcome, meaning the case is still hanging over them. There are a limited number of advocates trained in dealing with these cases, which is putting greater pressure on them and their diaries. Anecdotally, it has been suggested that jurors are acquitting in greater numbers as they feel removed from the witness; it is almost as if they are watching a film rather than relating to a real witness.

RESTRICTIONS ON EVIDENCE OR QUESTIONS RE SEXUAL HISTORY (YJCEA 1999, S 41)

4.81 The primary protection for complainants in sexual offences comes from YJCEA 1999, s 41. This restricts the questions that can be asked about previous sexual history unless it can be shown to fall under one of the gateways.

6 *R v Lubemba* [2014] EWCA Crim 2064; [2015] 1 WLR 1579.

4.82 An entire chapter could be devoted to s 41; for ease of reference, the legislation is set out here before a discussion on the protection it is designed to give.

> **'41 Restriction on evidence or questions about the complainant's sexual history.**
>
> (1) If at a trial a person is charged with a sexual offence, then, except with the leave of the court—
>
> (a) no evidence may be adduced, and
>
> (b) no question may be asked in cross-examination,
>
> by or on behalf of any accused at the trial about any sexual behaviour of the complainant.
>
> (2) The Court may give leave in relation to any evidence or question only on an application made by or on behalf of an accused and may not give such leave unless it is satisfied—
>
> (a) that subsection (3) or (5) applies, and
>
> (b) that a refusal of leave might have the result of rendering unsafe a conclusion of the jury or (as the case may be) the court on any relevant issue in the case.
>
> (3) This subsection applies if the evidence or question relates to a relevant issue in the case and either—
>
> (a) that issue is not an issue of consent or
>
> (b) it is an issue of consent and the sexual behaviour of the complainant to which the evidence or question relates is alleged to have taken place at or about the same time as the event which is the subject matter of the charge against the accused or
>
> (c) it is an issue of consent, and the sexual behaviour of the complainant to which the evidence or question relates is alleged to have been, in any respect, so similar—
>
> (i) to any sexual behaviour of the complainant which (according to evidence adduced or to be adduced by or on behalf of the accused) took place as part of the event which is the subject matter of the charge against the accused, or
>
> (ii) to any other sexual behaviour of the complainant which (according to such evidence) took place at or about the same time as that event,
>
> that the similarity cannot reasonably be explained as a coincidence.
>
> (4) For the purposes of subsection (3) no evidence or question shall be regarded as relating to a relevant issue in the case if it appears to the court to be reasonable to assume that the purpose (or main purpose) for which it would be adduced or asked is to establish or elicit material for impugning the credibility of the complainant as a witness.
>
> (5) This subsection applies if the evidence or question—

(a) relates to any evidence adduced by the prosecution about any sexual behaviour of the complainant and

(b) in the opinion of the court, would go no further than is necessary to enable the evidence adduced by the prosecution to be rebutted or explained by or on behalf of the accused.

(6) For the purposes of subsections (3) and (5), the evidence or question must relate to a specific instance (or specific instances) of alleged sexual behaviour on the part of the complainant (and accordingly, nothing in those subsections is capable of applying in relation to the evidence or question to the extent that it does not so relate).'

4.83 In simple terms, the legislation is designed to protect witnesses from the type of questioning designed to impugn their character rather than assist the jury with the issues.

4.84 There can be no questions about a complainant's previous sexual history unless it is of real relevance to the case; the test has been set out in *R v A (No 2)*:

> '31 As a matter of common sense, a prior sexual relationship between the complainant and the accused may, depending on the circumstances, be relevant to the issue of consent. It is a species of prospectant evidence which may throw light on the complainant's state of mind. It cannot, of course, prove that she consented on the occasion in question. Relevance and sufficiency of proof are different things; the fact that the accused, a week before an alleged murder, threatened to kill the deceased does not prove an intent to kill on the day in question, but it is logically relevant to that issue. After all, to be relevant, the evidence needs merely to have some tendency in logic and common sense to advance the proposition in issue. It is true that each decision to engage in sexual activity is always made afresh. On the other hand, the mind does not usually blot out memories. What one has been engaged on in the past may influence what choice one makes on a future occasion. Accordingly, a prior relationship between a complainant and an accused may sometimes be relevant to what decision was made on a particular occasion … there will be some cases where evidence of previous consensual sexual intercourse between the complainant and the defendant would be clearly relevant, but there will also be cases where such evidence would not be relevant. Where there has been a recent close and affectionate relationship between the complainant and the defendant, it is probable that the evidence will be relevant, not to advance the bare assertion that because she consented in the past, she consented on the occasion in question, but for the reason given by Professor Galvin, which is that evidence of such a relationship will show the complainant's specific mindset towards the defendant, namely her affection for him.'[7]

4.85 There is insufficient space to discuss the sheer volume of cases that have discussed s 41, but it is important to note that the courts have at the forefront of

7 *R v A (No 2)* [2001] UKHL 25; [2002] 1 AC 45.

their mind the protection of complainants from inappropriate questioning about their sexual behaviour.

PROTECTION FROM HARASSMENT ACT 1997 AND ASSOCIATED INJUNCTIONS

4.86 Not all offences within a domestic setting involve sexual offences or violence. Often, when a relationship breaks down, one partner cannot accept it and engages in behaviour that is commonly characterised as 'stalking'. Stalking is understood through the following acronym FOUR (as detailed on the CPS website): a pattern of fixated, obsessive, unwanted and repeated behaviours.

4.87 Stalking takes many forms; it principally involves persistently following or monitoring a person, but it does not necessarily mean that the perpetrator follows them in person. Rather, it can include forcing contact with the victim through any means, such as turning up unannounced at places they frequent, like their workplace or gym.

4.88 Protection from Harassment Act 1997, s 2A(3) sets out examples of acts associated with stalking. The listed behaviours are by no means exhaustive:

(a) following a person

(b) contacting, or attempting to contact, a person by any means

(c) publishing any statement or other material relating or purporting to relate to a person or purporting to originate from a person

(d) monitoring the use by a person of the internet, email, or any other form of electronic communication

(e) loitering in any place (whether public or private)

(f) interfering with any property in the possession of a person

(g) watching or spying on a person

4.89 Increasingly, in this digital age, stalking takes place over the internet and often via social media platforms, and advocates are routinely adjusting to deploying evidence from a wealth of sources, ranging from messenger platforms to surveillance apps, when presenting their cases.

4.90 Such behaviour by defendants, as in the case of harassment, undoubtedly has a substantial impact on many victims' mental health. Often, they report making significant changes to their daily routines, for example, changing the means by which they travel to work – bus rather than train, avoiding social gatherings with long-established friends, amending timings of regular appointments they attend; some even change phone numbers and, in extreme cases, move house. Victims routinely report feeling unable to travel alone and unsafe at home, which necessitates that they install additional and often expensive security measures.

In addition to those practical considerations, victim impact statements regularly document a deterioration in the victim's performance at work or in their studies due to the associated stress of this crime.

4.91 Given the above, bail conditions in such cases are closely considered, with the views of victims being a key consideration in the determination of whether to grant bail.

4.92 There are specific sentencing guidelines for stalking as provided for in the *Intimidatory Offences Definitive Guideline*.

4.93 In respect of ancillary applications, in addition to retraining orders, which are addressed later in this chapter, the Stalking Protection Act 2019 introduced Stalking Protection Orders: a civil order made on application to the magistrate's court by the police which requests both prohibitions and/or positive requirements to protect the victim from the risk of stalking. Breach of such an order is a criminal offence. Such orders are particularly useful where a case does not meet the threshold to commence criminal proceedings and allow for early police intervention.

4.94 Harassment is another key offence which falls under the umbrella of the Protection from Harassment Act 1997, under s 4 (putting people in fear of violence) and s 2 ('simple' harassment).

4.95 The s 2 offence is defined as causing alarm or distress to another, amounting to a course of conduct which must involve conduct on at least two occasions. It routinely involves a persistent and deliberate course of unacceptable conduct targeted at a person, which causes them to be both distressed and often fearful of the longer-term consequences.

4.96 The two instances (or more) do not have to involve the same type of behaviour on both occasions but must cause alarm or distress. As with stalking, harassment can take many forms, from the sending of abusive text messages to receiving unwanted letters, emails or visits.

4.97 It follows that the amount of occasions involved and the timing of these instances are key considerations. In a case where there are relatively few incidents spread far apart, it is less likely a court will be able to make a finding of a course of conduct: *DPP v Lau*.[8] Courts are urged to adopt a cautious approach in those cases and to carefully consider whether individual events do amount to a course of conduct, see *Pratt v DPP*.[9]

4.98 For the more serious offence, the prosecution has to prove that the course of conduct causes another to fear that violence will be used against them and that

8 *DPP v Lau* [2000] 1 FLR 799.
9 *Pratt v DPP* [2001] EWHC Admin 483.

the defendant knows or ought to know that their course of conduct will cause another to fear that violence would be used against them.

SENTENCING AND ANCILLARY REMEDIES

4.99 All Crown Court judges are instructed to use the Sentencing Council website, www.sentencingcouncil.org.uk.

4.100 This website is easily searchable and outlines the guidelines for all offences, if applicable. Not every offence has a guideline, and in those circumstances, the judge must still follow the same rubric: assessing culpability and harm, then considering aggravating and mitigating factors. In addition to sentencing guidelines, there are other key texts that judges and other professionals alike often rely upon in determining the most appropriate sentence. For example, *Banks on Sentence*, *Thomas' Sentencing Referencer*, and *Rook and Ward on Sexual Offences* are among the notable references.

4.101 The Sentencing Council's *Domestic abuse: overarching principles* states the following:

> 'The domestic context of the offending behaviour makes the offending more serious because it represents a violation of the trust and security that normally exists between people in an intimate or family relationship. Additionally, there may be a continuing threat to the victim's safety, and in the worst cases, a threat to their life or the lives of those around them.'

The CPS guidance on prosecuting domestic abuse also states:

> 'A victim's behaviour is never a justification for abuse perpetrated against them.
>
> Prosecutors should be alert to the potential for escalating risk. domestic abuse is rarely a one-off incident, and the cumulative and interlinked physical, psychological, sexual, emotional, or economic abuse has a particularly damaging effect on the victim and those around them. Domestic abuse is likely to become increasingly frequent and more serious the longer it continues and may result in death. Prosecutors should keep cases of domestic abuse under constant review, which includes assessing and reassessing the safety of victims and witnesses involved in the case through the police and specialist support agencies. Even minor offences have the potential to be followed by more serious incidents.
>
> Within the context of mutually violent relationships, it is important to consider that women are more likely to be injured and injured more severely than men.'[10]

10 CPS, 'Domestic Abuse' (last updated 6 February 2026), www.cps.gov.uk/prosecution-guidance/rdomestic-abuse.

4.102 An example for the Controlling and coercive behaviour guidelines is also set out here; aside from applying the overarching principles, the court must always categorise harm and culpability in order to reach a sentencing range – examples are below:

> **'Step 1 – Determining the offence category**
>
> The court should determine the offence category with reference only to the factors in the tables below. To determine the category, the court should assess *culpability* and the extent of *harm*.
>
> **Culpability**
>
> Where there are factors present from more than one category of culpability, the court should weigh those factors in order to decide which category most resembles the offender's case.
>
> *A – Higher culpability*
>
> - Conduct intended to maximise fear or distress
> - Persistent action over a prolonged period
> - Use of multiple methods of controlling or coercive behaviour
> - Sophisticated offence
> - Conduct intended to humiliate and degrade the victim
>
> *B – Medium culpability*
>
> - Conduct intended to cause some fear or distress
> - Scope and duration of offence that falls between categories A and C
> - All other cases that fall between categories A and C
>
> *C – Lesser culpability*
>
> - Offender's responsibility substantially reduced by mental disorder or learning disability.
> - The offence was limited in scope and duration
>
> **Harm**
>
> Where there are factors present from more than one category of harm, the court should weigh those factors in order to decide which category most resembles the offender's case.
>
> *Category 1*
>
> - Fear of violence on many occasions
> - Very serious alarm or distress which has a substantial adverse effect on the victim
> - Significant psychological harm
>
> *Category 2*
>
> - Fear of violence on at least two occasions
> - Serious alarm or distress which has a substantial adverse effect on the victim

Step 2 – Starting point and category range

Having determined the category at step one, the court should use the corresponding starting point to reach a sentence within the category range below. The starting point applies to all offenders irrespective of plea or previous convictions.

An adjustment from the starting point, upwards or downwards, may be necessary to reflect particular features of culpability and/or harm (for example, the presence of multiple factors within one category, the presence of factors from more than one category (where not already taken into account at step 1), or where a case falls close to a borderline between categories).'

4.103 Once a starting point has been identified, the court will look to statutory aggravating and mitigating factors to increase or decrease sentence. Such factors include

'*Statutory aggravating factors*

- Previous convictions, having regard to a) the *nature* of the offence to which the conviction relates and its *relevance* to the current offence and b) the *time* that has elapsed since the conviction
- Offence committed whilst on bail
- Offence motivated by, or demonstrating hostility based on any of the following characteristics or presumed characteristics of the victim: religion, race, disability, sexual orientation, or transgender identity

Other aggravating factors

- Steps taken to prevent the victim reporting an incident
- Steps taken to prevent the victim obtaining assistance
- A proven history of violence or threats by the offender in a domestic context
- Impact of offence on others, particularly children
- Exploiting contact arrangements with a child to commit the offence
- Victim is particularly vulnerable (not all vulnerabilities are immediately apparent)
- Victim left in debt, destitute or homeless
- Failure to comply with current court orders
- An offence committed on the licence or post-sentence supervision
- Offences taken into consideration

Factors reducing seriousness

- No previous convictions or no relevant/recent convictions
- Remorse
- Good character and/or exemplary conduct

- Serious medical conditions requiring urgent, intensive or long-term treatment
- Age and/or lack of maturity
- Mental disorder or learning disability (where not taken into account at step one)
- Sole or primary carer for dependent relatives
- Determination and/or demonstration of steps having been taken to address offending behaviour'

4.104 The court will then reduce the sentence further if the defendant has pleaded guilty at any stage of the proceedings.

4.105 All sentences follow the same rubric, considering harm and culpability, and it is important to note that any offence committed within a domestic context attracts a higher sentence as that is treated as an aggravating feature.

DOMESTIC ABUSE PROTECTION NOTICES AND ORDERS

4.106 The DAA 2021 allows for victims of DA or third parties, such as Chief Constables, to apply for a Domestic Abuse Protection Order. These are similar to Non-molestation Orders but can also be made by the Crown Court after a conviction at trial.

4.107 If the victim is applying, they apply to the Family Court, but third parties apply to the magistrates' court. Breach of such orders can result in criminal proceedings.

> **'27 Meaning of "domestic abuse protection order"**
>
> (1) In this Part, a "domestic abuse protection order" is an order which, for the purpose of preventing a person ("P") from being abusive towards a person aged 16 or over to whom P is personally connected—
>
> (a) prohibits P from doing things described in the order or
>
> (b) requires P to do things described in the order.
>
> (2) A domestic abuse protection order may be made—
>
> (a) on application (see section 28), or
>
> (b) in the course of certain proceedings (see section 31).
>
> (3) Section 32 sets out the conditions for making a domestic abuse protection order.
>
> **28 Domestic abuse protection orders on application**
>
> (1) A court may make a domestic abuse protection order under this section against a person ("P") on an application made to it in accordance with this section.

(2) An application for an order under this section may be made by—

(a) the person for whose protection the order is sought;

(b) the appropriate chief officer of Police (see subsection (4));

(c) a person specified in regulations made by the Secretary of State;

(d) any other person with the leave of the court to which the application is to be made.

(3) Where P is given a domestic abuse protection notice by a member of a relevant police force under section 22, the chief officer of Police in relation to that force must apply for a domestic abuse protection order against P.

(For further provision about such applications, see section 29.)

(4) The appropriate chief officer of Police is—

(a) in a case where subsection (3) applies, the chief officer of Police referred to in that subsection;

(b) in any other case, any of the following—

(i) the chief officer of Police of the force maintained for any police area in which P resides;

(ii) the chief officer of Police of any other force maintained for a police area who believes that P is in that police area or is intending to come to it;

(iii) the Chief Constable of the British Transport Police Force;

(iv) the Chief Constable of the Ministry of Defence Police.

(5) An application for an order under this section must be made to the family court, except where subsection (6) or (7) applies.

(6) An application made by a chief officer of Police for an order under this section must be made by complaint to a magistrates' court.'

4.108 The court must also consider the s 32 criteria as to whether such an order is necessary, and if they are so satisfied, on the balance of probabilities, the order can be made.

'32 Conditions for making an order

(1) The Court may make a domestic abuse protection order under section 28 or 31 against a person ("P") if conditions A and B are met.

(2) Condition A is that the court is satisfied on the balance of probabilities that P has been abusive towards a person aged 16 or over to whom P is personally connected.

(3) Condition B is that the order is necessary and proportionate to protect that person from domestic abuse, or the risk of domestic abuse, carried out by P.

…'

RESTRAINING ORDERS ON ACQUITTAL

4.109 From 1 December 2020, the court can order a Restraining Order upon conviction under Sentencing Act 2020, s 360 (previously Protection from Harassment Act 1997, s 5). From 1 December 2020, the court can also make a Restraining Order on acquittal under Protection from Harassment Act 1997, s 5A (previously Protection from Harassment Act 1997, s 5).

4.110 The purpose of this power is to ensure that even in cases where there is an acquittal of the court, a complainant has sufficient protection.

4.111 A Restraining Order after conviction will be made if the court feels there is a need to protect a person or people. It is designed to be a preventative measure, with criminal punishment following if it is breached. The case of *R v Khellaf*,[11] provided the following four principles that the court must take into account when considering ordering a restraining order:

(a) The court should consider the views of the person to be protected.

(b) No order should be made unless the judge concludes that it is necessary to protect the victim.

(c) The terms of the order should be proportionate to the harm which it is sought to protect.

(d) Particular care should be taken when children are involved to ensure that the order does not prevent contact between a parent and a child where such contact is otherwise appropriate.

4.112 Upon acquittal, the court can still make a Restraining Order; a defendant is not required to consent to such an order being made; the real test is whether the court thinks it necessary to protect a person. The prosecution must give notice to the court that they intend to apply for such an order. The judge, considering the order, may take into account the evidence they have heard in any trial. The prosecution is not limited to relying on the evidence adduced at trial; they may also refer to previous convictions, previous injunctions, hearsay evidence, and matters contained in crime reports that have not resulted in a criminal trial.

4.113 The powers are deliberately wide-ranging and are aimed at assisting those the court believes may be at risk. They carry the same punishment of imprisonment if breached.

4.114 CPS guidance[12] confirms any orders sought must must:

- only impose prohibitions and not positive requirements;

11 *R v Khellaf* [2016] EWCA Crim 1297.

12 CPS, 'Restraining Orders' (last updated 22 January 2025), www.cps.gov.uk/prosecution-guidance/restraining-orders.

- cover the range of behaviour undertaken by the defendant;
- relate clearly to the behaviour complained of;
- be realistic, reasonable and proportionate;
- be clear, concise and easy to understand by the defendant;
- be specific when referring to exclusion from an area, to include, for example, street names and/or clear boundaries, including maps.

4.115 The order can be sought for any duration the court thinks necessary, from a defined period, or indefinitely. A person subject to an order can apply to the court for its discharge.

CONCLUSION

4.116 We appreciate that this has been a whirlwind tour through DA and how it is dealt with in the criminal courts. The main learning point to take away is that there has been a sea change in how DA and the victims of it are dealt with in the courts. There is a greater emphasis on protecting victims and ensuring that they can give their evidence in the most comfortable manner possible.

4.117 A raft of special measures exist to protect victims when they are cross-examined, and even if the case results in an acquittal, the court still has the power to protect perceived victims of DA.

4.118 There is still a way to go, women are still predominantly the victims of abuse, and there are almost daily headlines of women murdered by abusive male partners; many reading this will recall the Labour MP Jess Phillips' annual practice where she spends five minutes in the House of Commons reading a list of women killed over the past 12 months where the perpetrator or suspect was a man known to them. Still, it is comforting to know such matters are being taken increasingly more seriously now. It is hoped that by challenging the abuse when it occurs at a lower level will lead to a reduction of the more serious abuse which often ends with devastating consequences such as those seen routinely in rape and murder cases.

CHAPTER 5

The Interaction Between Domestic Abuse, Controlling and Coercive Behaviour and Financial Remedies

5.01 This section will provide an overview of the law in this area so that its potential relevance is in the mind of the enquiring advocate or adviser when receiving a case.

5.02 *Author's note:* Financial remedies are a specialist aspect of family law and require evaluation in their own right by experts in that area. The authors of this book do not purport to be such experts. We are very grateful to Anita Mehta of 4PB for her invaluable assistance with this chapter, she having kindly agreed to become a guest contributor to enable us to embrace this important topic within this book. Ian and I considered it would be incomplete without reference to it. Anita has flagged key relevant factors herein but we, and she, would point out that there are limits to what can be addressed in this overview.

INTRODUCTION

5.03 The remedies for domestic abuse (DA) in the family justice system are injunctive relief and those of the Children Act 1989 when it comes to the safety of children. Financial remedies do not purport to offer a remedy for DA, as per Peel J, the lead judge in the Financial Remedy Court:

> 'It is not for the financial remedies court to impose a fine, a penalty, or damages upon a party for conduct. Nor is it for the financial remedies court to moralise or apportion blame in how the parties behaved towards each other during their time together.'[1]

5.04 That is notwithstanding the Domestic Abuse Act 2021 (DAA 2021) which makes it clear that DA can take many forms, and this includes economic abuse under s 1(3)(d) as explained in subs (4):

> '(3) Behaviour is "abusive" if it consists of any of the following—
>
> …
>
> (d) economic abuse (see subsection (4));

1 *N v J* [2024] EWFC 184, [38].

...

and it does not matter whether the behaviour consists of a single incident or a course of conduct.

(4) "Economic abuse" means any behaviour that has a substantial adverse effect on B's ability to—

(a) acquire, use or maintain money or other property, or

(b) obtain goods or services.'[2]

THE LIMITS OF PROTECTION

5.05 This chapter is about the division of finances *between married couples and civil partners* (collectively referred to as married couples below). Note, however: at the time of writing, the government has promised to introduce legislation to give unmarried couples rights and family law remedies. The authors of this book support the introduction of that legislation, as unmarried spouses and the children of those couples, are already financially vulnerable due to the lack of remedies and DA in all forms is not just the preserve of the married.

5.06 Moreover, as between married couples, High Court jurisprudence since 2020 has made clear that even very serious DA will not lead the Court to increase the scale of the award absent an evidenced financial consequence. Whether DA will impact the ultimate disposal of assets within a financial remedy outcome is an evolving area of interest.

PRACTICE NOTE

At the time of drafting, the government has just announced a consultation into financial remedies, which includes looking at the treatment of conduct. That review follows an increasing body of research in this area, notably including the report by Resolution *Domestic Abuse in Financial Remedy Proceedings*[3] and the report *Dividing property and finances on divorce: what happens in cases involving domestic abuse?*[4] which were both considered in the Law Commission scoping report published in December 2024.[5] Whilst it is impossible to know at the time of drafting what changes policymakers plan to make, practitioners need to be aware that this may be an area where either policymakers step in, or a case reaches the Court of Appeal concerning current High Court jurisprudence in respect of conduct.

2 DAA 2021, s 1(3)–(4).

3 *Domestic Abuse in Financial Remedy Proceedings* (Resolution, 2024) https://resolution.org.uk/wp-content/uploads/2024/10/Resolution_DAFRP_Report_ONLINE.pdf.

4 Emma Hitchings and Caroline Bryson, *Dividing property and finances on divorce: what happens in cases involving domestic abuse?* (University of Bristol, 2024).

5 Law Commission, *Financial Remedies on Divorce and Dissolution: A scoping report,* Law Com No 471 (18 December 2024), https://lawcom.gov.uk/project/financial-remedies-on-divorce/.

5.07 But remember – economic abuse can take many forms – it is a very effective form of coercive control. We encourage you to use your insight. What you are not usually permitted to plead in a financial remedies court you *CAN* plead in a children's court.

5.08 In the financial remedy proceedings, there are limits about what you can plead in respect of domestic abuse. However, it is still important that practitioners assess whether there is an ongoing abusive relationship between the parties in financial remedy cases, as this will impact on how the case is approached, including what measures need to be taken to prevent dissipation or concealment of funds, what forms of non-court dispute resolution (NCDR) are appropriate, how to formulate offers, draft orders and the appropriateness of the various types of remedy. There is a growing understanding amongst practitioners and the judiciary that NCDR, financial remedy litigation, and failing to comply with resulting court orders, can all be used as tools in ongoing abuse. This is especially so when the victim is forced to engage in concurrent litigation in respect of the children and injunctive relief.

HOW TO RECOGNISE SIGNS OF ECONOMIC ABUSE

5.09 There are many forms of economic abuse. Economic abuse may develop gradually and may be disguised as 'managing the finances'. Over time, the victim may find that their behaviour is completely controlled because of their financial dependence. It may only be when a legal team or financial adviser begins reviewing financial disclosure (perhaps in the course of separation) that the extent of the economic abuse becomes apparent.

5.10 Practitioners should be careful not to fall into stereotyping when thinking about economic abuse. It is well documented that the majority of coercive control is perpetrated by men, however it is not solely perpetrated by men. It is important to keep in mind that men can be the victims of this abuse.

5.11 It is also important to keep in mind that this abuse is not restricted to the person earning the income abusing the stay-at-home parent or spouse. The person generating the family income can still be the person who is economically abused by the other.

5.12 Think also of same sex couples. Do not allow gender assumptions to restrict your thinking with respect to roles. Be aware of cultural assumptions you might be making. We flag below dowry abuse but if English is not a client's first language and/or definitional roles within a marriage are impacted upon by culture or religion then financial independence may be restricted. Whether this amounts to controlling and coercive behaviour (CCB) and economic abuse is not a matter of assumption but of enquiry. It is part of getting to know your client's experiences and needs. Be curious, not judgmental.

Common warning signs during the relationship

5.13 What follows is not an exhaustive list, but one designed to trigger client/legal discussion. We endorse the use of the Surviving Economic Abuse screening tool,[6] which can help practitioners and clients detect and decide whether there has been economic abuse in the relationship. Consider:

- Isolation.
- Restriction of access to family, friends, or social networks, making the victim financially and emotionally dependent.
- Economic exploitation.
- Control of income, restriction of access to bank accounts, withholding of money, or confiscating financial resources.
- Monitoring and surveillance.
- Close monitoring of spending, demanding receipts, or limiting what the victim is allowed to buy.
- Sabotage of employment.
- Interference with work, discouraging career progression, or creating barriers to maintaining employment.
- Threats and intimidation.
- Use of money as leverage, including threats to cut off financial support or disclose sensitive financial information.
- Debt accumulation, accumulating debt in the victim's name, sometimes without their knowledge or consent, to exert control or create dependency.
- Mortgage abuse.[7]

Note, these behaviours are rarely isolated incidents, they form part of a broader pattern designed to make the victim subordinate.

PRACTICE NOTE

Practitioners should be alert to classic red flags as the financial picture starts to emerge, such as all the assets being in one party's name after a long marriage, assets being transferred to third parties around the time of separation, high liabilities in the name of a party who does not have the higher earning capacity, one party not having any access to their home, their own, or the children's possessions, their own or marital funds after separation.

6 Surviving Economic Abuse, 'Screening for Economic Abuse', https://survivingeconomicabuse.org/im-supporting-someone/information-for-womens-sector-professionals/screening-for-economic-abuse/.

7 Surviving Economic Abuse, *'Locked into a mortgage, locked out of my home': How perpetrators use joint mortgages as a form of economic abuse and how to stop them.* (September 2024), https://survivingeconomicabuse.org/wp-content/uploads/2024/09/SEA-Joint-Mortgages-Report-2024.pdf.

The impact of economic abuse

5.14 The effects of economic abuse can be devastating; victims can experience forms of emotional and psychological harm such as:

- anxiety and depression;
- loss of confidence and self-worth;
- feelings of helplessness or shame;
- fear of making independent decisions.

5.15 The impact of financial difficulties on victims and their children should also not be underestimated. For example, inability to develop their earning capacity, high debt, poor credit rating and lack of a pension, can have implications for the victim years after other scars from an abusive relationship have healed. Professor Emma Hitchings and Caroline Bryson found that: 'Up to five years after their divorce, female domestic abuse survivors continued to be more likely to be in financially precarious situations.'[8]

BARRIERS TO LEAVING THE RELATIONSHIP

5.16 It is becoming better understood that economic abuse can create significant barriers preventing victims leaving abusive relationships. This abuse can occur regardless of the level of the family assets and income; a gilded cage is still a cage. Fear of homelessness, poverty, or being unable to support their children often keep individuals trapped in harmful situations. It is not uncommon in cases of economic abuse, for the perpetrator to threaten the victim that they will 'have nothing' or be unable to care for themselves or their children if they leave. The fear engendered by such threats can have a significant controlling impact on the victim's behaviour. Note that immigrants and migrants, especially those with uncertain immigration status, limited family support and language barriers, are particularly vulnerable.

PRACTICE NOTE

Practitioners should be aware that, unlike other forms of DA, where leaving the relationship may reduce the victim's exposure to abusive behaviours, economic abuse can accelerate or start at the point of separation.

Pre-emptive steps

Victims need to consider what steps they take to meet their needs when leaving financially abusive relationships; they need to consider:

8 Emma Hitchings and Caroline Bryson, *Fair shares? Sorting out money and property on divorce* (Nuffield Foundation, 2025), https://www.nuffieldfoundation.org/project/fair-shares-sorting-out-money-and-property-on-divorce.

- Will the abuser allow them access to their own, or matrimonial funds, when they leave?
- Will the abuser restrict their access to funds for legal or financial advice?
- Do they need to create and protect (potentially hide) a fund to be able to leave safely and meet their, and their children's, needs?
- Will the abuser exploit their ability to pay the mortgage, by forcing them to pay all or more than their agreed share to avoid arrears and poor credit rating?

Think ahead.

QUANTUM OF THE AWARD

5.17 The Matrimonial Causes Act 1973 (MCA 1973) dates from 1973. Pending the outcome of the current consultation, it is case law that we look to, to explain how this statute, which is now over 50 years old, should be applied.

5.18 Case law explains that, when it comes to financial remedy proceedings between married couples, the court undertakes a two-stage exercise of computation of the parties' assets and liabilities, before considering how they should be distributed. When considering how to distribute the assets, the court will look for a fair outcome, applying the principles of sharing (dividing the assets generated by the parties' joint endeavour), meeting needs, or compensation. Although compensation has rarely been considered relevant by the court.

5.19 The court has regard to all the circumstances of the case, with the first consideration being the welfare of any minor of the family who has not attained the age of 18.[9] Section 25(2) sets out the matters the court should have particular regard to, and that includes: '(g) the conduct of each of the parties, if that conduct is such that it would in the opinion of the court be inequitable to disregard it.' On the rare occasions that DA has been taken into account in financial remedy proceedings, it has been as a result of the court finding that it is *conduct that is inequitable to disregard*.

The four categories of conduct argument

5.20 In *OG v AG*,[10] which predates the DAA 2021 and was not argued as a case involving abuse, Mostyn J identified four categories of conduct argument:

9 MCA 1973, s 25.
10 *OG v AG* [2020] EWFC 52, [34].

(a) gross and obvious personal conduct meted out by one party against the other. This includes economic misconduct, where one party economically oppresses the other for selfish or malicious reasons;

(b) '*add-back*' arguments, where one party has recklessly dissipated funds;

(c) litigation misconduct; and

(d) misconduct in failing to give full and frank disclosure.

The approach

5.21 In *Tsvetkov v Khayrova*,[11] Mr Justice Peel, as already noted, the lead judge in the Financial Remedy Court, set out the approach to running a conduct argument:

> '43. A party asserting conduct must, in my judgment, prove:
>
> i) the facts relied upon;
>
> ii) if established, that those facts meet the conduct threshold, which has consistently been set at a high or exceptional level; and
>
> iii) that there is an identifiable (even if not always easily measurable) negative financial impact upon the parties which has been generated by the alleged wrongdoing.
>
> A causative link between act/omission and financial loss is required. Sometimes the loss can be precisely quantified, sometimes it may require a broader evaluation. But I doubt very much that the quantification of loss can or should range beyond the financial consequences caused by the pleaded grounds.
>
> This is stage one.
>
> 44. If stage one is established, the court will go on to consider how the misconduct, and its financial consequences, should impact upon the outcome of the financial remedies proceedings, undertaking the familiar s25 exercise which requires balancing all the relevant factors.
>
> This is stage two.'

The facts (point i)

5.22 Proving the facts in these cases is not as easy as it sounds. Financial remedy proceedings do not usually contain the type of evidence that is commonplace in children proceedings. Evidence of a conviction is usually the best starting place. Otherwise, practitioners can apply for the judgment from

11 *Tsvetkov v Khayrova* [2023] EWFC 130.

the children proceedings to be admitted. The difficulty with both these solutions is that the criminal or children proceedings need to have concluded before the financial remedy proceedings start. As one way of overcoming this difficulty, Resolution has called for consideration of combined fact-finding hearings in children and financial proceedings.

The exceptionality threshold (point ii)

5.23 Practitioners are very aware of the significant gulf between how DA will be treated – sometimes in the same court by the same judge – within the financial remedy and children proceedings. To my mind (JDKC) this reveals how out of step practice in financial remedies cases is to the rest of the Family Court. We are told by our President that DA is a scourge on our society. We have case law, for example Hayden J in *F v M*,[12] endorsed by the Court of Appeal (see **Chapter 2** where this case was discussed at length), that identifies financial control as part of the weaponry of CCB. And yet, shift the court forum, and that insight and acceptance falls away? Its relevance is dismissed? That approach means that economic CCB can continue unabated in the throes of financial assessment and continue into and after distribution of family assets. 'Justice', where DA and CCB is concerned, should not be seen to have a double head within the Family Court.

5.24 Orders for no contact and even convictions for actual bodily harm (ABH), may not be considered sufficient to cross the exceptionality threshold. It is only the most extreme forms of DA that have crossed the threshold of being 'inequitable to disregard', in order to impact on the award:

- In *H v H (Financial Relief: Attempted Murder as conduct)*: conduct was recognised where the husband had been convicted of attempted murder of the wife.[13]
- In *K v L*: the husband had been convicted of the sexual abuse of his wife's grandchildren.[14]

5.25 Courts still routinely use the test advanced by Mr Mostyn QC (as he then was) to Mr Justice Burton in *S v S (Non-Matrimonial Property: Conduct)* to identify whether abuse has crossed the statutory threshold. This was formulated as conduct that elicits a '*gasp factor*'.[15] In that case the final incident between the parties, that led to the husband being convicted of ABH, was not considered sufficient to elicit the *gasp factor*.

5.26 However, this formulation of the statutory test has been criticised by some: including in *Seales v Seales (Ancillary Relief: Murder and Coercive Control as Conduct)*, where Master Bell commented that the 'gasp factor'

12 *F v M* [2021] EWFC 4.
13 *H v H (Financial Relief: Attempted Murder as conduct)* [2005] EWHC 2911 (Fam).
14 *K v L* [2010] EWCA Civ 125.
15 *S v S (Non-Matrimonial Property: Conduct)* [2006] EWHC 2793 (Fam).

threshold was, perhaps, too high.[16] Anita Mehta and Olivia Piercy, commenting on this test in the *Financial Remedy Journal*, opine:

> '... the "gasp factor" may be past its sell by date. It applies an outdated understanding of domestic abuse; one where there is a scale, with serious physical violence at the extreme end, and emotional abuse at the lesser end. The understanding of the Family Court in the private law arena has developed beyond this way of thinking.'[17]

Identifiable negative financial impact (point iii)

5.27 In respect of the first of his categories set out at **5.20** above, Mostyn J stated that:

> '... such conduct will only be taken into account in very rare circumstances. The authorities clearly indicate that such conduct would only be reflected where there is a financial consequence to its impact.'[18]

There is a question as to whether Macur LJ in *Goddard-Watts v Goddard-Watts*,[19] sitting in the Court of Appeal, departed from the approach of requiring a financial consequence of conduct, nevertheless this jurisprudence has been followed by other members of the High Court judiciary. Save in examples of money being transferred away from the family pot, or a complete loss of earning capacity due to life-changing injuries, it is exceptionally hard to provide concrete evidence to establish a financial impact.

5.28 In *N v J*, the year after *Tsvetkov*, Peel J found that:

> 'I accept that the statute does not specifically refer to a financial consequence, and it is therefore wise not to rule out completely the theoretical possibility of conduct being taken into account absent such a financial impact. Nevertheless, as the review of authorities above suggests, such cases will be vanishingly rare.'[20]

5.29 *JDKC note:* To inform any critique you have, do listen to Sir Nicholas reflecting on *OG v AG* and the following jurisprudence relating to cases involving DA on his podcast *Law & Disorder,*[21] for there we hear insight and are emboldened in the criticisms we make of the financial remedies approach to economic abuse and financially and emotionally abusive CCB.

16 *Seales v Seales (Ancillary Relief: Murder and Coercive Control as Conduct)* [2023] NIMaster 6.
17 Anita Mehta and Olivia Piercy, 'Is it Time to Consign the Gasp Factor to the History Books?', *Financial Remedy Journal* (18 October 2023).
18 *OG v AG* (n 10).
19 *Goddard-Watts v Goddard-Watts* [2023] EWCA Civ 115.
20 *N v J* (n 1), [39ii].
21 'The Misconduct Dilemma; how should abuse be reflected in financial remedies?', *Law & Disorder* (13 December 2025).

PRACTICE NOTE

Whilst the principal authors of this book may not have experience of financial remedies, they recognise the difficulty for victims of being able to specify the DA they have experienced and identify the financial impact in the early stages of legal advice or indeed by the first hearing. When victims have been traumatised, or are suffering from post-traumatic stress disorder, being able to identify what was abusive can take time. A trauma-informed approach to DA CCB requires sensitive handling of all aspects of CCB (referring back to Hayden J in *F v M*) and that includes economic control.

Pleading conduct

5.30 If you are considering pleading a conduct argument, you should take specialist advice on the issue, as failed attempts to run conduct can have cost implications for the victim. Should a party attempt to introduce DA into their submissions without making such a pleading, they are likely to invite criticism from the judge.

5.31 In *O v O*, Recorder Moys made this assessment of one party's attempt at doing just this:

> 'None of W's allegations were ever the subject of formal proceedings so that their alleged impact on the financial proceedings and/or reliance to a fair outcome could be spelled out.'[22]
>
> '"Conduct" allegations need to be properly pleaded at the earliest opportunity so that the person alleging the conduct is required to state "with particularised specificity" what the conduct allegations are, how those allegations meet the threshold for a conduct claim, and what the financial impact caused by the alleged conduct is so that the person accused of misconduct knows what case it is that he/she must meet.'[23]

PRACTICE NOTE

If you are going to continue on this course on the basis of informed client instructions notwithstanding the difficulties regarding the current state of law and practice, a summary of the conduct allegations, along with the financial impact, should be inserted in Box 4.4 of Form E. The other party is very likely to object to conduct being pleaded in the proceedings. Be prepared to make your arguments as to why it should not be excluded at the first hearing. If you get past that hearing, the court is likely to direct short statements and

22 *O v O* [2023] EWFC 161 (B), [55].
23 *O v O* (n 22), [60].

list a hearing specifically to determine whether the conduct argument should be allowed to proceed following the procedure identified in *Tsvetkov*. If there are relevant findings or evidence in other proceedings, ensure you have made an application to obtain it and are permitted to rely on it.

5.32 Until there is a change in the law or jurisprudence, the quantum of the award is not generally where practitioners in this field can make the most difference for victims. However, advisers can still make a significant holistic difference to clients where there is CCB as, once identified, better informed, self-aware protective steps can at least be taken.

DISSIPATION OF FAMILY ASSETS

5.33 It has regrettably been a common feature of financial remedy proceedings for as long as practitioners remember that one party to a marriage spends the family money,[24] or transfer assets away from the family pot before or around the time of separation to make sure the victim does not get their share. 'Adding-back' assets that have been recklessly dissipated is the second category of conduct identified by Mostyn J.

5.34 These cases often involve ferocious litigation with multiple applications and much manoeuvring; the abuser sometimes acts in person (despite financial resources) in order to gain perceived control over the proceedings. Whilst these behaviours have always existed, it is only now that we are starting to understand that this behaviour can be a continued form of abuse.

PRACTICE NOTE

It is always better to prevent the disposition of assets than to try and set aside dispositions that have already been incurred. If there are big transfers leaving a joint account, but there is still money left, you may be able to ask the bank itself to freeze the account. Just bear in mind that the account will be frozen for both accountholders. Alternatively, if the victim somehow gets advance notice that assets are about to be transferred, then immediately take specialist advice about whether an application for a freezing injunction is appropriate. There are strict conditions before a freezing injunction can be obtained, and there can be cost consequences resulting from applying when the conditions are not met. It is invariably prudent to invite the other party to undertake not to transfer the assets with a short timescale for reply. If they refuse to give the undertaking, that can form part of the evidence to apply for the injunction. If the money has already been transferred, consider whether an application pursuant to s 37 for the court to set aside the disposition is required.

24 See *Martin v Martin* (1978) Fam 12 CA Omerod J.

DOWRY ABUSE

5.35 Southall Black Sisters[25] is a pioneering organisation dedicated to helping black, minority and migrant women and girls. As part of its campaigning work, it has drawn attention to dowry abuse. This occurs where the dowry is taken or hidden, or the wife is abused because they have either not provided a dowry, or provided one which is considered by their husband to be insufficient. A dowry is usually intended for the next generation, or it is to be the financial security for the bride upon the breakdown of the relationship, which is why its removal has such ramifications. It should be borne in mind that there are occasions when the wife's family pay forms of dowry or mahr to the husband.

5.36 The complexity of this form of abuse stems from the fact that the dowry is often held by other members of the family who are not parties to proceedings. It is also frequently said to be outside the jurisdiction.

PRACTICE NOTE

There are no easy remedies to this form of abuse. The costs of pursuing the dowry often outweigh the amount of the dowry. Evidence of the amount of the dowry, and its existence within the jurisdiction is often the best place to start.

JOINT AND INDIVIDUAL DEBTS

5.37 Liabilities can be joint and several like mortgages, or they can be individual liabilities like credit cards or car loans. Both types of debts can be used to control and abuse victims. When it comes to mortgage abuse, the victim can find themselves trapped in circumstances where they have to pay all, or more than their share, of the mortgage or risk going into arrears and suffering the damaging impact this can have on future credit rating, or even facing repossession proceedings. This is particularly problematic if the victim is too scared to stay in the house for fear of the ongoing abuse, and/or where the abuser refuses to agree to remortgaging to obtain better interest rates.

5.38 Debts may also have been accumulated in the victim's name with, or without, their knowledge. At the point of separation, they can find themselves with liabilities that they are unable to pay.

25 https://southallblacksisters.org.uk/.

PRACTICE NOTE

The first point of call with mortgage abuse is to speak to the lender. There is detailed information on the Surviving Economic Abuse website on the steps that some mortgage providers will take.[26] As an adviser to a victim in this situation, you need to weigh up the risk of issuing court proceedings in circumstances where there can be cost consequences for not engaging with NCDR and attempts to settle first, and the fact that financial remedy litigation, where a final hearing is required, takes around 75 weeks on average in the South East. In these circumstances, there should be a focus on high-quality, focused NCDR, because unless policymakers step in, there is no way out of the joint mortgage until sale or transfer of the property.

5.39 In respect of individual liabilities, victims need to get specialist advice from debt advisers. There are schemes available, depending on the circumstances, that may allow write-off of coerced debts, provide respite, or allow the victim to challenge liability. The Financial Remedy Court cannot make an order that the abuser is responsible for debts in the victim's names, but it may make orders to apportion the assets to take them into account.

ENFORCEMENT

5.40 Again, there have been issues with enforcing financial remedy orders for a long time, it is only more recently that this is being understood as a possible ongoing form of abuse. The Law Commission made recommendations about this issue (which still have not been enacted) as long ago as 2016.[27] Regardless of the amount of assets, where there is an ongoing abusive relationship, consider whether the final order will allow the abuser to continue to control the victim.

PRACTICE NOTE

Abusers have long used any discretion in the drafting of the final order to frustrate the order. Advisers should make sure that there is no scope for abusers to be able to evade directions for sale of joint property. The research shows that victims end up walking away from the money they need because of how hard it is to get it from the abuser. As their adviser you may need to prioritise independent money over the amount of money. Think about ways that can achieved.

26 https://survivingeconomicabuse.org/.
27 Law Commission, *Enforcement of Family Financial Remedy Orders*, Law Com No 370 (2016).

CONCLUDING THOUGHTS

5.41 This chapter is written for a book addressing DA within the family justice system – we have viewed and analysed economic abuse through that lens. If you would like to develop your thinking, we recommend the Resolution report, as the next port of call. From this author's (JDKC's) perspective, I have been driven to the conclusion that the Financial Remedies Court is a dark place for victims of abuse. I recognise that this is by no means an accepted view in financial remedies circles. Indeed, it might even be thought of as controversial. But it seems to me that too little light from the Family Court's understanding of CCB has penetrated its walls, and that is not equitable nor just.

STOP PRESS

5.42 Just as our book was going to print, a judgment of Cusworth J was published,[28] where, in financial remedies proceedings there were findings (from the children's proceedings) that the wife had been coercively controlling to husband, which included acts of physical abuse and threats to kill. The police had also indicated they were going to take a prosecution forward. In his decision, Cusworth J said:

> '43. In my judgment, where a party has been found responsible for coercive controlling behaviour within a marriage, especially when that behaviour includes a significant element of violence, the negative financial impact may well not be easily measurable, and any loss will only usually be capable of a very broad evaluation at best. That does not however mean that such an impact will not be present. Whilst the statutory test – that the conduct must be such that it is "inequitable to disregard" – really means no more in ordinary language than that the behaviour should be taken into account if it would be unfair to ignore it, Peel J is right that the higher courts have set the threshold for applying s.25(2)(g) at a very high level. *Nonetheless, I consider that there is a real risk of unfairness to victims of violent or coercive controlling behaviour, if the lack of readily quantifiable financial loss prevents the courts from even considering the fairness of taking their assailant's behaviour into account in determining the outcome of a financial remedy application. Such behaviour may well have hard-to-predict but potentially far-reaching consequences, in some cases for the victim's prospects of achieving self-sufficiency, in others for a fair financial outcome in all of the circumstances. That does not mean that the fact of such behaviour will inevitably lead to a different award, but in the right case, it clearly should do.*'

We have said in the Preface that family law does not stand still and that it is every practitioner's duty to keep abreast of case law. *LP v MP* is a paradigm example evidencing the need for constant professional vigilance. Does this case signal

28 *LP v MP* [2025] EWFC 473 (22 November 2025).

that the jurisprudence in financial remedies cases will start to catch up with the rest of the family court? We hope so.

5.43 We wait with interest to see whether Resolution will start to campaign for a change to the law concerning the impact of DA on the outcome of financial proceedings for married and unmarried couples. It is down to policymakers to step in and fulfil the manifesto promise to give cohabitees rights. We wait to see if policymakers will indeed make changes in this field to improve experience and outcomes. We hope that, as awareness develops, better processes are developed so victims are not left so vulnerable. Watch this space.

CHAPTER 6

Allegations of Rape and Sexual Abuse

6.01 Allegations of sexual abuse are, sadly, an all too common feature of cases involving allegations of domestic abuse (DA) and require careful and sensitive consideration by the Family Court. It is in this area, in particular, where good practice lessons can be shared between family and crime practitioners for, whilst legal concepts and definitions may be unique to each specialism, managing the needs of vulnerable participants and exploring ways in which to anticipate and best manage the competing interests of the accused and accuser in a serious trial are issues each discipline has to grapple with.

6.02 For a number of years, sexual abuse has fallen squarely within the definition of DA and it is acknowledged to inflict untold physical, psychological and emotional harm upon its victims.

6.03 Despite the media occasionally reporting that the conviction rates for offences of rape (in the criminal jurisdiction) are extremely low, allegations of rape and sexual assault now feature regularly in the Family Court when the Court is dealing with allegations of DA. Unfortunately, the data on how many of those allegations are found established or rejected are less easy to collate. Lower courts, where the majority of private law cases of DA are litigated, do not routinely publish their judgments (and rarely, if ever, do we see reported decisions lower than county court judge/recorder level). As a result, identifying how many allegations of rape pass the civil binary test of proven or not on a balance of probabilities is impossible to state with any accuracy.

ALLOCATION

6.04 Having regard to the *Allocation and Gatekeeping Guidance – Private Law*, issued on 22 April 2014,[1] those exercising gatekeeping functions (a District Judge or a legal adviser, acting alone or together) are required to allocate all relevant family applications (as defined in the *Child Arrangements Programme*, para 23) to the lay justices (or at the First Hearing Dispute Resolution Appointment (FHDRA) by legal advisers) *unless* the case features certain issues.[2]

1 It is important to note that, at the time of writing, there is a consultation regarding updated Allocation Guidance. Whilst the 2014 Guidance remains in force, practitioners must have regard to any updates. The consultation documents can be found at: https://www.judiciary.uk/wp-content/uploads/2025/08/Combined-Allocation-and-Gatekeeping-Guidance-Consultation-Final.pdf.

2 Courts and Tribunals Judiciary, *President's Guidance on Allocation and Gatekeeping for Proceedings under Part II of the Children Act 1989 (Private Law)* (judicary.uk 2014), https://www.judiciary.uk/wp-content/uploads/2013/02/private-law-allocation-and-gatekeeping-guidance.pdf.

6.05 Specifically, if the matter meets the criteria set out in Part 1 of the Schedule to the Guidance, it should be allocated to a District Judge or District Judge (Magistrate's Court). If its complexity justifies allocation to a Circuit Judge, the District Judge should then reallocate it accordingly.[3] Part 1 to the Schedule of the 2014 Guidance defines such cases as involving any of the following:

> 'Allegations of significant physical, emotional or sexual abuse, or behaviours which have caused, or are at risk of causing, significant harm to the relevant child.
>
> Cases where significant factual matters are in issue (including substance misuse, domestic abuse, paternity, physical and/or mental health of relevant adults or children) such that a factfinding hearing lasting more than one day is likely and the necessity for expert evidence (i.e. beyond the expertise of CAFCASS and/or social worker) is likely to arise.
>
> Cases where the capacity of one of the parents is, or is likely to be, raised as an issue.
>
> Cases where there is a real possibility that the child will have to be joined as a party (see guidelines under rule 16.4 FPR 2010) &/or may be called to give evidence.
>
> Cases where there is, or is likely to be, a significant issue in relation to disclosure of documents to or from third parties or outside agencies.
>
> Cases where immigration issues are likely to be relevant and significant.
>
> Cases involving leave to remove children (permanently or temporarily) from the jurisdiction to Hague Convention and/or EU countries.
>
> Cases which involve significant issues to be determined in relation to the disclosure of information to one or other of the parties (e.g. where the Cafcass officer seeks to withhold information contained in a Safeguarding letter).
>
> Cases involving the enforcement of existing orders made by a District Judge or cases where a District Judge has previously made orders in relation to the same parties. Allocation should be to the same District Judge where practicable.
>
> Cases where there is a real possibility that Public Law Orders will be required, where the issues arising are of a type described in Part 1 or Part 2 of the Schedule to the President's Guidance on Allocation and Gatekeeping for Care, Supervision and other Part 4 proceedings.'[4]

6.06 If the case falls within the description in Part 2 of the Schedule to the Guidance, it should be allocated to either a District Judge, a District Judge

3 Courts and Tribunals Judiciary (n 2), para 25(c).

4 Courts and Tribunals Judiciary, *Schedule to the Allocation and Gatekeeping Guidance* (judicary.uk 2014), https://www.justice.gov.uk/documents/schedule-to-allocation-and-gatekeeping-guidance.pdf, Part 1.

(Magistrate's Court), a Circuit Judge or a High Court Judge.[5] Under Part 2, will be:

> 'Cases involving significant factual disputes (including allegations of abuse, violence, alleged or proven criminal activity, gravely inappropriate behaviours, sexual abuse, complex physical and/or mental health issues in relation to relevant adults or children) particularly where a fact finding hearing of 3 days or more is a real possibility and/or where it is likely that more than one expert (not including CAFCASS and/or social worker) will be involved.
>
> Cases where there are particularly difficult and unusual immigration or jurisdictional issues.
>
> Cases involving leave to remove (permanently or temporarily) from the jurisdiction to Hague Convention and/or EU countries which are factually or legally complex.
>
> Cases which appear to involve, or have the potential to involve, intractable opposition to contact.
>
> Cases seeking enforcement of existing Orders made by a Circuit Judge or Recorder or in cases where a Circuit Judge or Recorder has previously made orders in relation to the same parties. Allocation should be to the same Circuit Judge or Recorder where practicable.
>
> Circuit Judge (not District Judge): Cases seeking leave to remove from the jurisdiction [permanently or temporarily] outside of the Hague Convention/the EU. Where there are particular factual or legal complexities, the cases should ordinarily be allocated to the High Court following consultation with the DFJ.'[6]

6.07 In the latter scenario (if it falls under Part 2), the case should be allocated to a Circuit Judge or High Court Judge sitting in the Family Court, the FHDRA should be listed before a District Judge or District Judge (Magistrate's Court). If the gatekeeper, however, in discussion with the designated family judge, feels that it would be more appropriate to be conducted by a Circuit Judge or High Court Judge, it may be reallocated accordingly.[7]

PRACTICE NOTE

Allegations of *significant sexual abuse* which have caused, or are at risk of causing significant harm to the relevant child, and 'cases where *significant factual matters are in issue* ... such that a fact-finding hearing lasting *more than one* day is likely *and* the necessity for *expert evidence* (i.e. beyond the expertise of CAFCASS and/or social worker) is likely to arise' should be allocated to at least the District Judge level of the Family Court.[8]

5 Courts and Tribunals Judiciary (n 2), para 25(d).
6 Courts and Tribunals Judiciary (n 4), Part 2.
7 Courts and Tribunals Judiciary (n 2), para 26.
8 Courts and Tribunals Judiciary (n 4), Part 1.

6.08 The *Allocation and Gatekeeping Guidance – Private Law* offers little in the way of additional guidance as to what may constitute 'significant sexual abuse' and, therefore, it is likely that the Court will need some assistance in ensuring that the issue of allocation is dealt with appropriately at an early stage of the proceedings.[9] This process will initially take place without a hearing and in the absence of the parties.

PRACTICE NOTE

The criteria also refer to 'significant factual matters' being in issue, which would, we suggest, include controlling and coercive behaviour (CCB) as well as other complex relationship or child welfare issues. Does a party or the child have any disability or special needs?

Will the case last 'for more than one day'? Very likely so when one factors in time for two adults giving evidence as a minimum, at least one with special measures, potential breaks being required in listening and giving evidence, plus submissions from two parties. Query also if the CAFCASS officer will be required.

Consider, how does the requirement for expert evidence fit with the case (the criterion says 'and' expert evidence not 'or')? What expert evidence would be required so as to fulfil the test of necessity and proportionality at a fact-finding stage? The restrictions on the use of expert evidence have become tighter over the years but the criterion above has remained fixed. We suggest that, whilst one needs to be aware of that aspect, if the other elements are satisfied, it should not inhibit you from arguing for reallocation if that is the professional view you take having critically evaluated the seriousness of the allegation and the complexity of the litigation task to bring or defend it.

ALLOCATION AND COMPLEXITY

6.09 Practitioners must be familiar with the *Allocation and Gatekeeping Guidance – Private Law* so that they can be satisfied that the case in which they are engaged has been allocated to the appropriate level of Family Court.[10] Particular care should be taken with regard to cases which feature allegations of sexual abuse.

PRACTICE NOTE

Is it right that such cases should be allocated to magistrates for case management and hearing? This is where reference to the Sentencing

9 Courts and Tribunals Judiciary (n 2).
10 Courts and Tribunals Judiciary (n 2).

Council's Sentencing Guidelines may be informative: if criminal allegations of sexual abuse are considered so serious that magistrates should not be dealing with them in the criminal jurisdiction, is it right that magistrates deal with them in the family jurisdiction?

For example, has the justice's clerk or bench, undergone the training required in order to be conscious of the impact of trauma on recall, and anticipate the close management of the trial evidence needed in order not fall foul of case law on demeanour and cross-examination on sexual history?

PRACTICE NOTE

It is crucial that the application before the Court is sufficiently detailed to make plain the gravity of the allegations and their impact on the victim and the family so as to ensure that the Court can make the best decision it can on paper on allocation.

Otherwise:

- Too inexperienced a forum may be deciding an issue it is not skilled or trained enough to assess, leading to injustice if an allegation is found not proven when it should have been established.
- Valuable time may wasted, and emotions heightened, when the case is reallocated later down the line when evidence is filed and the gravity of the allegations makes it apparent that the case needs reallocation.

COMPLEXITY AND COUNSEL'S DUTY

6.10 Consider this issue: is it right that the counsel or solicitor currently conducting the advocacy (this includes you or the person you are instructing) continues to do so? Do you/they have the experience and skills required? To prosecute a rape trial in the criminal court requires specific training and accreditation – why should a victim have less qualified counsel in a family case?

PRACTICE NOTE

This is one of two practice notes on this issue. The second concludes this chapter. It warrants repetition as it is an important principle and yet, more often than not, it is seen in the breach rather than the observance.

Counsel must be aware of their obligations under the Code of Conduct to act within their competence. A professional's code of conduct includes a commitment to work within the limits of their training and competence to ensure public safety and maintain trust in their profession.

If a situation arises that falls outside their training, they must recognise the limitation and may need to seek support from colleagues or refuse the task they do not have the requisite skill to act on.

The bottom line is that when involved in this serious work one must keep the issue of allocation under active review and be prepared to make hard decisions as to the level of advocate and court required in order to secure the fairest trial for the parties, *especially when one may be unrepresented.*

THE DIFFERENCE BETWEEN THE CRIMINAL AND FAMILY COURT WHEN IT COMES TO SERIOUS ALLEGATIONS OF RAPE AND SEXUAL ABUSE

6.11 In *Re R (Children) (Care Proceedings: Fact-finding Hearing)*, the Court of Appeal, having considered the degree to which the Family Court should deploy criminal law concepts in its own evaluation of the same or similar behaviour, held as a matter of principle, that 'it was fundamentally wrong for the family court to be drawn into the analysis of factual evidence in proceedings relating to the welfare of children based on criminal law principles and concepts'.[11]

6.12 This case drew a valuable distinction between the purpose of the trials and what might be the same or similar in the criminal and family courts. Every family practitioner must grasp this. It enables an advocate to focus their arguments on necessity and proportionality when arguing for or against a fact-finding hearing being listed for a serious sex allegation against an adult as opposed to a child.

6.13 The Court of Appeal said, inter alia:

> 'The focus and purpose of a fact-finding investigation in the context of a case concerning the future welfare of children in the Family Court are wholly different to those applicable to the prosecution by the State of an individual before a criminal court. *The latter is concerned with the culpability and, if guilty, punishment for a specific criminal offence, whereas the former involves the determination facts, across a wide canvas, relating to past events in order to evaluate which of a range of options for the future care of a child best meets the requirements of his or her welfare.* Similarly, where facts fall to be determined in the course of ordinary civil litigation, the purpose of the exercise, which is to establish liability, operates in a wholly different context to a fact-finding process in family proceedings. Reduced to simple basics, in both criminal and civil proceedings the ultimate outcome of the litigation will be binary, either "guilty" or "not guilty", or "liable" or "not liable". In family proceedings, the outcome of a fact-finding hearing will normally be a narrative account of what the court has determined

11 *Re R (Children) (Care Proceedings: Fact-finding Hearing)* [2018] EWCA Civ 198, [67].

(on the balance of probabilities) has happened in the lives of a number of people and, often, over a significant period of time. *The primary purpose of the family process is to determine, as best that may be done, what has gone on in the past, so that that knowledge may inform the ultimate welfare evaluation where the court will choose which option is best for a child with the court's eyes open to such risks as the factual determination may have established.*'[12]

6.14 It is important to bear in mind the case of *A v B & Anor*, where the Court of Appeal, led by the President of the Family Division considered two conjoined appeals brought by mothers who had made allegations of DA, sexual abuse and rape.[13] The appeals raised a number of overarching issues regarding the approach that should be taken in the Family Court where allegations of rape are made in private children's law proceedings. The Court of Appeal dismissed the appeals. It warrants being read in full. We only quote that which is relevant to this chapter.

6.15 At para [20], the President endorsed the guidance in *Re H-N & Ors (Children) (Domestic Abuse: Finding of Fact Hearings)*[14] that strict criminal definitions should be avoided in the Family Court:

> 'In Re R and in Re H-N the Court of Appeal, and at High Court level Cobb J in F v M (2019) and Hayden J in F v M (2021), judges have been keen to prevent the Family Court becoming "bogged down" or "distracted", or for the true issues to be "obfuscated", by the legal technicality that would be introduced by definitions which were then to be applied as a matter of law. Whilst the focus of those decisions was upon the proposition that the definitions in question were those applicable under the criminal law, the mischief which, it has been held, should be avoided applies in equal measure to any alternative definitions that may be promulgated.'[15]

6.16 Note that the President continued to state that Knowles J was 'entirely correct in rejecting the assertion that the Family Court should import definitions of rape, sexual assault and consent (whether drawn from criminal law or elsewhere).'[16] Instead, the Court should follow the guidance as set out in the Family Procedure Rules 2010 (SI 2010/2955) and PD12J.

CONSENT

6.17 The issue of consent must be understood by those acting in the Family Court. Practitioners should make sure they are familiar with the family case law.

12 *Re R (Children) (Care Proceedings: Fact-finding Hearing)* (n 11), [62] (emphasis added).
13 *A v B & Anor* [2023] EWCA Civ 360.
14 *Re H-N & Ors (Children) (Domestic Abuse: Finding of Fact Hearings)* [2021] EWCA Civ 448.
15 *A v B & Anor* (n 13), [20].
16 *A v B & Anor* (n 13), [23].

We provide here just a few examples of what is a significant and important body of case law to call upon.

6.18 Cobb J gave judgment in the context of a Children Act appeal involving a finding of rape in *F v M (Appeal: Finding of Fact).*[17] The father appealed against a determination of fact made at the conclusion of a Finding of Fact Hearing that the subject child's conception had been as a result of rape. The mother claimed that after a short time engaged in the sexual act, she told the father she did not want him to continue and she did not want him to ejaculate inside her. The father denied that she ever asked him to 'stop', and said that prior to the initiation of sexual intercourse they had agreed he would not ejaculate inside of her. He maintained he had accidentally done so. The judge found that in failing to stop and withdraw before ejaculation, the father had raped the mother. The appeal was dismissed.

6.19 What we note as important is that the trial judge had heard evidence from both parties, and formed mixed views about the reliability and truthfulness of both parties. She had also analysed the contextual evidence, including the communications between the parties (see **Chapter 10** on social media where we set out the significance of this form of evidence), and was particularly struck by the consistency of the references by the mother in text messages to the fact she had pleaded with the father to 'stop'.

6.20 Cobb J said:

> '... In this case, the Judge's conclusion that M had been raped did not, however, depend upon a finding that the M had given conditional consent to penetration (i.e. "on the clear understanding that the man will not ejaculate within her vagina" but that F had made up his mind to do so). The Judge's conclusion was founded on the fact that part-way through the sexual act, M ceased to consent to the act ("stop, stop ...") and had made this known to F by requesting that he "stop". It is therefore not material to her finding of rape that there had been any discussion about ejaculation before the act of sexual intercourse (if there had been), nor that F had in fact ejaculated inside M's vagina. In short, as soon as M had withdrawn her consent to the sexual intercourse during the act, F's continued penetration of her became a serious sexual assault, which in the criminal law would, within the meaning of the Sexual Offences Act 2003, be rape.'[18]

6.21 Finally, and importantly, the Court noted that there are a number of reasons why the circumstances of the child's conception might ultimately be relevant to future child arrangements. It is why this is a *must-read* case:

17 *F v M (Appeal: Finding of Fact)* [2019] EWHC 3177 (Fam).
18 *F v M (Appeal: Finding of Fact)* (n 18), [27].

'… Quite irrespective, therefore, of whether F has committed the offence of "rape" or is otherwise criminally culpable, *there is a range of reasons why the circumstances of N's conception may ultimately be relevant to future child arrangements.* Specifically, it was regarded at an earlier case management hearing (and I agree with this direction) that *it would be important for there to be a determination of whether F's conduct towards M in the sexual act by which N was conceived was "violent or abusive", and in turn whether that conduct would be likely to be relevant in deciding whether to make a child arrangements order (see PD12J FPR 2010, para.4, para.5, and see further para.7 [ie does the statutory presumption apply having regard to any incident of domestic abuse?]).*'[19]

6.22 In *A & D v B, C & E* Knowles J analysed a number of propositions with regard to sexual history, rape myths, relevance of criminal concepts etc which are to be considered in any case where there are allegations of sexual assault which fall to be determined.[20]

6.23 Note that this is another *must-read* case. Knowles J is the DA lead and what she says has a significance beyond her role as a respected High Court judge. The propositions, together with Knowles J's conclusions were as follows. We take them in order as they are each such important concepts.

Whether the Family Court should apply a consistent definition of (i) rape, (ii) sexual assault or (iii) consent, making clear the difference between consent and submission[21]

6.24 Knowles J stated that:

'The correct starting point for the Family Court is that it must not import criminal definitions as an aid to fact-finding. The focus of the Family Court is to determine how the parents of a child behaved towards each other so as to be able to properly to assess risk and determine the welfare issues in each case.'[22]

6.25 The Court specifically had regard to the recent coming into force of the Domestic Abuse Act 2021 which replicated some provisions applicable in the criminal courts but noted that 'Parliament declined to legislate for a framework in the Family Court within which to determine allegations of rape and sexual assault, nor was it invited to do so during the passage of the Act'.[23]

19 *F v M (Appeal: Finding of Fact)* (n 18), [29] (emphasis added).
20 *A & D v B, C & E* [2022] EWHC 3089 (Fam).
21 *A & D v B, C & E* (n 20), [2].
22 *A & D v B, C & E* (n 20), [23].
23 *A & D v B, C & E* (n 20).

> 'At first instance, the Family Court determines allegations of rape and sexual assault without a legislative definition or framework. That is consistent with the purpose of a fact-finding exercise in family proceedings, which is to determine only such factual issues as are necessary to assess risk and to illuminate the welfare issues.'[24]

6.26 Knowles J highlighted what the Court of Appeal said in *Re H-N & Ors (Children) (Domestic Abuse: Finding of Fact Hearings)* at para [71], making clear that these comments are crucial in underscoring the clear distinction between the family and the criminal court:

> 'Behaviour which falls short of establishing "rape," for example, may nevertheless be profoundly abusive and should certainly not be ignored or met with a finding akin to "not guilty" in the family context. For example, in the context of the Family Court considering whether there has been a pattern of abusive behaviour, the borderline between "consent" and "submission" may be less significant than it would be in the criminal trial of an allegation of rape or sexual assault.'[25]

Knowles J thus reinforced the well-established principle in *Re R (Children) (Care Proceedings: Fact-finding Hearing)* that 'a family judge must consider a "wide canvas" and scrutinise the family relationships … over a period of time in order to arrive at a factual determination relevant to both risk and welfare'.[26]

Whether the failure to have a consistent approach to these issues is in breach of the mother's Article 6, 8 and 14 rights

6.27 Accepting that DA engages a complainant's rights under Articles 6, 8 and 14 of the European Convention on Human Rights, Knowles J highlighted the obligations placed upon Member States by the Council of Europe Convention on Preventing and Combating Violence Against Women and Domestic Violence ('the Istanbul Convention') which was ratified by the UK and entered into force on 1 November 2022. The extent of the obligation placed upon Member States is to take the necessary legislative or other measures to ensure that a variety of non-consensual vaginal, oral or anal penetration/acts of a sexual nature are criminalised. No obligation is placed on the Family Court.[27]

Whether the definitions of rape, sexual assault and consent used in the criminal justice system should be either a starting or finishing point for judges in the Family Court

6.28 Knowles J chose to respond to this issue alongside the below.

24 *A & D v B, C & E* (n 20), [24].
25 *Re H-N & Ors (Children) (Domestic Abuse: Finding of Fact Hearings)* (n 14), [71].
26 *Re R (Children) (Care Proceedings: Fact-finding Hearing)* (n 11), [62].
27 *A & D v B, C and E* (n 20), [40].

What the approach of the Family Court should be to a complainant's sexual history when determining allegations of rape and sexual assault

6.29 Knowles J stated that the:

> 'starting point [is] that the established approach to evidence in the family court can accommodate circumstances in which a parent, either making of facing allegations of sexual abuse, seeks to adduce evidence of the other person's sexual history, or their own sexual history or their shared sexual history'.[28]

She continued:

> '*The first step* must be to consider the admissibility of the evidence in question, which is determined by relevance. The question of relevance is one of fact, degree and proportionality.'[29]
>
> '*The second step*, where a party objects to the admission of otherwise relevant evidence, is to undertake a balancing exercise.'[30]

6.30 Knowles J examined these stages, noting that the decision of the Court of Appeal in *Dunn v Durham County Council* is relevant to both the first and second step:[31]

> 'What does that approach require? *First*, obligations in relation to disclosure and inspection arise only when the relevance test is satisfied. Relevance can include "train of inquiry" points which are not merely fishing expeditions. This is a matter of fact, degree and proportionality. *Secondly*, if the relevance test is satisfied it is for the party or person in possession of the document or who would be adversely affected by its disclosure or inspection to assert exemption from disclosure or inspection. *Thirdly*, any ensuing dispute falls to be determined. We determined ultimately by a balancing exercise, having regard to the fair trial rights of the other party and any person whose rights may require protection. It will generally involve a consideration of competing ECHR rights. *Fourthly*, the denial of disclosure or inspection is limited to circumstances here such denial is strictly necessary. *Fifthly*, in some cases, the balance may need to be struck by a limited or restricted order which respects a protected interest by such things as redaction, confidentiality rings, anonymity in the proceedings or such other order. Again, the limitation or restriction must satisfy the test of strict necessity.'[32]

28 *A & D v B, C and E* (n 20), [46].
29 *A & D v B, C and E* (n 20), [48].
30 *A & D v B, C and E* (n 20), [50].
31 *A & D v B, C and E* (n 20).
32 *Dunn v Durham County Council* [2012] EWCA Civ 1654, [23].

6.31 Knowles J found it was difficult to envisage circumstances in which an application by an alleged perpetrator of sexual abuse to adduce evidence of a complainant's sexual history with *another* individual would satisfy the test of relevance, although it was made clear that there is no absolute bar on adducing such evidence as it would be for the particular court to assess.

> 'More complicated is the question of relevance in relation to evidence of a complainant's sexual history with the alleged perpetrator. *The fact that adult parents had previously or subsequently engaged in consensual sexual activity of any sort does not mean that they were not raped or sexually assaulted on another occasion. However, evidence as to the parents' sexual relationship may be logically probative of an allegation of partnership rape or sexual assault. Thus, communications between the parties of a sexual nature may well be relevant as may communications between them either before or after the relevant incident or time period.* That approach is in keeping with the court's obligation to consider the wide canvas of evidence and its duty to have regard to patterns of behaviour – both of the complainant and the alleged perpetrator – as described in Re H-N. It does not give an alleged perpetrator permission to produce any material that they wish if it is irrelevant and, if relevant, where it fails to meet the approach articulated in [23] of Dunn v Durham County Council.
>
> Mr Metzer KC *invited me to state that there would be a strong presumption against the admission of evidence relating to a complainant's sexual history with an alleged perpetrator and to declare that the circumstances should be exceptional. I decline to do so.* First, that approach runs contrary to current practice in the family court which has been centred on relevance and is free from presumption or starting point. It also runs contrary to the basic principle that, by adopting an inquisitorial approach, the court requires the best relevant evidence before it to assess both the risk posed by a parent or the welfare best interests of the child. Second, and practically speaking, the Appellant's approach runs the risk of depriving the court of evidence relevant to its factual determination. I observe that there may well be circumstances in which evidence of sexual history as between partners is relevant to the court's assessment of the dynamic, their respective patterns of behaviour and the nature of their relationship.
>
> Based on the analysis above, *I do not regard it as necessary for a party wishing to rely on evidence of sexual history between partners to make a specific application to the court for permission to do so.* Practically speaking, this would add complexity and cost to already contentious children proceedings where a high proportion of litigants are self-representing.
>
> Though not addressed in either the written or oral argument because it is not a matter at large in these appeals, *I note that a complainant may wish to adduce evidence of an alleged perpetrator's sexual history with other individuals to demonstrate a pattern of allegedly abusive behaviour* (such evidence being described as similar fact evidence). The Court of Appeal in *R v P (Children: Similar Fact Evidence) [2020] EWCA Civ 1088* set out

the approach to be taken to the admissibility of such evidence at the case management stage in [19], and [23]-[24], emphasising the test of *relevance* and the need for the court to have available the best evidence to illuminate the subtle and persistent patterns of behaviour involved in coercive control, harassment and stalking.

In conclusion and to assist family judges in their case management task, I offer the following procedural framework, loosely based on that I articulated in Re M (A Child) (Private Law Children Proceedings: Case Management: Intimate Images) [2022] EWHC 986 (Fam), namely:

(a) If a party wishes to adduce evidence about a complainant's sexual history with a third party, a written application should be made in advance for permission to do so, supported by a witness statement;

(b) It is for the party making such an application to persuade the court of the relevance and necessity of such material to the specific factual issues which the court is required to determine.

(c) Any such application will require the court's adjudication preferably at a case management hearing.

(d) The court should apply the approach set out above at [45]-[49].

(e) If a party wishes to rely on evidence about sexual history between partners, they do not need to make a specific application to do so unless reliance is also placed on intimate images. In those circumstances, the party must issue an application in accordance with the guidance at [77]-[78] in Re M (Intimate Images).

(f) If a party objects to evidence of sexual history between parents/parties being filed, it should make an application to the court in advance, supported by a witness statement explaining why this material is either irrelevant or should not be admitted.

(g) Any such application will require the court's adjudication preferably at a case management hearing.

(h) The court should apply the approach set out above at [45]-[49].'[33]

Rape myths

6.32 Knowles J considered whether, when determining allegations of rape and/or sexual assault, judges in the Family Court should give themselves a warning about rape myths. Generally, such myths concern themselves with the behaviour or experiences of a complainant.

33 *Dunn v Durham County Council* (n 32), [54]–[58] emphasis added.

6.33 Knowles J referred to *Re H-N & Ors (Children (Domestic Abuse: Finding of Fact Hearings)* as having effectively highlighted the training available to family judges:

> 'Following the judgment of Russell J and at the request of the President, the Judicial College devised a freestanding sexual assault awareness training programme for Family judges. The programme draws heavily on the successful "serious sexual assault" programme for criminal judges. Since July 2020, it has been a mandatory requirement for all judges who hear any category of Family cases to undertake this programme. The programme, which is under constant review, includes elements in respect of psychological reactions to sexual assault and trauma, and has the benefit of contributions having been made by a number of victims of sexual assault discussing the impact that an attack has had upon them. In addition to the more general training in relation to domestic abuse, which is already in place for Magistrates, bespoke training suitable for the work they undertake in respect of sexual assault and trauma is in the process of being developed.
>
> This bespoke Family training feeds in turn into, and is further developed within, the extensive training programmes that are run in relation to domestic abuse by the Judicial College for the fee paid and salaried judges. These courses have been in place for some years and play a key role in both induction courses for newly appointed Family judges and continuation courses run for Family judges who are already in post.'[34]

6.34 Knowles J then commented:

> 'On the basis that I have found what follows of assistance in my own practice as the lead judge for domestic abuse, I draw the attention of family judges to *Chapter 6 of the Equal Treatment Bench Book (July 2022)* entitled "Gender". Under a subheading entitled *"Sexual Offences: Who is Affected?"*, there is information about sexual offences which includes several paragraphs addressing rape myths which may feature in criminal proceedings (see [74]-[91]). *Though written to assist those sitting in the criminal courts, there is much in that section which family judges may find useful.* The Equal Treatment Bench Book is publicly available on the judiciary.uk website at Equal Treatment Bench Book July 2022 revision (2) (judiciary.uk). Likewise, *the CPS Guidance on Rape and Sexual Offences at Annex A* provides a comprehensive guide to the unhelpful stereotypes which may cloud judicial thinking in cases involving sexual assault. It too is publicly available on the cps.gov.uk website and was last revised in *May 2021: Rape and Sexual Offences – Annex A: Tackling Rape Myths and Stereotypes | The Crown Prosecution Service (cps.gov.uk).*
>
> I have also come to the view that I should not produce a list of common rape myths or stereotypes or attempt to craft a standard self-direction about sexual assault stereotypes which a family judge might give her/himself. No list would

34 *Re H-N & Ors (Children) (Domestic Abuse: Finding of Fact Hearings)* (n 14), [67]–[68].

> be comprehensive. Further, it would run the risk of creating a rigid framework to which adherence would be given. That would deprive a family judge of the flexibility to think about what is apposite in the particular case, having been appropriately trained to recognise unhelpful stereotypes, and should they consider it necessary to do so, for a family judge to draw attention in her/his judgment to the manner in which they have guarded against applying any relevant stereotypes. Secondly, any self-direction I might devise would be equally inflexible because it cannot encompass the great variety of stereotypical thinking outlined, for example, in the two sources to which I have referred.'[35]

6.35 The judgment of Knowles J in *A & D v B, C & E* was subject to an appeal to the Court of Appeal in *A v B & C*.[36] The Court of Appeal comprised the President of the Family Division as well as Peter Jackson and Macur LJJ. Describing Knowles J's judgment as 'full and closely structured' the President, in giving the lead judgment, expressed his full agreement with what Knowles J said, with no intention 'to differ in any material particular from the more comprehensive analysis that has been provided by Knowles J'.[37] Peter Jackson LJ also agreed with the endorsement of Knowles J's approach.

PRACTICE NOTE

Code of Conduct

Cases involving allegations of anal, vaginal and/or oral rape are some of the most serious and sensitive an advocate and court is expected to manage. This is particularly so when one party may still be a caregiver to a vulnerable child and be vulnerable themselves; the impact of the trial has ramifications beyond the courtroom.

- The advocate MUST comply with their Code of Conduct in terms of competence.
- Advocates must, we suggest, be trained under the Family Law Bar Association (FLBA) and Bar Council Vulnerable Party scheme.
- Advocates must be familiar with the Advocates Toolkits and the *Equal Treatment Bench Book*.
- Advocates must apply their minds to the way in which the trial needs to be structured. They must be on good terms with participation steps that need to be taken in terms of trial management and the remit and conduct of cross-examination.

Too often, rates of pay for private law work are so low in legal aid terms or the client means are so limited that direct access fees are also modest, such that very junior counsel are instructed to act. That does not lessen the duty under the Code. If anything, it emphasises its importance.

35 *A & D v B, C & E* (n 20), [63]–[64] (emphasis added).
36 *A v B & C* [2023] EWCA Civ 360.
37 *A v B & C* (n 36), [4].

CHAPTER 7

Intimate Images

7.01 The ever-increasing accessibility of technology and the widespread use of social media has created a society which bears no resemblance to that of 35 years ago before the worldwide web was invented[1] and then access to it via widespread use of smartphones became commonplace. Whilst many of the technological and societal developments in recent decades are to be applauded, some are capable of being deployed with such malevolence, and, when that happens, the scars which are left behind are so deep that the victims never recover.

7.02 Debates take place on a daily basis regarding the sexualisation of society, and children in particular, and the impact that technology, social media and the internet have had on this. It was, therefore, only a matter of time before these issues crept into the home and found themselves a place within modern-day relationships between adults and between adults and children.

7.03 The days of meeting at a party on a night out or at some social function are slowly drawing to a close, often replaced by a swipe right on a mobile phone screen as dating moves online. Instead of speaking to someone face to face in a noisy bar, initial dialogue now takes place in a more remote fashion: via the instant messaging capabilities of the dating app of choice, or social media. 'Sliding into someone's DMs' has now replaced a conversation. And with this evolution comes a reduction of inhibition. Relationships start in the technological arena, and that arena continues to play a part in any ensuing relationship, however short or long that relationship may be.

7.04 Many children now also have, not only access to, but personal use of, a mobile. They can be tracked via it and their device can be used to record and monitor the actions of others – such as a parent.

7.05 The relevance of social media and mobile use to domestic abuse (DA), controlling and coercive behaviour (CCB) and stalking is self-evident. In this chapter we deal with intimate images – **Chapter 11** will then consider covert recording as a consequence of internet abuse.

1 Tim Berners-Lee, a British scientist, invented the World Wide Web (www) in 1989; it was originally conceived and developed to meet the demand for automated information-sharing between scientists in universities and institutes around the world. By the end of 1990, Tim Berners-Lee had the first Web server and browser up and running, demonstrating his ideas. He declined to patent his invention, wanting it to be accessible to all. By the end of 1994, the Web had 10,000 servers – 2,000 of which were commercial – and 10 million users. It has expanded exponentially since.

7.06 The use and misuse of intimate images has found its way into the Family Court arena. Whether used as a means of defending oneself against allegations of sexual abuse or as a litigation tactic to humiliate and embarrass an ex partner extending the reach of coercion and control directly into the courtroom.

7.07 In one of the first reported judgments concerning the use of intimate images in private law Children Act proceedings, *Re M (A Child: Private Law Children Proceedings: Case Management: Intimate Images)*, Knowles J observed that:

> 'anecdotal evidence suggests that the use of intimate images is becoming increasingly common in private law proceedings where allegations of domestic abuse (including sexual abuse) have been made and where the court has decided to determine the truth or otherwise of those allegations by holding a fact finding hearing …'[2]

PRACTICE NOTE

Re M (A Child: Private Law Children Proceedings: Case Management: Intimate Images) is a case every practitioner should read, not only where a party wishes to apply for the admission of intimate images, but also in connection with participation directions, an issue discussed in **Chapter 13**.

The importance of a careful reading of this authority is made clear by Mrs Justice Theis DBE in *D v R*: [Knowles J's summary in *Re M*] 'is required reading for any judge undertaking any hearing that involves allegations of domestic abuse'.[3]

DEFINITION

7.08 Careful not to trespass upon the definition of intimate images which can be found in the criminal law, Knowles J in *Re M* sought to offer a definition of intimate images for use in the Family Court. No doubt cognisant that the private law arena involves a high number of litigants-in-person, the Court clearly recognised that it is important that the definition of intimate images, from the Family Court's perspective, is unambiguous and easy to understand (and apply). The use of this definition of intimate images provides a clear benchmark for the Family Court to work from:

> '… when I use the term "intimate image" in the context of private law proceedings, I am describing an image of a person, whether an adult or a child, naked or partially naked. Such an image can include part of a person's

2 *Re M (A Child: Private Law Children Proceedings: Case Management: Intimate Images)* [2022] EWHC 986 (Fam), [3].
3 *D v R* [2023] EWHC 406 (Fam), [22].

body, clothed or unclothed, such as breasts, genitalia or the anus, which are generally regarded as private. Intimate images include those of a person engaged in what is normally regarded as private behaviour such as washing, urinating, masturbating or engaged in other sexual acts either alone or with another being.'[4]

7.09 Section 35 of the Criminal Justice and Courts Act 2015, which was subsequently amended by Domestic Abuse Act 2021, s 69 was repealed by the Online Safety Act 2023 but nevertheless provides a useful guide as to what a court may consider constitutes a private or sexual image:

'**35 Meaning of "private" and "sexual"**

(1) The following apply for the purposes of section 33.

(2) A photograph or film is "private" if it shows something that is not of a kind ordinarily seen in public.

(3) A photograph or film is "sexual" if—

(a) it shows all or part of an individual's exposed genitals or pubic area,

(b) it shows something that a reasonable person would consider to be sexual because of its nature, or

(c) its content, taken as a whole, is such that a reasonable person would consider it to be sexual.

(4) Subsection (5) applies in the case of—

(a) a photograph or film that consists of or includes a photographed or filmed image that has been altered in any way.

(b) a photograph or film that combines two or more photographed or filmed images, and

(c) a photograph or film that combines a photographed or filmed image with something else.

(5) The photograph or film is not private or sexual if—

(a) it does not consist of a photographed or filmed image that is itself private and sexual,

(b) it is only private or sexual by virtue of the alteration or combination mentioned in subsection (4), or

(c) it is only by virtue of the alteration or combination mentioned in subsection (4) that the person mentioned in section 33(1)(a) and (b) is shown as part of, or with, whatever makes the photograph or film private and sexual.'

7.10 The use of intimate images in proceedings represents a significant intrusion into the private life of the individuals concerned and it is therefore

4 *Re M* (n 2), [47].

unsurprising that Knowles J expressed grave concerns about their use in private law proceedings where allegations of DA are made. However, the creation and retention of intimate images in the context of a relationship is now commonplace and whilst it may come to represent a 'normal' feature of an intimate relationship for the mutual enjoyment of both willing parties, when that relationship breaks down the images have the potential to become deadly weapons capable of causing humiliation and embarrassment on a scale far more harmful than some other forms of DA. They may also represent the ultimate weapon in the arsenal of the controlling and coercive partner.

7.11 The recent jurisprudence has extolled the virtues of the Court being able to consider the parties' relationship as a whole when dealing with allegations of DA and, in particular, allegations of CCB; therefore, there will be some cases where the use of intimate images may represent an important part of the evidence which allows the Court to 'survey the wide canvas' of the relationship.

PRACTICE NOTE

Factors such as whether the photo was taken with the subject unawares, or whether the subject appears to be embarrassed or in discomfort may be relevant. Consider:

- Is the viewer's focus on the person or are they incidental to the content?
- Is the person being photographed aware of the person taking the photo? Are they engaged with the act of taking the image?
- Does the object person appear to be aware of the photo-taking act? If so, are they confident or distressed, etc?
- There can be many an innocent photograph taken in fun of someone in a bath or caught partially or fully undressed. But not all are. What is the intent and impact? Look at surrounding images, texts and factual chronology for context.
- Photos may have been taken between (then) consenting adults as part of sex play or may have been a result of dominance and oppression. What does the surrounding data suggest? Context is all.
- Whilst common sense may inform you as to what is a sexually explicit or intimate video or photograph, reference should be had to the Knowles J definition referred to above. It will need to be part of your submissions.

PROCEDURE: DEPLOYMENT

7.12 But how should such images be deployed and what safeguards should be in place to ensure that any intimate images relied upon are used proportionately and ensure the propriety of the proceedings? Knowles J offered some guidelines in *Re M* which have since been cited in subsequent decisions, most recently in the 2025 case of *S v B*.[5]

7.13 Rule 22.1 of the Family Procedure Rules 2010 (SI 2010/2955) (FPR) provides the Court with wide discretion to control the evidence it receives, allowing the Court to give directions as to the issues on which the Court requires evidence (rule 22.1(1)(a)), the nature of the evidence which it requires to decide those issues (rule 22.1(1)(b)) and the way in which the evidence is to be placed before the court (rule 22.1(1)(c)).

7.14 The first piece of advice which can be gleaned from *Re M* is thus:

> 'i. Sexually explicit or intimate videos and photographs should not be filed as part of evidence without a written application being made to the court in advance.'[6]

7.15 The tenor of this aspect of the guidance is that when making an application for permission to rely on sexually explicit or intimate videos or photographs, *the Court does not want to see the material at the outset* and prior to determining the application (of course, this would negate the serving of the application and defeat the whole purpose).

7.16 Additionally, any application should be accompanied by a schedule of the material, providing the following information to the Court:

- whether it is photographic or video evidence;
- the duration of any video evidence;
- a summary as to what the photograph or video shows;
- the relevance of the material to the issues before the Court.

By providing this detail, the Court is likely to be able to efficiently determine whether permission should be given.

7.17 The next point concerns the need for the Court to have sufficient time to consider the application:

> 'ii. Any such application will require the court's adjudication, preferably at an already listed case management hearing.'[7]

7.18 However obvious it may seem that the use of intimate images may be required in support of (or to defend) an allegation, *the use of such images is not a matter which can be agreed between the parties.* Knowles J is clear in the guidance that the Court *must* decide whether the use of intimate images is required and justified.

5 *S v B* [2025] EWFC 280 (B), [76].
6 *Re M* (n 2), [77(A)].
7 *Re M* (n 2), [77(B)].

7.19 The degree to which unrepresented litigants may be aware of this process, or if they are, choose to disregard it, is concerning.

7.20 Knowles J anticipated an application to use intimate images being part of a planned and listed hearing. However, with an increasing emphasis on reducing the number of hearings the Court holds in Children Act proceedings and the real possibility that, once the Court has determined that a Finding of Fact Hearing is necessary, further judicial case management may not take place until shortly before the Finding of Fact Hearing (or *at* the Finding of Fact Hearing), the reality is that the Court may be required to convene a hearing, of an appropriate length, to specifically deal with any such application.

PRACTICE NOTE

- Do not file and serve intimate images without court approval, even if the other side agree.
- The party seeking to adduce the intimate images needs to raise this matter, on notice at a case management hearing (CMH) or directions hearing.
- That party must ensure that the information the Court is likely to need (referred to above) is with the Court in good time and that the respondent to the application also has an appropriate amount of time to ensure that they are able to adequately respond.
- This must not be an 'ambush' application made at court or shortly before a hearing. It needs to be a properly prepared application, on notice, served with supporting documentation as set out below.
- This issue is taken so seriously by the court that it is *NOT* a matter to deal with on the basis of 'ask for forgiveness not permission'.

7.21 The third aspect of the guidance is that:

> 'iii. It is for the party making such an application to persuade the court of the *relevance* and *necessity* of such material to the specific factual issues which the court is required to determine.'[8]

7.22 In exercising this element of the Court's case management powers, the Court will need to have regard to the allegations it is being asked to determine at the Finding of Fact Hearing. As the culture of the Family Court moves away from the use of Scott Schedules – and pending the judiciary offering further guidance as to the most appropriate way to place allegations before the Family Court – *the Court is going to need to understand the nature of the allegations before it and how any intimate images relate to the allegations it is going to have to determine.*

8 *Re M* (n 2), [77(C)].

7.23 Additionally:

> 'iv. The court should carefully consider the relevance of the evidence to the issues in the case together with the likely *probative* value of any such evidence.'[9]

7.24 In order for the Court to properly consider the likely probative value of such evidence, it must be familiar with the facts of the case. This again reinforces the point that the Court must have sufficient time to prepare and consider the application; it is unlikely that a *short* case management hearing will be sufficient since the Court's attention is spread between a multitude of issues at such appointments.

7.25 See *S v B* for an example of where the Court found there to be a lack of probative value: the Court refused S's application for intimate images showing B's breasts to be introduced as evidence of her being a sex worker.[10]

PRACTICE NOTE

- It would be wise to direct the Court and one's opponents to the guidance in *Re M* early on in the hearing, specifically moulding your arguments (in support or against the application) around this authority.
- Do not assume knowledge. It is too serious an issue, and may have a profound and negative impact on the future management of the client or case if not dealt with properly.
- A trauma-informed court process requires proactive planning.

7.26 Further to relevance, necessity and probative value, the court will also need to consider the following:

> 'v. As part of its analysis and balancing exercise, the court will need to consider all the relevant factors including (i) any issues as to the vulnerability in relation to any of the parties and the likely impact on any such parties of the admission of such evidence and the manner in which it is used in the proceedings; and (ii) if it is able to do so at a preliminary stage, whether the application/use of such images is motivated, in whole or in part, by a desire to distress or harm a party.'[11]

7.27 It is likely that, by this stage of the proceedings, the Court is alive to issues of vulnerability (especially since it is obliged to treat an alleged victim of DA as vulnerable) and, therefore, this aspect of the analysis and balancing exercise should be relatively straightforward; however, you should not be afraid to remind yourself and the Court how your client's vulnerability manifests itself

9 *Re M* (n 2), [77(D)].
10 *S v B* (n 5), [76]–[77].
11 *Re M* (n 2), [77(E)].

and the impact that the application to adduce intimate images may have on that vulnerability.

PRACTICE NOTE

Particular care should be taken concerning participation arrangements for vulnerable witnesses. This is another aspect of a trauma-informed practice and court case management.

It may be useful at this point to recap your duties under Family Procedure Rules 2010 (SI 2010/2955), Practice Directions 12J (PD12J) and 3AA (PD3AA).

7.28 The Court's task in determining whether the application or use of intimate images is motivated, in whole or in part, by a desire to distress or harm a party is not a straightforward one. It may prove to be an 'own goal' for the party seeking to adduce the evidence.[12] A case which illustrates this is *S v B,* where His Honour Judge Willans found that S had applied to introduce an intimate image of B merely as a method of intimidation.

7.29 Unsurprisingly, the guidance in *Re M* indicated that a successful application would not be commonplace:

> 'vi. The circumstances in which a court will permit the inclusion in evidence of sexually explicit or intimate videos or photographs of any person are likely to be *rare*, in particular, in circumstances in which that person does not consent to such material being admitted.'[13]

7.30 But whilst the inclusion of such evidence is likely to be rare, there is no absolute bar to such material being adduced. Nor is the Court required to apply different rules relating to relevance. *The thrust of the guidance given by Knowles J is to ensure that well-established principles relating to necessity, proportionality and relevance are properly and thoroughly applied by the Court.*

7.31 Where the Court is inclined to permit the application, alternative means of viewing it should be considered:

> 'vii. Where the court is being asked to admit such material, the court should consider whether there may be a range of alternatives to the viewing of such material, for example but not limited to:
>
> a) seeking an admission/partial admission in respect of the alleged conduct.
>
> b) agreed transcripts and/or descriptions of any videos.
>
> c) playing only the audio track of any video recordings.

12 *S v B* (n 5), [78] and [80].
13 *Re M* (n 2), [77(F)].

d) using a still image rather than a video or a short excerpt from a longer video.

e) editing images to obscure intimate parts of the body.

f) extracting meta data as to the timing and location of the evidence.

g) focused and specific cross-examination on the issues.

h) consideration of the use of other evidence to prove the particular fact in issue instead.'[14]

PRACTICE NOTE

If an application to adduce intimate images is being contemplated, practitioners should be prepared to challenge their clients in order to ensure that:

- The application is properly motivated and is not intended to cause harm or humiliation to the other party.
- The intimate images are relevant to the issues which the Court has to determine. They should not be ancillary to the issues before the Court, nor should they serve a contextual purpose only. They should be *directly* relevant to the issues which the Court has to determine.
- Is there other evidence available which is capable of being placed before the Court which would obviate the need for intimate images to be adduced.
- Robust challenge of your client in the confines of a private and confidential conference on these issues is far better – and will make for a stronger application – than facing these issues for the first time on your feet.

It would also be wise to do the following, to assist the Court in their deliberations and to avoid unnecessary trauma for your client:

- Provide the Court with a written consideration of the alternatives listed at vii in advance of the hearing, enabling more efficient deliberations and, hopefully, a faster conclusion to the matter.
- Within this note, the Court will need to have sufficient details of the intimate images and information as to how these images are relevant within the wider context of the case.
- Your key words are *necessity, proportionality and relevance* for *each category* of images you seek to adduce

14 *Re M* (n 2), [77(G)].

HOW MUCH IS RELEVANT? IT'S NOT A CASE OF ONE IN, ALL IN

7.32 When considering alternative means of viewing the intimate material, the Court must have necessity at the forefront of its mind:

> 'viii. If the court decides to admit any sexually explicit or intimate images/videos for any purpose, care should be taken to limit the volume of such evidence to that which is necessary to fulfil the purpose for which it is admitted.'[15]

> PRACTICE NOTE
>
> It might be wise at this point to review the chapter on pleadings (**Chapter 12**) and its relevance to the issues in dispute. A re-read of *Re A*[16] and the guidelines within regarding pleading would also prove useful:
>
> - To what extent are these images necessary to the determination of the issues in this litigation – could the evidence be limited in any way in order to reduce the trauma caused by its admission into evidence?
> - Is the admission of the images proportionate?
> - Are they the only means to prove the point?
> - Where does the balance of harm lie in using them as opposed to not using them?

7.33 Again, this will require the Court to have a thorough knowledge of the case and be fully assisted with the issue of relevance.

WHO HAS TO VIEW IT?

7.34 In addition to limiting the volume of the evidence, the Court should consider limiting *who* should view the material:

> 'ix. The court should determine who can view the material that is to be admitted and limit this where necessary, bearing in mind its private character and the humiliation and harm caused to those both depicted and involved in the proceedings.'[17]

7.35 Practitioners must give some thought to the practicalities of adducing those images. For example, are they to be included in any witness bundle?; if they are to be used during the process of cross-examination, how are they going to be used?

15 *Re M* (n 2), [77(H)].
16 *Re A* [2015] EWFC 11.
17 *Re M* (n 2), [77(I)].

> 'x. If the evidence is considered relevant, a starting point would be to say that it should incorporate the lowest number of images, seen by as few people as necessary, and viewed in the least damaging way.'[18]

7.36 This is vitally important and practitioners must ensure that the Court gives careful consideration to who can have access to this highly sensitive material. Perpetrators of abuse may be seeking to rely upon such images or material to continue their abuse of the victim, or simply to be gratuitous. Practitioners must be alive to a number of issues such as this, weighing the evidential value of the material which is before the Court against the dynamic between the parties.

7.37 Those who feature in the material relied upon may not have already been exposed to the totality of it; it may have been covert or, if known of, thought to have been deleted and long since last viewed.

7.38 Watching it for the first time, or being required to review and be reminded of it and thus give instructions may be triggering. Additional harm may be caused. Do not overlook that and make that a point of submissions if arguing this is using the Court process to further abuse the alleged victim.

7.39 The Court will have PD 12J in mind and vulnerability awareness is required. The potential shame of thinking these images will be seen, not just by counsel and the judge, but court staff and administrators must be taken into account and ways to manage a circulation list thought about.

7.40 It may be that steps such as only permitting trial advocates and the trial judge to view the images should be considered.

HOW IS IT TO BE STORED?

7.41 Closely connected to the issue of *who* can access the material is the *security measures* regarding access to it:

> 'xi. It would be helpful to consider that the evidential security of such material can be maintained (for example, by using only password protected files) both within the hearing itself and outside it, and how the material is deployed within the proceedings.[19]
>
> xii. Specific consideration should be given to the protection and safeguards necessary in respect of any video evidence relied upon (for example, such evidence being made available on a single laptop and brought to court, or the distribution being limited to a core specified legal team on behalf of each party).'[20]

18 *Re M* (n 2), [77(J)].
19 *Re M* (n 2), [77(K)].
20 *Re M* (n 2), [77(J)].

7.42 The Court should be invited to give directions to ensure the security of the material, including how it is stored and transmitted. Storage of the material in particular should be given careful thought: do you wish to risk this material being leaked or being viewed by others who are not permitted?

WHEN IS IT TO BE DEPLOYED?

7.43 The Court should ensure that such material is put to the witnesses, only when it is *absolutely necessary* and with great care. It may need to be flagged as a course counsel is about to embark on.

7.44 Any advocate undertaking this work should have received training under the Family Law Bar Association (FLBA)/Bar Council programme. Gratuitous cross-examination must not be allowed.

7.45 The Court has wide case management powers and practitioners should not be afraid to call it to exercise them.

7.46 *How the evidence should be deployed during the course of the evidence will also require active (and ongoing) consideration by the court.* For example, It is likely that one party will seek to put the intimate images to the other party during the course of the evidence. Whilst this may be appropriate in the context of the individual case, the Court will be required to ensure that the cross-examination remains appropriate and does not stray into the realms of unnecessary questioning, embarrassment or humiliation. The Court should be invited to actively control the evidence at all times. We suggest the Court should check whether the advocates involved have received the FLBA/Bar Council training.

7.47 If your client is the one being questioned about the intimate images, you must ensure that the questions being put to your client are fair, balanced, appropriate and do not stray into areas which are unlikely to assist the Court in determining the issues before it. The tone of questioning is as important as the content. *You should not hesitate to intervene if the questioning becomes gratuitous, too lengthy and/or repetitive.*

PRACTICE NOTE

Apply your training on cross-examining vulnerable witnesses:

- Consider how a trauma-informed process applies to your work – eg should this area of cross-examination be flagged in the witness box as a topic – and factor in breaks.
- Consider the arrangements in and after court to support the client
- If you have not undertaken the training, you should have done and should do so now.

- Whether the cross-examiner is accredited under the Bar Council/FLBA training should be a matter you raise with the Court as part of your submissions if you are resisting the application. Even if it does not affect the determination of the issue (and it might), it will affect the way it is handled and, potentially, by whom.

CONCLUSIONS

7.48 The guidance given by Knowles J is comprehensive and offers practitioners and the judiciary alike a roadmap of relevant considerations when approaching an application to adduce intimate images. With the wide availability of technology and the tendency of many to live their lives in the digital world, the Family Court is likely to be increasingly called upon to control digital evidence placed before it.

7.49 As our understanding of DA continues to evolve, there is an increasing awareness that court proceedings can be used as a mechanism to continue abusive behaviour. This possibility must remain at the forefront of the Court's mind throughout proceedings, especially when considering whether to allow evidence to be adduced.

CHAPTER 8

Alienating Behaviours in the Family Justice System

8.01 Allegations of alienating behaviours engaged in by one parent with the intent or outcome of causing a rift between the other parent and the couple's children, often arise in family cases in connection with contact applications. They may form the grounds of an application by a parent who wants more contact than the other parent (or the child) will agree to. They can also arise as a rebuttal and counter attack to a claim of domestic abuse (DA) and/or controlling and coercive behaviour (CCB). In whatever context they arise, the determination of such allegations can consume a considerable amount of the scarce resources of an overstretched family justice system.

8.02 The complexity and controversy of such cases has been exacerbated by the different approaches taken by some family courts and practitioners when dealing with such issues. Too often, despite being faced with disputed allegations of DA (or even presented with past judicial findings of DA), allegations of so called 'parental alienation' seemingly operate as a 'trump card' leading to case management decisions to appoint an expert (usually a psychologist) in order to assist the court with such allegations. This is presumably motivated by a desire to obviate the delay, cost and time required for a contested judicial Finding of Fact Hearing. Such an approach has fuelled controversy, especially in conjunction with the use of the term 'parental alienation' without proper understanding of its limitations. Past wrongs caused by elevating so-called 'parental alienation' to a 'syndrome', and delegating assessment of such described and disputed parental conduct to a psychologist, has caused much damage to public confidence in private family court proceedings.

8.03 It should be axiomatic to say that the province of deciding disputed fact[1] lies with the judge within a hearing designed and constructed to permit transparent, balanced cross-examination of the allegations. That decision, arrived at on a balance of probabilities, then determines the factual premise upon which the Court, the parties and all professionals then proceed to assess risk and make welfare decisions. *Disputed fact is not for an expert to determine.* The expert, qualified to be regarded as such and to be appointed as an expert pursuant to Family Procedure Rules 2010 (SI 2010/2955) (FPR 2010), Part 25, may be asked

1 Clearly, not every adult dispute is relevant to a welfare determination regarding the children and litigation must be proportionate and necessary to inform welfare arrangements but, when allegations of DA or alienating conduct are made and denied, those allegations, if proven, may make a difference to the welfare decisions needing to be made for the children.

to assess risk on the basis of facts found to be proven but it is not for them to be asked, or to agree, to bypass the right to a fair trial principles under European Convention on Human Rights, Art 6.

8.04 Guidance released by the Family Justice Council in 2024, approved by the President, contained anecdotal evidence suggesting that the required changes in local practice are not consistently applied: some practitioners and courts are still preferring to continue with the use of psychologists or other experts to determine whether alienating behaviours are a feature of a case.[2]

8.05 Furthermore, there is a growing awareness of the interplay between allegations of DA and allegations of alienating behaviours. Practitioners must familiarise themselves with the term DARVO, short for 'Deny, Attack, and Reverse Victim and Offender' and its association with allegations of so-called parental alienation.

8.06 Thus, the purpose of this chapter is twofold:

- To provide a brief overview of the evolution of so-called parental alienation (PA) in the family justice system in order to understand what errors in good practice it gives rise to.
- To draw out lessons which can be learnt from those errors and offer guidance as to how such cases should be dealt with moving forward.

A (VERY) BRIEF HISTORY OF THE TERM 'PA'

8.07 Whilst the notion of a child preferring a relationship with one parent upon separation was first identified by Wallerstein and Kelly in 1976 (labelling the concept as 'parental estrangement'),[3] it was not until Dr Richard Gardner, a child psychiatrist, began to publish his 'research' on the concept that it gained considerable traction and set the family justice system in this country and others on a journey to try and resolve cases in which so-called PA was alleged.

8.08 Originally coined as a syndrome, 'Parental Alienation Syndrome' was defined by Gardner in the 1980s as, 'a psychological disturbance in which children are obsessed with deprecation and criticism of a parent – denigration that is unjustified and/or exaggerated'.[4]

2 Family Justice Council, *Family Justice Council Guidance on responding to a child's unexplained reluctance, resistance or refusal to spend time with a parent and allegations of alienating behaviour* (December 2024), https://www.judiciary.uk/wp-content/uploads/2024/12/Family-Justice-Council-Guidance-on-responding-to-allegations-of-alienating-behaviour-2024-1-1.pdf.

3 J S Wallerstein and J B Kelly, 'The effects of parental divorce: Experiences of the child in later latency' [1976] 46(2) American Journal of Orthopsychiatry 256–69, https://doi.org/10.1111/j.1939-0025.1976.tb00926.x.

4 R Gardner, 'Recent trends in divorce and custody litigation' [1985] 29(2) Academy Forum 3–7.

8.09 In 2000, the Court of Appeal heard a number of conjoined appeals in *Re L, V, M and H (Contact: Domestic Violence)*[5] during which the Court commissioned a report from Dr Clare Sturge and Dr Danya Glaser.[6] This case is familiar to practitioners as it recalibrated the way the Family Court treated allegations of DA when making welfare decisions for children. It has been dealt with at length in this regard in previous chapters of this book. *What is less known about this seminal case is that the Sturge/Glaser report also considered the issue of 'Parental Alienation Syndrome' (as it was then referred to), with the court at first instance having heard evidence from a proponent of Dr Richard Gardner, Dr Ludwig Lowenstein. Interestingly, Sturge and Glaser concluded that the 'syndrome' did not exist and was an unhelpful concept. This conclusion was endorsed by the Court of Appeal.*

8.10 In the years that followed, the Family Court continued to deal with cases in which PA was alleged, albeit there was increasing reluctance to refer to the concept as a syndrome. Nevertheless, some professionals working with families had less compunction about using the term and so it continued to linger. Soon, an industry of lawyers, psychologists and other professionals had grown around the concept of so-called PA.

8.11 In 2018, the Children and Family Court Advisory and Support Service (CAFCASS) Cymru commissioned a report by a number of academics which sought to provide an overview as to the academic and legal landscape regarding PA.[7] The authors of this report concluded:

- there was no commonly accepted definition of PA;
- there was a 'dearth of empirical evidence on the topic';
- research in the area was dominated by only a few authors who appeared to be polarised in their acceptance and rejection of the nature and prevalence of PA; and
- there was insufficient scientific substantiation regarding the identification, treatment and long-term effects of PA.

8.12 In an attempt to make things clearer, CAFCASS sought to introduce a working definition as to what PA was:[8]

> 'When a child's resistance/hostility towards one parent is not justified and is the result of psychological manipulation by the other parent.'

5 *Re L, V, M and H (Contact: Domestic Violence)* [2000] EWCA Civ 194.
6 Claire Sturge and Danya Glaser, 'Contact and Domestic Violence – the Experts' Court Report' [2000] 30 Family Law 615–25.
7 Julie Doughty, Nina Maxwell and Tom Slater, *Review of Research and Case Law on Parental Alienation* (April 2018), https://gov.wales/sites/default/files/publications/2018-05/review-of-research-and-case-law-on-parental-alienation.pdf.
8 Referred to by Peter Jackson LJ in *Re S (Parental Alienation: Cult)* [2020] EWCA Civ 568, [8].

8.13 When CAFCASS' then working definition was considered alongside the definition of PA Syndrome devised by Dr Richard Gardner (which was rejected by Sturge, Glaser and the Court of Appeal), there were some similarities which were not helpful at a time when the Family Court needed consistency and clarity when dealing with such cases. Arguably, this hindrance was not helped by CAFCASS' working definition receiving judicial endorsement by the Court of Appeal in *Re S (Parental Alienation: Cult)*.[9]

PRACTICE NOTE

A close reading of the case is required as the citation has too often been taken to refer to describing PA as a 'cult' when that is an incorrect and lazy reading of the judgment.[10]

8.14 In recent years, the way in which the family justice system is perceived to have balanced DA and PA has come under close scrutiny. Camps have formed ranging from those who campaign for increased awareness and recognition of PA as a psychological concept to those who decry it as a misconceived, gendered concept acting as a smokescreen to disguise DA and CCB. In between are many who simply argue for better practice, learning and outcomes in the Family Court when DA and PA are alleged. This increased awareness has ensured that the issue of alienating behaviours has remained near the top of the Family Court's agenda for a number of years and shows no sign of slipping downwards.

Moving from so called 'PA' to 'alienating behaviours'

8.15 In February 2023, the President of the Family Division handed down judgment in the case of *Re C (Parental Alienation: Instruction of Expert)*.[11] Whilst this judgment's main focus was upon the issue of experts in the Family Court (a topic which will be discussed later in this chapter), the President of the Family Division considered the terminology in use to describe PA. After consideration, the President endorsed the definition used by the Association of Clinical Psychologists UK: 'alienating behaviours' refer to those which cause 'the disruption or undermining of a parent/child relationship'.

8.16 Having encapsulated what the President believed 'alienating behaviours' to be, the Court went on to endorse the approach advocated by the Association of Clinical Psychologists, who made the following submission to the Court in *Re C (Parental Alienation: Instruction of Expert):*

9 *Re S (Parental Alienation: Cult)* (n 8), [8].

10 It was the mother's adherence to 'Universal Medicine', an organisation founded in Australia in 1999 by Serge Benhayon, that was held to be a 'cult' by the trial judge.

11 *Re C (Parental Alienation: Instruction of Expert)* [2023] EWHC 345 (Fam).

> 'Much like an allegation of domestic abuse; the decision about whether or not a parent has alienated a child is a question of fact for the court to resolve and not a diagnosis that can or should be offered by a psychologist. For these purposes, the ACP-UK wishes to emphasise that "parental alienation" is not a syndrome capable of being diagnosed, but a process of manipulation of children perpetrated by one parent against the other through, what are termed as "alienating behaviours." It is fundamentally a question of fact.'[12]

8.17 What followed was a three-stage test to determining the presence of alienating behaviours, which is now set out with the Family Justice Council guidance which is discussed later in this chapter:

> 'a court would need to be satisfied that *three elements are established* before it could conclude that alienating behaviours had occurred:
>
> (a) The child is refusing, resisting or reluctant to engage in a relationship with a parent or carer.
>
> (b) The refusal, resistance or reluctance is not consequent on the actions of the non-resident parent towards the child or the resident parent; and
>
> (c) The resident parent has engaged in behaviours that have directly or indirectly impacted on the child, leading to the child's refusal, resistance or reluctance to engage in a relationship with the other parent.'[13]

It is important to note that *all three elements must be proven on the balance of probabilities* with the burden of proof resting upon the person making the allegations.

PRACTICE NOTE

Do note that part 'b' of the test effectively introduces the conduct element between the parents – especially when DA and CCB may be a feature of it. By ensuring that the focus is on the behaviours related to the concept, the following benefits are hoped to materialise:

- The Court should be better able to steer those making such allegations towards the issues which the Court will need to resolve rather than litigating over the meaning of concepts and labels.
- The focus upon behaviours could deter the medicalisation of the concept and the desire for a 'diagnosis'.
- The Family Court should be able to deal with cases with a greater degree of consistency and predictability.
- Those who are called upon by the Family Court to assist in the management of cases, such as local authorities, the National Youth Advocacy Service (NYAS) and CAFCASS should all have a solid foundation from which to undertake their assessments, grounded in facts which have been determined by the Court.

12 *Re C* (n 11), [103].
13 Family Justice Council (n 2).

8.18 Practitioners might have hoped the President's decision in *Re C* provided them with a guiding light – a solution to resolve cases which practitioners and judges alike consider to be complex, difficult and time-consuming. However, within months of the President of the Family Division handing down his judgment in *Re C*, judgment was handed down by Keehan J in the long-running case of *Re A and B (Children: Parental Alienation) (No 5)*.[14] In the fifth and final judgment in this self-evidently difficult case, Keehan J sought to resolve the matter by having regard to the guidance given by the President in *Re C*. However, rather than merely applying such guidance, he used it to justify the fact that he had delegated the judicial function of determining PA to an expert. Specifically, he argued that the expert concerned had acted in accordance with the guidance given by the President by focusing upon the behaviours of the perpetrator. Not only was this application of the *Re C* guidance strange considering that the President had specifically disapproved of the use of an expert to delegate judicial functions, it is also unclear from the judgment how the court satisfied itself that the expert had in fact taken the approach described.

8.19 In an area of children's law which evokes controversy, inconsistency and fierce debate, we suggest that the approach taken by Keehan J may be said to have added to the confusion and gave continued licence to some professionals and courts to instruct unregulated experts to undertake community-based assessments that require the expert to evaluate conduct and behaviours (and ascribe consequences to these).

The present day

8.20 Following on from the President's decision in *Re C*, in August 2023 the Family Justice Council prepared draft *Guidance on Responding to Allegations of Alienating Behaviour*, which was released for consultation. Provoking one of the largest consultations in the history of the Family Justice Council, the final version of this guidance was published in December 2024. It came with this introduction:

> '**Foreword from the President of the Family Division and Chair of the Family Justice Council, Sir Andrew McFarlane:**
>
> The issue of parental alienation/alienating behaviours is a polarising one which has taken up much court time and public debate. This guidance note reflects the complexity and challenges of this area of family law. It has been long awaited.
>
> I approved this workstream for the Family Justice Council knowing how divisive this topic has become. In my view this guidance is required to ensure greater consistency of approach across the courts and to improve outcomes for children and families and to protect children and victims from litigation

14 *Re A and B (Children: Parental Alienation) (No 5)* [2023] EWHC 1864 (Fam).

abuse. It has my endorsement and I encourage everyone working within the Family Justice system to read it carefully.'[15]

The scope of the guidance

8.21 The scope of the guidance is wide, addressing the following:

- the litigation journey;
- case management;
- alienating behaviours and the three necessary elements to proving their existence;
- early robust case management of alienating behaviours allegations, encompassing:
  - fact finding hearings;
  - delay; and
  - next steps;
- the voice of the child in proceedings concerning alienating behaviours;
- welfare decisions where findings of alienating behaviour have been made, encompassing discussion of practical considerations and child friendly judgments;
- how to cultivate an understanding of 'Reluctance, Resistance and Refusal and Psychological Manipulation'; and
- the use of experts, including where there is a conflict of interest.

8.22 This guidance is a crucial piece of work which every practitioner must read and apply. It discusses the most significant and contentious areas that have bedevilled the family courts for decades.

Key concepts

8.23 The guidance introduces a number of key terms to describe the behaviours and emotions practitioners will need to be familiar with:

> '• *Attachment, affinity and alignment ("AAA")* – reasons why children may favour one parent over another, or reject a parent, which are typical emotional responses to parenting experiences and not the result of psychological manipulation by a parent.

15 Family Justice Council (n 2).

- *Appropriate justified rejection ("AJR")* – a situation where a child's rejection of a parent is an understandable response to that parent's behaviour towards the child and/or the other parent.
- *Alienating Behaviours ("AB")* – psychologically manipulative behaviours, intended or otherwise, by a parent towards a child which have resulted in the child's reluctance, resistance or refusal to spend time with the other parent.
- *Protective behaviours ("PB")* – behaviours by a parent towards a child in order to protect the child from exposure to abuse by the other parent, or from suffering harm (or greater harm) as a consequence of the other parent's abuse.
- *Reluctance, resistance or refusal ("RRR")* – behaviours by a child concerning their relationship with, or spending time with, a parent, which may have a variety of potential causes.'[16]

8.24 'AJR', 'PB' and 'RRR' are not necessarily new concepts and those familiar with this particular corner of children's law will have had experience of cases in which each have been raised. However, the guidance now gives these concepts a prominent position and so ought to ensure that the Court carefully explores whether there is an AJR or the use of PBs as part of its overall consideration.

8.25 With regard to the concept of PA, the guidance made several notable statements:

- It recognised that 'PA' and 'alienating behaviours' are terms which, due to contention over their meaning, 'serve to polarise opinion in a way that is often counterproductive to the best interests of children, and which shifts the focus away from the voice of the child'.[17]
- It stated that it aims to assist 'the court in determining the welfare of the child where allegations of "parental alienation" or "alienating behaviours" are made, by maintaining a *focus on the impact on the child rather than on parental behaviours per se*'.[18]
- It decisively stated that '"parental alienation syndrome" has no evidential basis and is considered a harmful pseudo-science' and warns that it is often a concept which is exploited in family proceedings despite the fact that, with proper forensic assessment, it becomes clear that it is actually quite rarely displayed.[19]
- It raised concerns that the concepts of alienating behaviours and the like have 'misplaced legitimacy'[20] in the Court and was clear to point out that,

16 Family Justice Council (n 2), p 4.
17 Family Justice Council (n 2), para 1.
18 Family Justice Council (n 2), emphasis added.
19 Family Justice Council (n 2), para 2.
20 Family Justice Council (n 2), para 4.

although it would use the terms 'PA' and 'alienating behaviours' for ease of understanding, this is not intended to give the concept legitimacy.[21]

- It also recognised that the behaviour is, nevertheless, an allegation which is increasingly raised in family proceedings and so endeavoured to provide guidance in order to assist the Court with this unfortunate reality.[22]

8.26 Crucially, despite noting a multitude of issues with the concepts of 'PA' and 'alienating behaviours', it noted that it was clear that, where found to exist, the harm these behaviours cause to a child can be significant and enduring, akin to other forms of emotional or psychological child abuse:

> 'Alienating Behaviours range in intensity and their impact on children, but these harms can be far reaching. They can affect a child's emotional, social and psychological development. Severed relationships and growing up with a false narrative can also have a harmful impact on a child's identity, self-worth and sense of safety in the world. Whilst the focus here is on the welfare outcomes for children, it is also important to recognise the very significant emotional impact on parents of the loss of a relationship with a child.'[23]

PRACTICE NOTE

A yellow flag (if not red) of concern should be placed against the name of anyone self-describing themselves as an expert in 'parental alienation'. That applies to legal professionals much as to psychologists, therapists or independent social workers. If they use the term 'parental alienation syndrome', run away fast.

We strongly suggest you look at any nominated expert's CV to see what organisations they are members of (and check past membership databases if you are in doubt).

Remember that research suggests that, as commonplace as such allegations have become, alienating behaviours which actually impact upon a child's relationship with the other parent are relatively rare.

What are alienating behaviours?

8.27 The Family Justice Council tells us that alienating behaviours are 'psychologically manipulative behaviours, intended or otherwise, by a parent towards a child *which have resulted* in the child's reluctance, resistance or refusal to spend time with the other parent'.[24]

21 Family Justice Council (n 2), para 5.
22 Family Justice Council (n 2), para 4.
23 Family Justice Council (n 2), para 6.
24 Family Justice Council (n 2), para 4.

PRACTICE NOTE

Readers will note the similarities to the working definition of PA with that previously used in the Family Court. But there is now an added component to part b of the three-stage test set out in *Re C* (and above at **8.17**).

Essentially, an extra phrase could be added to the original part b, thus:

> 'The refusal, resistance or reluctance is not consequent on the actions of the non-resident parent towards the child or the resident parent, *which may therefore be an appropriate justified rejection by the child or is not caused by any other factor such as the child's alignment, affinity or attachment.*'

This new 'formulation' remains similar to previous constructs of PA, however, it now seeks to place more focus upon actual behaviours which should assist the Court in dealing with such cases.

Allocation

8.28 Having received an application for an Order under Children Act 1989, s 8, the Court undertakes a key function in gatekeeping the application. This involves a District Judge and/or a legal adviser considering the papers and deciding to which level of the Family Court the case should be allocated.

8.29 At para 28 of the Family Justice Council Guidance:

> 'Where the alleged behaviour is mentioned in the original application or response, the Legal Adviser or Judge triaging the case will need to consider the nature, seriousness and complexity of the issues raised in deciding whether the matter can be retained by the Magistrates for case management under the allocation rules. The Legal Adviser or Judge triaging on issue should remind themselves of the elements that those making the allegations of Alienating Behaviours would be required to establish.'[25]

8.30 In order for proper and effective triaging to take place, the legal adviser or judge must have some understanding of alienating behaviours and what the person making the allegations is required to establish. This is an important stage in the proceedings. Proper and effective gatekeeping will ensure that cases in which alienating behaviours are *legitimately* raised are identified promptly so that case management decisions can be made without delay. The guidance envisages that the majority of private law matters which are allocated to magistrates will continue to be heard by magistrates. It is important to note that this does not

25 Family Justice Council (n 2), para 28.

mean allocation to an appropriate level of the Family Court cannot be revisited at a later stage in the proceedings. The guidance explains that:

> 'Where on initial scrutiny of the allegations it appears that one or more of the three elements is absent, or a court has already considered the allegations to be lacking in any solid evidential basis, the matter may remain with the Magistrates unless there are other matters contained in the application that would justify reallocation under the Family Procedure Rules (FPR). The Magistrates must thereafter keep allocation under review in accordance with the allocation guidelines at each stage of the proceedings.'[26]
>
> 'Where, after careful analysis of the information provided to the court in the documents, it appears that the three elements of alienating behaviour may be present, the case *must* be transferred for case management and determination by a judge.'[27]

PRACTICE NOTE

You must be alive to the following points when considering the issue of allocation in cases where alienating behaviours are alleged:

- They often feature allegations of other forms of abuse, such as DA (including sexual assault, physical assault, stalking and coercive behaviour) which complicate the factual matrix the Court may be required to determine.
- Allegations of DA and CCB are serious of and in themselves and cannot be 'ring fenced' from litigating allegations of alienation. The child may have been present or in the vicinity of the assaults and their welfare may have been (or is at risk of being) affected by the abuse of their primary carer. DA and CCB are abusive behaviours capable of causing significant harm to a child if they have been exposed to it within their home.
- If it is possible that alienation is present, the case *must* be transferred up. This reflects its complexity and seriousness.
- It may be useful to re-read the *Schedule to the Allocation and Gatekeeping Guidance – Private Law* which sets out that cases which appear to involve, or have the potential to involve, intractable opposition to contact *should* be allocated to a district judge but *may* be allocated to a circuit judge or High Court judge if sufficiently serious.[28]
- Remember – a mere *potential* to involve such issues is enough for the Court to consider the issue of allocation, and therefore allocate this matter to a district judge or above.

26 Family Justice Council (n 2), para 29.
27 Family Justice Council (n 2), para 28.
28 Courts and Tribunals Judiciary, *Schedule to the Allocation and Gatekeeping Guidance* (judicary.uk 2014), https://www.justice.gov.uk/documents/schedule-to-allocation-and-gatekeeping-guidance.pdf.

- Where a case has a significant litigation history, the *Schedule to the Allocation and Gatekeeping Guidance – Private Law* provides that cases seeking enforcement of existing Orders made by a circuit judge or a recorder *should* be allocated to a district judge but *may* be allocated to a circuit judge or High Court judge if sufficiently serious. If practicable, proceedings should be allocated to the same circuit judge or recorder.

8.31 It remains to be seen in practice how the Family Justice Council guidance fits with the *Allocation and Gatekeeping Guidance*. The bottom line is that practitioners have to become familiar with both. Considerable care must be taken and arguments prepared so that the Court can ensure that cases in which alienating behaviours are alleged are appropriately allocated.

8.32 Allocation of proceedings is a matter that requires ongoing consideration throughout a case: a decision made at the outset of the proceedings need not subsist for the duration of the proceedings. It has been acknowledged that proceedings concerning children can be dynamic.[29] Similarly, a decision that a Finding of Fact Hearing is not necessary may require reconsideration by the Court at a later stage of the proceedings.

8.33 In summary, great care should be taken when such cases are allocated to the magistrates' court. We would advise practitioners to apply the criteria above and be prepared to revisit allocation. On any analysis, there will be a fine line between the Court grappling with the issue of necessity and proportionality but doing so in a way that does not trespass near to a summary disposal of the allegations.

PRACTICE NOTE

In order to ensure that the Court can properly allocate proceedings from the outset, practitioners and litigants should ensure that sufficient information is included in the application to ensure that the Court can make a properly informed decision. Such information should address how they assert the three elements of alienating behaviour can be proven.

Necessity

8.34 The guidance from the Family Justice Council reminds practitioners (and the courts) that robust case management is important and no more so than

29 'Like dough sitting on a baker's proving shelf, a Family case that is waiting to be heard expands in size. Delay breeds more delay': Sir Andrew McFarlane, President of the Family Division, 'A View from The President's Chambers' (November 2022) https://www.judiciary.uk/guidance-and-resources/a-view-from-the-presidents-chambers-november-2022/.

in cases where alienating behaviours are alleged since if such allegations are raised as an issue for the first time late in proceedings, this can delay the entire proceedings. The guidance tells us, at para 33:

> 'Where [alienating behaviours] are raised after the initial stage in proceedings, it is important that the case is allocated/re-allocated to a judge to ascertain if there appears to be a solid evidential base *necessitating* judicial determination of the issue.'[30]

PRACTICE NOTE

- A judicial enquiry 'to ascertain if there is a solid evidential basis necessitating judicial determination of the issue' is not an invitation for the Court to undertake a summary trial. If necessary, you should be prepared to caution the Court against such a course of action.
- Rather, the Court must engage with the questions of necessity and proportionality in the same way as the Court considers whether a Finding of Fact Hearing is required in cases involving allegations of DA.
- Therefore, you should not shy away from referring the Court to the jurisprudence which guides the Court as to when a Finding of Fact Hearing may be considered necessary and proportionate (see **Chapter 5**). However, it is important to remember that, although the guidance set out in **Chapter 5** regarding necessity and proportionality is transferable here, the Court should also consider the evolution of any allegation of alienating behaviour.

8.35 A key piece of guidance regarding Finding of Fact Hearings is thus:

> 'A fact-finding hearing will only be required where it is relevant to the ultimate issues to be determined and where such a hearing is both necessary and proportionate. The court must carefully examine what, why and when the allegations of Alienating Behaviour were first reported to be an issue, mindful that allegations of Alienating Behaviour are sometimes raised as a response to allegations of domestic abuse.'[31]

8.36 The Family Justice Council devotes part of its guidance to the avoidance of default findings in cases in which alienating behaviours are alleged.[32] Simply because the child is demonstrating a reluctance, refusal or resistance to spend time with a parent does not necessarily mean that there are alienating behaviours. Rather, the Family Justice Council advises that the Court must adequately and safely consider all potential causal factors and explanations (including DA or

30 Family Justice Council (n 2), para 33, emphasis added.
31 Family Justice Council (n 2), para 49.
32 Family Justice Council (n 2), paras 61–64.

child abuse) when looking at the nexus between a child's reluctance, resistance or refusal and the behaviour of the parent.

8.37 The practitioner should be aware of, and ensure, the CAFCASS officer has applied the most current iteration of their *Domestic Abuse Practice Policy*, dated 10 December 2025 and published on 6 January 2026 (please refer to **Chapter 15** where this guidance is explored in detail). In particular:

> 'when assessing the reasons why a child does not want to spend time with a parent following separation, especially when a parent says they are experiencing alienating behaviours, [CAFCASS officer] must first consider whether the cause of this refusal is because the child is a victim of domestic abuse and harmful parenting or if there are other reasons for the child not wanting to spend time with that parent.'[33] (para 45)

CAFCASS should have applied and evidenced its guidance *Understanding why a child does not want to spend family time with a parent*.[34] Look up this material. It is very useful. Amongst other issues it expressly deals with: what children say; understanding their experiences; the impact of alienating behaviour on a child (Chapter 5); and the use of experts (Chapter 6).

PRACTICE NOTE

- Cases involving allegations of alienating behaviours are far from straightforward. The alleged behaviours can be highly nuanced and akin to CCB.
- It is important to ensure that the Court exercises great care in this exercise for it risks conflating the tests of necessity and proportionality with a summary disposal of the allegations.
- When the Court is called upon to undertake this preliminary exercise, it is likely that the evidential landscape will be far from complete. This is particularly the case when the Family Court is faced with significant numbers of litigants-in-person.
- Take heed of the behaviour of the child as that will better describe what the child is experiencing and why than a similar key word ('label'). Use and analyse the terms reluctance, refusal or resistance (RRR) and apply them to the chronology of the case resistance.

33 CAFCASS, *Domestic Abuse Practice Policy* (January 2026), https://www.cafcass.gov.uk/domestic-abuse-practice-policy, para 45.

34 CAFCASS, *Understanding why a child does not want to spent family time with a parent: A guide to assessment* (August 2025), https://www.cafcass.gov.uk/sites/default/files/2025-07/Understanding%20why%20a%20child%20does%20not%20want%20to%20spend%20family%20time%20with%20a%20parent.pdf.

- Take heed of the concept and potential reality of 'Deny, Attack, and Reverse Victim and Offender' (DARVO). Consider its relevance in the context of the litigation history.
- Remember to cross-apply case law – don't pigeonhole public and private law concepts – Children Act principles embrace both. For example, although in the context of public law proceedings, the Court of Appeal reminded practitioners that a premature disposal of a case was unfair and contrary to the interests of the children concerned.[35]
- Therefore, the Court must take care to ensure that it does not undertake a superficial and premature analysis at an early stage of the proceedings.

Evidence

8.38 As with any allegations made in the Family Court, the burden of proving the allegations rests upon the person making the allegations. Have in mind the type of behaviours that tend to suggest alienating behaviour such as:

- repeatedly or constantly criticising and belittling the other parent;
- unjustifiably limiting or restricting contact or undermining contact between the child and the other parent;
- forbidding discussion about the other parent;
- creating the impression that the other parent dislikes or does not love the child, or has harmed them or intends them harm; and/or
- denying emotional responsiveness to the other parent or spurning, terrorising, isolating, corrupting, or exploiting them.

8.39 These examples were set out in the Family Justice Council's consultation.[36] This list is not exhaustive and there are likely to be many more examples of behaviour which may amount to alienating behaviour which may also involve frustrating or undermining the extent to which the other parent can exercise parental responsibility in respect of the child.

8.40 The Family Justice Council makes a number of suggestions with regard to the evidence which the Court may wish to consider making directions on. These include:

- narrative statements;
- independent evidence (considering what evidence the trial court will need by way of disclosure, this may include medical records, social work records, school records and/or telephone records); and

35 *Re S-W (Children)* [2015] EWCA Civ 27.

36 Family Justice Council Consultation, *Draft guidance on Responding to allegations of alienating behaviour* (August 2023).

- schedules. (Following *Re H-N & Ors (Children) (Domestic Abuse: Finding of Fact Hearings),*[37] if a course of conduct is alleged, critical examination of that period and the events are likely to be relevant to disclosure.)

PRACTICE NOTE

Allegations of alienating behaviours may be highly nuanced and may not fit neatly into a schedule. In such circumstances, guidance given in **Chapter 2** relating to CCB may assist.[38]

PRACTICE NOTE

Pleading tips:

The following are examples of alleged conduct which may be appropriate to plead in a schedule of allegations:

- The resident parent has failed to make the child available to spend time with the non-resident parent in accordance with previous Orders of the Court without good reason (with a chronology of such failures).
- The resident parent has acted in such a way as to undermine the non-resident parent's parental responsibility such as enrolling them in a school without consent or consultation (or other such examples).
- The resident parent has unilaterally moved the child to a new location without consultation or consent.
- The resident parent speaks negatively of the non-resident parent to the child or allows them to be exposed to such negative comments.

Remember, when considering whether conduct would be appropriate in a schedule, bear in mind the three-stage test and the impact of the behaviour. Calibrating this behaviour against a neutral tether provides an anchor for argument. These three stages will be discussed further in this context, below.

8.41 It is unlikely that the totality of the alleged behaviour will be capable of being captured in a schedule of allegations and therefore, in preparation for a case in which such allegations are being made, both a schedule of allegations and a narrative statement should be contemplated.

8.42 However, as mentioned above, it is crucial that any evidence should be considered and pleaded in alignment with the three individual components of

37 *Re H-N & Ors (Children) (Domestic Abuse: Finding of Fact Hearings)* [2021] EWCA Civ 448.
38 See **Chapter 2, 2.14** onwards.

alienating behaviours set out above and refusal, resistance, reluctance and their triggers, causes and consequences.

8.43 For ease of reference, each element will be explored below with further guidance.

ELEMENT 1: THE CHILD IS REFUSING, RESISTING, OR RELUCTANT TO ENGAGE IN A RELATIONSHIP WITH A PARENT OR CARER

8.44 Whilst the Family Justice Council observes that if the child/children is/are spending time with the non-resident parent, alienation is unlikely to be found,[39] this will depend very much upon the circumstances of the case as it is possible that the child/children are spending time with the non-resident parent but that time fraught with difficulties or is being restricted or limited in some way.

8.45 It may be that a CAFCASS officer assesses the child at this point to determine their thoughts and feelings. However, it must be remembered that, although CAFCASS has a wealth of tools which may assist the Court, it is not an arbiter of fact.[40] The Court should, therefore, resist ordering such a report (unless it is necessary, as it sometimes is) so as to protect CAFCASS officers' role in proceedings from being compromised in this way.

> PRACTICE NOTE
>
> The authors of this book have often had proceedings where a CAFCASS officer was asked to give evidence at a Finding of Fact Hearing as it was appropriate in that case's particular context especially if they had provided a report which had moved from presentation of information to analysis and conclusion on disputed fact (and not on a contingent facts to be found basis).
>
> An application for recusal post-judgment may have a place where the CAFCASS officer has made a premature determination of behaviour (inconsistent with the Court's determination) and that premature view has impacted on interim decisions for the child and the trust and confidence in a parent.

39 Family Justice Council (n 2), para 39.
40 Family Justice Council (n 2), paras 40–41.

ELEMENT 2: THE CHILD'S RELUCTANCE, REFUSAL OR RESISTANCE IS NOT CONSEQUENT ON THE ACTIONS OF THE NON-RESIDENT PARENT TOWARDS THE CHILD OR THE RESIDENT PARENT

8.46 This is a key aspect for the Family Court to explore. Often, allegations of alienating behaviours are used as a 'defence' to allegations of DA. In such circumstances, the Family Court may be faced with two sets of allegations, each of which are capable of impacting upon the most appropriate arrangements for the child or of exposing the child to harm (or a risk of harm).

PRACTICE NOTE

Remember the impact of the binary test: if an allegation is not proven on a balance of probabilities, it has a value of 0 and is treated as if it did not happen. Not only does this fail to assist the maker of the unproven allegations but it may assist the person against whom it was made. For example, the opposing party may rely on the fact that an unproven allegation was made as an example of litigation conduct CCB.

Practitioners should think of this in advance and prepare their submissions accordingly.

8.47 Bear in mind that, although the Family Justice Council warns the Court to be cautious when invited to endorse a default finding that a parent who fails to establish allegations of DA or abuse of the child has therefore engaged in alienating behaviour, the Court does not always exercise such caution. For such a finding to have any basis in law, the Court would be required to find that, not only did the abuse as alleged not take place, but that such false allegations were advanced with the aim of disrupting the child's relationship with the other parent. The Family Justice Council opined that it will only constitute alienating behaviour if there is evidence that the child has been manipulated on the basis of those false allegations into an unjustified resistance or reluctance to engage with the allegedly abusive parent.

8.48 In the event that allegations of DA are proven, or there are other safeguarding issues which are found by the Court or otherwise evidenced, such findings may serve to explain why the child is reluctant, refusing or resisting to engage with the non-resident parent.

8.49 Practitioners should take care to explore the reasons why the child may be demonstrating a reluctance, refusal or resistance so that appropriate advice can be given at an early stage and in order to allow any potential hurdles to be addressed. If there are proven allegations (or admitted allegations) of DA, or the child has been exposed, or is likely to be exposed to, other forms of abusive behaviour, it is wise to consider whether allegations of alienating behaviour should be made. This is a matter which requires care.

ELEMENT 3: HAS ONE PARENT ENGAGED IN BEHAVIOURS THAT HAVE DIRECTLY OR INDIRECTLY IMPACTED ON THE CHILD, LEADING TO THE CHILD'S REFUSAL, RESISTANCE OR RELUCTANCE TO ENGAGE IN A RELATIONSHIP WITH THE OTHER PARENT

8.50 Arguably, the first two stages seek to lay the foundations before the Court is able to grapple with the fundamental issue: whether one parent is responsible for the child's refusal, resistance or reluctance to engage in a relationship with the other parent.

8.51 This is where evidence is key. Evidence can come in many forms and care should be taken to explore all avenues which may result in evidence being available for the Court. By way of an example, in a recent case in which one of the authors was involved, allegations were made against the non-resident parent which were the subject of a police investigation. At the conclusion of the police investigation, the police concluded that the children had been coached by the resident parent. The police evidence was invaluable. Their investigation had a depth and scope that the private paying litigant could not match. Schools can also hold important evidence, although it should be borne in mind that the child's school should be seen and protected as a neutral venue for the child and, therefore, great care should be exercised to maintain that neutrality. That assertion is, sadly, more often observed in the breach than obeyance and CPOMS (as the school safeguarding records are known) often produce a treasure trove of material about what narrative a parent has given to a teacher or what a child has said about home life and their perception of it. But schools can become unintentionally embroiled in parental personality power play – do not assume neutrality. Look at the evidence critically. What does it show about a parent's conduct, their narrative and its impact on the child? Evidence in the form of safeguarding logs (CPOMS) or school reports may offer an evidentially strong standpoint for the court to consider.

Case management decisions – should an expert be instructed?

8.52 As highlighted earlier in this chapter, the Family Justice Council's guidance emphasised the fact that 'it is inappropriate for experts to be asked to step into fact-finding or determination of Alienating Behaviours'.[41] Despite this, it may be necessary to have expert evidence from a psychologist expert when the Court comes to consider the welfare stage. This is in accordance with all we have said hitherto about the different responsibilities of the judge and the expert. It is for the judge to determine issues of disputed fact, not an expert.

41 Family Justice Council (n 2), para 108.

Alienation Experts? Psychologist? What's in a title?

8.53 The use of experts in cases where alienating behaviours is alleged has received scrutiny from a number of different quarters in recent years: the press and the media, as well as the courts have considered the role experts have to play in such cases.

8.54 In February 2023, the President of the Family Division handed down judgment in the aforementioned *Re C ('Parental Alienation': Instruction of Expert)*.[42] This was an appeal against a circuit judge decision with the central issue raised being 'of more general importance and relat[ing] to the instruction of experts in proceedings where there is an allegation of parental alienation'.[43] In particular, this concerned whether the expert who had been instructed in the case, a Melanie Gill, was qualified or otherwise to give expert evidence on the issues raised in their instruction. Such was the strength of feeling in this case, the Association of Clinical Psychologists was invited to intervene in the appeal.

8.55 During the course of the judgment, McFarlane P summarised the various guidance which had been offered by both the Family Justice Council and the British Psychological Society as well as setting out the submissions made by the Association of Clinical Psychologists. The judgment is important reading for any practitioner in this area. It provided the Court with the opportunity to draw together recent guidance and flag up key points in clear terms:[44]

- There is no definition of an 'expert' in family proceedings.
- Expert evidence will only be permitted in children proceedings 'if the court is of the opinion that the expert evidence is necessary to assist the court to resolve the proceedings justly'.[45]
- An expert witness may give factual evidence on a matter that he is not qualified to give expert evidence upon, but his opinion will only be admissible 'on any relevant matter on which he is qualified to give expert evidence'.[46]
- The question of whether an expert is qualified to give expert evidence is a matter for the Court in each individual case.
- The instruction and role of experts in the Family Court is already the subject of extensive coverage in the FPR 2010.
- *Certain categories of psychologist have a protected title which may only be used by those who are validly registered under the regulations.*
- It is not for the Family Court to prohibit the instruction of any unregulated psychologist. The current rules and guidance are clear and contain an

42 *Re C* (n 11).
43 *Re C* (n 11), [2].
44 *Re C* (n 11), [87] onwards.
45 *Re C* (n 11), [89].
46 *Re C* (n 11), [90].

element of flexibility. *The question of whether a proposed expert is entitled to be regarded as an expert remains one for the individual court.*

8.56 The concept of alienating behaviours is a highly controversial one: there are those who assert (with vigour) that it is a psychological condition requiring a psychologist to 'diagnose and treat' it whilst there are others who assert that it simply does not exist. For many years, the default position for the Family Court when dealing with such a case would be to permit the instruction of an expert. Notwithstanding the recent developments, in both the draft guidance from the Family Justice Council and in case law, there have been recent, reported, examples where the Family Court has approved the instruction of a psychologist in cases where PA has been alleged with such approval subsequently set aside on appeal (see *Re GB (Part 25 Application: Parental Alienation)*[47] and *Re A and B (Children: Expert's Reports)*[48]).

8.57 It is hoped that as the Family Court moves away from such a practice, the instances when the Family Court seeks to delegate its function to experts should reduce with the Court only turning to experts for assistance with the welfare outcomes for the child concerned.

8.58 In May 2022, the Family Justice Council issued *Interim Guidance in relation to expert witnesses in cases where there are allegations of alienating behaviours – conflicts of interest*[49] (Interim Guidance) which emphasised the importance of the expert being alert to potential conflicts of interest by quoting joint guidance given for psychologist expert witnesses by the Family Justice Council and the British Psychological Society:

> 'The expert witness' overriding duty is to the Court and to be impartial in their evidence; the impartiality of expert witnesses is essential to their evidence; if the psychologist has a view that is controversial as between experts or that might be derived from partiality, she or he must declare the extent of that interest. This is particularly relevant when a psychologist expert recommends an intervention or therapy that they or an associate would benefit financially from delivering. Whilst this may be experienced as helpful and facilitative to the court, this would be a clear conflict of interest and threat to the independence of their expert evidence.'[50]

47 *Re GB (Part 25 Application: Parental Alienation)* [2023] EWFC 150.

48 *Re A and B (Children: Expert's Reports)* [2024] EWHC 948 (Fam).

49 Family Justice Council, *Interim Guidance in relation to expert witnesses in cases where there are allegations of alienating behaviours – conflicts of interest* (May 2022), https://www.judiciary.uk/wp-content/uploads/2022/05/FJC-interim-Guidance-use-of-experts-in-cases-with-allegations-of-alienating-behaviours.pdf.

50 The British Psychological Society, *Psychologists as Expert Witnesses in the family courts in England and Wales: Standards, competencies and expectations* (May 2022), https://www.judiciary.uk/wp-content/uploads/2022/05/Psychologists-as-Expert-Witness-in-family-courts-in-England-and-Wales-standards-competencies-and-expectations-.pdf.

8.59 The Interim Guidance also reminds practitioners and courts alike of the President of the Family Division's memorandum – *Experts in the Family Court* – which set out the rigorous approach to be taken by the Family Court in admitting expert evidence and the need for a reliable body of knowledge or experience to underpin the expert's evidence.[51] We should not forget that the Family Court may only give permission to instruct an expert within family proceedings if it is of the opinion that the expert evidence is *necessary* to assist the Court to resolve the proceedings justly.

8.60 One particular difficulty that has often arisen in cases where alienating behaviour has been alleged is where an expert assessment has been undertaken which has 1) sought to determine whether alienating behaviour is present in a case and 2) concluded it is and 3) the 'expert' has recommended a programme of work or therapy which may or may not include the child which only they can deliver (or they recommend that this is most appropriately delivered by them).

8.61 Practitioners must be alive to the joint guidance given by the Family Justice Council and the British Psychological Society: *Psychologists as Expert Witnesses in the Family Courts in England and Wales: Standards, competencies and expectations*.[52] Amongst other things, this guidance makes it explicit that the use of an expert in this way would be a clear conflict of interest and a threat to the independence of the expert evidence. *It must not happen.*

8.62 The inappropriate use of (unregulated) experts was highlighted in *O v C*,[53] in which Judd J acceded to an application by the mother to set aside findings of fact made by a district judge five years earlier. In making findings of PA, the Court relied upon a report prepared by an unregulated 'expert'. As a result of those findings, the children were removed from the care of the mother and placed in the father's care, with the mother only having limited contact with the children. Relying upon the decision *Re C (Parental Alienation: Instruction of Expert)*,[54] the mother asserted that the Court's delegation of its function to Ms Gill (the 'expert') was inappropriate and not regarded as acceptable practice now. Judd J concluded that the findings of PA made by the district judge could not be regarded as having proper status today, with the court observing, at [31]:

> '… there are no findings with a solid foundation that the mother alienated the children even though the judge expressed it as such, and accordingly no findings to actually set aside.
>
> For the avoidance of doubt, I make it clear that what the judge expressed to be findings based on Ms Gill's assessment should not stand as such in any further assessment going forward.'

51 President of the Family Division, *President's Memorandum: Experts in the Family Court* (October 2021), https://www.judiciary.uk/wp-content/uploads/2021/10/PFD-Memo-Experts.pdf.
52 The British Psychological Society (n 50).
53 *O v C* [2025] EWFC 334.
54 *Re C* (n 11).

PRACTICE NOTE

- Do not look for an expert who specialises in 'PA' or any of the associated terminology. In fact, view that as an alert point of concern (see Practice Note at the outset of this chapter).
- A regulated clinical psychologist is likely to have sufficient expertise to undertake an expert assessment and offer an expert opinion. The reasons are self-evident and the guidance issued by the Family Justice Council and British Psychological Society make it plain why this is so.
- *Re C ('Parental Alienation': Instruction of Experts)* can now be read with *O v C*. The authors contend that the appropriate course to adopt is that only regulated experts should be instructed by the Court and only for the expertise that it is within their domain to provide in order not to trespass on the Court's exclusive responsibility to determine disputed fact.[55]
- CAFCASS reissued and updated its *Domestic Abuse Practice Policy* as of 10 December 2025 and it contains a hyperlink to the guidance *Understanding why a child does not want to spend family time,* which is effectively endorsed with the update. Chapter 6 deals with the instruction of experts and specifically exhorts practitioners to adopt the Family Justice Council guidance. It flags that 'individuals identifying themselves as parental alienation "experts" are unregulated and should not be appointed as psychological experts'.

Case management decisions – should the child be joined

8.63 As well as the provision of evidence, there are other steps the Court may wish to consider when dealing with a case in which alienating behaviour is alleged. A significant case management decision the Court will need to determine is the role of the child within the proceedings. The guidance suggests that the Family Court may wish to consider the joinder of the child and whether the making of additional directions should be postponed pending joinder.

8.64 Rule 16.2 of the FPR 2010 provides: '(1) The court may make a child a party to proceedings if it considers it is in the best interests of the child to do so.'

8.65 Practice Direction 16A (PD16A) of the FPR 2010 then sets out the circumstances when a child/children should be made a party to the proceedings. Those circumstances assist practitioners and the Court to determine whether the issue of joinder is in the best interests of the child. Paragraph 7.1 provides:

55 *Re C* (n 11).

'Making the child a party to the proceedings is a step that will be taken only in cases which involve an issue of significant difficulty and consequently will occur in only a minority of cases. Before taking the decision to make the child a party, consideration should be given to whether an alternative route might be preferable, such as asking an officer of the Service or a Welsh family proceedings officer to carry out further work or by making a referral to social services or, possibly, by obtaining expert evidence.'

PRACTICE NOTE

- In the current climate in which the Family Court operates, there is an eagerness to reduce the amount of expert evidence placed before the Court, with a continuing focus upon the definition of necessity.
- In addition, the remit of the expert must be strictly prescribed if their role is to be of value and not trespass upon the Family Justice Council guidance.
- The other issue is who sources and pays for any expert and who drafts the letter of instruction. With unrepresented parties the Court must grapple with the practicalities and costs. This, in turn, may impact on necessity and proportionality.

8.66 Paragraph 7.2 of PD16A reminds us that the decision to join the child as a party to the proceedings is a decision which 'will always be exclusively that of the court'. It is a judicial decision.

8.67 There are some areas of England which have developed a practice that a child can only be joined to proceedings if a CAFCASS Service Manager, having spoken to the judge in the absence of the parties and received a summary of the case, consents to such joinder.

8.68 Such a delegation of the judicial responsibility is arguably wrong in law, serves to undermine the transparency of the proceedings for those engaged in them and means that a decision to join the child as a party to the proceedings is not exclusively that of the Court. Unfortunately, however, such a practice is likely to continue, whilst the resources available to the Family Court remain strained.

8.69 With CAFCASS resources under pressure, the Court may wish to consider the appointment of a guardian from other sources: for example, NYAS is able to accept appointments to represent children, with NYAS caseworkers able to be allocated.

8.70 Paragraph 7.2 of PD16A further sets out a number of circumstances, by way of guidance, which may justify the joinder of the child as a party. Not all the factors are set out below, but rather those which are relevant where alienating behaviours are a feature of the proceedings:

'(a) where an officer of the Service or Welsh family proceedings officer has notified the court that in the opinion of that officer the child should be made a party;

(b) where the child has a standpoint or interest which is inconsistent with or incapable of being represented by any of the adult parties;

(c) where there is an intractable dispute over residence or contact, including where all contact has ceased, or where there is irrational but implacable hostility to contact or where the child may be suffering harm associated with the contact dispute;

(d) where the views and wishes of the child cannot be adequately met by a report to the court.'

PRACTICE NOTE

In a case where alienating behaviours are alleged, the child's ascertainable wishes and feelings may not be easily discerned and may require several pieces of work to be undertaken over a period of time, particularly once a factual matrix has been determined by the Court.

It is on the question of evaluating 'wishes and feelings' before a fact-find that many a CAFCASS officer has floundered by straying into providing views on whether the child's wishes and feelings are their own or influenced by external factors.

Public law

8.71 Whilst allegations of alienating behaviour are often a feature of private law proceedings, practitioners should be alive to the reality that findings of alienating behaviour are capable of crossing the threshold as set out in Children Act 1989, s 31(2). The Family Justice Council recognises that the harm caused by alienating behaviours can be significant and enduring, like other forms of emotional and psychological abuse.[56]

8.72 Practitioners must remain alive to the fact that findings of alienating behaviour may give rise to the possibility of public law proceedings and, in such circumstances, practitioners should be fully familiar with the provisions of Children Act 1989, s 37 and the Court's powers to direct a local authority investigation into the child's circumstances. Upon directing such an investigation, practitioners must be aware that the Court also has the power to make an interim care order if it is satisfied that there are reasonable grounds to believe that the test in s 31(2) is made out – note the lower test of 'reasonable grounds to believe' is applicable. The making of an interim care order in such circumstances *does not*

56 Family Justice Council (n 2), para 6.

result in private law proceedings becoming public law proceedings: they remain private law proceedings until such time as the local authority brings their own application for a public law order.

Welfare decisions

8.73 Cases in which alienating behaviour has been established can present the Court with a number of challenges when it comes to considering the most appropriate welfare outcome for the children. Such decisions are, fundamentally, welfare decisions. The Family Court is likely to require some assistance in undertaking this welfare evaluation, whether that be from a social work perspective or other expert evidence.

8.74 Given the debates which rage on in some quarters of the Family Justice System as to what PA is/what alienating behaviours are, it is crucial that any welfare decision (and assessment which informs such a decision) is rooted in an established factual matrix. The Family Justice Council's guidance offers limited assistance to the Family Court and practitioners regarding how the welfare stage of such cases should be approached.

8.75 CAFCASS has devised a number of tools designed to assist Family Court advisers and guardians in assessing the most appropriate welfare outcome.[57] It is beyond the scope of this book to delve into each of these tools and offer a critique of them, however, although practitioners should familiarise themselves with these tools, a degree of caution is required. Earlier in the chapter, we offered a brief overview of the controversy and polarisation which has dominated this area. Some of the tools previously used by CAFCASS were rooted in the literature and research which can be traced back to the 'research' of Dr Richard Gardner and those who have sought to build upon the work he did.[58] This may require practitioners to drill down into the guidance that is being relied upon or applied.

8.76 As mentioned in August 2025, CAFCASS published *Understanding why a child does not want to spend family time with a parent: A guide to assessment.* This is a useful document for those who seek to challenge, or otherwise understand, CAFCASS' approach.[59] The guidance is part of the CAFCASS Child Impact Assessment Framework, which 'provides guidance and practice aids to support Family Court Advisors in their thinking for children and their families

57 CAFCASS, *Child Impact Assessment Framework (CIAF)*, https://www.cafcass.gov.uk/professionals/our-resources-professionals/child-impact-assessment-framework-ciaf.

58 An example can be seen in: CAFCASS, *Understanding why a child does not want to spent family time with a parent: A guide to assessment* (August 2025), https://www.cafcass.gov.uk/sites/default/files/2025-07/Understanding%20why%20a%20child%20does%20not%20want%20to%20spend%20family%20time%20with%20a%20parent.pdf. In this document, Family Court advisers are directed to literature which considers the reformulation of parental alienation syndrome.

59 CAFCASS (n 58).

in both public and private law proceedings' with the purpose being 'to support Cafcass practitioners in understanding the reasons for the children's views'.[60]

8.77 Of course, as part of any welfare analysis undertaken by a professional working in the Family Court, or indeed, the Family Court itself, the Welfare Checklist, as set out in Children Act 1989, s 1(3) is the lodestar. A particularly tricky aspect of the Welfare Checklist in the context of a case where alienating behaviours are involved can be found in s 1(3)(a) which requires the Court to have regard to the child's ascertainable wishes and feelings (considered in light of their age and understanding). In *Re H (Children)*, the Court of Appeal quoted Parker J at [43]:

> 'I have more than once stressed in this case, as in others, that the word used in the Children Act about wishes and feelings is "ascertainable" and not "expressed." "Ascertainable" often means that the Court has to look at actions rather than words.'[61]

8.78 The level of care that is required was also expressed by HHJ Wildblood KC in *Re A (Children) (Parental Alienation)*, when the Court summarised the difficulty in relying upon a child's wishes and feelings in a case where alienation is a feature:

> 'There is an obvious difficulty about how to approach the expressed wishes and feelings of children who are living in an alienated environment such as this. If children who have been alienated are asked whether they wish to have a relationship with a non-resident parent there is a likelihood that the alienation they have experienced will lead them to say "no." Therefore, in this type of case, the approach to the wishes and feelings of children has had to be approached with considerable care and professionalism. To respond simply on the basis of what children say in this type of situation is manifestly superficial and naïve. The children in this case have been expressing wishes that they should see their father for many years now. The lack of an effective and early enquiry into what was happening within this family meant that there was no effective intervention. That, in turn, has led to the children's expressed wishes being reinforced in their minds. It has also resulted in the mother being able to say 'we should listen to the children,' rather than addressing the underlying difficulties.'[62]

8.79 It is correct that children should always be given the opportunity to express their views in their own proceedings, with CAFCASS recognising that it is their right to do so, but this has to be viewed in the context of the particular circumstances of the case.[63] This caveat was recognised by the President of the Family Division in the case of *Re L (A Child)*:

60 CAFCASS (n 58), p 3.
61 *Re H (Children)* [2014] EWCA Civ 733, [43].
62 *Re A (Children) (Parental Alienation)* [2019] 9 WLUK 445, [13(ix)].
63 CAFCASS (n 58), p 6.

'Whilst it is a fundamental principle, applicable to every case, that the child who is the subject of the proceedings shall be heard, the manner and degree to which the child is heard will vary from case to case. Further, it is important to bear in mind that each element in the welfare checklist is subject to the overarching requirement in CA 1989, s1(1) that the welfare of the child must be the court's paramount consideration.'[64]

Change of living arrangements

8.80 Changing the child's living arrangements represents a fundamental change in that child's life. To those who have been involved in cases where alienating behaviours are alleged – or indeed, proven – seeking to change the child's living arrangements will often be raised as one of the ways, if not the only way, of resolving the difficulties which have arisen.

8.81 In contemplating such a step, the Family Court is highly likely to have appointed a guardian to represent the child, having regard to the circumstances when such an appointment should be made (see above). There may also be an expert opinion before the Court.

8.82 When the Court is considering changing the living arrangements of a child, CAFCASS recommends that the guardian/Family Court adviser should consider the need for supervision in line with CAFCASS' policy as well as a referral to the local authority, preparation of a risk assessment pursuant to Children Act 1989, s 16A and/or a recommendation to the Court that it should direct an investigation pursuant to Children Act 1989, s 37.[65] It is recommended that all of these steps be considered before making a recommendation to change the child's living arrangements.

8.83 Changing the living arrangements of a child has often been referred to as 'a judicial weapon of last resort' and an 'essential weapon or tool'.[66] However, the President of the Family Division, McFarlane P has sought to step away from such a characterisation. In the case of *Re L (A Child)*, the President distanced himself from the language as, in the President's view, it 'risks moving the focus of the decision-making away from the welfare of the child which must be the court's paramount consideration'.[67] The President repeated that 'the court cannot put a gloss on to the paramountcy principle'[68] in Children Act 1989, s 1.

64 *Re L (A Child)* [2019] EWHC 867 (Fam), [61].
65 CAFCASS (n 58), p 7.
66 Per Thorpe LJ and Coleridge J in *Re A (Children)* [2009] EWCA Civ 1141.
67 *Re L* (n 64), [54].
68 *Re L* (n 64), [59].

8.84 The President goes on to summarise the test which the Court must apply when considering whether to change the child's living arrangements:

> '... The test is, and must always be, based on a comprehensive analysis of the child's welfare and a determination of where the welfare balance points in terms of outcome. It is important to note that the welfare provisions in CA 1989, s1 are precisely the same provisions as those applying in public law children cases where a local authority may seek the court's authorisation to remove a child from parental care either to place them with another relative or another relative or in alternative care arrangements. Where, in private law proceedings, the choice, as here, is between care by one parent and care by another parent against whom there are no significant findings, one might anticipate that the threshold triggering a change of residence would, if anything, be lower than that justifying the permanent removal of a child from a family into foster care. Use of phrases such as "last resort" or "draconian" cannot and should not indicate a different or enhanced welfare test. What is required is for the judge to consider all the circumstances in the case that are relevant to the issue of welfare, consider those elements in the s1(3) welfare check list which apply on the facts of the case and then, taking all those matters into account, determine which of the various options best meets the child's welfare needs.'[69]

8.85 There are a number of reported decisions in which this outcome has either been contemplated by the Court or implemented by the Court, although these predate the implementation of the Family Justice Council's guidance. Some pertinent cases are set out at the end of this chapter which make for important reading and which may not have been covered elsewhere in this chapter in any or sufficient detail.

CONCLUSIONS

8.86 Alienating behaviours continue to represent a difficult and contentious area for family practitioners and the judiciary alike. Even with clear direction from the judiciary and the Family Justice Council, difficulties remain in approaching this issue with any degree of consistency in practice.

8.87 The fact remains that, regardless of the continuing and polarising debates which surround this issue, on a daily basis the Family Court is faced with cases in which at least one party raises the issue of alienating behaviour. It is crucial that the Family Court and those who work within have tools at their disposal in order to ensure that cases are resolved expeditiously but effectively.

69 *Re L* (n 64), [59].

CASE LAW

Re S (Cult: Parental Alienation) [2020] EWCA Civ 568

8.88 A Court of Appeal decision against a first instance decision by a circuit judge in which the court refused a father's application for a child arrangements order that the nine-year-old move to live with him. Notwithstanding the court making findings that the father had been alienated from the child, the judge at first instance did not alter the child arrangements. Giving the lead judgment, Peter Jackson LJ set out the law concerning PA as it was at the time the judgment was handed down.

8.89 The Court of Appeal effectively endorsed the working definition which had been used by CAFCASS:

> 'When a child's resistance/hostility towards one parent is not justified and is the result of psychological manipulation by the other parent.'

Whilst this working definition does bear some similarity to the current definition of 'alienating behaviour' the Court of Appeal made a number of observations about the management of such cases.

8.90 Perhaps hinting that it is the Court's function to determine allegations of alienating behaviours, the Court of Appeal observed that where a process of alienation is found to exist, there is a spectrum of severity and an assessment of all aspects of the child's welfare is required, with the Court required to consider all of the circumstances and choose the best welfare solution (see [10]). The overall approach the Court should take – which we say is just as relevant now in light of the Family Justice Council guidance – is set out, at [13], with the succinctness and eloquence we have come to expect from Peter Jackson LJ:

> 'In summary, in a situation of parental alienation the obligation on the court is to respond with exceptional diligence and take whatever effective measures are available. The situation calls for judicial resolve because the line of least resistance is likely to be less stressful for the child and for the court in the short term. But it does not represent a solution to the problem. Inaction will probably reinforce the position of the stronger party at the expense of the weaker party and the bar will be raised for the next attempt at intervention. Above all, the obligation on the court is to keep the child's medium to long term welfare at the forefront of its mind and wherever possible to uphold the child and parent's right to respect for family life before it is breached. In making its overall welfare decision the court must therefore be alert to early signs of alienation. What will amount to effective action will be a matter of judgement, but it is emphatically not necessary to wait for serious, worse still irreparable, harm to be done before appropriate action is taken. It is easier to conclude that decisive action was needed after it has become too late to take it.'

Re L (A Child) [2019] EWHC 867 (Fam)

8.91 Often deployed – or at least contemplated – in cases where alienating behaviours are proven, a change of a child's living arrangements was once considered to be a draconian step,[70] this is no longer the case. The decision of the President of the Family Division, Sir Andrew McFarlane in this case offered guidance as to the correct approach the Court should take when considering a change to a child's living arrangements. In so doing, the President sought to step away from the language used in *Re A (Residence Order)* and set out the appropriate test for the Court to apply:

> 'Having considered the authorities to which I have referred, and others, there is, in my view, a danger in placing too much emphasis on the phrase "last resort" used by Thorpe LJ and Coleridge J in Re A. It is well established that the court cannot put a gloss on to the paramountcy principle in CA 1989, s1. I do not read the judgments in Re A as purporting to do that.' (See further at **8.84**.)

It is important to observe that the approach of McFarlane P in *Re L (A Child)* was endorsed by the Court of Appeal in *Re S (Cult: Parental Alienation)*.

Re C (Parental Alienation: Instruction of Experts) [2023] EWHC 345 (Fam)

8.92 A key decision by the President of the Family Division, Sir Andrew McFarlane who heard an appeal from a decision by a circuit judge. Whilst the substance of the appeal related to the fact-finding which had been undertaken, the President identified that 'the central issue raised [was] of more general importance and relate[d] to the instruction of experts in proceedings where there [was] an allegation of parental alienation'. The Court was assisted by the Association of Clinical Psychologists during this hearing, which provided written and oral submissions.

8.93 The key points of this judgment can be easily summarised:

- Whether an expert is sufficiently qualified to give expert evidence to the Court is a matter for the Court having considered the expert's qualifications and experience.
- It is permissible for an expert who is not regulated by a professional body to be used.[71]

70 See Thorpe LJ in *Re A (Residence Order)* [2009] EWCA Civ 1141, [21].

71 Although the authors of this book contend that only regulated experts should be used in Children Act proceedings.

- PA is a matter for the Court to determine. In arriving at this view, the President accepted and endorsed the submission of the Association of Clinical Psychologists at [103]:

> 'Much like an allegation of domestic abuse; the decision about whether or not a parent has alienated a child is a question of fact for the Court to resolve and not a diagnosis that can or should be offered by a psychologist. For these purposes, the ACP-UK wishes to emphasise that "parental alienation" is not a syndrome capable of being diagnosed, but a process of manipulation of children perpetrated by one parent against the other through, what are termed as, "alienating behaviours." It is, fundamentally, a question of fact.'

CHAPTER 9

Injunctive Relief in the Family Court

INTRODUCTION

9.01 The jurisdiction of the Family Court is wide-ranging, with its protective grasp reaching far beyond the protection and welfare of children. Up and down the country, on a daily basis, family courts will be seized of applications made for injunctions to regulate relationships between family members, partners, spouses, former partners and former spouses. With an ever-increasing awareness of domestic abuse (DA) within intimate and familial relationships, along with the insidious and constantly evolving nature of it, it can be no surprise that the work the Family Court does in this area is increasing. In the period of January to March 2025, there was an increase of 5 per cent in applications to the Family Court compared with the same period in 2024. The number of orders made by the Family Court increased by 1 per cent compared with a year earlier. Moving beyond percentage figures (which can often fail to demonstrate the gravity of a problem), between January and March 2025, the Family Court was invited to make 9,222 injunctive orders.[1]

9.02 Injunctive relief in the Family Court, in the context of DA and for the purposes of this chapter, consists of applications for Non-Molestation Orders and Occupation Orders. According to statistics published by the Ministry of Justice, the number of applications for Occupation Orders has decreased by 3 per cent compared to the same period in 2024.[2] However, the increase in the number of applications for Non-Molestation Orders is alarming and, whilst it is not the purpose of this text to offer an explanation for this increase,[3] it is obvious that this area continues to have a significant role to play in the work of the Family Court. In fact, between January and March 2025, applications for Non-Molestation Orders made up 84 per cent of the total applications for injunctive relief made to the Court, presenting a significant challenge for the Family Court in terms of resource allocation.[4]

1 'Family Court Statistics Quarterly: January to March 2025' (Gov.uk, June 2025), https://www.gov.uk/government/statistics/family-court-statistics-quarterly-january-to-march-2025/family-court-statistics-quarterly-january-to-march-2025#domestic-violence-remedy-orders.

2 'Family Court Statistics Quarterly: January to March 2025' (n 1).

3 Arguably, this is linked to the coming into force of the Legal Aid, Sentencing and Punishment of Offenders Act 2012 which restricted the availability of legal aid in private children law proceedings unless there was (amongst other things) evidence of DA. Legal aid for applications for Non-Molestation Orders was unchanged but made easier by the removal of the application fee payable to HM Courts and Tribunal Service for such applications.

4 President of the Family Division, *Practice Guidance: Non Molestation Injunctions under the Family Law Act 1996* (July 2023), https://www.judiciary.uk/wp-content/uploads/2023/07/Practice-Guidance-Non-Molestation-Injunctions.pdf.

9.03 This chapter offers a practical overview of the law relating to Non-Molestation Orders, Occupation Orders, Domestic Abuse Prevention Notices and Orders as well as other forms of injunctive relief intended to protect and support victims of domestic abuse.

NON-MOLESTATION ORDERS

9.04 The power for the Family Court to make a Non-Molestation Order can be found in Family Law Act 1996 (FLA 1996), s 42.

Molestation: what does that mean?

9.05 We may all have an idea of what constitutes molestation, but the reality is that there is no statutory definition under the FLA 1996. This was not an oversight by those drafting this legislation; the absence of a statutory definition is conscious and deliberate. Before the FLA 1996 came into force, the Law Commission considered this issue, saying (we have italicised points of particular note to us):

> 'Molestation is an umbrella term which covers a wide range of behaviour. Although there is no statutory definition of molestation, the concept is well established and recognised by the courts. *Molestation includes but is wider than violence. It encompasses any form of serious pestering or harassment and applies to any conduct which could properly be regarded as such a degree of harassment as to the call for the intervention of the court* … In the working paper we asked whether the term "molestation" should be defined by statute. The overwhelming view of respondents was that any reform of the law in this area should not reduce the current level of protection from molestation. *There was no evidence of problems having been caused in practice by the lack of a statutory definition. Some concern was expressed that a definition might become over restrictive or that it could lead to borderline disputes.* Consequently, we recommend that the courts should continue to have power to grant protection against all forms of molestation, including violence, and *we further recommend that there should be no statutory definition of molestation*.'[5]

9.06 Of course, the perpetrator's abusive behaviour by way of molestation may take any of the forms set out in the definition of DA in Domestic Abuse Act 2021 (DAA 2021), s 1, or any combination of them. This section is so critical to an understanding that we set it out, in the context of this chapter, below:

> **'Domestic Abuse Act 2021, s 1: Definition of "domestic abuse"**
>
> (1) This section defines "domestic abuse" for the purposes of this Act.

5 *Family Law, Domestic Violence and Occupation of the Family Home* (Law Com No 207, 1992), para 3.1 (emphasis added).

(2) Behaviour of a person ("A") towards another person ("B") is "domestic abuse" if—

(a) A and B are each aged 16 or over and are personally connected to each other, and

(b) the behaviour is abusive.

(3) Behaviour is "abusive" if it consists of any of the following—

(a) physical or sexual abuse;

(b) violent or threatening behaviour;

(c) controlling or coercive behaviour;

(d) economic abuse (see subsection (4));

(e) psychological, emotional or other abuse;

and it does not matter whether the behaviour consists of a single incident or a course of conduct.

(4) "Economic abuse" means any behaviour that has a substantial adverse effect on B's ability to—

(a) acquire, use or maintain money or other property, or

(b) obtain goods or services.

(5) For the purposes of this Act A's behaviour may be behaviour "towards" B despite the fact that it consists of conduct directed at another person (for example, B's child).'

PRACTICE NOTE

Note that whilst the Act set out categories of 'domestic abuse', *it did not offer up a definition of 'molestation'.*

Case law can assist with examples of the interpretation of the word 'molestation'. But remember – even with case law guidance, *what is or is not considered to be molestation may be subjective, case- and fact-dependent.*

That affords a high degree of discretion and demands adaptability in legal thinking. We need to be alert to new ways of misbehaving to one another as technology advances as well as the emergence of culturally diverse and non-heterosexual needs. Family law is a responsive jurisdiction – it's our task to apply and adapt it to fit society's needs and those who are vulnerable.

9.07 Whilst it is vital to be aware of what the authorities say with respect to the definition of molestation, it is recommended that the following authorities are used as a *guide* rather than an exhaustive list of what constitutes molestation.

9.08 The Court has grappled with the meaning of molestation for decades. This case from 1973 is a case in point. In *Vaughan v Vaughan* Davies LJ sought to define it:

'There are two different definitions … "meddle hostilely or injuriously" … "to cause trouble to; to vex, annoy, put to inconvenience." It seems to me that, in the circumstances of this case, taking into consideration this lady's health, of which the husband was to some degree aware, and taking into consideration the fact that he knew she was frightened of him, molestation has plainly been made out in this case.'[6]

9.09 In the same case, Stephenson LJ offered a different perspective:

'"Molest" is a wide, plain word which I should be reluctant to define or paraphrase. If I had to find one synonym for it, I should select "pester." Whether communication amounts to molestation is a question of fact and degree. I have no doubt that what this man did … to this woman, with the knowledge of his past conduct which both of them had, was to molest her."[7]

9.10 A decade later, Ormerod LJ, in *Horner v Horner*, described molestation as: '… [A]ny conduct which can properly be regarded as such a degree of harassment as to call for the intervention of the court.'[8]

9.11 And in a 1988 article for the Family Law Journal, HHJ Fricker observed that molestation is: 'deliberate conduct which substantially interferes with the applicant or the child, whether by violence, intimidation, harassment, pestering or interference sufficiently serious to warrant intervention by the court.'[9]

9.12 Many cases followed, the jurisprudence of which was drawn together in 2020 by the President of the Family Division in *Re Al M (Non-Molestation Application)*. We have underlined some stand out lines but the judgment must be read as a whole:[10]

'It is common ground that there is no definition of "molestation" in the FLA 1996. Reference has been made by all parties to the case law both prior to the implementation of the 1996 Act and thereafter. In particular, *C v C (Non-Molestation Order: Jurisdiction) [1998] 1 FLR 554*, Sir Stephen Brown P held that molestation:

"implies some quite deliberate conduct which is aimed at a high degree of harassment of the other party, so as to justify the intervention of the court…It does not include enforcing an invasion of privacy per se; there has to be some conduct which clearly harasses and affects the applicant to such a degree that the intervention of the court is called for."

6 *Vaughan v Vaughan* [1973] 1 WLR 1159 (CA).
7 *Vaughan* (n 6).
8 *Horner v Horner* [1983] 4 FLR 50, [51G].
9 HHJ Fricker, 'Molestation and Harassment after Patel v Patel' [1988] Fam Law 395, at 399.
10 *Re Al M (Non-Molestation Application)* [2020] EWHC 3305 (Fam).

From Sir Stephen Brown's analysis, *it is clear that the impact upon the applicant of the behaviour is an important element in deciding whether or not some quite deliberate conduct clearly harasses her or him*. (Although in *C v C [2001] EWCA Civ 1625*, an order was made controlling conduct which "was calculated to cause alarm and distress to the mother", *the courts have held that the respondent's intention is not a necessary element in establishing conduct which amounts to molestation.*

In *Re T (A Child) [2017] EWCA Civ 1889*, having referred to the earlier authorities, I urged caution against attempts to narrow down the definition of "molestation":

> "27. In the decades that have followed those judicial utterances those sitting in the Family Court have, on a day by day, case by case basis, deployed good sense and judgment in determining whether or not particular conduct amounts to 'molestation'. In my view this court should continue to be very wary of offering any further precision in the definition."

Later in the same judgment I went on to state:

> "42. When determining whether or not particular conduct is sufficient to justify granting a non-molestation order, the primary focus, as established in the consistent approach of earlier authority, is upon the 'harassment' or 'alarm and distress' caused to those on the receiving end. It must be conduct of 'such a degree of harassment as to call for the intervention of the court.' Although in C v C the phrase 'was calculated to cause alarm and distress' was used, none of the authorities require that a positive intent to molest must be established."

What is needed to justify the intervention of the court is some form of deliberate conduct which has the effect on the applicant of harassment to such a degree that the court's protection is called for. The negative impact on the applicant can include elements of psychological and/or emotional harm. The conduct of the respondent, whilst being deliberate, does not need to have been with the intention of causing that harm.'[11]

9.13 There are common threads woven through the authorities as to what molestation means and what the Court should have regard to when deciding whether particular conduct amounts to molestation. This section does not seek to set out each and every authority on this subject. Those referred to above offer a comprehensive overview of how the meaning of molestation has evolved and offer practitioners guidance as to what may amount to molestation. Pervading through all of the authorities is a reluctance to set out firm and immovable guidance as to what molestation is; indeed, the President of the Family Division

11 *Re Al M* (n 10), [31]–[35] (emphasis added).

in *Re AI M* demonstrated why one should be wary of interpretation by way of a precise (and hence restrictive) definition.

9.14 The message is important and bears repetition – each family unit or relationship is different and unique; one person's idea of molestation may not reflect the views of another. The approach taken in any one case must continue to be flexible and adaptable, reflective of the very wide discretion the Family Court enjoys.

PRACTICE NOTE

We direct practitioners' attention to the Home Office Statutory Guidance, issued in July 2022.[12] Chapter 3 provides a conduct list (for lack of a better phrase) which operates as a helpful, and thought provoking, checklist of types of behaviours which the client may have experienced but may not immediately classify as molestation and abuse. Crucially, although some of the listed behaviours may be subtle, they are clearly pernicious and controlling, potentially causing the recipient significant distress.

Who can apply for a Non-Molestation Order?

9.15 In light of the special nature of family relationships, the Law Commission felt that the scope of injunctions in family proceedings needed to be extended, saying that, 'when problems arise in close family relationships, the strength of emotions involved can cause unique reactions which may at times be irrational and obsessive'.[13] At the time of the Law Commission's review of the law, injunctive relief was only available to spouses and cohabitants in the family jurisdiction. The Law Commission identified that, whilst the reactions referred to earlier, 'may most commonly arise between spouses and cohabitants,' it was recognised that, 'they can also occur in many other close relationships which give rise to similar stresses and strains and in which the people concerned will often continue to be involved with one another'.

9.16 It is against this backdrop that the FLA 1996 provides the Court with a list of people who may make an application for a Non-Molestation Order. This was further widened by the Domestic Violence, Crime and Victims Act 2004 and therefore serves to extend the jurisdiction of the Family Court.

9.17 Referring to them as an 'associated person', FLA 1996, s 62(3) provides a list of those who the Act considers could be associated with another person:

'(a) they are or have been married to each other;

12 Home Office, *Domestic Abuse – Statutory Guidance* (July 2022), https://assets.publishing.service.gov.uk/media/62c6df068fa8f54e855dfe31/Domestic_Abuse_Act_2021_Statutory_Guidance.pdf.

13 Law Com No 207, 1992 (n 5).

(aa) they are or have been civil partners of each other;

(b) they are cohabitants or former cohabitants;

(c) they live or have lived in the same household, otherwise than merely by reason of one of them being the other's employee, tenant, lodger or boarder;

(d) they are relatives;

(e) they have agreed to marry one another (whether or not that agreement has been terminated);

(ea) they have or have had an intimate personal relationship with each other which is or was of significant duration;[14]

(eza) they have entered into a civil partnership agreement (as defined by section 73 of the Civil Partnership Act 2004) (whether or not that agreement has been terminated);

(f) in relation to any child, they are both persons falling within subsection (4); or

(g) they are parties to the same family proceedings (other than proceedings under this Part).'

9.18 Section 43 of the FLA 1996 allows for a child under the age of 16 to apply for a Non-Molestation Order (or an Occupation Order) but leave of the Court is required. The Court may grant leave only if it is satisfied that the child has sufficient understanding to make the proposed application for a Non-Molestation Order or an Occupation Order (s 43(2)).

9.19 An example of how the Court approaches an application for a Non-Molestation Order by a child under the age of 16 can be seen in the Family Court decision of His Honour Judge Clive Baker in *D v T*,[15] with the Court having heard evidence from the applicant to satisfy itself that the applicant had sufficient understanding to make the proposed application. Observing that 'children below the age of 16 are inherently unlikely or unable to fall within one of the other categories of associated persons as defined by section 63(3)' (other than having or having had an intimate personal relationship with each other which was of significant duration), HHJ Clive Baker expressed the view that:

> 'any determination as to whether a particular application falls within the statutory criteria must be set in the context of the circumstances of the case and indeed relevant characteristics of the applicant and respondent.'[16]

14 NB As part of HHJ Clive Baker's research for his judgment in *D v T* [2023] EWFC 97, the Court observed, at [14]–[16], that 'intimate personal relationship … of significant duration' was not defined in the Act, or in case law. In the Parliamentary debates during the passage of the Domestic Violence, Crime and Victims Act 2004, the government's intention was said to be to define it 'in the broadest terms and it would be for the court in individual circumstances to determine whether it applied'.

15 *D v T* [2023] EWFC 97.

16 *D v T* [2023] EWFC 97, [25].

EX PARTE OR INTER PARTE? EX PARTE ORDERS/WITHOUT NOTICE HEARINGS

9.20 The vast majority of applications for Non-Molestation Orders – and, to a lesser extent, applications for Occupation Orders – begin life as an ex parte/without notice application. This means that the application is made without the respondent being informed of the application or being present at the hearing. Whether they should be informed/present or not is a real issue to be grappled with by the practitioner.

9.21 The power for the Court to make a Non-Molestation Order or an Occupation Order without notice to the respondent can be found in FLA 1996, s 45. The statutory test for the exercise of the Court's power to make an ex parte order is summarised in the opening lines of s 45(1) of the Act: 'whether it is just and convenient to do so.'

9.22 At first blush, it may be considered that the bar to be applied is relatively low, however, a series of authorities have sought to offer guidance as to when it would be appropriate for the Family Court to exercise its powers and make an order without notice to the respondent.

9.23 In *R v R*, Peter Jackson J (as he then was) presided over an appeal against a case management order made by a district judge in proceedings under the FLA 1996, with Peter Jackson J taking the opportunity to highlight a number of important principles which are applicable to all such cases:[17]

> '(1) The default position of a judge faced with a without notice application should always be "Why?", not "Why not?" As has been repeatedly stated, without notice orders can only be made in exceptional circumstances and with proper consideration for the rights of the absent party.
>
> (2) The court should use its sweeping powers under the Family Law Act 1996 with caution, particularly at a one-sided hearing. Where an order is made, it is the responsibility of the court (and, where applicable, the lawyers) to ensure that it is accurately drafted. This consideration applies with special force when a breach of the order will amount to a criminal offence.
>
> (3) Extra injunctive provisions such as exclusion areas and orders prohibiting any direct communication between parties should not be routinely included in Non-Molestation Orders. They are serious infringements of a person's freedom of action and require specific evidence to justify them.
>
> (4) The power to penalise non-compliance with case management orders should be used firmly but fairly, in a way that supports the overriding objective rather than defeating it. The court should apply the rules (here specifically FPR r.4.6) with that aim.
>
> (5) The court should be on guard against the potential for unfairness arising from the Legal Aid, Sentencing and Punishment of Offenders Act 2012,

17 *R v R* [2014] EWFC 48.

whereby the applicant is entitled to legal representation as a result of unproven allegations, while the respondent is not. In this case, the fact that one party had no legal advice at any stage was critical to the outcome.'[18]

9.24 During his tenure as President of the Family Division, Sir James Munby published Practice Guidance regarding the duration of ex parte (without notice) orders.[19] This guidance was given following the Magistrates' Association and the National Bench Chairs' Forum asking whether it was proper to grant an ex parte Non-Molestation Order for an indefinite period. On a strict interpretation of the statutory provisions, the making of an indefinite ex parte Non-Molestation Order is open to the Court. However, Sir James Munby expressed the view that the making of an indefinite ex parte Non-Molestation Order was wrong in principle. Drawing together a number of authorities, the then-President distilled the relevant principles as being:

'i. An ex parte (without notice) injunctive order must never be made without limit of time. There must be a fixed end date. It is not sufficient merely to specify a return day. The order must specify on its face and in clear terms precisely when it expires.

ii. The order must also fix a return day. The order must specify the date, time and place of the hearing on the return day. The return day should normally be no more than 14 days after the date when the order was made. How long the hearing on the return day should be listed for must be a matter for the discretion of the judge. However … often a short listing may well be appropriate.

iii. Careful consideration needs to be given to the duration of any order made ex parte (without notice). Many orders will be of short duration, typically no more than 14 days. But in appropriate cases involving personal protection, such as non-molestation injunctions granted in accordance with Part IV of the Family Law Act 1996, the order itself can be for a longer period, such as 6 of even 12 months, provided that the order specifies a return day within no more than 14 days. This must be a matter for the discretion of the judge, but a period longer than 6 months is likely to be appropriate only where the allegation is of long term abuse or where some other good reason is shown. Conversely, a period shorter than 6 months may be appropriate in a case where there appears to be a one-off problem that may subside in weeks rather than months.

iv. The order must make it clear that (a) it was made in the absence of the respondent and that the court has considered only the evidence of the applicant and (b) the court has made no finding of fact. Where the evidence is written, it must be identified in the order. Where, exceptionally, the court has received oral or other evidence (eg, a photograph) that evidence should be recorded on the face of the order or reduced to writing and served with the order.

18 *R v R* (n 17).

19 President of the Family Division, *Family Court Duration of Ex Parte (Without Notice) Orders*, Practice Guidance (January 2017).

v. Where the order has been made in accordance with Part IV of the Family Law Act 1996 it must recite the court has had regard to sections 45(1) and (2) of the Act.

vi. The order (see FPR 18.10(3)) "must contain a statement of the right to make an application to set aside or vary the order under rule 18.11." The phrase "liberty to apply" is not sufficient for this purpose. The order must spell out that the respondent is entitled, without waiting for the return day, to apply to set aside or vary the order.

vii. If the respondent does apply to set aside or vary the order the court must list the application as a matter of urgency, within a matter of days at most.'[20]

9.25 In *Practice Guidance: Non-Molestation Injunctions*, the President of the Family Division (Sir Andrew McFarlane) updated the above guidance concerning the making of ex parte/without notice orders by making the following observations:[21]

(a) When applying the 'just and convenient' test as set out in FLA 1996, s 45, the Court's approach must be informed by a modern understanding of DA, including the definition set out in DAA 2021, s 1.

(b) Whilst FLA 1996, s 45 does not establish a test of necessity, a without notice order should only be made without notice to the respondent in exceptional circumstances.

(c) In all cases where an order is made without notice, the Court must list a hearing which the respondent should attend.

9.26 Therefore, whilst the statutory test may still be considered a relatively low test, guidance emanating from a number of judgments as well as practice guidance issued by the President of the Family Division has sought to ensure that the Family Court only makes an ex parte/without notice order in exceptional circumstances.

9.27 In the decision of *DS v AC*, Lieven J offered a summary of the principles which could be drawn from the FLA 1996 and the case law:

'a. On a without notice application the court must consider whether there is a risk of significant harm attributable to the Respondent if the order is not granted immediately, s45(2)(a);

b. And whether the Applicant would be deterred or prevented from making the application if the order is not made immediately; s45(2)(b);

c. A without notice order should only be made in exceptional circumstances and with proper consideration for the rights of the absent party, *R v R* at [1];

20 Practice Guidance (n 19).
21 President of the Family Division, *Practice Guidance: Non Molestation Injunctions under the Family Law Act 1996* (July 2023), https://www.judiciary.uk/wp-content/uploads/2023/07/Practice-Guidance-Non-Molestation-Injunctions.pdf.

d. The Court should use its powers under the FLA with caution, particularly at a one-sided hearing, or necessarily on a paper consideration without the other party having notice, *R v R* [1];

e. "molestation" does not imply necessarily either violence or threats of violence, but can cover any degree of harassment that calls for the intervention of the court, *Horner v Horner* at 51G;

f. The primary focus of the court should be upon the "harassment" or "alarm and distress" caused to those on the receiving end, *Re T (A Child)*; and

g. There does not have to be a positive intent to molest, *Re T* at [42].'[22]

9.28 Lieven J considered it important that these principles are applied properly with orders not simply being granted by default.

PRACTICE NOTE

The statement in support of an ex parte application must not just deal with the acts of alleged molestation which the applicant relies upon to justify an order being granted, but must also set out:

(a) why it is urgent, and

(b) why it must be made without notice to the respondent.

These are distinct and important separate points that are often not properly addressed in applications.

- Supportive corroborative evidence, such as social media screenshots, police reports, police crime report numbers or GP attendances should be attached to the statement.
- It is poor practice to expect that the Court will be prepared to listen to oral submissions adducing evidence that could and should have been put in statement form. Otherwise, the reasons for an ex parte order will not be transparent to the absent respondent who is fixed with a serious order.
- If (and this is a big if) there is good reason why material relevant to the application was not in the statement, then reasons for the omission must be given, it must be reduced to writing at court, sworn, and leave of the Court must be given in order to adduce it.
- Too often ex parte injunctions, the application and evidence, are dealt with by non-legally trained administrative staff with limited information to hand. In our submissions in *Re T* in *Re H-N & Ors*[23] we identified the commonplace use in busy, cash-strapped, high street legal aid firms of using a junior member of staff to take this 'over the counter' work and take instructions with limited client knowledge, insufficient time

22 *DS v AC* [2023] EWFC 46, [23].
23 *Re H-N & Ors (Children) (Domestic Abuse: Finding of Fact Hearings)* [2021] EWCA Civ 448.

and training and reduce the client's history to 'the first, the last and the worst' incident. Given the trauma involved in recall and the likelihood that rape, in particular, is hard to express to a stranger, such an approach has serious potential consequences.

- An inadequately prepared injunctive application can have serious adverse credibility ramifications for a client who later supplements it, claiming controlling and coercive behaviour (CCB) or other serious acts of abuse.

PRACTICE NOTE

- Subject to an assessment of means carried out by the Legal Aid Agency, legal aid is available for those applying for a Non-Molestation Order.
- An application for a Non-Molestation Order is made on form FL401 accompanied by a statement of evidence in support of the application (see the Family Procedure Rules 2010 (SI 2010/2955) (FPR 2010), r 10.2) and a draft Order.

A statement of evidence must address the following points:

- If applicable, why the application is being made with urgency and without notice to the respondent.
- How the applicant and the respondent are associated, by reference to FLA 1996, s 63(3).
- The history of the parties' relationship, including any children of the family.
- The conduct which gives rise to the application and how that conduct amounts to molestation. Do NOT use 'the first, last and worst' reductive approach to evidence.
- Be frank about what limitations may have impacted on acquiring all relevant potential content of the statement.
- The effect of that molestation upon the applicant and any relevant children.
- The nature of the protection sought under the Non-Molestation Order, with some justification as to why each provision is required.
- Identify what options have been tried to avoid the need for court proceedings.
- Identify supportive evidence, whether from screenshots of social media use, the police, neighbours, photographs etc and either attach them to the statement OR say they exist and are being acquired and will be provided as soon as they are available.

- If further information comes to light after the statement has been prepared, for example, at court (often the first time the advocate has met the client and spent time with them) reduce it to writing, even if handwritten, explain within it why it was not in the original statement and seek leave to file it.

Also note the following:

- There is no longer a court fee payable to HM Courts and Tribunal Service.
- Form FL415 – Statement of Service must be filed at court once service has been effected upon the respondent.
- The steps set out in FPR 2010, r 10.10 must be followed in order to ensure that the Non-Molestation Order is notified to the police.
- In accordance with FPR 2010, r 10.5, all hearings in relation to the application for a Non-Molestation Order are held in private unless the Court directs otherwise.

A ROUND UP

PRACTICE NOTE

- Remember that the primary aim of a Non-Molestation Order is to protect the victim from harm, with any sentence imposed for breach being primarily concerned with ensuring that the order is complied with and that it achieves the protection that it was intended to achieve.
- For the Family Court the focus is on protection, not punishment.

UNDERTAKINGS

9.29 The provision of undertakings to the Court can be a useful way to resolve an application under the FLA 1996, with s 46(1) of the Act giving the Court the power to accept an undertaking.

What is an undertaking?

9.30 An undertaking is a formal promise given to the Court which can contain the same terms which would otherwise be contained in a Non-Molestation Order or an Occupation Order.

9.31 However, as no power of arrest can be attached to an undertaking given in these circumstances (FLA 1996, s 46(2)), the options to enforce an undertaking are limited to bringing contempt proceedings which arguably reduces the protection offered to the person seeking protection due to the difficulties which may be encountered in bringing such proceedings.

When can the Court accept undertakings?

9.32 With respect to an application for an Occupation Order, the Court is prohibited from accepting an undertaking to resolve an application for an Occupation Order if a power of arrest would otherwise be attached to the order – see FLA 1996, s 46(3).

9.33 Whilst undertakings can be a useful mechanism to resolve proceedings with respect to an application for a Non-Molestation Order, the Court cannot accept an undertaking – regardless of an agreement reached between the parties – in circumstances where the respondent to the application has used or threatened violence against the applicant or a relevant child and it would be necessary to make a Non-Molestation Order in order to protect the applicant or a relevant child.

9.34 Note that the wording of FLA 1996, s 46(3A) is deliberately wide:

> 'The court shall not accept an undertaking under subsection (1) instead of making a non-molestation order where it appears to the court that—
>
> (a) the respondent has used or threatened violence against the applicant or a relevant child; and
>
> (b) for the protection of the applicant or child it is necessary to make a non-molestation order so that any breach may be punishable under section 42A.'

9.35 'Where it appears to the court' offers the Court wide discretion: the Court need not make findings of fact as to the use or threatened use of violence.

9.36 Allegations of such conduct should lead the Court to the conclusion that it is prohibited from accepting an undertaking. However, the reality of busy court lists and an overwhelmed Family Court means that judges and magistrates may be keen to accept undertakings to resolve otherwise disputed applications in circumstances where there are allegations of violence or threats to use violence.

PRACTICE NOTE

Balance the following with your client and make a record of the discussion and advice.

Possible advantages:

- The Court is not required to make any findings of fact against the respondent and therefore, there is no need for the Court to conduct a full hearing. As a result, proceedings are likely to be over more quickly and with less expense and client time used on preparing evidence. This is especially attractive for advocates when trying to get before the judge on a heavily listed application day and a long wait for a trial date.

- The applicant is not required to go through the process of giving evidence.
- An undertaking can be given without any admission as to the events complained of.
- Mutual undertakings can often be negotiated.
- Proceedings can be less confrontational and adversarial.

Possible disadvantages:

- Beware of short-termism and expediency – look at the case overall.
- When serious allegations have been made and are denied or countered with allegations of contact resistance (or 'so called alienation', as is commonly raised) the determination of the allegations may (or will) affect the welfare decision for a child, accepting an undertaking may, therefore, be 'kicking the can down the road'.
- Court pressure, or that from your opponent, may tempt you into avoiding confronting s 46(3A). Don't allow this to happen. You must draw the Court's attention to s 46(3A) along with the commentary contained in the *Family Court Practice* which offers further clarity as to whether the court has any discretion.[24]
- If contact is simmering as an issue (and it often is) a Finding of Fact Hearing may be necessary to resolve serious allegations. If so, trading undertakings is avoiding confronting the problem that has to be grasped and adds delay to resolution rather than avoiding it.

Practical points

9.37 Any undertaking given to the Court should be on the correct form, Form N117. If the court is invited to accept undertakings from both parties to an application, separate forms should be used.

9.38 For cases where the other party is acting in person, a useful guide is to refer to the Resolution publication, *Good Practice Guide to Working with Litigants in Person*.[25]

24 *Family Court Practice (The Red Book)*, para 2.650[1]. The *Red Book* is a comprehensive guide to the procedures, statute and key precedent within all areas of family law, published annually by LexisNexis.

25 Resolution, *Good Practice Guide to Working with Litigants in Person* (2024), https://resolution.org.uk/wp-content/uploads/2024/10/GPG2024_WorkingWithLitigantsInPerson_Sept2024_24-09-24.pdf.

9.39 In order to preserve the enforcement options available to the Court, proper service must be effected upon the person giving the undertaking to the Court. Good practice should see the party giving the undertaking being provided with a copy of the undertaking before leaving court. Alternatively, service can be effected by posting a copy or by personal service.

9.40 Make sure the order drawn up reflects the evidence before the Court and the circumstances that led to the undertakings being taken – especially if s 46(3A) may apply.

9.41 Be clear about the duration of the undertaking.

What are the Court's responsibilities?

9.42 As an undertaking is a formal promise to the Court (note – not to the applicant), there are a number of steps the Court should take:

(a) The Court should actively consider the terms of the undertaking and approve them before inviting the person giving the promise to sign it.

(b) The Court must ensure that the person giving an undertaking understands the promise they are giving to the Court as well as the consequences they may face in the event of a breach.

(c) The Court should consider how long the undertakings should last for.

9.43 Upon the Court accepting the undertaking, the court clerk should endorse upon the Court's copy of the undertaking the manner in which it was served upon the person giving it.

9.44 Courts should be reluctant to accept an undertaking from a person who is not present, although the Court is able to accept such an undertaking via a party's legal representative. It is, therefore, incumbent upon the legal representative to have full instructions on the point and be able to offer the Court the reassurance that their respondent client understands both the terms of the undertaking and the consequences of breaching it.

PRACTICE NOTE

If the respondent client isn't present this should be recorded on the face of the order and the undertaking.

Making the order in the represented respondent's absence places a heavy burden on the legal representative who may find themselves in the unenviable position of being a witness in any subsequent committal proceedings.

DURATION OF A NON-MOLESTATION ORDER

9.45 By virtue of FLA 1996, s 42(7), the Court may make a Non-Molestation Order for a specified period of time, or until further order. Of particular relevance is whether the order was made ex parte or inter partes.

9.46 Having regard to the guidance issued by the President of the Family Division in July 2023, the principles summarised by Cobb J are added to:

- An ex parte order must have a fixed end date, which shall clearly be set out on its face.
- The ex parte order can be for a substantial period, such as 6 or even 12 months, but the return date must be listed within 28 days at most.[26]

> PRACTICE NOTE
>
> If an ex parte order is made it is good practice to make provision in the order for the respondent to have leave to apply to vary or discharge the order on short notice upon written application with grounds identified in a sworn statement to be served on the applicant and the Court.

9.47 In practice, although courts have the ability to make a Non-Molestation Order of indefinite duration, such orders, whether ex parte or inter parte, are uncommon and duration has been the subject of judicial debate in a number of reported cases, both before and after the coming into force of the FLA 1996.

9.48 In *Galan v Galan*, Slade LJ, sitting in the Court of Appeal, confirmed that 'normally an order for a short, fixed period will be the appropriate order, if any, for the court to make' and that, while an order unlimited in time will not normally be appropriate, there is nothing in the 1996 Act which expressly limits the discretion of the Court as regards the duration of the order.[27]

9.49 The debate regarding the use of Non-Molestation Orders indefinitely began with the decision in *M v W (Non-Molestation Order: Duration)* when Cazalet J stated that:

> '… the object of non-molestation orders is designed to give a breathing space for the parties and, unless there are *exceptional or unusual circumstances*, it should be for a specified period of time. If this latter course is not taken then many years go by and a party may find himself or herself suddenly arrested under an order made many years previously when much has since changed and the original order has lost the substance of its main purpose.'[28]

26 *Practice Guidance: Non-Molestation Injunctions* (n 21).
27 *Galan v Galan* [1985] FLR 905.
28 *M v W (Non-Molestation Order: Duration)* [2000] 1 FLR 107, [109D] (emphasis added).

9.50 However, considering the same issue whilst sitting in the Court of Appeal, Hale LJ overruled the decision in *M v W* in *Re B-J (A Child) (Non-Molestation Orders: Power of Arrest)*, stating that the use of 'exceptional or unusual' as a 'test' was too restrictive:

> 'In my judgment, therefore, the guidance given in *M v W* as to the duration of non-molestation orders, wise though it may have been in the individual case, is too restrictive and does not represent the intention of Parliament … To seek to limit the great variety of factual circumstances in which these orders may be needed by such words as "exceptional or unusual" is to invite just the sort of argument which took place in this court in respect of an order which was clearly justified in the circumstances of the case in the interests of the little girl concerned …'[29]
>
> '… A non-molestation order is indeed sometimes, even often, designed to give a breathing space after which the tensions between the parties may settle down so that it is no longer needed. But in other cases, it may be appropriate for a much longer period, and it is not helpful to oblige the courts to consider whether such cases are "exceptional" or "unusual"…'[30]
>
> '… There are obviously cases, of which this is one, in which the continuing feelings between parties who separated long ago are such that a long term or indefinite order is justified.'[31]

9.51 A High Court decision by Cobb J in *Manjra v Shaikh*,[32] drew together the authorities in the context of an appeal against the making of an indefinite Non-Molestation Order and considered them in the light of amendments made to the FLA 1996 by the Domestic Violence, Crime and Victims Act 2004 (with s 1 of the 2004 Act introducing a new s 42A into the FLA 1996 which imported a criminal sanction for breach of a Non-Molestation Order) as well as guidance issued by the then President of the Family Division, Munby P:

> 'i. The Family Law Act 1996 contemplates first and foremost that an order may be made for a specified period, or until "further order"; the expectation is that if there is no end date specified in the order, there will be an order bringing the injunction to an end;
>
> ii. Adherence to the Practice Guidance issued by the President of the Family Division is essential for all ex parte orders, and the principles should apply equally to on notice orders;[33]
>
> iii. It is, and has been for some time, good practice for orders to stipulate an end date; that date is likely to be no more than 12 months following the making of the order;

29 *Re B-J (A Child) (Non-Molestation Orders: Power of Arrest)* [2001] 1 All ER 235, [35].
30 *Re B-J (A Child) (Non-Molestation Orders: Power of Arrest)* (n 29), [29].
31 *Re B-J (A Child) (Non-Molestation Orders: Power of Arrest)* (n 29), [33].
32 *Manjra v Shaikh* [2020] EWHC 1805 (Fam).
33 Cobb J had regard to the *Family Court Duration of Ex Parte (Without Notice) Orders* (n 19) which has now been superseded by *Practice Guidance: Non Molestation Injunctions under the Family Law Act 1996* (n 19).

iv. There may still be circumstances where the court is entitled to conclude that a Non-Molestation Order for a longer, or even an indefinite period, is justified; Hale LJ deprecated the suggestion that these orders should be made only "exceptionally." It is suggested by Cobb J that the circumstances in which such orders are made will include cases where there is evidence of persistent molestation after the initial injunctive order; put another way, there may be cases where the court takes the view, on the facts that the requirement for protection from abuse has no foreseeable end date".'[34]

9.52 Whilst it has to be acknowledged that the majority of Non-Molestation Orders made are for a prescribed period of time – usually six months to a year – there are occasions when a longer period of injunctive protection is required. The judgment of Hale LJ in *Re B-J (A Child) (Non-Molestation Orders: Power of Arrest)* serves to remind us, as practitioners, that there are an infinite number of circumstances which may befall a family or individual and the role of the Family Court is to consider the particular set of circumstances before it: slavish adherence to a test of 'exceptional' or 'unusual' runs the risk of shifting the focus from the needs of the person before the Court to what those words actually mean.[35]

IMPLEMENTATION OF A NON-MOLESTATION ORDER

9.53 Once the Court has made a Non-Molestation Order, there are a number of steps which must be taken in order to ensure that the order is enforceable.

Service: ex parte orders

9.54 If an application for a Non-Molestation Order is made on notice, FPR 2010, r 10.3 requires the applicant to personally serve upon the respondent:

(a) a copy of the application together with any statement in support; and

(b) notice of any hearing or directions appointment set by the Court.

Service must take place not less than two days before the hearing or within another period directed by the Court.

PRACTICE NOTE:

- FPR 2010, r 10.3(1A) prohibits the application being personally served upon the respondent by the applicant.
- If the applicant acts in person, r 10.3(2) extends the option for the applicant to ask the Court Office to serve the applicant.
- The use of a process server to effect personal service is considered a reasonable, necessary and proportionate disbursement on the applicant's legal aid certificate.

34 *Manjra v Shaikh* (n 32), [22].

35 *Re B-J (A Child) (Non-Molestation Orders: Power of Arrest)* (n 29).

9.55 The issue of service of court orders was considered by the President of the Family Division in *Re P (Service on Parent in a Refuge)*[36] where guidance was given as to the practice to be adopted when court orders need to be served upon a person who is thought to be residing in a women's refuge. It is important to note that this guidance ought to apply equally to men's refuges and other refuge environments.

9.56 Pending more detailed consideration by the FPR committee, the President gave the following guidance, which should be applied when court orders and other documents must be served on an individual who is thought to be residing in a refuge:

'i. Where a person to be served is thought to be residing in a refuge, the court should only require personal service at the address of the refuge in circumstances which are truly exceptional and urgent.

ii. In all other cases, an alternative means of service, as sanctioned by FPR 2010, Part 6, should be used. Such alternative means include:

 a. Personal service at an alternative location;

 b. Service on the party's legal representative;

 c. Service via post at a PO Box or office address provided by the refuge for this purpose;

 d. Service via email and/or text and/or WhatsApp or other electronic messaging service in circumstances where the resident is known to use these means of communication.

e. Service by post via a third party whom the court is confident will provide the resident of the refuge with the documents.

iii. Where service is to be via post at a PO Box or office address provided by the refuge for this purpose, the CEO or director of the refuge should be required to confirm that any material thus served will be promptly brought to the attention of the person to be served.

iv. When considering arrangements for service on a person who is residing at a refuge, the court should at all times be mindful of its duty under DAA 2021, s63 and FPR, Part 3A and 3AA to make participation directions with respect to an individual who is, or is at risk of being, a victim of domestic abuse.

v. When considering arrangements for service on a person who is residing at a refuge who is a migrant woman, the court should pay additional attention to the need to ensure that any court orders are appropriately translated.

vi. The alleged perpetrator or their representative must never, themselves, personally serve a resident at a refuge.

vii. Where, because of the exceptional and urgent nature of the circumstances, it is considered necessary for the court to order personal service of court documents on a resident at a refuge, the court must be alive to the factors set

36 *Re P (Service on Parent in a Refuge)* [2023] EWHC 471 (Fam).

out at paragraph 34 above and should consider contacting the CEO or the director of the refuge to make appropriate arrangements.

viii. Where personal service is to be made at a refuge, it should be undertaken by a court bailiff or the Tipstaff and, where possible, using female officers in plain clothing.

ix. The address of a refuge must never be disclosed to the alleged perpetrator or to their solicitor, even if an undertaking is offered.

x. Any formal contact with a refuge, and other orders requiring information, should engage with the CEO or director of the refuge. It will never be appropriate for individual refuge staff members to be required by court order to disclose confidential information.'[37]

9.57 It is important to note that this guidance is applicable to all forms of service. Typically, the need to personally serve orders urgently is likely to arise in cases concerning Non-Molestation Orders, Occupation Orders or other forms of injunctive relief. Such a need may also arise in Children Act proceedings and, therefore, practitioners should ensure that they are familiar with this guidance.

9.58 Parties should be aware of the guidance on the security implications involved where one party is in a refuge, as set out by the Children and Family Court Advisory and Support Service (CAFCASS) in its recent *Domestic Abuse Practice Policy* document (10 December 2025), which directs practitioners to 'be aware of Practice Direction 6D of the Family Procedure Rules 2010 which deals with Service of court papers where there are reasonable grounds to believe that a person is residing in a refuge'.[38]

9.59 Security also has an impact on contact arrangements. See para 25 for the following:

'Where the resident parent and child are currently living in a refuge or other confidential, protective accommodation due to a report of domestic abuse by the other parent, practitioners must clearly set out the risks that exist to the court of directing any form of spending time arrangements (in person and other forms of contact including letters, telephone and video contact) that could compromise the confidentiality of the location and therefore safety of the parent and child. Also, if it is necessary for someone to be living in a refuge for their safety, then the criteria for risk of harm or further harm will have been established. In these cases, it is necessary for an assessment of harm and risk of harm to be completed before any spending time arrangements are recommended to the court. In the unusual circumstance, where a parent is living in a refuge with their child/ren and "time with" has not been suspended, then a referral should be made urgently to children's social care together with a 16A risk assessment to the court, which should

37 *Re P (Service on Parent in a Refuge)* (n 36), [46].

38 CAFCASS, Domestic Abuse Practice Policy (January 2026), https://www.cafcass.gov.uk/domestic-abuse-practice-policy, para 26.

recommend suspension of any interim "time with" arrangements while a full assessment of what is safe for the child is completed.'[39]

This serves as stark reminder that practicalities in terms of case administration cannot be divorced form the central issue of concern being litigated – namely the safety and security of the participants and the welfare of the child. Make sure your practice is as well interlinked.

Notification to the police

9.60 A breach of a Non-Molestation Order is a criminal offence (see subsequent section) and so, upon a Non-Molestation Order being made, the police must be notified in order to ensure the enforceability of the order.

When the Court makes a Non-Molestation Order (or an Occupation Order with a power of arrest attached to it), the applicant must serve upon the police force with responsibility for the applicant's address (or other such police force as the court may direct):[40]

(a) a copy of the order, and

(b) 'A statement showing that the Respondent has been served with the order or informed of its terms (whether by being present when the order was made or by telephone or otherwise)'.[41]

9.61 In circumstances where the applicant is acting in person and asks for the Court to effect service upon the police, or the Court has made the Non-Molestation Order of its own motion, the Court must provide a copy of the order and a statement showing that the respondent has been served with the order or informed of its terms.[42]

PRACTICE NOTE

- These service points are *crucial* to ensure that the Non-Molestation Order is enforceable in all respects.
- Failure to follow these steps is likely to result in the order being unenforceable, thereby exposing the applicant to avoidable risk (not to mention the possibility of professional consequences).

39 CAFCASS (n 38), para 25.
40 FPR 2010, r 10.10(1)(ii).
41 FPR 2010, r 10.10(2).
42 FPR 2010, r 10.10(3)(b).

Breach of a Non-Molestation Order

9.62 Whilst breach of a Non-Molestation Order is a criminal offence, there are two options available to deal with any breach.

The first – and now the most uncommon – option is for the Court to deal with any breach of a Non-Molestation Order, under the civil jurisdiction, as contempt.

The second is for the matter to be dealt with by the criminal court as a criminal offence for which the respondent has been arrested. Pursuing both is problematic. A common theme running through the authorities on the issue of sentencing for contempt is that 'great care must be taken if there are concurrent criminal or civil proceedings, to ensure that sentences in two or more courts do not punish twice for the same thing'.[43]

Civil remedy

9.63 As breach of a Non-Molestation Order is a criminal offence, and therefore within the criminal courts' jurisdiction, the Family Court no longer has the power to attach a power of arrest to a Non-Molestation Order.[44]

9.64 However, breach of a Non-Molestation Order is considered to be a contempt of court and is therefore punishable as such, carrying a maximum sentence of two years' imprisonment.[45] Here, the Family Court can seek to enforce the Non-Molestation Order as a contempt of court, unless the matter is being pursued as a criminal matter – FLA 1996, s 42A(3) and (4). In *Hale v Tanner,* Hale LJ, sitting in the Court of Appeal, offered some guidance, which can be summarised as:[46]

(a) An application to commit for contempt was previously the only enforcement procedure available for breach of a Non-Molestation Order under s 42.

(b) The full range of criminal sentencing options is not available.

(c) Custody is not automatic.

(d) There is a power to fine, and a power to suspend a custodial sentence, which should nevertheless not affect the length of the sentence, that is, you do not make the sentence longer because you are going to suspend it.

(e) The length of the sentence depends on the Court's objectives, which will always include marking the Court's disapproval of the disobedience of its order and securing compliance with it in the future.

43 *H v O* [2004] EWCA Civ 1691, [39].
44 See the Domestic Violence, Crime and Victims Act 2004, Sch 10, para 38 and *FD (Inherent Jurisdiction: Power of Arrest)* [2016] EWHC 2358 (Fam).
45 Contempt of Court Act 1981, s 14.
46 *Hale v Tanner* [2000] 1 WLR 2377.

(f) The length of the committal has to bear some relationship to the maximum statutory sentence of two years.

(g) The Court has to bear in mind the context, which may be aggravating or mitigating.

9.65 Hale LJ went on to say:

> '... In many cases the court will have to bear in mind that there are concurrent proceedings in another court based on either the same facts, or some of the same facts, which are before the court on the contempt proceedings. The court cannot ignore those parallel proceedings. It may have to take into account their outcome in considering what the practical effect is upon the contempt proceedings. They do have different purposes and often the overlap is not exact, but nevertheless the court will not want, in effect, the contemnor to suffer punishment twice for the same events.'[47]

9.66 This guidance was expanded upon by the Court of Appeal, headed up by the then President of the Family Division in the case of *Lomas v Parle*, who acknowledged that 'it is not difficult for a persistent course of domestic violence (sic) to generate concurrent proceedings in three courts'.[48] The guidance seeks to supplement that given in *Hale v Tanner* and can be distilled into the following points:

(a) With regards to passing sentences, the criminal courts and the Family Court do not share the same objective and operate in different ranges. As stated above, whilst the criminal courts can pass a sentence of up to five years, a judge in the Family Court is restricted to a maximum of two years.

(b) An important objective for the judiciary in the Family Court is to uphold the authority of the Court by demonstrating that its orders cannot be flouted with impunity.

(c) The first court to sentence must not anticipate or allow for a likely future sentence. It is for the second court to sentence to reflect the prior sentence in its judgment in order to ensure that the defendant is not twice punished for the same act.

(d) It is essential that the second court to sentence is fully informed of the factors and circumstances reflected in the first sentence.

(e) The first court to sentence has an obligation to ensure that the basis of its sentence is fully expressed and that a transcript of its judgment is made available to the second court.

(f) Any application to commit in the Family Court should be issued promptly after the alleged breach and listed without delay to ensure that, if proved, the

47 *Hale v* Tanner (n 46), [34].
48 *Lomas v Parle* [2003] EWCA Civ 1804, [42].

contempt will have been punished before any sentence in parallel criminal proceeding.

(g) Judges should, as far as possible, ensure that sentences passed for breaches of Non-Molestation Orders are not manifestly discrepant with sentences for harassment charged under Protection from Harassment Act 1997, ss 3, 4 or 5 (noting that, the more serious the offence, the less scope there will be to maintain any relationship between family and criminal court sentences).

(h) Sentences of imprisonment do not necessarily deter repetition. Consideration should be given to the Court directing attendance at programmes designed to address DA and emotional management.

9.67 When the Court of Appeal handed down judgment in *Lomas v Parle*, the Domestic Violence, Crime and Victims Bill had just been published. The Court of Appeal suggested that the Bill provided an opportunity to reconsider how breaches of injunctions may be more efficiently handled by the Court.

9.68 The Domestic Violence, Crime and Victims Act 2004 amended the FLA 1996, creating s 42A. This section makes breach of a Non-Molestation Order a criminal offence, punishable by up to five years' imprisonment. Therefore, whilst the guidance offered by the Court of Appeal in *Hale v Tanner* and *Lomas v Parle* is useful and provides a helpful steer to ensure that any breach is dealt with proportionately if charged with a criminal offence arising out of the same conduct, it must now be viewed through the lens of the criminal court being able to deal specifically with breach of a Non-Molestation Order.

Criminal remedy

9.69 In many ways, dealing with a breach of a Non-Molestation Order through a criminal remedy is a much more straightforward endeavour – and the most common form of punishing a breach of such an Order. It may be said that the use of the criminal law to punish a breach of a Non-Molestation Order undermines the autonomy of the victim to choose the method of punishment if the Crown Prosecution Service vigorously pursues criminal breach. However, the reality is more likely to be one of relief for the victim as it allows for the delegation of dealing with a breach of such an order.

9.70 As mentioned above, the Domestic Violence, Crime and Victims Act 2004 inserted a new s 42A into the FLA 1996. It is important to closely consider this legislation and its key points:

(a) It is a defence to an allegation of breach of a Non-Molestation Order to assert that the defendant had a reasonable excuse for breaching the order:

> '(1) A person who without reasonable excuse does anything that he is prohibited from doing by a non-molestation order is guilty of an offence.'

(b) In relation to a Non-Molestation Order made without notice to the respondent, it is essential that all practical points are addressed (set out earlier in this chapter) and service is properly effected and evidenced:

> '(2) In the case of a non-molestation order made by virtue of section 45(1), a person can be guilty of an offence under this section only in respect of conduct engaged in at a time when he was aware of the existence of the order.'

(c) The inclusion of the following provisions serves to limit the circumstances which may arise where conduct may fall to be punished twice: in the criminal courts and the Family Court. Although unlikely to arise, it is possible that prosecution for a breach of a Non-Molestation Order is problematic (perhaps due to ineffective service of the order) but gives rise to potential criminal liability for other offences.

> '(3) Where a person is convicted of an offence under this section in respect of any conduct, that conduct is not punishable as a contempt of court.
>
> '(4) A person cannot be convicted of an offence under this section in respect of any conduct which has been punished as a contempt of court.'

(d) With a statutory maximum sentence of five years' imprisonment available, the options for the criminal courts are more extensive than those available to the Family Court and may include fines, imprisonment and a wide variety of community orders.[49]

> '(5) A person guilty of an offence under this section is liable—
>
> (a) On conviction on indictment, to imprisonment for a term not exceeding five years, or a fine, or both;
>
> (b) On summary conviction, to imprisonment for a term not exceeding the general limit in a magistrates' court, or a fine not exceeding the statutory maximum, or both.'

PRACTICE NOTE

Astute practitioners will want to be aware of the extent to which Domestic Abuse Protection Orders (DAPOs) may assist them if the pilot is running in their area as this scheme can offer protection and covers actions that would typically require both a Non Molestation Order and an Occupation Order (see the end of this chapter for information on this initiative).

49 Whilst the purpose of this chapter is not to offer a detailed analysis of the criminal law insofar as it relates to breaching a Non-Molestation Order, the Sentencing Council offer comprehensive guidelines to the criminal courts which may be a worthwhile reference tool when advising those who have breached a Non-Molestation Order.

OCCUPATION ORDERS

9.71 An Occupation Order is a more complicated injunctive order as it serves to regulate the occupation of the family home, by the making of declarations or orders. It does not seek to regulate the ownership of the family home and is intended to be a temporary order. There are a variety of orders the Court can make, all of which depend upon the circumstances of the person seeking the order. Whilst usually sought by a victim of DA, the Family Court is able to make an Occupation Order in a wide variety of circumstances.

9.72 By and large, applications for Occupation Orders are not as commonplace in the Family Court when compared to applications for Non-Molestation Orders, with the use of the former being far more consistent in terms of the number of applications being issued.

9.73 An Occupation Order has two potential uses:

(a) It can confer the right to occupy the home to a party who has no entitlement to otherwise occupy the home.

(b) It can regulate, or even exclude a party from the home even if they have sole entitlement to occupy the home.

9.74 Arguably, more complicated than the law relating to Non-Molestation Orders, there is a comprehensive statutory regime governing the availability and making of Occupation Orders. Sections 33–41 of the FLA 1996 set out the comprehensive statutory regime. The purposes of this section will be to explore each of those sections as well as offering guidance on the law and practice in this particular area.

Who can apply for an Occupation Order?

9.75 An application for an Occupation Order may be freestanding or be within other family proceedings. However, the Family Court is unable to make an Occupation Order of its own motion as it does not have the power to do so (FLA 1996, s 39(2)).

9.76 As a result of the Law Commission concluding that it was more difficult to justify excluding from or otherwise interfering with a respondent's enjoyment of their property when the applicant enjoyed no such rights themselves, the categories of those entitled to apply for an Occupation Order are much more limited. There is no reference to an 'associated person', but rather a much narrower category: 'entitled' or 'non-entitled' applicants.

Section 33

9.77 An Occupation Order made pursuant to FLA 1996, s 33 is only available to those who are entitled to occupy the home either by virtue of s 33 or having acquired home rights pursuant to FLA 1996, s 30. Having satisfied the definition of an entitled person, as set out in s 33(1)(a), an applicant seeking an Occupation Order is able to seek an order, or a declaration, in respect of the home.

9.78 Given the range of orders available, as set out in s 33(3), as well as the ability to make declarations pursuant to s 33(4), a wide range of circumstances are catered for and can serve to offer a person requiring protection with almost a bespoke order designed to best meet their needs and offer them the greatest protection.

9.79 Orders can be made preventing the respondent from changing locks at the home, requiring the respondent to leave the whole or part of the home, or to only occupy the home at various times.

PRACTICE NOTE

- With the client, think about the size and daily use of the house for its occupants.
- Consider tension points (kitchen, bathroom, TV).
- Construct a hierarchy of vulnerability and need.
- Think through options. Who does what when? Who needs what from their occupancy? Is it vital for work, school, family support, childcare?
- Who has lived there the longest (ie occupation history)?
- Who has the means to find alternative accommodation either with family, friends or renting?

Duration

9.80 Section 33(10) of the Act imposes no maximum duration for an Occupation Order made under s 33. Whilst practically the Family Court tends to make an order under this section with a duration of six months, it is unlikely that the Court will consider making an Occupation Order until a further order unless there are exceptional circumstances. Whilst there is an inevitable distinction to be drawn between Non-Molestation Orders and Occupation Orders, practitioners may find the authorities dealing with indefinite Non-Molestation Orders offer some guidance as to factors the Family Court may take into consideration.

9.81 With the ever-increasing pressure on Family Court listing, however, an Occupation Order made at the outset of the proceedings may remain in place for the duration of the proceedings, until such time as the Court is able to adjudicate upon all matters. This may mean that the Occupation Order remains in place for a period far in excess of what the circumstances of the particular case may justify. The Court may be invited to reconsider the need for the continuation of the Occupation Order during the course of the proceedings which may require a reconsideration of the balance of harm test.

What does the Court consider?

9.82 The Family Court's power to make an Occupation Order is not a mandatory one, it is a discretionary power. In deciding whether to exercise this discretionary power, the Court has two available routes open to it: the application of a *balance of harm test* (FLA 1996, s 33(7)) or the exercise of the *Court's discretion* (FLA 1996, s 33(6)).

9.83 The Court of Appeal provided clarity as to how the Family Court should approach applications for an Occupation Order in the case of *Chalmers v John* with Thorpe LJ giving the lead judgment.[50]

PRACTICE NOTE

The relevant stages can be summarised as:

(a) Does the evidence establish that the applicant or any relevant child is likely to suffer significant harm attributable to conduct of the respondent if an order is not made?

(b) If the answer to Step One is 'yes', the Court must make an order unless, balancing one harm against the other, the harm to the respondent or the child is likely to be as great – this is known as the 'balance of harm test'.

(c) If the answer to Step One is 'no', the Court enters the realms of its discretion, as set out in s 33(6). The Court must exercise a broad discretion having regard to all of the circumstances of the case, particularly those factors set out in the statutory checklist within subparas (a)–(d), although the Court is not limited to these and should consider all of the circumstances of the case[51] – this is known as the 'discretionary test'.

The balance of harm test; s 33(7)

'(7) If it appears to the court that the applicant or any relevant child is likely to suffer significant harm attributable to conduct of the respondent if an order under this section containing one or more of the provisions mentioned in subsection (3) is not made, the court shall make the order unless it appears to it that–

50 *Chalmers v Johns* [1999] 1 FLR 392.

51 *Re L (Children) (Occupation order: absence of domestic violence)* [2012] EWCA Civ 721.

(a) the respondent or any relevant child is likely to suffer significant harm if the order is made; and

(b) the harm likely to be suffered by the respondent or child in that event is as great as, or greater than, the harm attributable to conduct of the respondent which is likely to be suffered by the applicant or child if the order is not made.'

9.84 The test for the Family Court to undertake is a simple balancing exercise, with the Family Court's task being to determine where the greater harm will lie if the Court were to make an Occupation Order.

(a) The Court's task is to assess the effect of the conduct on the applicant or any relevant children, rather than look at the intention of the respondent.[52]

(b) In the absence of significant harm, the Court should only grant an Occupation Order which excludes a party with a right of occupation from the home in exceptional circumstances in light of the draconian nature of the order.[53]

(c) The applicable standard of proof when approaching the Balance of Harm test is the simple balance of probabilities. This can be inferred from the use of the word 'likely' in the Act. In cases brought under the Children Act 1989, the courts have held that the word 'likely' means 'a real possibility' which is to be established on the balance of probabilities.[54]

9.85 A useful illustration of the balance of harm test at play can be seen in the case of *B v B (Occupation Order)*.[55] In this case, the wife was forced to flee the family home as a result of the husband's use of serious violence against her. The wife and the parties' baby were housed in local authority bed and breakfast accommodation. The husband remained in the family home with his six-year-old son from a previous relationship. The court at first instance made an Occupation Order in favour of the wife but the husband appealed. The Court of Appeal held that all that the baby needed was to be securely with the wife. Although the wife's present accommodation was unsuitable, it was likely to be temporary as she would be considered homeless and therefore, in priority need for accommodation. In applying the balance of harm test, the Court found that if the husband was ordered out of the home, it would cause his six-year-old son significant harm, changing school for the fifth time in 18 months and would be disruptive and damaging to his mental and emotional health. The Court of Appeal was careful to point out that the Court would not and could not be tolerant of the husband's conduct and that perpetrators of DA cannot be expected to remain in shared accommodation. However, in applying the balance of harm test, the fact that the six-year-old son was not a child of both parties was a critical factor and swung the balance in favour of the husband.

52 *G v G (Occupation Order: Conduct)* [2000] 2 FLR 36, CA.

53 *G v G (Occupation Order: Conduct)* (n 52).

54 See *Re H (Threshold Criteria: Standard of Proof)* [1996] 1 All ER 1 and *Re B (Sexual Abuse: Standard of Proof)* [2008] UKHL 35.

55 *B v B (Occupation Order)* [1999] 1 FLR 715.

The discretionary test; s 33(6)

9.86 In the event that the Court is not persuaded that the balance of harm test justifies the making of an Occupation Order, it can consider whether, as a matter of discretion, the Court should make an Occupation Order. Section 33(6) of the Family Law Act 1996 provides:

> '(6) In deciding whether to exercise its powers under subsection (3) and (if so) in what manner, the court shall have regard to all the circumstances including—
>
> (a) the housing needs and housing resources of each of the parties and of any relevant child;
>
> (b) the financial resources of each of the parties;
>
> (c) the likely effect of any order, or of any decision by the court not to exercise its powers under subsection (3), on the health, safety or well-being of the parties and of any relevant child; and
>
> (d) the conduct of the parties in relation to each other and otherwise.'

9.87 However, this list is not an exhaustive list of the factors the Family Court will take into consideration when deciding whether to exercise its discretion. The Court of Appeal considered the factors the Court can take into consideration in *Re L (Children) (Occupation order: absence of domestic violence)*.[56]

9.88 In regard to s 33(6)(a), the applicant's statement should set out details of the parties' current home in terms of its size, number of rooms and other facilities as well as location and proximity to schools, family and other support networks. The statement should explore the options realistically available to the parties should they move to a different property.

9.89 When responding to s 33(6)(b), the financial resources of each of the parties, the applicant should seek to provide the Court with as much detail as they can and support any evidence with bank statements and other relevant information. The extent to which the applicant can do this for both parties may be limited; if this is the case, the applicant should explain why.

9.90 Section 33(6)(c) requires the Court to have a good understanding of these factors for it is not being asked to make an objective assessment, but rather a subjective one.

9.91 Finally, in regard to s 33(6)(d), the Court will need to have specific details of the alleged conduct. The Court should be informed of any ongoing criminal investigations into such allegations, as well as where the investigation is at and whether there are any bail conditions in place against one party or another. If there has been a history of DA reported to other agencies or services, such as a

56 *Re L (Children) (Occupation order: absence of domestic violence)* (n 51).

GP, hospital or support service, details of this should be given. In short, if there is any corroborative evidence available to support a party's assertions, this should be placed before the Court.

PRACTICE NOTE

It is important to note the following:

- There is nothing in s 33(6) which limits the Court's discretion to make an Occupation Order to cases in which there has been physical violence.[57] The subsection is broadly drafted, covering not just cases in which there is violence but also all manner of other problems that can occur when a relationship has run into difficulties.
- There is no authority establishing that a spouse can only be excluded from the home if reprehensible conduct on his or her behalf is found.
- The Court is not required to make findings on all disputed issues.
- What the judge has to do is make findings on the matters that are relevant to the exercise of their discretion.
- An applicant bringing an application for an Occupation Order which may fall to be considered under s 33(6) of the Act should ensure that they prepare a detailed statement, setting out *all of the circumstances* that the applicant considers are relevant to the decision the Court will have to make.
- It is important that such a statement addresses, *in detail and with any supporting evidence,* the factors set out in s 33(6) of the Act. However, such a statement should not be confined to those four factors.

Section 35: former spouse or civil partner

9.92 Section 35 applies only to *former* spouses or *former* civil partners; current spouses/civil partners have home rights under FLA 1996, s 30 and could apply for an Occupation Order under s 33 of the Act. However, as home rights come to an end upon divorce or dissolution of the civil partnership, any remedy after that point lies within s 35. Equally, if the adults are former or current cohabitants then one turns to s 36 for the relevant occupation provision (which will be discussed in due course).

9.93 *Three conditions must be satisfied* in order for the Family Court to make an Occupation Order pursuant to s 35 of the Act:

57 Also have regard to the Court of Appeal decisions in *Grubb v Grubb* [2009] EWCA Civ 976 and *Dolan v Corby* [2011] EWCA Civ 1664.

1. The applicant must be a former spouse or civil partner with no existing right to occupy;
2. the respondent must not be entitled to occupy the property; and[58]
3. the property was, or was intended to, be the parties' home.

PRACTICE NOTE

In making an Occupation Order under s 35 of the Act, the Court must make a declaration in accordance with either s 35(3) or (4). This important aspect *must not* be omitted when drafting the order.

The practical effect of both the declaratory and regulatory aspects of the order is that the same level of protection is offered to non-entitled applicants as is offered to entitled applicants, albeit the duration of the order is not the same.

9.94 As with the Court's approach to an Occupation Order under s 33 of the Act, the Court will have regard to a *balance of harm* test. This is set out at s 35(8) of the Act and is, in essence, the same test applicable to an order under s 33. Regard should be had to the earlier commentary on how the Court should approach such a test.

9.95 If the balance of harm test concludes in the applicant's favour, the Court *must* make an Occupation Order; the only discretion the Court has then relates to the precise terms and the duration of the order.

9.96 As with an order made under s 33, should the balance of harm test fail to fall in the applicant's favour, the Court retains a *discretion* to make an Occupation Order and should go on to consider the factors set out in s 35(6)(a)–(g).

9.97 In considering these factors, the Court should have particular regard to (a)–(e). Whilst the length of the parties' separation and the time which has elapsed since the parties' divorce can be significant factors, the Court has confirmed that the needs of the children can outweigh those factors.[59]

9.98 Upon the Court concluding that it should make an Occupation Order, the Court must go on to determine whether the respondent's occupation of the property requires regulation. The options available to the Family Court are set out in s 35(5).

58 FLA 1996, s 63(1) defines a 'dwelling-house' for the purposes of an Occupation Order as including (a) any building, or part of a building which is occupied as a dwelling, (b) any caravan, house-boat or structure which is occupied as a dwelling, and any yard, garden, garage or outhouse belonging to it and occupied with it.

59 See *S v F (Occupation Order)* [2000] 2 FCR 365 (Fam Div), [372].

Duration of an order under s 35

9.99 Note this distinction – whilst an Occupation Order can be made under s 33 of the Act with no maximum duration, the same cannot be said when the order is made under s 35. Section 35(10) gives the Court the power to make an Occupation Order under s 35 for a maximum period of six months which can be extended on any number of occasions, albeit only by a maximum of six months at a time.

Section 36: current or former cohabitants

9.100 This section of the FLA 1996 is broadly similar to s 35, but whereas s 35 applies only to former *spouses* or former *civil partners,* s 36 applies when the parties are current or former cohabitants.

9.101 Whilst there is a broad degree of overlap between ss 35 and 36 of the Act, there are some differences which are worthy of note. When drafting the legislation, Parliament sought to emphasise the distinction in the quality of the relationship with those who have made a public commitment by way of marriage or civil partnership. This might now seem dated but this is where the law is at.

9.102 Therefore, in addition to the common factors with ss 33 and 35, the Court is also obliged to consider the additional factors set out in s 36(6)(e)–(i).

9.103 In determining an application under this section, the Court must still consider the factors common with applications under the other sections, along with the balance of harm test. However, an important distinction arises.

PRACTICE NOTE

Insofar as the balance of harm test is concerned, if this falls in favour of the applicant, *it does not serve as a presumption in favour of making the order* as it does under the other sections. It is merely a further consideration.

Duration of an order under s 36

9.104 Pursuant to s 36(10) of the Act, an Occupation Order made under s 36 is limited to a maximum period of six months. Whilst this can be extended by the Court, it can only be extended once for a further maximum period of six months. As such, the maximum period of protection offered by the Court under s 36 is 12 months.

Sections 37 and 38: when neither party is entitled to occupation

9.105 Orders under ss 37 and 38 of the Act may be made when neither party is entitled to occupy the home. Section 37 of the Act relates to spouses, former spouses, civil partners and former civil partners but note it relates only to the matrimonial home. Similar provisions are set out in s 38 with respect to cohabitants and former cohabitants.

9.106 With respect to s 37, the Court must apply the balance of harm test. In the event that the balance of harm test falls in favour of the applicant, the Court *must* make an Occupation Order. In the event that the balance of harm does not fall in favour of the applicant, the Court's remaining discretion is guided by the factors set out in s 33(6) of the Act. This is largely in line with the approach taken to Orders made under s 35.

9.107 With respect to s 38, which applies to current or former cohabitants, whilst the Court should still apply the balance of harm test, the Court is simply required to have regard to it and the factors which are set out in s 38(4). This is largely in line with the approach taken to orders made under s 36 of the Act.

9.108 Whether the order is made under s 37 or s 38 of the Act, as neither party is entitled to occupy the home, there is no requirement for the Family Court to make any declaratory orders.

Duration of orders made under ss 37 and 38

9.109 The durations of Occupation Orders made under these sections directly relate to the duration of the orders set out in ss 35 and 36 of the Act.

9.110 In the event that an Occupation Order is made pursuant to s 37, s 37(5) gives the Court the power to make an Occupation Order for a maximum period of six months, although this can be extended on any number of occasions, by amounts not exceeding six months.

9.111 In the event that an Occupation Order is made pursuant to s 38, pursuant to s 38(6) the order is limited to a maximum period of six months. Whilst this can be extended by the Court, it can only be extended once for a further maximum period of six months. As such, the maximum period of protection offered by the Court under s 38 is 12 months.

Breach of an Occupation Order

9.112 Unlike a breach of a Non-Molestation Order, breach of an Occupation Order made by the Court is *not* a criminal offence. However, upon considering whether to make an Occupation Order, FLA 1996, s 42(4A) requires the Court to consider whether it should also make a Non-Molestation Order.[60]

9.113 Section 47 of the Act provides the Court with the power to attach a power of arrest to an Occupation Order with s 47(2)(a)–(b) providing that the Court makes an Occupation Order and the respondent has used or threatened violence against the applicant or a relevant child.

9.114 In relation to an Occupation Order made *without notice* to the respondent, the Court can only attach a power of arrest to such an order if it appears to the Court that:

(a) the respondent has used or threatened violence against the applicant or a relevant child; and

(b) there is a risk of significant harm to the applicant or the child, attributable to the conduct of the respondent, if the power of arrest is not attached to those provisions immediately.[61]

9.115 In the event of a breach, and in circumstances where there is a power of arrest attached to the order, a police officer can arrest any person without warrant whom they have reasonable cause to suspect is in breach of any such provision.

PRACTICE NOTE

A power of arrest attached to an Occupation Order need not be for the same duration as the Occupation Order itself· This enables the Court to ensure the respondent's compliance with the order.[62]

9.116 Upon a respondent to an Occupation Order being arrested, they must be brought before the Court for punishment for contempt within 24 hours of the arrest whereupon the respondent may then be remanded on bail or in custody pending the contempt proceedings or dealt with in respect of the breach.[63] Rule 10.11(3)(a) of the FPR 2010 states that the matter must be dealt with within 14 days beginning with the date of the arrest unless the Court directs otherwise. Rule 10.11(3)(b) requires the arrested person to be given at least two days' notice of the hearing (this is mandatory).

60 We have seen that breach of a Non-Molestation Order is a criminal offence and, if there was a degree of overlap in the provisions of both the Non-Molestation Order and the Occupation Order, the effect may be that breach of the Occupation Order is criminalised by virtue of the breach of the Non-Molestation Order.

61 See FLA 1996, s 47(3).

62 See *Re B-J (Power of Arrest)* [2000] 2 FLR 443, CA.

63 See FLA 1996, s 47(7). Note that, in calculating the 24-hour period, no account is to be taken of Christmas Day, Good Friday or any Sunday, those being the days when courts do not generally sit.

PRACTICE NOTE

It is important that the initial statement in support of such an application is sufficiently detailed so that the Court is appraised of the respondent's conduct towards the applicant and any relevant child, with the statement demonstrating how that conduct gives rise to the risk of significant harm (and what that harm is likely to be).

Note that the Court is not required to make findings of fact at this stage, but it must be sufficiently informed so as to ensure that sufficient protection is provided for.

Checklist

Listed below are some key issues to consider whilst making an application for an Occupation Order.

- Subject to an assessment of means carried out by the Legal Aid Agency, legal aid is available for those applying for an Occupation Order.
- Ensure that any application for an Occupation Order is made on form FL401, accompanied by a statement of evidence and a draft order.[64] Also note that there is no longer a court fee payable to HM Courts and Tribunal Service for such an application.
- It is important to correctly identify the category of applicant that your client falls under in order to apply under the corresponding section of the Act, and subsequently, to ensure that the relevant evidence for that category is included in the statement of evidence.
- If the Occupation Order contains one or more provisions to which a power of arrest is attached, each provision must be set out in a separate paragraph and must not include a provision within the same paragraph to which there is no power of arrest attached.
- If the Occupation Order has a power of arrest attached to any part of it, the steps set out in FPR 2010, r 10.10 must be followed in order to ensure that the police are notified of the Occupation Order.
- Do note that, in accordance with FPR 2010, r 10.5, all hearings in relation to the application for an Occupation Order are held in private unless the Court directs otherwise.
- A Statement of Service, on Form FL415, must be filed at court once service has been effected upon the respondent.[65]

64 In the event that the application is made without notice, r 10.2(4) requires the witness statement to address the reasons why notice has not been given.

65 See r.10.3 of the FPR 2010 in relation to service of the order.

DOMESTIC ABUSE PROTECTION NOTICES AND ORDERS

9.117 For many years, practitioners have looked to the FLA 1996 for injunctive relief to protect those who are victims of DA. With the coming into force of the DAA 2021, a new form of injunctive relief was introduced. Whilst there is no express intention to repeal Non-Molestation Orders or Occupation Orders, it is intended that there will be a gradual switch from Non-Molestation Orders to Domestic Abuse Protection Orders (DAPOs). According to DAA 2021, s 27, a DAPO prevents an individual from being abusive to another person who is over the age of 16 and to whom they are personally connected.

9.118 Section 32 of the DAA 2021 sets out the conditions which must be satisfied on the balance of probabilities before an order can be made. In determining whether condition A is satisfied, the Court will have regard to the definition of DA set out in DAA 2021, s 1. The behaviour *may take any form as set out in the statutory definition or any combination of those behaviours.* Section 35 provides examples of the type and nature of provisions which may be made by the Court. They are, however, examples only and do not represent an exhaustive list of the provisions which the Court can impose. Section 35(3) provides the Court with a wide discretion and places no limit upon the provisions which the Court can make.

9.119 The Home Office Guidance[66] provides a list of other provisions which the Court is open to impose restriction on:

- Contacting or interacting with the victim via third parties. For example, the children, partner, other family members, friends or co-workers of the victim.
- Hacking, monitoring or controlling the social media accounts, email, phone, computer or other personal devices of the victim.
- Engaging in any form of surveillance of the victim by any means.
- Interfering with or restricting the victim's access to goods, services or property.
- Damaging or threatening to damage properly belonging to the victim.
- Cancelling or procuring goods or services in the name or account of the victim or intentionally running up bills or debts in the name of the victim (with or without the knowledge of the victim).
- Interfering with, restricting the victim's access to, or deliberately frustrating the disposal of joint assets.
- Sharing or publishing, or threatening to share or publish, personal information or images relating to the victim.

66 Home Office, *Controlling or Coercive Behaviour Statutory Guidance Framework* (5 April 2023) https://assets.publishing.service.gov.uk/media/642d3f9e7de82b001231364d/Controlling_or_Coercive_Behaviour_Statutory_Guidance_-_final.pdf.

- Creating manipulated or synthetic material online related to the victim.
- Making reference to the victim on social media either directly or indirectly.

9.120 If the Court imposes a positive requirement for the perpetrator to do something, it must specify the person who is responsible for supervising compliance.[67] Prior to making such an order, the Court must receive evidence about its suitability and enforceability from the person to be specified in s 36(2).[68]

PRACTICE NOTE

A wide definition:

A moot point that possibly only precedent will illuminate is that DAPO protection is wider than that of Non-Molestation Order protection – certainly its specificity is striking but there's nothing unhelpful in that – it directs minds to specific types of behaviour that might bypass the person who has the first line duty of taking instructions (see again the alert as to the dangers of the 'first/ last/ worst' approach referred to under Non-Molestation Orders).

Other practical points:

- Note the restrictions on the availability of DAPOs. At the time of writing, their use is limited to pilot areas (Manchester, Croydon, Sutton or Bromley). Whilst the perpetrator must live within the pilot area, the victim does not need to.
- An application for a DAPO may be made on a freestanding basis in proceedings which are already before the Family Court or by the Court's own motion in ongoing proceedings.
- The implementation of DAPOs remains in its infancy. Practitioners must be on the alert for updates.

Prohibitions, restrictions and positive requirements

9.121 The prohibitions, restrictions and positive requirements are significantly wider than those available for a Non-Molestation Order. In fact, a DAPO can regulate conduct which would typically require both a Non-Molestation Order and an Occupation Order.

9.122 When considering what the provisions of the order should be, the Court must consider what may be necessary to protect the victim.[69] The provisions may include prohibitive, restrictive or positive requirements.

67 DAA 2021, s 36(2).
68 DAA 2021, s 36(3).
69 DAA 2021, s 35(2).

9.123 It might be a (positive) sign of the times that this developing protective limb pays specific regard to the following at s 36(1) when considering the requirements a DAPO imposes on someone:

'(a) conflict with the person's religious beliefs;

(b) interference with the person's work or with the person's attendance at an educational establishment;

(c) conflict with the requirements of any other court order or injunction to which the person may be subject.'

9.124 However, it remains open to the Court to make the order notwithstanding s 36(1) if it concludes that it is not practicable to avoid.

Without notice applications

9.125 Given the nature of the protection required, the Court is often faced with an urgent application. Section 34 of the DAA 2021 allows the Court to make a Domestic Abuse Protection Notice (DAPN) in circumstances where the Court considers it is 'just and convenient' to do so (NB *the same test applicable for without notice Non-Molestation Orders).*

9.126 When considering whether to make a DAPO on a without notice basis, the Court must have regard to all of the circumstances set out in s 31(3).

9.127 Having made an order on a without notice basis, the Court must give the person against whom the order was made an opportunity to make representations about the order as soon as is just and convenient and at a hearing on notice.[70]

Duration

9.128 Pursuant to DAA 2021, s 38(3), the length of the DAPO must be specified in the order, whether that be for a specified period,[71] until a specified event[72] (s 38(3)(b)) or until further order.[73] This has the effect of vesting in the Court the power to make a DAPO for an indefinite period.

9.129 Different provisions of the DAPO may have different durations which must be specified in the order.[74] However, the use of electronic monitoring has a maximum duration of 12 months.[75]

70 DAA 2021, s 34(4)(a) and (b).
71 DAA 2021, s 38(3)(a).
72 DAA 2021, s 38(3)(b).
73 DAA 2021, s 38(3)(c).
74 DAA 2021, s 38(4).
75 DAA 2021, s 38(5).

Notification requirements

9.130 Section 41 of the DAA 2021 sets out the obligations placed upon those who are subject to a DAPO. Those who are made subject to a DAPO must notify the police of their name and address within three days of the order being made.[76] Any changes to the home address throughout the duration of the DAPO must also be notified to the police within three days.[77]

9.131 Upon notification, the perpetrator should receive a written acknowledgment.[78] Practitioners should hold on to a copy of the written acknowledgment (or it should be provided to the person protected by the order) in the event that notification becomes an issue.

9.132 Failure to comply with the notification requirements relating to the DAPO without reasonable excuse, or providing false information to the police in purported compliance with the requirements of a DAPO is a criminal offence pursuant to DAA 2021, s 43(1), with the offence being triable either way and carrying a sentence of up to five years' imprisonment.

Variation/discharge

9.133 An application for variation or discharge can be made by the victim, perpetrator, the third party who applied for the order, the police where the perpetrator resides or the police in an area where the perpetrator may be moving to.[79] It must be addressed to the Court that made the order.[80] The Court can also discharge or vary the DAPO of its own motion.[81]

DOMESTIC ABUSE PROTECTION NOTICES

9.134 Since DAPOs require a court hearing to be valid, it is important that the police have an emergency power to protect an abused individual in the interim. This protection is called a Domestic Abuse Protection Notice (DAPN) and allows a police officer to arrest the subject of the order without warrant should they have reasonable grounds to believe that they are breaching the order.

9.135 Part 3 of the DAA 2021 sets out the statutory regime for both DAPOs and DAPNs. Section 22 provides that a DAPN can be made where:

(a) the intended subject of the order is over 18 years old;

76 DAA 2021, s 41(2).
77 DAA 2021, s 41(5). The meaning of 'home address' is set out in s 56.
78 DAA 2021, s 42(4).
79 DAA 2021, s 44(3).
80 DAA 2021, s 45(1).
81 DAA 2021, s 44(2)(b).

(b) the person whom the order protects is aged 16 or over;

(c) the latter two individuals are 'personally connected';

(d) a senior police officer has reasonable grounds to believe that the intended subject of the order has been abusive towards the person the order seeks to protect (this is known as Condition A);

(e) the senior police officer has reasonable grounds to believe that it is necessary to make a DAPN to protect an individual from DA, or the risk of DA, carried out by the intended subject of the order (this is known as Condition B).

9.136 Section 24 sets out several factors which must be considered by a senior police officer when deciding whether it is appropriate to make a DAPN:

(a) the welfare of anyone under 18 whose interests may be affected by the notice;

(b) the views of the person the notice is meant to protect;

(c) any statements or objections made by the person the notice is directed at;

(d) if the notice concerns shared premises, the views of any relevant occupants.

PRACTICE NOTE

Section 25 sets out how a DAPN must be drafted. An important point here is that a requirement once a DAPN is made is that an application for a DAPO is heard in the magistrates' court within 48 hours of the DAPN being made. The intended subject of the order must be given notice of this application and the date and time of the hearing.

9.137 In the event of a breach of a DAPN the subject of the order must be held in custody and brought before a magistrates' court within 24 hours of the arrest, unless the hearing to determine a DAPO is due to take place within this period, in which case their breach would be considered at this hearing.

PARTING WORDS

9.138 This chapter is dense and long, reflecting the care that needs to be taken when applying for, or resisting, the aforementioned orders. Whilst these protections are commonplace, they often mark the first point of contact between a family and a lawyer or courtroom. The applications tend to be decided at short notice and by a time-pressed tribunal. Yet the making of them can profoundly reshape a home and the dynamics within a family. The orders we have described in this chapter are serious ones and so we urge practitioners to approach them with the attention to detail, specificity of instructions and supportive evidence that they warrant.

CHAPTER 10

Taking Instructions and Gathering Evidence

THE RELEVANCE OF TEXT MESSAGING, SOCIAL MEDIA AND ELECTRONIC EVIDENCE

10.01 A key aspect of the evidential landscape which is often overlooked until much later in the process (and often some way into the proceedings) is the presence of text messages, social media material, email correspondence, internet searches, photographs, videos, voice recordings, notes, and so on. A huge number of people conduct and record their lives (and those who are in communication with them) through their mobile devices, providing a contemporaneous, unfiltered window into the lives of the participants. This can often become fertile ground for cross-examination many months, sometimes years later, when the content has long been forgotten by them. This is the evidence that can make or break a pleaded case when what has been said in carefully crafted solicitors letters, client statements or pleadings is tested against the unvarnished reality of the life lived within the family.

10.02 What any one person chooses to say on oath, whether in statement form or the witness box, often pales into insignificance when their social media activity is exposed. The extent of an individual's power and reach through internet use is only as limited as the user's imagination. That imagination provides scope for abuse and exploitation.

10.03 As Cobb J (as he then was) observed In *Re A (Capacity: Social Media and Internet Use: Best Interests)*:

> 'There were particular and unique characteristics of social media networking and internet use which distinguished it from other forms of contact and care. In the online environment, there was significant scope for harassment, bullying, exposure to harmful content, sexual grooming, exploitation, encouragement of self harm, access to dangerous individuals and/or information – all of which might not be so readily apparent if contact was in person.'[1]

10.04 The forensic value of social media content is self-evident (whether it enhances or shatters your case). It provides evidence of the 'real time' encounters, actions, thoughts and feelings most proximate to the allegations in question,

1 *Re A (Capacity: Social Media and Internet Use: Best Interests)* [2019] EWCOP 2.

generally recorded at a point before the investigative and legal process began. Given how long a period may expire between the events in question, the initiating court application and the trial, contemporaneous evidence often becomes the key evidential foundation for the Court to determine who did what, when, why and with what consequences.

> PRACTICE NOTE
>
> The short resume of sample case law in this chapter makes the simple but fundamental point that expectations of the client in terms of the reliability of, and judicial reception and perception of their oral evidence, need to be approached with professional caution and forensic and legal preparation.
>
> No practitioner should go into the trial without a clear understanding of the case law they will seek to rely upon either in protection of their client's case or attack on the opponent's case.
>
> Case law and a proper appreciation of the risks and benefits of contemporaneous social media evidence are the cornerstones of client survival, if not client success.

SAMPLE CASE LIBRARY (WHICH EVERY PRACTITIONER MUST UPDATE)

10.05 As Baroness Hale cautioned in *Re B*:

> '… there are specific risks to which the court must be alive. Allegations of abuse are not being made by a neutral and expert Local Authority which has nothing to gain by making them, but by a parent who is seeking to gain an advantage in the battle against the other parent. This does not mean that they are false but it does increase the risk of misinterpretation, exaggeration or downright fabrication.'[2]

10.06 Peter Jackson J also made some key observations in *Lancashire County Council v The Children & Ors*:

> 'Where repeated accounts are given the court must think carefully about the significance or otherwise of any reported discrepancies. They may arise for a number of reasons. One possibility is of course that they are lies designed to hide culpability. Another is that they are lies told for other reasons. Further possibilities include faulty recollection or confusion at the time of stress or where the importance of accuracy is not fully appreciated, or there may be inaccuracy or mistake in the record-keeping or recollection of the person

2 *Re B* [2008] UKHL 35, [29].

hearing and relaying the account. The possible effect of delay and repeated questioning upon memory should also be considered, as should the effect of one person on hearing accounts given by another. As memory fades, a desire to iron out wrinkles may not be unnatural; a process that might inelegantly be described as "story-creep" may occur without any necessary inferences of bad faith.'[3]

10.07 Whilst not given in the context of family law litigation, all practitioners should make themselves familiar with the line of authority that begins with *Gestmin* and continues to be updated as our use of social media proliferates and outpaces the precedents we have as our library. Artificial intelligence (AI) and manipulated, faked images and communications, will be the next challenge for the family justice system to grapple with.

10.08 In *Gestmin SGPS SA v Credit Suisse (UK) Ltd & Anor* Leggatt J had some very potent things to say about testimony based on memory, which are quoted in full below (we have italicised the phrases that leapt out to us).[4] These words of warning remain apposite over a decade later (by way of example, in *Lachaux v Lachaux* Mr Justice Mostyn considered the guidance in *Gestmin* and approved it[5]).

> 'An obvious difficulty which affects allegations and oral evidence based on recollection of events which occurred several years ago is the unreliability of human memory.
>
> While everyone knows that memory is fallible, I do not believe that the legal system has sufficiently absorbed the lessons of a century of psychological research into the nature of memory and the unreliability of eyewitness testimony. One of the most important lessons of such research is that in everyday life *we are not aware of the extent to which our own and other people's memories are unreliable and believe our memories to be more faithful than they are. Two common (and related) errors are to suppose: (1) that the stronger and more vivid is our feeling or experience of recollection, the more likely the recollection is to be accurate; and (2) that the more confident another person is in their recollection, the more likely their recollection is to be accurate.*
>
> Underlying both these errors is a faulty model of memory as a mental record which is fixed at the time of experience of an event and then fades (more or less slowly) over time. In fact, psychological research has demonstrated that memories are fluid and malleable, being constantly rewritten whenever they are retrieved. This is true even of so-called "flashbulb" memories, that is memories of experiencing or learning of a particularly shocking or traumatic event. (The very description, "flashbulb" memory, is in fact misleading,

3 *Lancashire County Council v The Children & Ors* [2014] EWHC 3 (Fam).
4 *Gestmin SGPS SA v Credit Suisse (UK) Ltd & Anor* [2013] EWHC 3560 (Comm) (15 November 2013).
5 *Lachaux v Lachaux* [2017] EWHC 385 (Fam).

reflecting as it does the misconception that memory operates like a camera or other device that makes a fixed record of an experience.) External information can intrude into a witness's memory, as can his or her own thoughts and beliefs, and both can cause dramatic changes in recollection. Events can come to be recalled as memories which did not happen at all or which happened to someone else (referred to in the literature as a failure of source memory).

Memory is especially unreliable when it comes to recalling past beliefs. *Our memories of past beliefs are revised to make them more consistent with our present beliefs.* Studies have also shown that memory is particularly vulnerable to interference and alteration when a person is presented with new information or suggestions about an event in circumstances where his or her memory of it is already weak due to the passage of time.

The process of civil litigation itself subjects the memories of witnesses to powerful biases. The nature of litigation is such that witnesses often have a stake in a particular version of events. This is obvious where the witness is a party or has a tie of loyalty (such as an employment relationship) to a party to the proceedings. Other, more subtle influences include allegiances created by the process of preparing a witness statement and of coming to court to give evidence for one side in the dispute. A desire to assist, or at least not to prejudice, the party who has called the witness or that party's lawyers, as well as a natural desire to give a good impression in a public forum, can be significant motivating forces.

Considerable interference with memory is also introduced in civil litigation by the procedure of preparing for trial. A witness is asked to make a statement, often (as in the present case) when a long time has already elapsed since the relevant events. *The statement is usually drafted for the witness by a lawyer who is inevitably conscious of the significance for the issues in the case of what the witness does nor does not say. The statement is made after the witness's memory has been "refreshed" by reading documents. The documents considered often include statements of case and other argumentative material as well as documents which the witness did not see at the time or which came into existence after the events which he or she is being asked to recall. The statement may go through several iterations before it is finalised. Then, usually months later, the witness will be asked to re-read his or her statement and review documents again before giving evidence in court. The effect of this process is to establish in the mind of the witness the matters recorded in his or her own statement and other written material, whether they be true or false, and to cause the witness's memory of events to be based increasingly on this material and later interpretations of it rather than on the original experience of the events.*'[6]

6 *Gestmin SGPS SA v Credit Suisse (UK) Ltd & Anor* (n 4) [15]-[20].

PRACTICE NOTE

When one adds the impact of trauma on a victim's ability to process and retain a memory of events and the impact of that trauma on the victim's capacity to recall and retell abusive experiences in court, one begins to see how many barriers there are to live evidence in the witness box being of value in the way we have historically understood it to be.

10.09 Next, see *Re ABC (Children: Overlaying Child),*[7] where Mr Justice Keehan says:

> 'When considering the "wide canvas" of evidence the following section of the speech of Lord Nicholls in *Re H and R (Child Sexual Abuse: Standard of Proof) [1996] 1 FLR 80* remains relevant …
>
> The evidence of the parents and of any other carers is of the utmost importance. It is essential that the court forms a clear assessment of their credibility and reliability. They must have the fullest opportunity to take part in the hearing and the court is likely to place considerable weight on the evidence and the impression it forms of them (see *Re W and another (Non-accidental injury) [2003] [2] FCR 346.*
>
> The process by which the facts are judicially determined is further complicated for the potent reason Leggatt J, as he then was, set out in *Gestmin SGPS SA v Credit Suisse (UK) Ltd & Anor [2013] EWHC 3560 (Comm) (15 November 2013)*, [paragraphs 15- 21] in relation to testimony based on memory:
>
>> "An obvious difficulty which affects allegations and oral evidence based on recollection of events which occurred several years ago is the unreliability of human memory. While everyone knows that memory is fallible, I do not believe that the legal system has sufficiently absorbed the lessons of a century of psychological research into the nature of memory and the unreliability of eyewitness testimony. One of the most important lessons of such research is that in everyday life we are not aware of the extent to which our own and other people's memories are unreliable and believe our memories to be more faithful than they are. Two common (and related) errors are to suppose: (1) that the stronger and more vivid is our feeling or experience of recollection, the more likely the recollection is to be accurate; and (2) that the more confident another person is in their recollection, the more likely their recollection is to be accurate."
>
> Leggat LJ additionally made the following observations as to demeanour in *R (on the application of SS) (Sri Lanka) v The Secretary of State for the Home Department [2018] EWCA Civ 1391*:

7 *Re ABC (Children: Overlaying Child)* [2020] EWFC 57.

> "36. Generally speaking, it is no longer considered that inability to assess the demeanour of witnesses puts appellate judges 'in a permanent position of disadvantage as against the trial judge'.

That is because it has increasingly been recognised that it is usually unreliable and often dangerous to draw a conclusion from a witness's demeanour as to the likelihood that the witness is telling the truth. The reasons for this were explained by MacKenna J in words which Lord Devlin later adopted in their entirety and Lord Bingham quoted with approval:

> "I question whether the respect given to our findings of fact based on the demeanour of the witnesses is always deserved. *I doubt my own ability, and sometimes that of other judges, to discern from a witness's demeanour, or the tone of his voice, whether he is telling the truth. He speaks hesitantly. Is that the mark of a cautious man, whose statements are for that reason to be respected, or is he taking time to fabricate? Is the emphatic witness putting on an act to deceive me, or is he speaking from the fullness of his heart, knowing that he is right? Is he likely to be more truthful if he looks me straight in the face than if he casts his eyes on the ground perhaps from shyness or a natural timidity? For my part I rely on these considerations as little as I can help.*
>
> 40. This is not to say that judges (or jurors) lack the ability to tell whether witnesses are lying. Still less does it follow that there is no value in oral evidence. But research confirms that people do not in fact generally rely on demeanour to detect deception but on the fact that liars are more likely to tell stories that are illogical, implausible, internally inconsistent and contain fewer details than persons telling the truth: see Minzner, 'Detecting Lies Using Demeanor, Bias and Context' (2008) 29 Cardozo LR 2557. *One of the main potential benefits of cross-examination is that skillful questioning can expose inconsistencies in false stories.*"'[8]

10.10 In the case of *Re X (Children: Alleged Physical Abuse)*,[9] HHJ Sharpe summarised the decision of Peter Jackson LJ in *Re S (A Child: Findings of Fact)*,[10] giving the judgment of the court in which the Court of Appeal identified the benefits of adopting a *chronological* structure by which to set out the genesis and subsequent evolution of the accounts given in order to enable a proper evaluation of the cogency and veracity of a child's allegations, particularly in a situation where the process of evidence building has been criticised at trial. HHJ Sharpe quoted this section of Peter Jackson LJ's judgment in *Re S*:

> 'It would in my view have assisted the Judge if he had identified and focused on the chapters of time covered by the evidence. These might conveniently have been arranged under these headings: the background, the first accounts,

8 *Re ABC* (n 7), [18]–[22].
9 *Re X (Children: Alleged Physical Abuse)* [2024] EWFC 305 (B)
10 *Re S (A Child: Findings of Fact)* [2023] EWCA Civ 346.

the ABE process, [the child's] subsequent statements. This approach would have allowed the Judge to focus on the situation [the child] found herself in at various stages and to address [the alleged perpetrator's] case effectively.'[11]

10.11 Given that in any proceedings, a reasonable starting point is that the parties' mobile phones are likely to be an important source of contemporaneous evidence which traverses a number of different medias – written material, pictures, videos, audio, internet searches – this chapter will offer guidance about the use of text messaging, social media and other electronic material.

FIRST PRINCIPLES

10.12 As practitioners, we have all been in situations where a carefully constructed case has been undermined (or destroyed) by the late disclosure of a text message or a social media post. Whilst this risk can usually be anticipated by early directions for discovery, what is less easy to anticipate is how *vast* the data may be and how to hone in on what is relevant and proportionate to the allegations and issue at large.[12] This is particularly daunting in a family 'justice' system buckling under the pressure of the work it faces, with legal aid rates non-existent or derisory for this exercise.

First meeting

10.13 At an initial meeting with your client, whilst trying to get to grips with the strengths and weaknesses of their case, it is important to identify what evidence there is to support or undermine their position so as to enable you to give early, clear advice.

PRACTICE NOTE

Inviting your client to guide you through their mobile phones – text messages, social media accounts, photographs, and so on – does not represent an intrusion into their lives (arguably, that horse has already bolted given your involvement and it is much better for this preliminary exercise to be undertaken in the privacy of your offices, bound by duties of confidentiality and privilege). This exercise may prove hugely rewarding, yielding a huge amount of information which will require review to distil the relevant from the irrelevant.

Be very VERY careful with how you manage the ethics of this early review. An unscrupulous client may delete that which is shown to you if it becomes

11 *Re S* (n 10), [34].

12 One of the writers has had recent experience of a Finding of Fact Hearing where a huge proportion of the parties' relationship was undertaken by text message. This resulted in a bundle of over 14,000 pages of messages covering every aspect of the parties' relationship.

clear it runs counter to their case. You may need screenshots to be taken and sent to you as, if you have seen something that runs counter to your client's case and they later deny its existence you may be compromised in continuing to act for them. Make sure that you not only give a warning regarding not deleting data but that you record that warning in writing and have it signed by the client.

10.14 What may have started life as an innocuous text message[13] or a social media post several years earlier may now carry a very different meaning some years later, especially in the context of cases in which controlling and coercive behaviour is alleged. If there are text messages or other media on the device, it is important that this data is secured promptly and exhibited to any narrative statement.

PRACTICE NOTE

The importance of prompt and efficient disclosure is multi-layered:

1. It alerts the other side and the Court at the earliest possible stage that this material is available, thereby allowing the Court to exercise its case management powers in a timely and efficient manner.
2. It provides the client with a proper opportunity to explain to the Court why this material is relevant to the issues which the Court is going to have to determine.
3. The downside is that it can lead to a tit for tat 'show and tell' of selective texts which can only be properly evaluated when the surrounding data is known – and that may not be so beneficial for your client. Context is everything.

Procedure

10.15 In cases where domestic abuse (DA) is alleged, the complainant will be required to file and serve a statement in order to provide the Court with sufficient detail to enable the Court to consider the necessity of a Finding of Fact Hearing (see **Chapter 14**). In reality, this provides the first real opportunity to place details of the relevant evidence before the Court, including screenshots of any messages or social media posts and any audio/visual material. *It is unlikely that the totality of the electronic material will be capable of being filed, served and exhibited at this stage.*

13 Screenshots of text messages which are not – or cannot – be supported by the actual device should be viewed with some scepticism. A single internet search will reveal a number of websites where convincing screenshots can be created – right down to the date, time and network.

PRACTICE NOTE

- The Court is unlikely to have sufficient time to explore this evidence in detail at a preliminary stage given the pressures on listing and the raft of case management issues that need to be grappled with at either the first hearing or subsequent case management hearing. However, sometimes the Court is particularly alive to the issues in the case and is able to list the matter for an appropriate duration to enable it to grapple with the issues.
- Keep the initial statement succinct, drawing the Court's attention to the evidence which is available and that which might need to be made available by focused directions.

10.16 If the totality of the electronic evidence is not known/capable of being adduced within the initial statement (either due to volume or the need for it to be extracted professionally), an application should be made for the Court to adjudicate upon it – preferably at a hearing which is already listed.

PRACTICE NOTE

- Think about the window of time that will be most relevant to the issues that need to be determined (proportionality) as they may affect the welfare decision for the children (necessity).
- If the parties' relationship was of some length, the relevance/necessity/proportionality test is going to be a high hurdle to surmount. Perhaps, consider a time frame or a key word search. Prepare your answer as the Court will want to know how you intend to do this.
- Obtain the client's signed instructions on this application. Advise the client that only they know what is on their device at this stage and it is they who need to have confidence it will tell the story they say it does. Every text has at least two 'bank' sources – held by the sender and the receiver – what will its mirror image say?
- Give the client the option to backtrack before making the application. If they proceed, make it their decision. Warn them you can only give advice on the basis of what they tell you.
- If your opponent is the first to raise media disclosure, put the test to them to meet: necessity, proportionality, relevance, cost, a right to rebuttal.
- It shouldn't be a fishing expedition. Consider what has been served to platform the application – is there an application/statement/Practice Direction compliant document setting out how such disclosure is relevant to the issues which the Court is being invited to determine and is there some merit in their argument?

PHOTOGRAPHS, VIDEOS AND AUDIO

10.17 It was Cesar Romero who once said that 'the camera never lies' and it is true that the advent of photography has allowed light to be cast where there only used to be darkness: a picture can tell a story absent any words. *But* technology has advanced beyond Cesar Romero's dreams (or nightmares). Pictures can (and do) lie – revenge porn, superimposed images and sophisticated edit functions have changed the raw images' potential.

10.18 Similarly, video footage and audio can be captured surreptitiously, at the touch of a button. Children and adults can be recorded and often are clandestinely, or they are set up.

10.19 The use of photographs, video footage and audio in evidence can be compelling: instead of merely relying on statements written through lawyers long after the events in question, the Court can relive the parties' experiences by watching or listening to recordings of an incident or seeing in vivid detail the injuries sustained or damage caused during a domestically abusive incident. The words – with the accompanying aggression, vitriol and hatred – sounding out from a recording can be illuminating.

10.20 Consideration ought to be given to obtaining transcripts of any video or audio recordings in order to assist the Court follow the evidence. Invariably, the obtaining of transcripts will require a direction from the Court, particularly if the costs of preparing such transcripts are to be considered a reasonable, necessary and proportionate disbursement upon the legal aid certificates of at least one of the parties.

PRACTICE NOTE

If one of the parties does not have legal aid, that party may not be able to contribute towards the costs of the evidence that the court is directing. In those circumstances, it falls to the Court to undertake an assessment of that party's financial circumstances. If this party is the victim of DA, steps should be taken to ensure that this exercise is not undertaken in the full glare of a hearing where the perpetrator can legitimately access details about their victim's financial circumstances.

All the above assumes English is the first language of the user. If it is not, translation costs will need to be contemplated.

Another practical issue which is often overlooked is the need for the Court to be able to access the evidence: equipment available in the courtroom is not always capable of playing video footage or audio recordings. Such facilities must be available for the Court to consider the evidence, as well as provide the parties with an opportunity to explain it whilst giving evidence.

PROVENANCE

10.21 In this technological age, good provenance of social media data cannot be assumed. Smartphones now offer the ability to edit messages for a short period of time after they have been sent with some common messaging platforms allowing sent messages to be deleted for all users in the event it has been delivered to the recipient but not yet read.

10.22 Even more concerning, there are a number of web-based platforms which allow people to 'fake' text messages so that they are completely indiscernible from authentic screenshots. In the authors' experience this can and does happen. By way of a recent example, in a public law case a parent appended to a statement a copy of a 'screenshot' of a text message they had allegedly received from a professional in order to prove that the individual had kept a particular appointment. It looked genuine but no trace of the message could be found on either the sender or receiver's mobile and ultimately it transpired that one of the parties had manufactured it using an internet 'mock up' site. It was only because the author was aware of the possibility of such websites being used that the issue was pursued with some degree of determination.

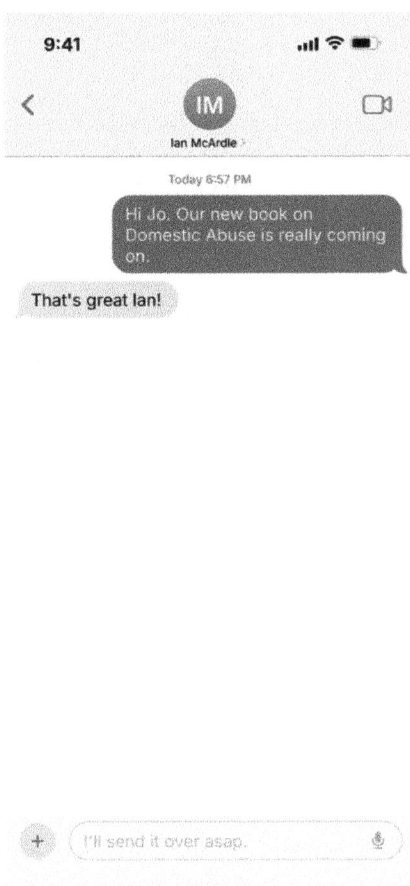

10.23 In light of these technological advances, it is therefore essential that, when receiving text messages (whether they are from your client in support of their case, or from the other side seeking to advance their own position), their provenance must be carefully considered. Was the date and time an auto stamp or is it a client set system (look and check). Of course, if the Court ultimately concludes that the text messages or other media adduced in evidence have been altered or falsified in order to affect the overall narrative, the implications are pretty obvious. Above is an example of a screenshot created using a website which was found in seconds. It is not an actual text message exchange between two of the authors of this book but highlights how easy – and how convincing – this can be.

PRACTICE NOTE

Applications to see mobile data need not always be planned. They can be part of an 'ambush' cross-examination.

It is not unknown (and it is something at least two of the authors of this book have done more than once) to ask to see the opposing party's mobile device when they are in the witness box, asking them to unlock it and hand it over, for example to check if contact was maintained with a victim after a non-molestation order was made forbidding it.

If they refuse to comply, make it plain, there and then, to the witness and to the judge, that you will be inviting the Court to draw an adverse inference from their refusal. Then reissue the request to the witness.

THE OVERLAP BETWEEN CRIME AND FAMILY

10.24 There are those cases where the information held on a mobile device is of such critical evidential importance that it requires professional extraction, or has already been the subject of a criminal investigation. If there is a parallel police investigation (that has not yet concluded or is waiting for the trial in the Family Court to complete) then you are going to face potential objection from the police to disclosure pre-charge.

PRACTICE NOTE

The police may also have been selective in their search terms in a way that is not compatible with the broad remit of the Family Court. Do not assume what the police think is relevant to a possible prosecution encompasses all of your client's interests. Check the criteria applied. What search terms were used? What period was covered? What people/contact numbers were scoped in the search? What images were the focus? Often, the family practitioner will want to see the aftermath of the key incident not just the build up. It may save a lot of time waiting for an incomplete product if you know pre-receipt that it will need to be redone.

10.25 It is a herculean task to gain access to mobile phones held by the police in order to extract the data independently for the family proceedings if the phone data download has not yet been completed by the police. The police will not want anything done to the mobile phone/device which could contaminate the integrity of the evidential source.

10.26 The Court of Appeal (CA) gave guidance on the correct procedure for extracting relevant social media evidence in public law proceedings, particularly when the extraction is not performed by the police. In *Re P, H-L (Children) (Mobile Phone Extraction)* the CA considered how the rights of third parties should be protected when data and material are extracted from parties' mobile phones following the instruction of a mobile phone expert.[14] The CA acknowledged that the Family Procedure Rules 2010 (SI 2010/2955) do not provide a complete framework within which the answers to every question can be found and, where there is a gap, recourse is to be had, where appropriate, to the Civil Procedure Rules 1998 (SI 1998/3132) which provide a more detailed code for disclosure and inspection of documents.

10.27 King LJ cited the President's guidance in *Re H-N & Ors (Children) (Domestic Abuse: Finding of Fact Hearings)* but drew a distinction between the President's disapproval of the Family Court importing criminal concepts and principles and the adoption of practices tried and tested in the criminal court such as the scope of cross-examination.[15] In the latter, good practice in the Crown Court could be drawn upon in the Family Court. King LJ held that, where there is insufficient or absent guidance, this type of procedural matter (extracting mobile phone data involving third parties) was one where a judge could draw upon good practice in the criminal court in order to inform the conduct of the Family Court proceedings.

10.28 The CA endorsed the reference to the *Attorney General Guidelines on Disclosure 2013*,[16] but cautioned against the need to 'painstakingly go through Annex A of the AG Guidelines'[17] reminding practitioners that:

> '... Rather, the court's focus will be on the relevance of the material as a whole and in making case management orders which are not only proportionate in terms of cost and management, but which also protect so far as is possible the privacy rights of any third parties in much the same way as is done by the police under the AG Guidelines.'[18]

14 *Re P, H-L (Children) (Mobile Phone Extraction)* [2023] EWCA Civ 206.

15 *Re H-N & Ors (Children) (Domestic Abuse: Finding of Fact Hearings)* [2021] EWCA Civ 448.

16 *Attorney General Guidelines on Disclosure 2013* (gov.uk, 2013), https://www.gov.uk/government/publications/attorney-generals-guidelines-on-disclosure-2013.

17 *Re P, H-L (Children) (Mobile Phone Extraction)* (n 14), [65].

18 *Re P, H-L (Children) (Mobile Phone Extraction)* (n 14).

10.29 Ultimately, the CA endorsed the need for a proportionate approach to be taken to mobile phone extraction, for example, extraction covering only the period of time which is required, with there also being a requirement for the extraction report to undergo any sift for relevance or any redaction.

10.30 Whilst this decision emanated from the public law arena of children law, it is likely that the principles arising from it will also be applied in the private law arena, given the comments made by King LJ at [69] that 'contentious litigation in all jurisdictions is having to find ways to deal with the avalanche of material downloaded from mobile phones and social media sites'.[19]

10.31 In private law proceedings, we would suggest that such a process would be best undertaken by those instructed on behalf of the child (assuming that the Court has determined that the child should be joined to the proceedings) given their neutrality within the proceedings.

FINAL WORD

10.32 Gone are the days when the Court only had oral evidence to rely upon when making significant decisions. The Court now has the benefit of receiving evidence in a variety of forms. Used correctly, text messages, social media posts, photographs and other forms of electronic evidence provide the Court with a unique and detailed insight into the lives and behaviours of the parties before it.

10.33 The proper use of this evidence can be instrumental in the Court preferring one case over another and can provide a telling insight into the parties' conduct when they are away from the court arena.

19 *Re P, H-L (Children) (Mobile Phone Extraction)* (n 14), [69].

CHAPTER 11

Covert Recording

'Advances in technology empower anyone with a mobile phone or a tablet to make recordings that would be the envy of yesterday's spies.'[1]

11.01 We live in a technological age. An age where someone's every movement can be monitored, recorded and broadcast for the world to see in a matter of seconds. Whilst we have considered the evolution of technology in the Family Court in the context of intimate images, there is another area which is also problematic and likely to be more widespread (if it is not already). Whilst the use of covert recordings in the Family Court can offer significant evidential value and allow the Court to survey a wider canvas in terms of the relationships it has to consider, the harm that such recordings can cause can be widespread and significant.

11.02 There are many reasons why someone would want to record their interactions with others and professionals, particularly when they anticipate imminent court proceedings or are wishing to collate evidence for future court proceedings or for some other purpose. Such reasons can include a desire to secure an accurate (and immediate) account of a meeting, allowing them to challenge inaccuracies in official minutes as well as gathering evidence for use in contemplated court proceedings.

11.03 It was in 2016 that Mr Justice Peter Jackson (as he then was) uttered the words quoted above. The following year, the former President of the Family Division, Sir James Munby, gave the lead judgment in the case of *Re B (A Child)*.[2] In this case, the Court of Appeal was given some assistance by the Association of Lawyers for Children and the Transparency Project, the latter having already offered some general guidance in December 2015.[3] However, concerned by the absence of any authoritative guidance, the Court of Appeal emphasised the need for:

'consideration to be given to what is a topic of growing significance for family courts in relation to which there is, at present, surprisingly little authority and no adequate guidance.'[4]

1 *M v F (Covert Recording of Children)* [2016] EWFC 29, [1].
2 *Re B (A Child)* [2017] EWCA Civ 1579.
3 *Parents Recording Social Workers – A Guidance Note for Parents and Professionals* (The Transparency Project, 2015), https://transparencyproject.org.uk/guidance-on-parents-recording-meetings-with-social-workers-2/. (Now withdrawn.)
4 The Transparency Project (n 3), para 35.

11.04 Specifically, the Court of Appeal extended an invitation to the Family Justice Council to take the first step and consider the whole question of covert recording from a multi-disciplinary viewpoint. In May 2025, the Family Justice Council released guidance entitled, *Family Justice Council Guidance on Covert Recordings in Family Law proceedings concerning children.*[5] This publication is of enormous aid in an area of litigation which was previously uncharted territory. It is expected that this will merely be the first of many publications to tackle this issue; the President of the Family Division, Sir Andrew McFarlane, stated in his foreword to the guidance that:

> 'This has been a growing area for the courts to consider with little guidance available to judges or other professionals. This guidance from the Family Justice Council (FJC) explores the issues and examines the consequences arising from the use of covert recordings by private individuals and sets out guidance that we hope will lead to greater consistency in approach.
>
> Whilst some covert recordings have been found to have evidential value, the secret nature of covert recordings can intrude on the privacy of parents, children and professionals, causing harm and often leading to concerns about the accuracy of the recording. It is hoped that this guidance will encourage professional bodies and organisations in the Family Justice System to consider developing their own guidance on the use of covert and overt recordings.'[6]

11.05 Covert recording is often a feature of cases in which domestic abuse (DA) is alleged – it can serve to evidence domestically abusive behaviour as well as expose professional viewpoints on contentious issues. The purpose of this chapter is not to encourage the use of covert recording but rather offer a commentary of the law as it currently stands and seek to guide practitioners through the all-too-uncomfortable territory of a client revealing that they have a cache of covert recordings which they seek to rely upon in proceedings.

PRACTICE NOTE

It is useful to be aware of the four appendixes attached to the Family Justice Council guidance:

- Appendix 1: Summary of General Principles and Case Management considerations.
- Appendix 2: Nagalro Guidance on Recording Meetings between a Practitioner and Client with Template Letters.

5 Family Justice Council, *Family Justice Council Guidance on Covert Recordings in Family Law proceedings concerning children* (May 2025), https://www.judiciary.uk/wp-content/uploads/2025/05/Covert-recordings-in-Family-Law-proceedings-concerning-children-Family-Justice-Council-Guidance.pdf.

6 Family Justice Council (n 5), p 4.

- Appendix 3: Guidance relating to case management of intimate images: Extract from *M (A Child: Private Law Children Proceedings: Case Management: Intimate Images)* [2022] EWHC 986 (Fam).
- Appendix 4: Summary Guidance for Litigants in family proceedings.

Appendix 4 is likely to be particularly useful as a guide you can recommend to clients.

WHAT IS A COVERT RECORDING?

11.06 Covert recordings are, quite simply, 'any recordings made without the express knowledge and permission of the people being recorded, whether by video or audio'.[7] In this day and age, it is relatively easy to covertly record conversations on devices which many of us carry around on a daily basis, and which may be easily concealed. Or, a simple Google search reveals a vast array of devices capable of being concealed inside clothing, teddy bears or within the home environment.

11.07 Within the Family Court, experience tells us that the issue of covert recording is more likely to arise during a private law dispute, when levels of trust and co-operation between separating parents are at an all-time low. However, it can also arise in the public law arena.

11.08 A common form of covert recording in the private law sphere is likely to include handovers of contact. Those of us who deal with such cases will no doubt recall many clients explaining to us that they feel insecure and unsafe when meeting with their former partner to conduct handovers with their child and have resorted to recording the handover on their mobile phone, which is secreted in their pocket. Covert recordings can also evidence incidents of DA, or simply provide the Court with an unadulterated and raw view of a party's (or witness's) demeanour away from the glare of the Court.

11.09 Covert recordings will be considered hearsay evidence, and the recordings will be considered as 'documents' to which evidential rules apply. Only when it is the act of recording covertly, rather than a reliance upon the contents of the recording, that is being relied upon are the rules relating to hearsay unlikely to be applicable.

THE THREE TYPES OF COVERT RECORDING

11.10 In the Family Justice Council's guidance, three distinct types of covert recordings are identified:

7 Family Justice Council (n 5), para 1.2.

(a) the covert recording of professionals;

(b) the covert recording of other family members; and

(c) the covert recording of children.[8]

Covert recording: professionals

11.11 The Family Justice Council have identified the following examples of reasons why a parent may engage in the covert recording of a professional during family proceedings:

> '• They do not trust or do not want to rely on the notes of the meeting and/or they may not want to wait for the notes of the meeting to be sent to them. It may be that they have previous experiences of not having received any notes when others have, or received notes that they do agree with. They may have found it hard to challenge inaccuracies or omissions in the past;
>
> • They want to gather evidence for later use in court proceedings;
>
> • They want to use recording for other reasons, such as to circulate information as part of a campaign, for example on social media. This might not be their original intention when making the recording.'[9]

11.12 Anecdotally, the covert recording of professionals is highly likely to create a deep sense of unease when in family proceedings, with far-reaching ramifications for the lay client who has undertaken the covert recording (see later in this chapter). However, it is the covert recording of professionals that highlighted the way in which evidence obtained covertly can significantly alter not only judicial perspectives of a case but also the outcomes. This was brought into sharp focus in the case of *Medway Council v A & Ors (Learning Disability)*.[10]

11.13 In this case, the mother had a learning disability and was placed, alongside her baby, in a poorly matched foster placement. A number of allegations were made by the local authority about the mother's conduct in the foster placement, which formed part of the Court's adjudication at the final hearing. At the final hearing, it became apparent that the mother had covertly recorded the foster carer and a number of covert recordings and transcripts were adduced which proved instrumental in the dismissal of the allegations. The circuit judge made these comments in her judgment:

> 'It is salutary and sobering to consider that there are many children in foster care, and many parents in parent and baby foster placements, and there will be occasions when parents complain about their treatment in those placements, but that it is the frequent practice in care proceedings not to require the foster carer to attend court, but to rely upon their notes and the

8 Family Justice Council (n 5), para 1.4.

9 Family Justice Council (n 5), para 3.2.

10 *Medway Council v A & Ors (Learning Disability)* [2015] EWFC B66; See also *Re F (Care Proceedings: Failure of Expert)* [2016] EWHC 2149 (Fam).

social worker's evidence. In the light of *Re A 2015* and *Re J 2015*, and an example such as this case, it will be all the more important to consider with a sharp focus the nature of the evidence that the court needs to consider, and best evidence in particular. In this case, the parents' allegations were frankly treated dismissively from the outset. But for this court's willingness to permit the consideration and transcription of the records, despite the extreme lateness that they were provided, in combination with the requirement that the foster carer attend to give evidence … it would have been impossible to gain a just and proper understanding of this case.'[11]

11.14 Indeed, it has become clear in recent years that professionals may not always carry out their work to an adequate standard. Candidly, in the aforementioned case of *Re B*, Munby P (as he then was) stated that:

> 'It needs to be accepted, with honesty and candour, that there have been in recent years in the family courts shocking examples of professional malpractice which have been established only because of the covert recording of the relevant individual …'[12]

11.15 Whilst the possibility of professional malpractice must remain a possibility – as has been demonstrated by a number of reported cases – the starting point for the Court ought to be that a professional has acted properly and they should be able to defend whatever they say because they are working to a professional standard and likely subject to professional regulation.

11.16 CAFCASS gives advice to its practitioners that they should always be transparent in their work and there is no legal reason why a parent should not record their own interview.[13] However, CAFCASS advises that, if a recording is made, the Family Court adviser should inform the parent that they will include in their report that the interview was recorded.[14] This would flag the presence of the recording to the other party (parties) as well as the Court.

11.17 Whilst the recording of a meeting with a professional should not be necessary, there are occasions when the recording of such a meeting has probative evidential value.

Covert recording: individuals

11.18 There are additional reasons why separating parents will covertly record each other, or their children. These can include that:

11 *Medway Council v A & Ors (Learning Disability)* (n 10), [114].
12 *Re B (A Child)* (n 2), [12].
13 Family Justice Council, *Draft Covert Recordings in Family Law Proceedings Concerning Children: Family Justice Council Guidance*, https://www.nagalro.com/_userfiles/pages/files/covert_recording_guidance_for_consultation_final_91122.pdf, p 6.
14 Family Justice Council (n 13).

- there may be a history of allegations being made of a domestically abusive nature and therefore, the covert recording serves to offer some protection from allegations;
- they want to gather evidence for later use.

11.19 This issue is more likely to arise in the context of a private law dispute between separated parents and is particularly relevant in cases where there are allegations of DA which are a live issue before the Court. In many such cases, whilst the Court may try and provide for interim arrangements for contact which are safe for all concerned, there may be times when the parents come into contact with each other. As mentioned at the beginning of this chapter, a key example is child arrangements handovers. During those periods, either party may feel the need to covertly record the handover in order to offer themselves a degree of protection against the making of further allegations or to evidence the inappropriate behaviour of the other party in furtherance of their own case before the Court.

11.20 It has been acknowledged by the Court of Appeal that the use of covert recording can be a form of abuse and amount to intimidation. In the case of *Re C*, the father had covertly recorded handovers and discussions with the mother.[15] Whilst the father had previously agreed not to record handovers, he reneged on that agreement and continued to do so. The recordings (along with transcripts) were adduced but it became apparent that the recordings had been edited as they did not match the transcripts which had been prepared.

PRACTICE NOTE

As with other forms of digital evidence, care must be taken by practitioners when reviewing evidence produced by parties. It is prudent to pay close attention to time stamps, metadata and other anomalies which may be indicators of tampering.

Although no official guidance on identifying tampered-with evidence in the Family Court has been published, it may be useful to refer to **Chapter 10** ('Taking Instructions and Gathering Evidence') where this issue is explored in more detail. It is the authors' hope that, as evidence tampering becomes increasingly easy to achieve through websites and editing technology, authoritative guidance on identifying fake evidence will soon be published.

11.21 The Court of Appeal held that covert recording can be a form of abuse, albeit a form of abuse that is highly fact-specific, with the Court going further to say that a party cannot simply argue that because the recording was covert, it could not be capable of causing harm or amounting to abuse. Specifically, the Court of Appeal stated that:

15 *Re C* [2015] EWCA Civ 1096.

> 'The District Judge, having had the benefit of reading the Recorder's finding of fact judgment and her findings in relation to the previous recordings as well as having heard the parties give evidence, was in my judgment, entitled to conclude that the use of recording equipment in the context of the case overall amounts to a form of intimidation and is abusive and is therefore capable of being the subject of an injunction. The danger of such recordings as an evidential tool can be seen in the use the father made of them in the earlier hearings.'[16]

PRACTICE NOTE

It is important to note that the covert recording of someone else can give rise to DA injunctions, as noted above in *Re C*. If a client becomes subject to an application for the admission of covert recording, carefully consider whether the conduct of the recording person would justify an injunction such as a non-molestation order (see **Chapter 9**). Equally, if your client is the recording person, it would be wise to be prepared to defend an application for an injunction from the other side.

Covert recording: children

11.22 At the heart of every private law dispute lies a child, or children. They are often viewed (wrongly) as the pawn in the game. Often, one (or both) of the parents lose sight of the child and become so embroiled in the dispute with the other party that they may try to involve the child in covert recording.

11.23 The harm which can be occasioned to the child – as well as the Court's perception of the parents – and the consequences of covert recording were illustrated in the case of *M v F (Covert Recording of Children).*[17] In this case, the father's partner sewed recording devices into the lining of the child's clothing in order to record conversations. A number of meetings with professionals were also covertly recorded.

11.24 Insofar as the proceedings were concerned, Peter Jackson J made a number of observations about the consequences for the proceedings 'of a large mass of material being produced at a late stage'.[18] In this particular case, Peter Jackson J pointed out that the following were the outcomes of the father's attempt to rely upon covert recordings:

(a) The covert recordings further damaged the relationships between the adults in his child's life.

16 *Re C* (n 15), [59].
17 *M v F (Covert Recording of Children)* (n 1).
18 *M v F (Covert Recording of Children)* (n 1), [5].

(b) It highlighted to the Court the father's inability to trust professionals.

(c) It created a secret which may affect the child's relationship in the future both with her father and stepmother.

(d) It put at risk the family's standing in the community since those who interacted with the child are not likely to react positively to the discovery that they may have been captured on covert recordings.

(e) The covert recordings involved an enormous waste of time, especially due to the need to transcribe the recordings.

(f) Since none of the recordings ended up being of benefit to the father in his submissions, he wasted a significant amount of legal costs including having to pay £1,500 for the recordings to be transcribed and being ordered to pay £9,240 to the mother for time wasted.

11.25 Ultimately, the father's recordings disclosed no useful information at all and, instead, led the Court to decide that the child should be moved to the care of her mother instead since the father was clearly incapable of meeting his child's emotional needs as a primary carer.[19]

11.26 Objectively, all of these consequences are applicable to any case in which covert recordings fall to be considered. It is the balance to be struck between these consequences and the evidential value of the recordings which will inform any decision as to whether covert recordings should be adduced.

11.27 In a more recent example, Mr Justice Poole in *Re A (A Child) (Hague Convention: Wrongful Retention)* dismissed the father's application to rely on recordings of contact between the father and the child on the basis that:

> '… they had been made covertly and the father had sole control over what was recorded and could have steered recorded conversations with his child to suit his purpose. Hence, the evidence would be of very little weight. Further, the use of covert recordings, including of contact with a child, was a breach of trust with the child and the other parent and should be strongly discouraged by the court.'[20]

11.28 It is unclear if Poole J listened to the recordings as part of his evaluation that the recordings held little evidential weight. Nevertheless, the factors identified by the Court (the father having sole control over what was recorded and could steer the conversation) are part and parcel of the Court's consideration regarding the weight to be given to the recording.

11.29 Ultimately, however, whilst covert recording does represent a breach of trust, this does not in of itself render it inadmissible or of limited weight. It may

19 *M v F (Covert Recording of Children)* (n 1), [4].
20 *Re A (A Child) (Hague Convention: Wrongful Retention)* [2021] EWHC 1204 (Fam), [20].

prove significant in informing the overall welfare analysis and/or, in the words of HHJ Lazarus in *Medway Council v A & Ors (Learning Disability)*, offer the Court 'a just and proper understanding of the case'.[21]

PRACTICE NOTE

In the context of a case in which there are allegations of DA, the Court should be invited to give careful consideration to the evidential value of the covert recording before arriving at a summary determination regarding its weight. In a case where coercive and controlling behaviour is alleged, the Court may find valuable evidence in covert recordings which assist it in seeing – through a clearer lens – the true relationship between the parties.

ARE COVERT RECORDINGS LAWFUL?

11.30 The consideration of covert recordings in this section relates to the covert recording of conversations between individuals and meetings involving professionals. It does not refer to the covert recording of court hearings. The recording of a court hearing without permission from the court is strictly prohibited and amounts to a contempt of court pursuant to Contempt of Court Act 1981, s 9. This includes remote hearings.

11.31 There are limited restraints upon private individuals making covert recordings insofar as the law is concerned. All recordings made after 25 May 2018 are now subject to the provisions of the UK General Data Protection Regulation (UK GDPR) (Regulation (EU) 2016/679 of the European Parliament and of the Council), tailored by the Data Protection Act 2018. It is important to note that the making, retention and distribution of a recording constitutes processing personal data.

11.32 However, if personal data (ie recordings) are processed in the course of a purely personal or household activity with no connection to a professional or commercial activity, it will usually be considered outside of the scope of the UK GDPR. In other words, covert recordings made in a family/private context are neither legal nor illegal: their admissibility in family proceedings depends on the discretion of the Court after weighing various factors, an issue which will be explored in more detail later on in this chapter. The legality of a covert recording is, therefore, fact-specific.

11.33 What can be said with definitiveness if that: THE USE OF COVERT RECORDINGS IS NOT TO BE ENCOURAGED. The use of covert recordings in proceedings concerning children can be a game of Russian roulette: whilst on the one hand, the person seeking to adduce covert recordings into evidence may

21 *Medway Council v A & Ors (Learning Disability)* (n 10) [114].

feel particularly strongly that they will be vindicated and the recordings will serve to enhance their case; on the other hand, they may find that the trust the Court, professionals and the other side has in them is irreparably damaged.

11.34 Although potentially outside the scope of the UK GDPR, in the ordinary sense of the words, covert recordings do represent a significant invasion of privacy and are unlikely to promote a child's welfare. Indeed, in the Association of Lawyers for Children's review of the Family Justice Council's draft guidance, it expressed the feeling that the guidance wasn't clear enough in stating that 'covert recording of children, parents and professionals by private individuals in child welfare cases is firmly discouraged'.[22]

11.35 Essentially, if considering recording someone covertly, the starting point should be: don't! As Peter Jackson J said in *M v F (Covert Recording of Children)*:

> 'It is almost always likely to be wrong for a recording device to be placed on a child for the purpose of gathering evidence in family proceedings, whether or not the child is aware of its presence.'[23]

ADDUCING COVERT RECORDINGS

11.36 If a litigant seeks to adduce covert recordings as evidence into proceedings, they should bring the matter to the attention of the Court so that the Court can exercise its case management powers (and do so in a timely manner).

11.37 The party seeking to adduce the covert recordings should make an application to the Court, on notice to the other parties, which provides the following information:

(a) The nature of the recording, with detail as to the context, whether the recording is edited and the date and time of such recording.

(b) The methodology of the recording and why it was obtained covertly.

(c) The relevance of the contents to the issues in the proceedings.[24]

11.38 It is often the case that the person seeking to rely upon the recordings wishes for other professionals involved to listen/view the recordings. If a Family Court adviser from CAFCASS is asked to view or listen to the recordings, the expectation from CAFCASS is that the material should not be viewed or listened to until the Court has determined whether the material is admissible.

22 Association of Lawyers for Children, *Comments and response to the Family Justice Council's draft guidance entitled 'Covert Recordings in Family Law Proceedings Concerning Children'* (12 December 2022), https://www.alc.org.uk/uploads/images/FJC-Covert-recordings-ALC-response-2.pdf.

23 *M v F (Covert Recording of Children)* (n 1), [1].

24 Family Justice Council (n 5), para 4.18.

PRACTICE NOTE

For the avoidance of doubt, the same advice applies to you as a practitioner. Great caution should be taken when deciding whether to view or listen to a covert recording before a decision has been made on admissibility. If in doubt, don't do it. Think first and think through the consequences. Reflect on the Family Justice Council procedure set out below at **11.39**. How are you going to engage with this when you are in court. Ask the questions: what is its relevance (see **11.42**) and potential probative value (**11.44**)? Let these issues inform your decision.

PROCEDURE

11.39 The Family Justice Council guidance helpfully sets out the issues which the Court must make directions upon before a proper assessment of admissibility can be made:

- 'The method of disclosure of the recordings to the other parties, including whether transcripts are required.
- Establishing the full scope of the recordings, how they came about, and which recordings fall to be considered.
- Establishing authenticity if in dispute, including any issues relating to editing.
- Establishing the probative value of the recordings to relevant issues in dispute.
- Consideration of implications for the welfare of the parties, and in particular the child if having been the subject of covert recordings.
- Consideration of costs arising from the application.
- Any further hearing to determine the issue of admissibility.'[25]

11.40 Transcripts of any recordings may be a useful tool for the Court. However, transcription can be expensive and for this to be considered a reasonable, necessary and proportionate disbursement upon any legal aid certificate, an order from the Court will be required.

11.41 The importance of case management and early decision-making cannot be understated. Indeed, some of the principles set out by Knowles J in the case of *Re M (A Child: Private Law Children Proceedings: Case Management: Intimate Images)*, discussed in **Chapter 7,** are equally applicable here.[26]

25 Family Justice Council (n 5), para 4.3.
26 *Re M (A Child: Private Law Children Proceedings: Case Management: Intimate Images)* [2022] EWHC 986 (Fam).

Relevance

11.42 Before the Court engages in full consideration of the recordings themselves, it should be satisfied that the content of the recording is relevant to the issues to be determined in proceedings. The test for deciding 'relevance' was expressed by the House of Lords in *Director of Public Prosecutions v Kilbourne*:

> 'Your Lordships have been concerned with four concepts in the law of evidence: (i) relevance; (ii) admissibility; (iii) corroboration; (iv) weight. The first two terms are frequently, and in many circumstances legitimately, used interchangeably; but I think it makes for clarity if they are kept separately, since some relevant evidence is inadmissible and some admissible evidence is irrelevant … *Evidence is relevant if it is logically probative or disprobative of some matter which requires proof.*'[27]

11.43 The use of covert recording may not just be relevant to the subject matter of the recording. The relevance may lie in the conduct of the person who recorded covertly and/or in relation to the child's welfare. However, just because the Court has found the covert recording to be relevant, that does not mean that any 'weight' will be attached to it.[28] The following factors must also be considered.

Probative value

11.44 If the covert recording has been found to be relevant, the next issue to consider is whether it has any probative value. The Family Justice Council indicates that this involves two questions:

- Does the recording go to proving what was either said or done by the subject of the recording?
- Does the recording go to proving the truth of something said?[29]

11.45 This isn't to say that caution should be thrown to the wind if one of these questions is answered positively. One must still consider the context of the recording and whether what was said was manipulated in any way by the recorder, for example by asking specifically worded questions. But generally speaking, as stated in *Singh v Singh & Ors:*

> 'There can be great value in what is said in such circumstances, where the parties plainly know the truth of the matters they are discussing and are talking (at least on one side) freely about them.'[30]

27 *Director of Public Prosecutions v Kilbourne* [1973] 1 All ER 440, emphasis added.
28 See *Re B (A Child)* (n 2).
29 Family Justice Council (n 5), para 4.26.
30 *Singh v Singh & Ors* [2016] EWHC 1432 (Ch), [11].

Authenticity

11.46 As noted previously in regard to *Re C*, the Court must also consider whether the covert recording is authentic.[31] This will involve interrogating various aspects of the nature of the recording, including:

- *Its length* – if the recording is merely an isolated section of a conversation/action, rather than a recording of the entire interaction between the recorder and another individual, this may raise alarm bells.
- *Metadata* – whether the original metadata is still intact or whether there is evidence of it having been edited.
- *Timestamps* – whether the timestamp on the recording matches the date/time on which the recorder claims it was made. Indeed, ask yourself whether the date is even one that exists (for example, if a recording has been dated the 30 February this may indicate the tampering of evidence!).

11.47 It may be that the other party (who may also be the subject of the recording) disputes authenticity. In this context, the Court must consider the validity of their arguments.

PRACTICE NOTE

At this point, the Court may order that an independent expert create a transcript of the covert recording. Having a transcript of an original recording can be extremely useful where, later on in proceedings, a party accuses another of tampering with the evidence *during* proceedings, or – God forbid – the recording is 'lost'.

Furthermore, it is worth bearing in mind that, where covert recordings are particularly voluminous or complex, the Court may order a forensic expert to report on its authenticity. This will inevitably have a huge impact on costs and so the client should be informed of this possibility early on if you think this is likely.

How the recording was obtained

11.48 It has already been noted that covert recordings are, per se, neither lawful nor unlawful – it depends on the context. However, the Court does have the power to find a covert recording inadmissible if it considers that it was obtained through unlawful means.

11.49 This is by no means an easy task:

31 Do refer to **Chapter 10** for a recap on the tampering of evidence.

'In exercising that power, the court will be guided by what is "necessary for disposing fairly of the [proceedings]", and will take into account the importance of the evidence, "the conduct of the parties", and any other relevant factors, including the normal case management aspects. Ultimately, this requires the court to carry out a balancing exercise.'[32]

11.50 The Information Commissioner's Office (ICO) has elaborated upon this test. According to the ICO, there will be a lawful basis for a covert recording where:

- there is a 'legitimate interest', or 'purpose' for the covert recording;
- the making and sharing of the recording is necessary for this purpose; and
- within a balancing exercise, the importance of this purpose overrides the interests of the individual who is the subject of the recording.[33]

THE DECISION OF THE COURT

11.51 It is a balancing of all of the aforementioned factors which will influence the Court's decision upon whether a covert recording should be admitted as evidence.

PRACTICE NOTE

As a practitioner it would be wise to base your submissions regarding covert recordings (whether in favour of admission or not) upon the aforementioned factors. Demonstrate that you have engaged with the tests. Make your agreement based on them. Give the judge a toolkit to follow. Do the hard work for them because this will be an anxiety-provoking application.

SPECIFIC CONSIDERATIONS WHERE CHILDREN ARE INVOLVED

11.52 Should the Court admit a covert recording of a child/children as evidence, there will be further issues for you to resolve in your role as a practitioner.

11.53 Firstly, where the subject of a covert recording is a child (or children), thought will need to go into how the child is informed of the existence of such evidence (if indeed it is deemed appropriate to inform them at all). Whilst

32 *Imerman v Tchenguiz* [2010] EWCA Civ 908; [2011] 1 All ER 555, [177].

33 Information Commissioner's Office, 'Step 4: Access Necessity and Proportionality', https://ico.org.uk/for-organisations/uk-gdpr-guidance-and-resources/childrens-information/childrens-code-guidance-and-resources/dpia-tools/online-retail/step-4-assess-necessity-and-proportionality/. Please note that this guidance is due to be updated after this book goes to print, following the Data (Use and Access) Act 2025 which came into force on 19 June 2025.

conducting research, the Family Justice Council interviewed young people to ascertain how they would feel if they discovered a parent had covertly recorded them. The results were overwhelmingly negative, with young people expressing feelings of:

> '... betrayal and discomfort, raised concerns about the clear potential for manipulation and coercion, seeing such recordings as a breach of trust and violation.'[34]

11.54 Bearing this in mind, it is clear that the child's welfare must be considered when deciding how, when and crucially, *if*, they should be informed of the existence of such recordings.

11.55 Firstly, the Court will need to decide whether it is appropriate that the child is informed at all. This will involve the consideration of a variety of factors including:

- whether informing the child is likely to cause more harm than not doing so;
- whether knowledge of the covert recordings is likely to damage the child's relationship with one or both of their parents; and
- the likelihood that the child will discover the existence of the covert recording through another means in the future – such a discovery could greatly impact the child's trust in the justice system and indeed, their parents.

11.56 The latter was a key consideration in *M v F*:

> 'She is also at risk of harm arising from the recordings. I accept the Guardian's compelling assessment that it would be extremely damaging for Tara if the information comes to her in future in some uncontrolled way, something that is likely to cause her confusion or distress and seriously affect her ability to trust people ...'[35]

11.57 Once a decision has been made upon whether the child should be informed, the manner in which they are informed will need to be considered.

PRACTICE NOTE

Think about *where* the child should be informed, *who* should be present, the *level of detail* required to be communicated and the *phrasing* of this information, preferably in a way which minimises the damage this could have upon the child's relationship with their parents. Among other things, the age, temperament and character of the child are likely to impact the appropriate answers to these questions.

34 Family Justice Council (n 5), para 8.2.
35 *M v F (Covert Recording of Children)* [2016] EWFC 29; [2016] WLR(D) 275, [5(iii)].

Children take breach of their privacy very seriously. It can make them feel unsafe and let down when they find out they have been recorded. Factor that into the preparation. Are they old enough to demand to see/listen to it? Has there been a decision on that? What is in their best interest?

If the child has a court-appointed children's guardian for the proceedings, the guardian is likely to be able to advise on these issues. If the child does not have a guardian, it may be wise to consider whether an application for the appointment of a guardian should be made.

11.58 Another issue the Court may face following the admission of covert recordings of children is whether the child/children will be required to give oral evidence on the nature and/or authenticity of the recordings. In determining whether this is appropriate the Court will weigh up the importance of the child's evidence against the potential harm to the child in giving such evidence. The Family Justice Council lists the following factors as being relevant to this assessment:

'• The child's wishes and feelings about giving evidence.
- The child's particular needs and abilities.
- The age, maturity, vulnerability, understanding, capacity, and competence of the child.
- The support or lack of support the child has.
- The quality and importance of the child's evidence.
- The views of the guardian who should have discussed the issue with the child and those with parental responsibility.
- The impact that may be had on later care arrangements.'[36]

PRACTICE NOTE

An application for a child to give evidence in relation to a covert recording should be made on the C2 Form. One of the first things the Court will do in response to such an application is to urgently consider whether the child requires legal representation and/or should be appointed a guardian if they have not already been appointed one.

A BETTER WAY

11.59 It's clear that, although in some cases the making and use of covert recordings is extremely useful, in others it can be somewhat of a minefield.

36 Family Justice Council (n 5), para 5.8.

This begs the question of whether there is a better way to obtain such evidence. Quite simply, the Family Justice Council's response to this is to change the word 'covert' to 'overt'.

11.60 By informing the subject of the recording that you wish to record them, and consequently gaining their consent, many of the issues inherent in covert recordings would be nullified. As mentioned at the beginning of this chapter, some organisations such as CAFCASS have already released guidance to their employees that their meetings with parents can, and perhaps should, be recorded. Such a decision will mean that both the recorder and the subject are in control of the evidence and have knowledge of whether the recording that ends up being presented to court, is indeed the original recording.

11.61 Of course, any organisation proposing to do this would need to set clear boundaries and procedures in order to protect both parties. Although beyond the scope of this book, the Family Justice Council guidance is a useful resource on this point.[37]

PRACTICE NOTE

Overt or covert or in between?

Recording is a hybrid act because it's derived from commonplace practice not targeted – for example the commonplace 'halo' video recordings often used at entrances to homes, recording visitors. Is that covert or overt?

Overt recording is not just something which could be explored in the context of meetings with professionals; clients who wish to evidence the other parent's behaviour could ask for permission to record them also.

This will have to be a decision for the client as to whether they think that the individual's behaviour will change once on camera, negating the usefulness of the recording completely. But in some circumstances, by gaining the consent of the individual to record them, your client may well be able to produce recorded evidence which not only supports their position, but also (by the fact that it is overt and with consent) negates many of the Court's potential grievances with admitting recordings.

The latter outcome is perhaps more likely where the agreed recording is to be ongoing, for example, at every handover. Whilst the other parent may act differently in the first couple of handovers, the awareness of being recorded (and its impact on their behaviour) may fade over time, ultimately revealing their true colours.

37 Family Justice Council (n 5), para 33 onwards.

11.62 This chapter has aimed to provide a useful overview of the use of covert recordings within family proceedings. As a final point, should you be instructed by a client who is finding it difficult to understand the nature and judicial treatment of covert recordings, the authors highly recommend that you provide them with Appendix 4 of the Family Justice Council's Guidance, Summary Guidance for Litigants in family proceedings. This sets out the content of this chapter in non-legal, plain English, which may greatly reassure an anxious client.[38]

38 Family Justice Council (n 5), Appendix 4.

CHAPTER 12

Pleading Domestic Abuse

12.01 The Family Procedure Rules 2010 (SI 2010/2955) (FPR 2010) provide the procedural mechanism which enables the Family Court to deal with all cases by reference to the overriding objective. There are several sections which are important to highlight before focus shifts to the specific context of pleading domestic abuse (DA). Primarily, the overriding objective ensures that the Family Court deals with cases justly, having regard to any welfare issues involved.[1]

12.02 The Rules go on to offer guidance as to how a case is dealt with justly so far as practicable, which include:

> '(a) ensuring that it is dealt with expeditiously and fairly;
>
> (b) dealing with the case in ways which are proportionate to the nature, importance and complexity of the issues;
>
> (c) ensuing that the parties are on an equal footing;
>
> (d) saving expense; and
>
> (e) allowing to it an appropriate share of the court's resources, while taking into account the need to allot resources to other cases.'[2]

12.03 It is also important to bear in mind that the Family Court has wide powers to control the evidence it receives, which are set out in FPR 2010, r 22.1:

> '22.1
>
> (1) The court may control the evidence by giving directions as to—
>
> (a) the issues on which it requires evidence;
>
> (b) the nature of the evidence which it requires to decide those issues; and
>
> (c) the way in which the evidence is to be placed before the court.
>
> (2) The court may use its power under this rule to exclude evidence that would otherwise be admissible.
>
> (3) The court may permit a party to adduce evidence, or to seek to rely on a document, in respect of which that party has failed to comply with the requirements of this Part.
>
> (4) The court may limit cross-examination.'[3]

1 FPR 2010, r 1.1.
2 FPR 2010, r 1.1(2)(a)–(e).
3 FPR 2010, r 22.1.

INQUISITORIAL OR ADVERSARIAL?

12.04 Now that the scene has been set, the first issue to consider in the context of DA is whether the approach of the court should be inquisitorial or adversarial. Practice Direction 12J tells us this:

> 'The court should, wherever practicable, make findings of fact as to the nature and degree of any domestic abuse which is established and its effect on the child, the child's parents and any other relevant person …'[4]

12.05 A relevant Finding of Fact Hearing can take an *inquisitorial* process, with an inquisitorial approach, having considerable advantages over an adversarial approach.[5] An inquisitorial approach encourages a holistic review of the case, enabling improved identification of the issues and the evidence required to determine them as well as better monitoring of the protection of the victim and the arrangements for the children.

12.06 However, in reality it would be hard to think of many cases that do not feel, certainly from the perspective of the parents involved, adversarial. There is an unattractive tendency in private law proceedings, far more so than public law matters in the authors' views, for legal teams to make the trial process, and the litigation that underpins it, adversarial in tone, content and approach. Such an approach is to be deprecated and challenged.

12.07 The core task for the practitioner is to extract the best evidence from the client so that the Court can make an informed (crucially, a trauma-informed) decision for the benefit of the client and the children who are the subject of the application. This is all the more important when we consider that the adult and child are still living with adult conflict and its consequences.

PRACTICE NOTE

Be proactive – assist the Court in the exercise of its discretion.

Take a default inquisitorial approach guided by:

- reviewing contemporaneous supporting records, eg mobile data, social media, other agency information (housing, police), accounts from friends and family (texts sent to them may assist), neighbours, school, community/religious leaders;
- considering the dynamic of non-native UK speakers from a cultural, religious and language perspective:
  - Would they be constrained from talking to a male GP or male police officer, for example?

4 PD12J, para 29.
5 PD12J, para 28.

   - Are they dependent on the partner or partner's family for shelter, food, security, status?
- for non-English speakers, their accessibility to the evidence:
   - incorporate a trauma-informed client relationship as part of your client care and evidence framing approach;
   - be alert to the risks of memory reframing where a traumatic incident is alleged.
- adopting the tone towards your opponent and conducting yourself in and out of court in the way you want to see mirrored back. Do not accept discourtesy. Deal with it early and firmly. We all hate those cases that we dread dealing with in our diary or inbox, so don't avoid the issue – grapple with it.

THE PLEADING FORMAT OF ALLEGATIONS OF DOMESTIC ABUSE

12.08 The mechanism by which allegations are put before the Court for determination has been the subject of considerable focus in recent years and, notwithstanding the benefits that an inquisitorial approach brings to the process, the way in which the allegations are placed before the Court is an important feature of the case. It will determine the scope of the trial, the length of the trial and the limits of cross-examination.

12.09 The use of Scott Schedules (or schedules of allegations) in the Family Court to plead allegations of DA is commonplace, with family courts up and down the country making directions for them to be prepared. One can see the attraction in theory: a short, concise document in tabular form which includes the allegations summarised, the evidence in support of such allegations referenced and the respondent's response to such allegations. In practice, such documents are rarely short nor concise and, moreover, as our understanding of DA has developed, the limitations of pleadings through a list format have become plain. The default option of *'first, last, worst' or 'choose your best 10'* is to be strongly deprecated as it prevents the Court from assessing the relationship as a whole.

12.10 The use of Scott Schedules is specifically referenced in Practice Direction 12J, with the Court being directed to consider:

> '… whether the key facts in dispute can be contained in a schedule or a table (known as a Scott Schedule) which sets out what the applicant complains of or alleges, what the respondent says in relation to each individual allegation or complaint; the allegations in the schedule should be focused on the factual issues to be tried; and if so, whether it is practicable for this schedule to be completed at the first hearing, with the assistance of the judge …'[6]

6 PD12J, para 19(c).

12.11 The Court of Appeal considered the continuing utility of Scott Schedules in the decision of *Re H-N & Ors (Children) (Domestic Abuse: Finding of Fact Hearings)* and had this to say:

> 'One striking feature of the dozen oral submissions heard during the hearing of these appeals was that there was effective unanimity that the value of Scott Schedules in domestic abuse cases had declined to the extent that, in the view of some, they were now a potential barrier to fairness and good process, rather than an aid.
>
> Concern about the utility of Scott Schedules was raised on two different bases: one of principle and the other more pragmatic. The principled concern arose from an asserted need for the court to focus on the wider context of whether there has been a pattern of coercive and controlling behaviour, as opposed to a list of specific factual incidents that are tied to a particular date and time. Abusive, coercive and controlling behaviour is likely to have a cumulative impact upon its victims which would not be identified simply by separate and isolated consideration of individual incidents.
>
> The second, more pragmatic criticism is not unrelated to the first. As an example in one of these four appeals, the parties were required to "limit" the allegations to be tried to ten and the judge at trial further reduced the focus of the hearing by directing that only three would be tried. It was submitted that that very process of directed selection, produces a false portrayal of the couple's relationship. If such an applicant succeeds in proving the three remaining allegations, there is a risk that the court will move forward on the basis that those three episodes are the only matters "proved" and therefore the only facts upon which any adverse assessment of the perpetrator's future risk falls to be made. By reducing and then further reducing its field of focus, the court is said to have robbed itself of a vantage point from which to view the quality of the alleged perpetrator's behaviour as a whole and, importantly, removed consideration of whether there was a pattern of coercive and controlling behaviour from its assessment.
>
> For our part, we see the force of these criticisms and consider that serious thought is now needed to develop a different way of summarising and organising the matters that are to be tried at a fact-finding hearing so that the case that a respondent has to meet is clearly spelled out, but the process of organisation and summary does not so distort the focus of the court proceedings that the question of whether there has been a pattern of behaviour or a course of abusive conduct is not before the court when it should be. This is an important point. Everyone agrees.
>
> The Harm Panel has expressed a similar view and noted that "reducing a long and complicated history of abuse into neat and discrete descriptions is challenging and can itself result in minimisation of the abuse (Chapter 5.4), and that by limiting the number of allegations the court is not exposed to 'more subtle and persistent patterns of behaviour" (Chapter 7.5.1). So too did Hayden J in *F v M* in his Post Script.'[7]

7 *Re H-N & Ors (Children) (Domestic Abuse: Finding of Fact Hearings)* [2021] EWCA Civ 448, [43]–[47].

12.12 The comments made in, and endorsed by, the Court of Appeal in *Re H-N & Ors* were a culmination of observations made in recent years as to the utility of Scott Schedules.

12.13 Indeed, Baker J (as he then was) in the case of *Re LG (Re-opening of Fact-Finding)* cautioned as to the risk the Court and practitioners faced when allegations were contained within a schedule, with the following observation:

> 'Not infrequently, a party alleging domestic violence is directed to identify and rely on a few allegations as "specimen" allegations on which to seek findings. In taking this course, however, parties and the court must be careful to ensure that significant issues are not overlooked. Sometimes a pattern of harassment and other forms of domestic abuse is only discernible by conducting a broader examination of the allegations.'[8]

12.14 Whilst Hayden J declined to give prescriptive guidance on the use of Scott Schedules in the case of *F v M*, the judge did observe – in the context of coercive and controlling behaviour – that, whilst the Court could see the advantages of 'carefully marshalling the evidence and honing the allegations',[9] the Court could also see how a particularly insidious form of DA, such as controlling and coercive behaviour 'may not easily be captured by the more formulaic discipline of a Scott Schedule'.[10] Further, Hayden J cautioned that 'an intense focus on particular and specified incidents may be a counterproductive exercise', carrying the risk of obscuring the serious nature of harm perpetrated in a pattern of behaviour.[11]

12.15 The Court of Appeal in *Re H-N & Ors* did not go as far as hoped by many of the parties and intervenors in addressing which pleading format was the most helpful to a busy court. The Court of Appeal concluded that:

(a) 'The value of Scott Schedules in domestic abuse cases had declined to the extent that, in the view of some, they were *a potential barrier to fairness and good practice, rather than an aid*.'[12]

(b) There were a number of principled and pragmatic concerns in relation to Scott Schedules raised by the parties.

(c) 'The principled concern arose from an asserted need for the court to focus on the wider context on whether there has been a pattern of coercive and controlling behaviour, as opposed to a list of specific factual incidents that are tied to a particular date and time.'[13]

(d) 'Serious thought is now needed to develop a different way of summarising and organising the matters that are to be tried at a fact-finding hearing'[14] without

8 *Re LG (Re-opening of Fact-Finding)* [2017] EWHC 2626 (Fam), [27].
9 *F v M* [2021] EWFC 4, post script.
10 *F v M* (n 9).
11 *F v M* (n 9).
12 *Re H-N & Ors* (n 7), [43] (emphasis added).
13 *Re H-N & Ors* (n 7), [44].
14 *Re H-N & Ors* (n 7), [46].

limiting the number of allegations or minimising the abuse. Suggestions include a 'threshold' type document as in public law proceedings, formal pleadings of particulars of claim as seen in civil proceedings and a narrative statement in a prescribed form.

(e) However, such work was not for the Court of Appeal.

ALTERNATIVES TO SCOTT SCHEDULES

12.16 Practitioners still await authoritative guidance as to the alternative way of pleading allegations in the Family Court. Until then, cases will continue to proceed through the Family Court. So, how can cases be properly presented (and responded to) so that the Court is able to ensure that no child-relevant aspect of the parties' relationship is overlooked and, therefore, any assessment of risk is predicated upon a thorough overview of the parties' relationship?

PRACTICE NOTE

Keep in the forefront of your mind:

- the child's past experiences and future needs are the focus;
- the Family Court is not the place to relive the dying throes of a toxic adult relationship;
- the Court needs to make decisions that will impact upon its assessment of the welfare of the child;
- the Children Act 1989, s 1(3) welfare checklist is a useful reference tool to hone drafting, preparation and submissions on scope of the Finding of Fact Hearing.

12.17 During the course of submissions before the Court of Appeal in *Re H-N & Ors*, the Court was invited to consider three potential alternative ways to a Scott Schedule of pleading a case in which DA was alleged: a s 31-type threshold pleading, civil style Particulars of Claim and a narrative statement.[15]

12.18 Of the four options which were referenced by the Court of Appeal, the authors would say that none of them are perfect. However, the options that follow offer the most flexibility and accuracy, albeit to varying degrees.

A 'threshold' type document, similar to that used in public children law proceedings

12.19 Whilst the use of such a document might enable the case to be pleaded in a succinct way, the utility of such a document will largely depend upon focused

15 *Re H-N & Ors* (n 7).

instructions and careful legal review of their relevance. Why? Because whilst there is now a clear, statutory definition of DA, it is a wide-ranging definition which encompasses many different aspects of conduct. Whilst some aspects of DA can clearly be identified as domestically abusive, there are some aspects which are not so obvious unless or until one stands back and considers the behaviour as a whole and/or considers the impact of this conduct on the victim. This feature of a case has not been lost on the senior courts, with both the High Court and the Court of Appeal observing the importance of taking a step back and considering the relationship as a whole.

12.20 Keep in the forefront of your mind the clear guidance given by the (former) President of the Family Division, Sir James Munby in the case of *Re A* on the essentials of pleading a case.[16] The pertinent observations made by Munby P in this case are quoted below:

> 'The first fundamentally important point relates to the matter of fact-finding and proof. I emphasise, as I have already said, that is for the local authority to prove, on a balance of probabilities, the upon which it seeks to rely. I draw attention to what, in *Re A (A Child) (No 2) [2011] EWCA Civ 12, [2011] 1 FCR 141*, para 26, I described as:
>
> > "the elementary proposition that findings of fact must be based on evidence (including inferences that can properly be drawn from the evidence) and not on suspicion or speculation."
>
> This carries with it two important practical and procedural consequences.
>
> The first is that the local authority, if its case is challenged on some factual point, must adduce proper evidence to establish what it seeks to prove. Much material to be found in local authority case records or social work chronologies is hearsay, often second- or third-hand hearsay. Hearsay evidence is, of course, admissible in family proceedings. But, and as the present case so vividly demonstrates, a local authority who is unwilling or unable to produce the witness who can speak of such matters first-hand, may find itself in great, or indeed insuperable, difficulties if a parent not merely puts the matter in issue but goes into the witness box to deny it. As I remarked in my second View from the President's Chamber, [2013] Fam Law 680:
>
> > "Of course the court can act on the basis of evidence that is hearsay. But direct evidence from those can speak to what they have themselves seen and heard is more compelling and less open to cross-examination. Too often far too much time is taken by cross-examination directed to little more than demonstrating that no-one giving evidence in court is able to speak of their own knowledge, and that all are dependent on

16 *Re A* [2015] EWFC 11.

> the assumed accuracy of what is recorded, sometimes at third of fourth hand, in the local authority's files."

... The second practical and procedural point goes to the formulation of threshold and proposed findings of fact. The schedule of findings in the present case contains, as we shall see, allegations in relation to the father that "he appears to have" lied or colluded, that various people have "stated" or "reported" things, and that "there is an allegation". With all respect to counsel, this form of allegation, which one sees far too often in such documents, is wrong and should never be used. It confuses the crucial distinction, once upon a time, though no longer, spelt out in the rules of pleading and well understood, between an assertion of fact and the evidence needed to prove the assertion. What do the words "he appears to have lied" or "X reports that he did Y" mean? More important, where does it take one? The relevant allegation is not that "he appears to have lied" or "X reports"; the relevant allegation, if there is evidence to support it, it is surely that "he lied" or "he did Y."

Failure to understand these principles and to analyse the case accordingly can lead, as here, to the unwelcome realisation that a seemingly impressive case is, in truth, a tottering edifice built on inadequate foundations.

The second fundamentally important point is the need to link the facts relied upon by the local authority with its case ... the need to demonstrate *why*, as the local authority asserts, facts A + B + C justify the conclusion that the child has suffered, or is at risk of suffering, significant harm of types X, Y or Z. Sometimes the linkage will be obvious, as where the facts proved establish physical harm. But the linkage may be very much less obvious where the allegation is only that the child is at risk of suffering emotional harm or, as in the present case, at risk of suffering neglect. In the present case, as we shall see, an important element of the local authority's case was that the father "lacks honesty with professionals", "minimises matters of importance" and "is immature and lacks insight of the issues of importance". Maybe. But how does this feed into a conclusion that A is at risk of neglect? The conclusion does not follow naturally from the premise. The local authority's evidence and submissions must set out the argument and explain explicitly why it is said that, in the particular case, the conclusions indeed follow from the facts. Here, as we shall see, the local authority conspicuously failed to do so.'[17]

12.21 The decision in *Re A* did not create any new legal principles or offer a new way of approaching the determination of a factual matrix but what it did do, superbly, was to require the advocate to think forensically about the case.

17 *Re* A (n 16), [8]–[12].

PRACTICE NOTE

Whilst the *Re A* guidance was given in the context of public law proceedings, the main principles are equally applicable to a situation where the Court is being asked to make findings of abuse which are likely to inform the future welfare arrangements for the child/children concerned:

- state the fact you rely upon;
- identify and cite the primary source of the evidence that proves that fact;
- link the fact to harm or risk of harm.

Use this structure to challenge your pleadings and to challenge any allegations made against you.

REMEMBER: What are the key issues in the case that must be litigated in a fact-finding hearing to enable a welfare decision to be made for the children that does not expose them to harm? That is the lodestar that should guide practitioners.

REMEMBER: Family proceedings are civil proceedings – ask for better and further particulars if the pleading is deficient. This is an effective tool and can be disconcerting for your opponent.

Formal pleadings by way of particulars of claim as seen in civil proceedings

12.22 The authors have not seen this used despite it being mentioned in *Re H-N & Ors* as a potential option.[18] This is not a natural forum for those who practise in family law and in that lack of familiarity lie dangers for the unwary in trying to tie multi-layered family dynamics to formal and formulaic civil pleadings. If it is to be used, we strongly reiterate the advice given above regarding distilling the harm alleged, evidence relied upon and issue as the focus of the claim. The 'Practice Notes' will remain relevant.

A narrative statement

12.23 There are considerable benefits to the use of a *focused* narrative statement in cases where the Court is called upon to determine allegations of DA. A narrative statement allows the person alleging DA to set out with specificity the DA they allege and to exhibit relevant material (such as photographs, screenshots etc). And, in their own words, it allows the person to clearly explain to the Court

18 *Re H-N & Ors* (n 7).

the effect the DA has had upon them and the children concerned, which can be an important determining factor.

12.24 The benefit of a narrative statement at an early stage in the proceedings is likely to be of considerable assistance to the Court. Not only will such a statement allow the Court to consider the necessity and proportionality of a Finding of Fact Hearing (see earlier part of this chapter) but it will also provide useful information for the Court when exercising its case management with regard to any such Finding of Fact Hearing.

12.25 In order to ensure that the narrative statement is of maximum assistance to the Court, a balance needs to be struck between the length of any such statement and ensuring that the statement sets out the case in full.

Language

12.26 The preparation of a narrative statement is incredibly important and the significance of this vital piece of evidence should not be lost at any stage of the proceedings. Any statement made by the client represents their opportunity to tell the Court what they have experienced, how it has affected them and, importantly, why all of that is relevant to the issues that the Court has to determine.

12.27 The statement should be written in the client's own style (when/if they give live evidence to the Court, you almost want the statement to 'come alive' in the witness box rather than leaving the tribunal wondering if the person in the statement and the person in the witness box are one in the same!). Use the vocabulary and the terminology that the client uses. Do not think that the Court must have a statement in 'proper' English. Language is a powerful tool – in a DA case, diluting the language runs the risk of diluting the impact the alleged behaviours have had on the client – which is the very thing that the Court needs to have regard to.

12.28 The *President's Memorandum: Witness Statements*, issued by the President of the Family Division on 10 November 2021[19] sought to remind practitioners of the contents of Practice Direction 22A of the Family Procedure Rules and in particular, para 4.1 which provides:

> '4.1 … the affidavit/statement *must*, if practicable be in the maker's own words, it should be expressed in the first person …'[20]

The word 'must' is deliberately italicised to emphasise that this is a requirement.

19 Judiciary of England and Wales, *President's Memorandum: Witness Statements* (2021), https://www.judiciary.uk/wp-content/uploads/2022/07/PFD-memo-on-witness-statements-12112021.pdf.
20 Practice Direction 22A, para 4.1 (emphasis added).

Interpretation

12.29 For some time, there have been differing practices on the ways in which witness statements have been prepared and presented to the Court when English isn't the client's first language and a translator has been required to enable them to participate in proceedings. Is it created in the client's language then translated into English or vice versa with a paragraph at the end of the English version of the witness statement to confirm that it has been read to and understood by the witness in their own language?

12.30 We now have the answer. Paragraph 23 of Practice Direction 32 (PD 32) of the Civil Procedure Rules 1998 (SI 1998/3132) (CPR) states that if a witness statement is in a foreign language, the party relying on it must have it translated, file the original foreign language statement with the Court, and have the translator sign the original statement to certify the translation's accuracy.[21] The translation must be a certified, accurate representation of the witness's evidence, ensuring the Court can understand and rely on the information.

12.31 Specifically:

- a witness statement must be drafted in that witness's own language as well as their own words;[22]
- the witness statement must contain details as to the process by which it was prepared. For example, face to face, telephone and/or through an interpreter;[23]
- the foreign language witness statement must be translated by the party relying upon it, the foreign language statement filed with the Court and the original statement signed by the translator and certifying that the translation is accurate;[24]
- the witness statement must include the date of translation.[25]

12.32 Please also note the contents of Practice Direction 22 (Statements of Truth).[26]

- Paragraph 2.1 of Practice Direction 22 contains the new form of wording for the statement of truth verifying a statement of case.
- Paragraph 2.2 contains the form of wording for the statement of truth verifying a witness statement. Paragraph 2.2 also states that the statement of truth on the witness statement should be provided in the language of the witness statement.

21 CPR Practice Direction 32, para 23.2.
22 CPR Practice Direction 32, para 18.10.
23 CPR Practice Direction 32, para 18.1(5).
24 CPR Practice Direction 32, para 23.3.
25 CPR Practice Direction 32, para 17.2(6).
26 CPR Practice Direction 22.

- Paragraph 2.4 stipulates that a statement of truth must be in the witness's own language.
- Paragraph 2.5 states that a statement of truth must be dated with the date on which it was signed.

PRACTICE NOTE

- When English is not a client's first language, the words to describe DA may simply not exist in that person's first language. There may also be shame attached to reporting their experiences which can lead to inconsistent accounts and behaviours. Race, culture and religion can all play a part in how abuse is considered and reported so take the time to try to understand what they have experienced. Take an inquisitorial approach.
- Check that religious/cultural restrictions have not impacted on the translation. Specifically, and by way of example, a female client must be comfortable recounting her experiences to a male interpreter.
- Make sure that the account is one the client can give from their own experiences – not one 'guided' by an elder/partner to protect reputations or social standing in the community.
- Check who is accompanying the client to conferences and why. Take instructions in private, save with an interpreter present.
- Ensure the correct dialect is used (not simply the main language of the country of origin).
- Use the client's own words, do not paraphrase and do not anglicise. Do not 'legalese'. This is *their* account – it stands as chief oral evidence. How would the client best express themselves in the witness box?

Length

12.33 Do not forget the President's words in his *President's Memorandum: Witness Statements*[27] which identified that:

> 'As a general standard, a witness statement should not exceed 15 pages in length (excluding exhibits). This page limit is a statement of best practice and does not derogate from the limit of 25 pages in PD27A para 5.2A.1 which should be regarded as a maximum.'[28]

27 CPR Practice Direction 22.
28 Judiciary of England and Wales (n 19).

12.34 The authors do not invite practitioners to disregard this Memorandum, which was prepared in an attempt to strike a balance between dealing with cases proportionately but also justly. However, it has to be acknowledged that trying to distil a long, abusive relationship into a statement limited in length may prove to be a difficult task.

12.35 Unrepresented litigants routinely file very lengthy discourses. When in doubt, include a paragraph in any order that defines the maximum length of the document as well as font size and spacing – this sounds extreme but it is often done.

Cognitive limitations

12.36 Be alert to cognitive issues that may impact on the client's ability to recall, process and recount experiences. If in doubt, raise those issues and apply for permission to obtain a cognitive assessment. Whilst this is frequently a step taken in the public children law arena, it is not often taken in the private children law arena. Practitioners must be alive to this.

Neurodivergence

12.37 Be alert to neurodivergent differences which may impact on the client's ability to recall, process and recount experiences. In January 2025, the Family Justice Council published *Family Justice Council Guidance on Neurodiversity in the Family Justice System for Practitioners* in which it is acknowledged that available evidence suggests that neurodivergence is overrepresented among court users and the fact that it is often underdiagnosed is likely to further mask its prevalence in those accessing family justice.[29] The Family Justice Council recognises the way in which a failure to recognise and take into account neurodivergence impacts children and families within the family justice system in two key, and intertwined, ways:

(a) by way of assessments undertaken before, during and after proceedings, or as part of dispute resolution; and

(b) by way of barriers to participation in proceedings, which in turn restrict access to justice and to a fair trial.

12.38 It is beyond the scope of this book to do a deep dive into this guidance, although it is important reading for practitioners and judiciary alike. Neurodiversity may add an additional layer of vulnerability which practitioners should be alive to.

29 Family Justice Council, *Family Justice Council Guidance on Neurodiversity in the Family Justice System for Practitioners* (January 2025), https://www.judiciary.uk/wp-content/uploads/2025/01/Family-Justice-Council-Guidance-on-Neurodiversity-in-the-Family-Justice-System-for-Practitioners.pdf.

PRACTICE NOTE

A summary:

- Be aware of barriers to getting the most reliable narrative from the client and make adjustments accordingly.
- Use the client's own words and phraseology in the statement – it's their evidence, not the solicitor's.
- Use their language to draft their statement if English isn't their first language.
- Treat the statement as the client's evidence in chief (as that is what it is) – how would they explain their history and concerns (relevant to the children) to the judge?
- Don't use legalese in the statement.
- Don't use ten words when five will do.
- If information is now known that wasn't included in the non-molestation statement or initiating C100/C1a application, then explain why (with a traumatised client, revealing experiences of rape or coerced filmed sex, for example, may take time as trust develops between the victim and their lawyer).
- If the client has cognitive limitations or is neurodivergent, make that explicit.
- Get the client to check every paragraph (initial each paragraph in the solicitor's copy if needs be). Don't simply dispatch and ask for it to be signed and dated at the end. Each statement is an important document and should be treated as such.

12.39 For an example of how a judge has decided to use a narrative of their own recourse in setting out findings, consider Peel J's approach in *Re JK (A Child) (Domestic Abuse: Findings of Fact Hearing)*.[30] This judgment was handed down following a Finding of Fact Hearing concerning allegations of coercive and controlling behaviour. The Court found that the father had been physically abusive towards the mother and his behaviour amounted to controlling and coercive behaviour. The father used various forms of threat, intimidation, financial control and manipulation to exert power over the mother. The Court used the guidance in PD12J and discussed how to apply *Re H-N & Ors*.[31]

12.40 Poole J gave a narrative account of his findings as opposed to relying solely on the parties' Scott Schedules and noted that a focus on specified allegations

30 *Re JK (A Child) (Domestic Abuse: Findings of Fact Hearing)* [2021] EWHC 1367 (Fam).
31 *Re H-N & Ors* (n 7).

would not do justice to the case. Observing that the Court of Appeal in *Re H-N & Ors* did not give strict guidelines as to how the courts might case manage and hear allegations of DA, Poole J highlighted the Court's recommendations at para [58] of *Re H-N & Ors*. He pointed out that, following *Re H-N & Ors)*, once it has been determined that a Finding of Fact Hearing was necessary:

> '… it would have been helpful to have had, in addition to the witness evidence, concise statements on behalf of each party including (a) a summary of the nature of the relationship, (b) a list of the forms of domestic abuse that the evidence is said to establish, (c) a list of key specific incidents said to be probative of a pattern of coercion and/or control; (d) a list of any other specific incidents so serious that they justify determination irrespective of any alleged pattern of coercive and/or controlling behaviour. The court would have needed to know which specific allegations listed at (d) were admitted or disputed, but in my view there would have been no need to have formal responses to the other sections of the statements.
>
> As it is, and in the light of *Re H-N and Others (Children) (Domestic Abuse: Finding of Fact Hearings),* the primary issues requiring my determination are the allegations of patterns of behaviours said to constitute coercion and/or control. However, in this case the specific allegations of physical assault do require discrete determination because they are part of the alleged pattern of coercion and control. The use and threat of physical violence was, it is alleged, a significant element in the father's exercise of coercion and control. I shall therefore consider the specific allegations of physical violence alongside the allegations of patterns of abuse. In doing so slavish adherence to Schedules will not be helpful. Accordingly, I shall set out my findings in narrative form.'[32]

12.41 The President's Guidance, *Fact-finding hearing and domestic abuse in Private Law children law proceedings – Guidance for Judges and Magistrates* was published on 5 May 2022.[33] Written with authority and clarity by Macur LJ, and approved by the President, it is essential reading. In the Guidance, Macur LJ also acknowledges that *Re H-N & Ors* 'cautioned against Scott Schedules' but reasserts that it didn't rule out schedules per se.[34] This approach was proposed: allegations that can be clearly defined (such as a specific incident of police abuse) might have a place in a schedule, but allegations that look at patterns of behaviour might need a broad overview that is conveyed better by a statement. He stated that, 'A hybrid of the two, dividing types of behaviour into clusters to provide an overview akin to a threshold document in public law might be appropriate'.[35]

32 *Re JK (A Child) (Domestic Abuse: Findings of Fact Hearing)* (n 30), [27]–[28].
33 President's Guidance, *Fact-finding hearing and domestic abuse in Private Law children law proceedings – Guidance for Judges and Magistrates* (2022), https://www.judiciary.uk/guidance-and-resources/fact-finding-hearings-and-domestic-abuse-in-private-law-children-proceedings-guidance-for-judges-and-magistrates/.
34 President's Guidance (n 33), para 9.
35 President's Guidance (n 33), para 10.

12.42 *Re B-B (Domestic Abuse: Fact-Findings)* is the Finding of Fact judgment which was remitted by the Court of Appeal to the High Court following the conjoined appeals which were reported as *Re H-N & Ors*.[36] This case was then known as *B-B* and is discussed in *Re H-N & Ors*.[37] Cobb J found that the father's behaviour was abusive towards the mother in a number of ways.[38] This judgment sets out the Court's approach in subsequent Finding of Fact Hearings in relation to the parties' cross-allegations of DA. Cobb J considered the issues in a holistic way, noting the patterns of behaviour of both parents during the length of their relationship. He did so by 'clustering' the allegations into forms of alleged abuse. The judge proceeded, as the Court of Appeal contemplated he should, on the basis that the Court should consider whether a pattern of coercive and/or controlling behaviour can be demonstrated on the evidence, rather than being merely focused on any singular particular factual incident.

PRACTICE NOTE

Final Words:

- Pleadings are the most focused, succinct and accessible way for the court to consider the remit of the case they are being asked to consider.
- Pleadings are the way in which you can identify the relevance of a client's allegation to welfare and the client's defence to it.
- Do not think of them as a form to be completed.
- Use them to hone your case and the evidence you rely upon.
- Use them to think tactically on the relevance, necessity and proportionality of the evidence.

36 *Re B-B (Domestic Abuse: Fact-Findings)* [2022] EWHC 108 (Fam); *Re H-N & Ors* (n 7).
37 *Re H-N & Ors* (n 7), [79] and [115].
38 *Re H-N & Ors* (n 7), [62]–[81].

CHAPTER 13

Participation in the Family Court

INTRODUCTION

13.01 Within the confines of an intimate relationship, few will contemplate a situation whereby they have to share the minutiae of that relationship in front of strangers; to participate in a post-mortem of that relationship when the wounds that it has left behind have yet to heal. And yet, this is what is often required in the Family Court, particularly when the Court is having to view the parties' relationship through the lens of future arrangements for any child.

13.02 There is growing awareness that the Family Court process itself can be used – and is used – as a tool through which abusive behaviours can continue to be perpetrated. But how can those who have been exposed to domestic abuse (DA) be protected by the Family Court whilst also ensuring that sufficient information is obtained by the Family Court in order to properly discharge its obligations?

13.03 The extent to which experiences of domestic abuse (DA) can impact upon the evidence of a victim must remain at the forefront of practitioner's minds as well as the judges or magistrates hearing such cases. Practitioners should pay heed to the observations of Mrs Justice Judd in *Re M (A Child)*:

> 'The reason it was so important for the judge to give very careful consideration to the question of vulnerability in this case is because a *vulnerable person may not act in the same way as someone more independent or confident if they are exploited or abused in a relationship.* Such an individual may be so anxious for the relationship to succeed that *they accept treatment that others would not. They may be easy to exploit. They may not even realise what is happening to them, and will cling to the dream of a happy family and relationship …*
>
> Here it is quite clear from reading the transcript of the hearing and judgment that in rejecting a number (although not all) of the mother's allegations against the father the judge relied very much on the fact she wanted to be in a relationship with the father, she tried to get him back when he rejected her, and that she engaged in sex with him after occasions when she said he had raped or abused her. These reasons may well hold good in many cases, but most definitely not all. In some cases, it is a very unsafe premise upon which to base findings of fact, especially if the alleged victim is vulnerable or dependent as the mother said she was here. Further, it seems to me that the judge's disbelief that the mother would have remained in an abusive

relationship led her to conclude the mother was lying about it. This tainted the whole of her evidence and was a thread which ran throughout the case.'[1]

PRACTICE NOTE

Ensuring proper and effective participation in cases where DA is a feature (alleged or otherwise) is not an aspiration. It is a requirement and a necessary and a fundamental tenet of the principles enshrined in Article 6 of the European Convention on Human Rights. It must not be overlooked.

13.04 As explored in this chapter, you will likely find that the legal framework surrounding vulnerability and participation is relatively straightforward. However, time and again, practitioners and courts fail to give any (or sufficient) consideration to the statutory obligations the Court has to consider in relation to this crucial issue. It is for this reason that there is a steady stream of case law regarding the issue of vulnerability and participation, with many published decisions arising from appeals where courts, at first instance, have failed to consider this issue. At the end of this chapter, some of those cases will be summarised so as to remind practitioners of some of the pitfalls that we should not be falling into and to encourage better practice moving forward. But, as with other areas discussed in this book, this is only a sample of relevant cases since case law moves forwards all the time. *Readers must, therefore, keep abreast of developments.*

STARTING POINT

13.05 Since the coming into force of the Domestic Abuse Act 2021 (DAA 2021), s 63 provides a statutory footing for the principle of vulnerability in the context of DA, with s 63(2) providing that:

> 'Rules of court must provide that where P is, or is at risk of being, a victim of domestic abuse carried out by a person listed in subsection (3), it is to be assumed that the following matters are likely to be diminished by reason of vulnerability—
>
> (a) The quality of P's evidence;
>
> (b) Where P is a party to the proceedings, P's participation in the proceedings.'

13.06 This must be the starting point for practitioners. In the context of cases involving allegations of DA, in light of this assumption, there is no need to unpick this any further. It is not an assumption that the (alleged) perpetrator can attempt to displace and the wording of the statutory provision does not require the victim to establish that they are a victim of DA in order to fall under the assumption

1 *Re M (A Child)* [2021] EWHC 3225 (Fam), [82]–[83] (emphasis added).

– there simply needs to be a risk that they are a victim of DA. The presence of allegations – particularly allegations which are a live feature in the proceedings – gives rise to the risk.

PRACTICE NOTE

DAA 2021, s 63(2) imposes a mandatory assumption which the Court must make unless the victim essentially opts out (see s 64(4)). This assumption triggers arrangements for participation directions and special measures.

13.07 Having established vulnerability, Family Procedure Rules 2010 (SI 2010/2955) (FPR 2010), r 3A.2A(3) requires the Court to consider whether it is necessary to make one or more participation directions.

PARTICIPATION DIRECTIONS

13.08 In order to assist the Court in considering whether to make one or more participation directions, the Court *must* have regard to the factors set out in r 3A.7. It is vital that practitioners are familiar with these factors and therefore, given their importance, they are set out here in full:

‘(a) the impact of any actual or perceived intimidation, including the behaviour towards the party or witness on the part of—

(i) any other party or other witness to the proceedings or members of the family or associates of that other party or other witness; or

(ii) any members of the family of the family of the party or witness;

(b) whether the party or witness—

(i) suffers from any mental disorder or otherwise has a significant impairment of intelligence or social functioning;

(ii) has a physical disability or suffers from a physical disorder; or

(iii) is undergoing medical treatment;

(c) the nature and extent of the information before the court;

(d) the issues arising in the proceedings including (but not limited to) any concerns arising in relation to abuse;

(e) whether a matter is contentious;

(f) the age, maturity and understanding of the party or witness;

(g) the social and cultural background and ethnic origins of the party or witness;

(h) the domestic circumstances and religious beliefs of the party or witness;

(i) any questions which the court is putting or causing to be put to a witness in accordance with section 31G(6) of the 1984 Act;

(j) any characteristic of the party or witness which is relevant to the participation direction which may be made;

(k) whether any measure is available to the court;

(l) the costs of any available measure;

(m) any other matter set out in Practice Direction 3AA.'[2]

PRACTICE NOTE

The language used in DAA 2021, s 63 and FPR 2010, Pt 3A and PD3AA is such that participation directions are a mandatory consideration for the Court. The word 'must' is used within both the Act and throughout the Rule. It is the Court's obligation to consider vulnerability.

13.09 Having regard to the sheer number – as well as the breadth – of factors which the Court *must* have regard to when deciding whether to make one or more participation directions, the Court has the discretion to ensure that participation directions can adapt to the issues in each particular case.

13.10 Practice Direction 3AA (PD3AA) of the FPR 2010 is crucial reading for practitioners and must form an integral part of the practitioners' toolkit. It sets out the practice and procedure to be followed:

> 'to achieve a fair hearing by providing for appropriate measures to be put in place to ensure that the participation of parties and the quality of the evidence of the parties and other witnesses is not diminished by reason of their vulnerability.'[3]

13.11 Paragraph 1.4 of PD3AA emphasises the collective responsibility of all of those involved in the proceedings to ensure that those who are vulnerable are able to participate effectively:

> 'All parties and their representatives are required to work with the court and each other to ensure that each party or witness can participate in proceedings without the quality of their evidence being diminished and without being put in fear or distress by reason of their vulnerability as defined with reference to the circumstances of each person and to the nature of the proceedings.'[4]

13.12 The application of this part of the Practice Direction was illuminated by Judd J in the case of *K v L and M*[5] at [62] and summarised (and built upon)

2 FPR 2010, r 3A.7.
3 FPR 2010, PD3AA. para 1.2.
4 FPR 2010, PD3AA. para 1.4.
5 *K v L and M* [2021] EWHC 3225 (Fam).

by Peel J in *GK v PR*[6] at [31], albeit with the suggestion that the obligation or duty upon the Court is, in effect, delegated (at least, in part) to any legal representatives who are instructed in the case:

> 'I agree with Judd J who said in *K v L and M [2021] EWHC 3225 (Fam)* at [62] that the obligation to consider vulnerability is upon the court, not least because the rules so mandate. The extent of that obligation, or duty, must depend on the context, the issues, the nature of the allegations, the way in which case management has taken place and submissions by legal representatives. When parties are represented, and in particular where a ground rules hearing has taken place, then I would expect the judge to need to do no more than cast a brief overview over the proposed arrangements.'[7]

13.13 However, in the case of *BF v LE* Lieven J observed that:

> 'Although the Domestic Abuse Act 2021 was not in existence as at September 2019 … PD3A … was. The caselaw is clear that there is a *proactive duty on judges to consider whether special measures are required. The fact that the alleged victim of abuse does not request them, even if represented, does not relieve the judge of that proactive duty,* see the caselaw cited above. FPR3A, although perhaps not in such quite strong terms as subsequent Rules and the Domestic Abuse Act, still imposes a proactive duty on judges to consider the need for participation directions.'[8]

GROUND RULES HEARING

13.14 An often-overlooked requirement in cases where vulnerability arises is that of a Ground Rules Hearing. Paragraph 5.2 of PD3AA provides that there shall be a Ground Rules Hearing prior to any hearing at which evidence is to be heard. A Ground Rules Hearing is defined in the *Equal Treatment Bench Book*:

> 'Ground rules hearings provide an opportunity to plan any adaptations to questioning and/or the conduct of the hearing that may be necessary to facilitate the evidence of a vulnerable person.'[9]

13.15 Paragraphs 5.3 through to 5.7 of PD3AA guide the matters which need to be considered at a Ground Rules Hearing. Of particular relevance is para 5.5:

> 'In all cases in which it is proposed that a vulnerable party, vulnerable witness or protected party is to be cross-examined (whether before or during a hearing) the court must consider whether to make participation directions,

6 *GK v PR* [2021] EWFC 106.
7 *GK v PR* (n.7), [31].
8 *BF v LE* [2023] EWHC 2009 (Fam), [77].
9 Judicial College, *Equal Treatment Bench Book* (July 2024, updated May 2025), p 52, para 137.

including prescribing the manner in which the person is to be cross-examined. The court must consider whether to direct that-

a) any question that can be asked by one advocate should not be repeated by another without the permission of the court;

b) questions or topics to be put in cross-examination should be agreed prior to the hearing;

c) questions to be put in cross-examination should be put by one legal representative or advocate alone, or, if appropriate, by the judge; and

d) the taking of evidence should be managed in any other way.'[10]

13.16 The *Equal Treatment Bench Book* recommends that the Ground Rules Hearing should take place as early as possible and, if at all possible, before the day of the hearing which will enable the advocates to prepare and, if necessary, to adjust their approach.[11] Furthermore, the judge should state what the ground rules are, the rules should be recorded and the advocates must abide by them.[12]

PRACTICE NOTE

The Ground Rules Hearing does not need to be a separate hearing, but it warrants close preparation and its outcomes must be recorded on the face of the resulting order.

13.17 The likelihood is that alleged victims of DA will be required to give evidence to the Family Court – whether that be within a Finding of Fact Hearing or a final hearing – and therefore face cross-examination. It is important to note that the considerations set out in para 5.5 of PD3AA *must* be considered by the Court.

13.18 Best practice would dictate that it should be recorded on the face of the resulting court order that the Court has considered these factors and whether the Court is taking any steps as a result.

13.19 In the Court of Appeal decision of *Re N (A Child)* the importance of applying the procedures was made clear:

> 'In my judgment, Part 3A and its accompanying Practice Direction provide a specific structure designed to give effective access to the court, and to ensure a fair trial for those people who fall into the category of vulnerable witness. A wholesale failure to apply the Part 3 procedure to a vulnerable witness must, in my mind, make it highly likely that the resulting trial will be judged to have been unfair.'[13]

10 PD3AA, para 5.5.
11 Judicial College (n 9), para 141.
12 Judicial College (n 9), para 146.
13 *Re N (A Child)* [2019] EWCA Civ 1997, [51].

13.20 Whilst those who practise this aspect of family law ought to be familiar with the toolkits available via the Advocate's Gateway,[14] PD3AA sets the expectation that all advocates – including litigants-in-person – are expected to be familiar with and to use the techniques employed by the toolkits and the approach of the Advocacy Training Council.

PRACTICE NOTE

In reality, it is unlikely that litigants-in-person will be familiar with and use the techniques employed in the toolkits. The obligation upon the Court and legal representatives involved is to make sure that each party engages with these crucial guidelines. This will need to be proactively raised with an unrepresented litigant in good time for them to think about the issue.

13.21 The Court of Appeal considered the provisions regarding vulnerability in *Re S (Vulnerability Party: Fairness of Proceedings)*.[15] It highlighted that, in recent years, courts and tribunals across the English and Welsh legal system have recognised the need to make due provision for vulnerable persons to participate in proceedings. Giving the lead judgment of the court, Baker LJ referred to FPR 2010, r 3A and PD3AA as '"comprehensive provisions" which are of "fundamental importance to the administration of family justice".'[16]

13.22 The Court of Appeal then offered practice guidance (we have italicised phrases that seemed key to us):

> 'It is equally clear that the duty to identify any party or witness who is a vulnerable person and to assist the court to ensure that each part or witness can participate in proceedings without the quality of their evidence being diminished, extends to all parties to the proceedings and their representatives. It will almost invariably be one of the parties or their representatives, rather than the court, who first identifies that a party or witness is or may be vulnerable. *We consider that good practice requires the parties' representatives actively to address the question of whether a party is vulnerable at the outset of care proceedings.* Indeed, as social workers will as a matter of course be looking for vulnerabilities in families as part of their practice, it is to be hoped that this issue will be identified before care proceedings are started. *We recognise, however, that it is often not easy to identify vulnerabilities and that professionals dealing with urgent and difficult situations in families will have to contend with a large number of issues. For that reason, we consider that, to comply with the obligation under rule 3A.9, the judge conducting the case management hearing at the start of care proceedings should as a matter of course investigate whether there are, or may be, issues engaging Part 3A of the rules and that the parties' advocates should as far as practicable be in*

14 The Advocate's Gateway: https://www.theadvocatesgateway.org.
15 *Re S (Vulnerability Party: Fairness of Proceedings)* [2022] EWCA Civ 8.
16 *Re S (Vulnerability Party: Fairness of Proceedings)* (n 15), [38].

a position to respond. Furthermore, rule 3A.9 stipulates that the court's duty continues to the end of the proceedings. There will therefore be other points at which the court may have to address the issue, for example, when another party is joined to the proceedings'.[17]

13.23 The decision in *Re S (Vulnerability Party: Fairness of Proceedings)* was clearly in the context of public law proceedings but the principles are no different and pervade the private law jurisdiction as well as the public law jurisdiction. As it points out, social workers engaged with families before the court hearing can (and should) be alive to the issue of vulnerability, as should those employed by the Children and Family Court Advisory and Support Service (CAFCASS) – whether that be as Family Court advisers preparing reports pursuant to Children Act 1989, s 7 or guardians appointed pursuant to FPR 2010, r 16.

PRACTICE NOTE

Within public law proceedings, the issue of the vulnerability of the parents is likely to feature from the outset of proceedings, particularly where the local authority plead DA as a threshold allegation or cite a history of sexual or physical abuse in the paternal background. But it may not be framed as having an impact on the adult vulnerability as the focus will be on the impact of abuse on the child, not on the adult.

Often in such cases, the local authority may not be required to identify who is the perpetrator and who is the victim. Then it becomes the practitioner's duty to draw the threads out and to think proactively about what the history reveals in terms of each adult's vulnerability in proceedings if their Article 6 and 8 rights are to be respected and protected.

PARTICIPATION IN PRACTICE

13.24 Whilst we have explored the obligation upon the Court – and the parties – to engage with the issue of vulnerability, how that translates to practice is important. What can the Court put in place to ensure that a party or witness who is vulnerable is able to participate fully and meaningfully in the proceedings? In short, there are many options available.

13.25 The Court may make directions relating to:

(a) the structure and/or timing of the hearing, including a later start – or earlier finish – to the Court sitting day;

(b) the nature and formality of the language to be used during the hearing;

(c) whether separate entrances/exits to the court building are required and to include separate waiting areas;

17 Re S *(Vulnerability Party: Fairness of Proceedings)* (n 15), [39] emphasis added.

(d) the use of screens to ensure that the party or witness is unable to see a particular person in the courtroom;

(e) the use of a live video-link so that they need not be physically present in the courtroom (to include the use of remote hearing facilities);

(f) the use of an intermediary;

(g) the use of a Qualified Legal Representative for unrepresented parties;

13.26 There is no hard and fast rule with respect to particular participation directions. Each case is unique, and so the directions which may be required in order to ensure proper and effective participation by all will be too. Additionally, there may be a menu of participation directions which are considered necessary in order to ensure that all parties and witnesses can participate effectively. It is vital for the integrity and fairness of the process that all participation directions which are required are sought and implemented.

QUALIFIED LEGAL REPRESENTATIVES

13.27 Sections 66 and 67 of the DAA 2021 amended the Matrimonial and Family Proceedings Act 1984, making provision for the appointment of a Qualified Legal Representative (QLR) to cross-examine relevant witnesses so that alleged victims do not face cross-examination by their own alleged abusers. Although it was introduced for cases issued after 21 July 2022, the fees were so derisory in the first instance that the QLR was an illusionary service for too long. Fortunately, the rates are now more reasonable (just), and we are starting to see the scheme in practice.[18] Anecdotal evidence suggests standards of service are variable, but benefit is still gained by the Court. As a minimum, use of a QLR takes the burden off the judge having to take the lead.

13.28 The creation of the QLR scheme arose from a growing recognition amongst the judiciary, practitioners, DA specialists and government that court procedures did not adequately protect victims of abuse in the family and civil courts.[19]

What is a Qualified Legal Representative?

13.29 The role of a QLR is summarised in the guidance as ensuring that, 'the fairness of the proceedings is maintained, by carrying out the cross-examination which the prohibited party is prohibited from performing'.[20]

18 The rates are broadly similar to the rates of pay under the Legal Aid Agency's Family Advocacy Scheme for Private Law Children Matters.

19 Ministry of Justice, *Statutory Guidance: Qualified Legal Representative appointed by the court* (updated June 2024), https://assets.publishing.service.gov.uk/media/665ef0d98f90ef31c23ebdb0/Qualified_legal_representative_appointed_by_the_Court_Statutory_guidance.pdf, p 7.

20 Ministry of Justice (n 19), p 11.

13.30 The intention is to prevent alleged abusers from cross-examining alleged victims (and alleged victims from having to cross-examine alleged abusers) in the all too common scenario of one or both of the parties being legally unrepresented in proceedings. However, a QLR is not responsible to the party that they are asking questions on behalf of; instead, they are accountable to the Court.

13.31 QLRs can be either solicitors or barristers who hold a current practising certificate. However, a recent judgment suggests that a QLR must not be representing one of the parties as a solicitor or barrister in concurrent proceedings as this would be a conflict of interest. In *K v P (Criminal Solicitor as Court-Appointed QLR)* a wife applied for the discharging of her husband's QLR in family proceedings because this QLR was also representing the husband in criminal proceedings concerning DA.[21] Her application was granted, the Court accepting her submissions that this jeopardised the QLR's independence and conflicted with the spirit of the QLR scheme which is to protect and minimise the distress of alleged victims of abuse during proceedings.

13.32 HM Courts and Tribunal Service require those who register as QLRs to have undertaken advocacy and vulnerable witness training or have made a commitment to undergo such training within six months of registering for the scheme. However, it is unclear whether any checks are undertaken to determine whether QLRs have undertaken this training. Furthermore, the availability of this training for QLRs is limited with only the Family Law Bar Association offering this training to family barristers in conjunction with the Inns of Court College of Advocacy.

The law: when is a party entitled to a Qualified Legal Representative?

13.33 The legislation only impacts family proceedings issued on or after 21 July 2022. There are likely to be some proceedings which are still ongoing from before that date. In those cases, the previous rules continue to prevail.

13.34 Section 65 of the DAA 2021 inserted Pt 4B into the Matrimonial and Family Proceedings Act 1984. A short summary of the provisions of Pt 4B is as set out below:

13.35 Under ss 31R–31T,[22] a party will automatically be entitled to a QLR when:

- one party has been convicted of/given a caution for/is charged with an offence against the other party;

21 *K v P (Criminal Solicitor as Court-Appointed QLR)* [2025] EWFC 321.

22 See DAA 2021, s 65 where Pt 4B of Matrimonial and Family Proceedings Act 1984 is copied, and then navigate to ss 31R–31T.

- there is an on-notice protective injunction in place between the parties; or
- one party has evidence of DA. The list of the specified evidence is found in Sch 3 to The Prohibition of Cross-Examination in Person (Civil and Family Proceedings) Regulations 2022 (SI 2022/568).

13.36 Even if there is not an automatic prohibition, the Court may nevertheless give a direction prohibiting cross-examination either on application by a party or of its own motion.[23]

13.37 The test laid out in s 31U(1)(b) states that the Court will make such a direction where it appears that:

- the quality condition or the significant distress condition is met, and
- it would not be contrary to the interest of justice to give the direction.[24]

The quality condition is met if the evidence is likely to be diminished without but would be improved with the use of a QLR.[25] Quality of the evidence is defined in the statute as 'completeness, coherence and accuracy'.[26] Coherence is further defined as meaning the ability to give answers which 'address the questions' and 'can be understood, both individually and collectively'.[27]

13.38 The second condition – significant distress – is met if the cross-examination is likely to cause significant distress, this level of distress is likely to be more significant than if questioned by a QLR[28] and it would not be contrary to the interests of justice to give such a direction.[29] This might be as a result of the litigant-in-person being expected to cross-examine an expert or for reasons other than DA.

13.39 The Court is to have regard to, among other things, the list of factors set out at s 31U(5): the views of the witness as to whom they would be most comfortable being cross-examined by; the views of the party due to cross-examine the witness as to whether they are comfortable fulfilling this role; the nature of the questions; any behaviour between the party and witness which has been confirmed in a Finding of Fact Hearing (from the party towards the witness and vice versa); the behaviour of the witness and the party (respectively) during proceedings, whether in relation to the witness/party or generally; any form of relationship between the party and witness.[30]

13.40 Further, the Court must also specifically consider whether there is a suitable alternative means for the witness to be cross-examined or of obtaining

23 Matrimonial and Family Proceedings Act 1984, s 31U(1)–(4).
24 Matrimonial and Family Proceedings Act 1984, s 31U(1)(b).
25 Matrimonial and Family Proceedings Act 1984, s 31U(2).
26 Matrimonial and Family Proceedings Act 1984, s 31U(6).
27 Matrimonial and Family Proceedings Act 1984, s 31U(7).
28 Matrimonial and Family Proceedings Act 1984, s 31U(3).
29 Matrimonial and Family Proceedings Act 1984, s 31U(1)(b)(ii).
30 Matrimonial and Family Proceedings Act 1984, s 31U(5).

the evidence that might have been given under cross-examination.[31] Interestingly, Practice Direction 3AB explicitly states that the judge conducting the cross-examination is not a satisfactory alternative.[32] Notwithstanding this, this often remains an alternative utilised by the Court. In fact, the Explanatory Note to the DAA 2021 includes a judge putting questions to a witness as a specific example of a 'satisfactory alternative means'.[33]

13.41 A decision under s 31U to direct a QLR is binding until the relevant witness is discharged.[34] It may be revoked by the Court before then if it is in the interests of justice to do so. If there is an application by a party for revocation, it should only be revoked if there has been a material change of circumstances.

PRACTICE NOTE

It is sensible for practitioners to consider whether a QLR will be necessary at the earliest stages of any proceedings. This will not only be for cases where the other side is already a litigant-in-person, but also where either party indicates that they may not be represented at the next hearing.

If a party unexpectedly becomes unrepresented prior to a hearing where a QLR would be necessary, then it is likely to cause the hearing to be ineffective if not dealt with sooner. Given the pressures faced by the Family Court, it is crucial that this is drawn to the Court's attention as soon as possible.

13.42 The directions for instructing a QLR are set out in Practice Direction 3AB.[35] In summary:

- invite the party to arrange for a QLR and specify the date by which the party must notify the Court of the identity and contact details of this representative;
- if the party states that they do not want or are unable to make such arrangements, or fails to notify the Court by the date specified, the Court must consider whether it is necessary in the interests of justice for the witness to be cross-examined by a court-appointed QLR;
- if so, the Court must choose and appoint a QLR from the Court-maintained list of QLRs and make directions for such appointments.

13.43 Even if there is an order for a court-appointed QLR, there is no guarantee that one will be available and therefore, practitioners ought to give some thought to how the hearing can proceed in the absence of a QLR.

31 Matrimonial and Family Proceedings Act 1984, s 31W(2).
32 FPR 2010, PD3AB, para 5.3.
33 Explanatory Note to the DAA 2021, *Commentary on Provisions of Act,* para 270.
34 DAA 2021, s 65: s 31V of Pt 4B.
35 FPR 2010, PD3AB, para 6.2.

13.44 The President of the Family Division in his *View from the President's Chambers* in July 2023 provided the following suggestions of how to approach cases where no QLRs are found (although it will be for the judge in each individual case to decide how to proceed).[36]

(a) If no QLR is found within 28 days, the Court should list the case for directions and direct that some summary information is provided by HM Courts and Tribunals Service about the difficulties that have been encountered.[37]

(b) There is no guidance as to the test to be applied for the termination of a QLR appointment, but the President suggests a similar focus on whether it is in the 'interests of justice' to do so and consideration of the overriding objective (both the need to deal with matters expeditiously and fairly as well as to ensure that parties are on an equal footing).[38]

(c) Time should be taken to consider whether there is a suitable alternative, eg directly instructing an advocate.[39]

(d) If the appointment is discharged, short reasons should be recorded for doing so.[40]

(e) The guidance that the judge conducting cross-examination is not a satisfactory alternative 'does not trump the overriding objective'. Ultimately, the Court may have to deploy the judge in such way when it is the 'only way to deal with the case, justly, expeditiously and fairly in the absence of a QLR'.[41]

13.45 Ultimately, the Court may find itself in the unenviable position of having to go through all the procedural steps, before returning to the practice that was one of the catalysts for the introduction of QLRs in the first place.

13.46 Although there have been improvements in the availability of QLRs, the scheme is far from perfect and there are occasions when the Court is unable to appoint a QLR. In February 2024, the President of the Family Division handed down judgment in *Re Z (Prohibition on Cross-examination: No QLR)* in order to consider, 'the approach that a judge or magistrates sitting in the Family Court should adopt when the court has directed that a Qualified Legal Representative [QLR] should be appointed for a party in accordance with Part 4B of the Matrimonial and Family Proceedings 1984, yet, despite a diligent search by the court office, no QLR can be found'.[42]

13.47 In this judgment, the President set out the rates of remuneration applicable to a court-appointed QLR which happen to be broadly consistent with the rates of

36 Sir Andrew McFarlane, 'A View from The President's Chambers: July 2023' (2023), https://www.judiciary.uk/guidance-andresources/a-view-from-the-presidents-chambers-july-2023/, paras 16–20.
37 Sir Andrew McFarlane (n 36), para 17.
38 Sir Andrew McFarlane (n 36), para 18.
39 Sir Andrew McFarlane (n 36), para 19.
40 Sir Andrew McFarlane (n 36).
41 Sir Andrew McFarlane (n 36), para 20.
42 *Re Z (Prohibition on Cross-examination: No QLR)* [2024] EWFC 22, [1].

remuneration available to those who undertake legally aided private law work.[43] The rates of pay available to practitioners – whether that be under the QLR scheme or via legal aid – are low and do not reflect the level of work that is required in order to discharge professional obligations. Understandably, the rates offered do not attract many experienced practitioners, which results in these difficult cases often being dealt with by very junior or under-qualified/inexperienced practitioners. Whilst the rates available to those doing QLR work have increased slightly with the coming into force of The Prohibition of Cross-Examination in Person (Fees of Court-Appointed Qualified Legal Representatives) (Amendment) Regulations 2023 (SI 2023/1319), they remain derisory.[44]

13.48 In *Re Z (Prohibition on Cross-examination: No QLR)*, the President offered his own account of the difficulties he faced when dealing with a case in which there was no QLR available and the task of cross-examination fell to the Court. He President observed:

> '… I found the task of asking the questions to be a particularly burdensome, unnatural and tricky one. As neither party was represented, as the judge I found myself first of all asking questions to tease out further details "in chief", as it were, from the first of the parties to give evidence before then putting to them most of the questions that the other party wished to have put. The process was then reversed when the other party entered the witness box. Over the course of a full court day, I therefore ended up asking all of the questions.'[45]

13.49 The President went on to explain why he had described the process as 'tricky':

> 'I have used the word "tricky" to describe the process as, when undertaking questioning, the court has to tread a narrow path between, on the one side, ensuring the witness' evidence is adequately tested by the points that the other party wishes to raise, but, on the other, ensuring that the judge does not enter the arena or be seen in any way to be promoting the case of one side or the other.'[46]

PRACTICE NOTE

Practitioners should be under no illusion that these cases are difficult. Finding of Fact Hearings are likely to be particularly difficult given the subject matter that the Court is dealing with.

The reality is that the alleged victim of DA will be represented and therefore, the task of prosecuting the case is likely to fall to a legal representative (both in terms of preparing for the hearing and conducting the hearing).

43 *Re Z* (n 42), [16].
44 The Prohibition of Cross-Examination in Person (Fees of Court-Appointed Qualified Legal Representatives) (Amendment) Regulations 2023 (SI 2023/1319).
45 *Re Z* (n 42), [28].
46 *Re Z* (n 42), [29].

Roles of a Qualified Legal Representative

13.50 Whether acting as a QLR or not, practitioners should be aware of the roles and responsibilities which befall a QLR. The role of the QLR is different to the usual role of a legal representative. However, there are no 'black' and 'white' rules which govern the role and the exercise of it – rather, there is a field of 'grey.' The responsibilities of the QLR extend beyond simply turning up at court and cross-examining a witness.

13.51 According to the statutory guidance:

> '… the court-appointed qualified legal representative's central purpose is to ensure that the fairness of the proceedings is maintained, by carrying out the cross-examination which the prohibited party is prohibited from performing.'[47]

It is worthy of note that a QLR is not responsible to the prohibited party but is required to cross-examine 'in the interests of the party'.[48]

13.52 The statutory guidance seeks to explain this:

> 'Although they will advance the interests of the prohibited party during the cross examination, *the QLR must not attempt to present the prohibited party's entire case and should not take instructions from the prohibited party in the manner that a party's own lawyer ordinarily would.* However, the QLR is expected, in most cases, to meet with the prohibited party to elicit relevant information that will form the basis of the cross-examination and inform the drafting of the position statement.'[49]

13.53 In order to assist practitioners, the Family Law Bar Association circulated guidance to its members in July 2023 which summarised its understanding of a QLR's responsibilities. We take it as our template. We can do no better than to set this out, in part, here because it is so central to practitioners understanding a QLR's role and duties:

> 'i. [A QLR] will be appointed by the court and not the client and may be required to act with more limited information as to the nature of the case and the matters in issue. Accordingly, [a QLR] will be placed in a situation that will be alien to normal practice and additional considerations will apply.
>
> ii. It is apparent from the statutory scheme that in relation to the appointment of a [QLR]:
>
> - Your appointment is made in the interests of justice;
> - you are not the representative of the court that appoints you; and

47 Ministry of Justice (n 19), p 11.
48 Ministry of Justice (n 19), p 9, para 1.4.2.
49 Ministry of Justice (n 19), p 11 (emphasis added).

- whilst not responsible to him or her, you are appointed to represent the interests of the party relevant to the cross-examination you are to undertake.

iii. The role of a court appointed QLR is undoubtedly limited to the proper performance of their duty as a cross-examiner of a particular witness. Therefore, it should not be thought that a QLR has a free-ranging remit to conduct the trial on the prohibited party's behalf. Their professional duty and their statutory duty is to ensure that they are in a position properly to conduct the cross-examination. The important thing to note is that the QLR must ensure that s/he performs his/her duty in accordance with the words of the statute.

iv. As a court-appointed QLR, you will not have a contractual relationship with the client and, therefore, the Bar Council standard contractual terms (or chambers's equivalent terms) will not apply.

v. Your core duties will continue to apply. In particular, those of most relevance to you as a court-appointed QLR are your duties to the court (CD1), to act with honesty and integrity (CD3) and to maintain your independence (CD4). In certain circumstances, the principle of client confidentiality (CD6) may also be engaged.

vi. It is essential that only legal representatives with appropriate experience should be appointed. The BSB Handbook provisions prevent counsel from accepting any instructions if to do so would cause him to be professionally embarrassed, which includes having insufficient experience or competence to handle such a matter … do not accept an appointment as a QLR if you consider you do not have sufficient experience.

vii. In carrying out your duties to the Prohibited Party, it is important that you are clear as to the purpose and the parameters of any questions you ask of the witness(es). It is not difficult to foresee a situation where questions asked without the benefit of detailed instructions from the party may receive answers which may either harm his or her case or open-up previously unexplored and unhelpful areas of evidence. Given the limitations upon your role and the more restricted input that you receive from the Prohibited Party, this situation may, in some cases, be unavoidable. However, if you make the prohibited party aware of the nature of the questions you intend to ask, the danger of this arising will be mitigated. Where it does then occur, you are less likely to be at fault.

viii. Where you are appointed by the court, your appointment terminates at the conclusion of the proceedings or when the court so orders. The witness(es) you are required to cross-examine should be named in the order appointing you. However, there remains the possibility that the judge may intervene during the trial to make a direction preventing the party from cross-examining other witnesses. Where the task of a court appointed QLR is extended in this way, it is important that you obtain certainty from the trial judge as to the basis on which you are appointed to act by ensuring each witness is named in a further order. You must be careful to ensure that you remain within the scope of the duties and obligations of a court appointed QLR and do not become the instructed advocate in the ordinary sense. You should also ensure that the Prohibited Party is aware and understands that this is the case.

ix. The Court is likely to direct the QLR to attend a pre-trial ground rules hearing. Where there is a point of law or admissibility which can be properly taken within the scope of your appointment, you should make the appropriate submissions, whether of your own volition or at the invitation of the trial judge. This would include, for example, questions relating to the sexual history of the witness or whether a particular line of cross-examination may raise the need for further disclosure of evidence. It will be your duty to raise in advance any points of law or procedure relevant to the conduct of the cross-examination.

x. You should also make representations concerning any proposed participation directions that will have an impact on the conduct of your cross-examination.

xi. The QLR will need to meet with the prohibited party to understand the essence of the prohibited party's case and agree with the prohibited party and/or the Court the issues that will be covered in the cross-examination.

xii. You should ask the prohibited party to confirm whether he or she stands by the account given in a police interview or in a statement made to the court. If the prohibited party has provided a police interview and a statement, you should consider whether there are any significant differences between the content of the interview and the statement, and if so, ask the party what case he or she is to run at the trial.

xiii. A prohibited party's refusal to be represented may have its origin in mental health issues. In such cases you may not be able to obtain any assistance from the party and may also not be assisted by comments in interview or a completed statement. In such circumstances you may not be able to do more than advance such submissions and put to the witness such lines of challenge as are apparent to you from the papers and are appropriate to your appointment. Where this arises, the QLR must bring to the court's attention any issues relating to the prohibited party's capacity to participate fully in and understand the proceedings. The qualified legal representative must also alert the court to the potential need for participation directions or special measures such as a registered intermediary.

xiv. As a court appointed QLR you should seek such further information as is required (from the court, the other party and the prohibited party you are appointed to assist) in order to be able to properly fulfil your role. This will include obtaining and familiarising yourself with the relevant papers in the case. This may include obtaining and considering additional papers relevant to the prohibited party's case. It will also require the issues in the party's case to be identified with sufficient clarity to enable you to discharge the duty of putting that case to the witness(es). You may seek guidance from Court as to the apparent issues in the case.

xv. Information sought from the prohibited party should be limited to such matters as will be relied upon in evidence during their case. You should not seek instructions from the party as to the conduct of the case more generally.

xvi. Where the party does not co-operate in identifying the issues in the case, you are entitled to rely on an account given in interview, or on the content of a statement, insofar as the party has confirmed that its contents reflect his or her case.

xvii. Where the prohibited party does not cooperate, the qualified legal representative may have to confine the cross-examination to matters that the judge directs are relevant as far as can be ascertained from the court papers in the proceedings. The QLR should then relay what these matters are to the prohibited party.

xviii. The extent to which a positive case can or should be put in cross-examination is to be assessed in accordance with the usual principles and is a matter in respect of which you must exercise your judgment.

xix. The overall extent of the cross-examination is likewise a matter for you to assess in light of all relevant circumstances. However, to effectively protect the prohibited party's article 6 and article 8 rights, the QLR must put the essence of the prohibited party's case to the witness on those parts of the witness' case that may have a significant impact on the outcome of the proceedings.

xx. The prohibited party may suggest questions to the QLR that he or she wishes to be put to the witness. Although the QLR may take such suggestions into consideration, ultimately questions should only be put to the witness if they relate to the essence of the prohibited party's case, and they are on those parts of the witness' case which may have a significant impact on the outcome of the proceedings.

xxi. The QLR must ensure that he or she is fully conversant with the evidence and issues in the case and has obtained sufficient information about the prohibited party's case to be able to cross-examine and test the evidence effectively.

xxii. The QLR must ensure that the cross-examination carried out provides the court with sufficient information to reach a conclusion on the issues that arise during the case.

xxiii. It is recommended that the QLR should prepare a brief position statement to help identify and narrow the issues that will be the focus of the cross-examination.

xxiv. Many of the issues that may arise can only be taken on a case-by-case basis. You should bear in mind the limitations of your role and be alert not to stray into acting as the prohibited party's legal representative generally. The two roles are different and latter falls outwith the scope of your appointment.

xxv. The QLR must make clear that they cannot give advice or represent the prohibited party throughout the case but are appointed by the court to carry out a very limited role. The QLR cannot help with preparing documentation or assist in complying with directions.

xxvi. The court appointed QLR will need to explain to the prohibited party that they cannot promise the confidentiality that usually attaches to lawyer-client relationships (legal professional privilege) and that there are obligations in family proceedings to disclose material that is unhelpful to the prohibited party's case.

xxvii. Should you become unable to fulfil your role as a QLR, you should inform the court immediately so an alternative QLR can be appointed. The termination of your appointment occurs by the making of a further court order.'[50]

50 Family Law Bar Association, *The Role of the Qualified Legal Representative in Family Court Proceedings* (July 2023), https://www.alc.org.uk/uploads/images/QLR_doc_v3.pdf.

What are NOT the responsibilities of a Qualified Legal Representative?

13.54 As explained above, the duties of a QLR are limited to the cross-examination of the witness(es), preparation for those cross-examinations, and occasionally, to the drafting of legal submissions and ancillary applications.

13.55 It may be that the Court will ask the QLR to perform other tasks, such as the drafting of court orders or assist in negotiations between the parties or to liaise with CAFCASS or a local authority. Do not permit this.

(a) The role of a QLR is not governed by a chambers' or firm's normal terms and conditions. The QLR may be freelance and not associated with a chamber or firm at all.

(b) The QLR should not be undertaking any task that might fall outside of the scope of their professional insurance in cases where there is no professional client and no contractual relationship with the client under the direct access scheme, especially if they are not authorised to conduct work on a direct access basis. To do so may put them in breach of their professional conduct responsibilities.

13.56 There are many tasks that could be seen as preparatory to the conduct of a cross-examination. It is impossible to list them all here. As set out above, these will have to be considered on a case-by-case basis. A QLR must be trusted to use their professional judgment in these 'grey' areas. It is easy to see how, in discussion with the unrepresented party, it might become apparent that they need documents that have not yet been produced to conduct a competent cross-examination or that further witnesses who have not yet been warned appear to be necessary. The latter – seeking further evidence, advancing the case or 'representing' the party further – is not their role.

13.57 The Court will need to be alive to the witnesses, and the documents, that might be needed and make disclosure and attendance directions before the QLR is allocated. The Court must not rely on litigants representing themselves to know what they should be seeking by way of disclosure orders.

13.58 In our view, any case that is likely to need a QLR will require the Court to actively case manage and think ahead to what the QLR will require. Otherwise, the duties on the QLR that we set out earlier may lead to the QLR having to make applications to adjourn the case.

13.59 Those who work in the Family Court on a daily basis, as well as those who are signed up to the scheme, will recognise the sheer number of appointments which the Court is called upon to secure. Demand far outstrips supply.

PRACTICE NOTE

Anticipating and managing the vulnerability of a participant in a case is a non-delegable duty of each practitioner. This is a 'must do' not 'should do' responsibility under statute, rules and case law.

Remember that vulnerability may not be confined to the applicant and respondent but also to witnesses. Make it known if you are accredited to cross-examine vulnerable witnesses under a certified scheme (such as the Family Law Bar Association/Bar Council training) or parallel training.

Enquire as to who asking questions, or proposing to ask questions, of a vulnerable person, is accredited. If they are not, raise this with the Court.

Trained or not, all family practitioners should make themselves aware of the guidance in the Advocacy Toolkit Library. The role the QLR can play in making a court hearing a trauma-informed, Article 6-compliant, process is vitally important.

But, it is important for practitioners to be aware that QLRs must not attempt to present the entirety of the case for the prohibited party and to ensure that the Court conducts matters in such a way that it does not impose a duty on the QLR that it is not theirs to shoulder.

The practitioner must be alert to the pressures brought to bear upon the QLR by the unrepresented party, or indeed, if the Court calls upon a QLR to do more than is strictly required by their role in order to alleviate some of the pressures upon the Court.

13.60 A key aspect of the QLR's role is independence. But what can be done if there is a concern that this independence is, or may be, compromised? Such a situation arose and was considered by the President of the Family Division in *K v P (Criminal Solicitor as Court-Appointed QLR)*[51] when a QLR was appointed to cross-examine the mother on behalf of the father who was a litigant-in-person in the family proceedings. It transpired that the QLR was also instructed by the father in criminal proceedings arising out of DA allegations within which the mother was the main prosecution witness. The mother objected to the father's criminal solicitor continuing in the role of QLR in the Family Court and she applied for an order to discharge his appointment. The President was assisted by submissions from the Association of QLRs, the Association of Lawyers for Children and the Right to Equality and offered guidance to practitioners:

- There should not be a blanket prohibition upon any court-appointed QLR who is also instructed as a solicitor or barrister for the same party in parallel criminal proceedings.

51 *K v P (Criminal Solicitor as Court-Appointed QLR)* (n 21).

- The Family Court does have the power to terminate a QLR appointment and should take the following factors into account when making such a decision:
  - Is the appearance or actuality of QLR independence compromised?
  - Is the protective purpose of the QLR undermined?
  - Is there a perceived or actual conflict of interest?
  - Does it create a material imbalance of disclosure or cross-jurisdictional knowledge?

CONCLUDING REMARKS

13.61 Effective and proper participation in proceedings is a cornerstone of fairness. Those who are vulnerable, whether that be by virtue of their lived experiences or some other reason, must be able to participate effectively in proceedings concerning them and their children.

13.62 As the case law demonstrates, the Court remains obliged to ensure that issues of vulnerability and participation are appropriately addressed within proceedings. As with other aspects of proceedings, the Court may look to other representatives in the case and rely upon them but that does not absolve the Court of its responsibility.

13.63 Many of the reported decisions highlight the importance of ensuring compliance with the provisions; many of the appellate decisions amply (and somewhat ironically) demonstrate that the Court's approach (and often, failure) to properly deal with vulnerability and participation can leave subsequent factual and welfare decisions vulnerable to appeal.

13.64 Much work is still to be done to ensure that those representing victims of DA and other vulnerable parties are appropriately trained. The Family Law Bar Association, in association with the Inns of Court College of Advocacy, have devised and delivered training to its members for free. This training is essential. Yet, whilst initial take up for this training appeared encouraging, recently enthusiasm has waned. This training – and equivalents which may, in time be offered to solicitors and legal executives – is crucial and must be undertaken by all those seeking to represent those who are vulnerable; those who do not complete this training may end up finding themselves overlooked by the Court when decisions are made regarding cross-examination of vulnerable witnesses and other critical case management decisions.

CHAPTER 14

Finding of Fact Hearings: Necessity and Proportionality

14.01 Finding of Fact Hearings represent a significant event in any proceedings concerning the welfare of a child; they provide an opportunity for the Court to determine the factual matrix which will inform welfare arrangements for the child and often arise in the private law arena in the context of domestic abuse (DA). Proceedings can have collateral impact on the adult protagonists – affirmative and cathartic or abusive. The practitioner's duty is to be aware of trauma-informed practice and trial management to avoid the latter, which may impact on relationships long after the Court has ceased to be involved. Proceedings must focus on the necessary litigation to determine decisions for the child's welfare but the Court may find itself having to determine allegations that do not directly involve the child but rather 'set the scene' as to the nature and context of the parental relationship to which the children have been exposed to in order to ensure that any risk the children face going forward is determined and, if possible, managed.

14.02 *The driving focus will always be: will the allegations that the Court is asked to determine, if proven, impact upon the arrangements for the children and their welfare?* The answer to this question should always be 'yes.'

14.03 Because fact-finding hearings may involve allegations in which the child has not been directly involved, the Court has to have a keen eye on necessity and proportionality – a topic that has been frequently commented upon within a number of authorities.

14.04 Per Cobb J (as he then was) in *Re B-B*:

> 'Fact-finding in cases concerning alleged domestic abuse are almost always time-consuming and challenging for judges and magistrates; the responsibility placed on the lay and/or professional judiciary to conduct a fair, thorough and above all a considerate and respectful hearing is indeed "weighty" (*Re H-N* at [6]) particularly where the factual issues are often complex, emotions are invariably raw, and the stakes are so high.'[1]

14.05 Per Peter Jackson LJ in *Re H-D-H (Children)*, the decisions taken day-in day-out whether to hold a fact-finding hearing '... are not always easy decisions

1 *Re B-B* [2022] EWHC 108 (Fam), [13].

and the factors typically do not all point the same way: most decisions will have their downsides'.[2]

14.06 Per Peter Jackson LJ in *Re L (Relocation: Second Appeal)*:

> 'The correct approach to allegations of domestic abuse is set out in PD12J. It sets out a clear and helpful framework to ensure that full consideration is given to the grave effects of domestic abuse, and that proper weight is given to abuse where it is proved. At the same time, the framework requires an exercise of judgement by the court in each case where the issue may arise. Few relationships lack instances of bad behaviour on the part of one or both parties at some time and it is a rare family case that does not contain complaints by one party against the other, and often complaints are made by both. Yet not all such behaviour will amount to "domestic abuse", where "coercive behaviour" is defined as behaviour that is "used to harm, punish or frighten the victim ..." and "controlling behaviour" as behaviour "designed to make a person subordinate ..." In cases where the alleged behaviour does not have this character it is likely to be unnecessary and disproportionate for detailed findings of fact to be made about the complaints; indeed in such cases it will not be in the interests of the child or of justice for the court to allow itself to become another battleground for adult conflict.
>
> The task of identifying cases where allegations of domestic abuse require findings of fact to be made (either as part of main hearing or at a separate fact-finding hearing) is the stock-in-trade of judges in the Family Court, who see private law disputes at every point on the spectrum of seriousness and are constantly making evaluations of this kind. In doing so, they will have assistance from Cafcass, from the parties, and on occasion from their representatives'. [3]

14.07 The approach taken by Peter Jackson LJ in *Re L (Relocation: Second Appeal)* was cited with approval in *Re H-N & Ors (Children) (Domestic Abuse: Finding of Fact Hearings)* to the general effect that: '... not all directive, assertive, stubborn, or selfish behaviour, will be "abuse" in the context of proceedings concerning the welfare of a child; much will turn on the *intention* of the perpetrator of the alleged abuse and on the harmful *impact* of the behaviour'.[4]

Note the key words we have highlighted.

PRACTICE DIRECTION 12J (PD12J)

14.08 PD12J is the 'guidebook' for the court – and practitioners – when considering whether it is both necessary and proportionate to determine disputed

2 *Re H-D-H (Children)* [2021] EWCA Civ 1192, [23].
3 *Re L (Relocation: Second Appeal)* [2017] EWCA Civ 2121, [61]–[62].
4 *Re H-N & Ors (Children) (Domestic Abuse: Finding of Fact Hearings)* [2021] EWCA Civ 448, [32] (emphasis added).

allegations of DA. Whilst supplemented by case law, it is to PD12J practitioners must first turn.

14.09 Paragraph 5 of PD12J takes the Court through each of the factors which should be considered. This is important for practitioners to be aware of in order to allow proper submissions to be made to the Court, which are grounded in both the evidence and the principles which the Court must take into account:

> 'The court must, at all stages of the proceedings, and specifically at the First Hearing Dispute Resolution Appointment ('FHDRA'), consider whether DA is raised as an issue, either by the parties or by Cafcass or CAFCASS Cymru or otherwise, and if so must –
>
> - identify at the earliest opportunity (usually at the FHDRA) the factual and welfare issues involved;
> - consider the nature of any allegation, admission or evidence of domestic abuse, and the extent to which it would be likely to be relevant in deciding whether to make a child arrangements order and, if so, in what terms;
> - give directions to enable contested relevant factual and welfare issues to be tried as soon as possible and fairly;
> - ensure that where domestic abuse is admitted or proven, any child arrangements order in place protects the safety and wellbeing of the child and the parent with whom the child is living, and does not expose either of them to the risk of further harm; and
> - ensure that any interim child arrangements order (i.e. considered by the court before determination of the facts, and in the absence of admission) is only made having followed the guidance in paragraphs 25-27 below.'

14.10 In particular, the Court must be satisfied that any contact ordered with a parent who has perpetrated DA does not expose the child and/or other parent to the risk of harm and is in the best interests of the child. The duty of the Court to consider PD12J cannot be overstated – in fact, decisions may become vulnerable to appeal if PD12J is ignored.[5]

NECESSITY

14.11 Paragraph 16 of PD12J then sets out the circumstances in which the Court may consider a Finding of Fact Hearing in relation to any disputed allegation of DA to be necessary:

> '(a) in order to provide a factual basis for any welfare report or for assessment of the factors set out in paragraphs 36 and 37 below;[6]

5 *Re J (A Child)* [2024] EWFC 77 (B).

6 PD12J, paras 36 and 37 set out the 'factors to be taken into account when determining whether to make child arrangements orders in all cases where domestic abuse has occurred' and shall be explored later in this book.

(b) in order to provide a basis for an accurate assessment of risk;

(c) before it can consider any final welfare-based order(s) in relation to child arrangements; or

(d) before it considers the need for a domestic abuse intervention.'

14.12 Paragraph 17 of PD12J invites the Court to consider all of the evidence before it – or which could be before it – in order to consider the necessity of a Finding of Fact Hearing:

> 'In determining whether it is necessary to conduct a fact-finding hearing, the court should consider –
>
> (a) the views of the parties and of Cafcass or CAFCASS Cymru;
>
> (b) whether there are admissions by a party which provide a sufficient factual basis on which to proceed;
>
> (c) if a party is in receipt of legal aid, whether the evidence required to be provided to obtain legal aid provides a sufficient factual basis on which to proceed;
>
> (d) whether there is other evidence available to the court that provides a sufficient factual basis on which to proceed;
>
> (e) whether the factors set out in paragraphs 36 and 37 below can be determined without a fact-finding hearing;
>
> (f) the nature of the evidence required to resolve disputed allegations;
>
> (g) whether the nature and extent of the allegations, if proven, would be relevant to the issue before the court; and
>
> (h) whether a separate fact-finding hearing would be necessary and proportionate in all the circumstances of the case.'

14.13 It is important to note that PD12J is *guidance*, but it is not legally binding as Court of Appeal decisions are – albeit given, it is the Road Ahead Guidance[7] as was, for example, expressly referred to by the Court of Appeal in *Re H-N & Ors*,[8] and all practitioners are now exhorted to adopt subsequent guidance issued, the distinction might seem a narrow one.[9]

14.14 In *Re H-N & Ors*, the Court of Appeal considered the guidance contained in PD12J and summarised the 'proper approach':

> 'i) The first stage is to consider the nature of the allegations and the extent to which it is likely to be relevant in deciding whether to make a child arrangements order and if so in what terms (PD12J.5).

7 Sir Andrew McFarlane, President of the Family Division, *The Family Court and COVID 19: The Road Ahead*, https://www.judiciary.uk/wp-content/uploads/2020/06/The-Road-Ahead_FINAL.pdf.

8 *Re H-N & Ors* (n 4).

9 Per Lieven J in *TRC v NS* [2024] EWHC 80 (Fam), at [32].

ii) In deciding whether to have a finding of fact hearing the court should have in mind its purposes (PD12J.16) which is, in broad terms, to provide a basis of assessment of risk and therefore the impact of the alleged abuse on the child or children.

iii) Careful consideration must be given to PD12J.17 as to whether it is "necessary" to have a finding of fact hearing, including whether there is other evidence which provides a sufficient factual basis to proceed and importantly, the relevance to the issue before the court if the allegations are proved.

iv) Under PD12J.17(h) the court has to consider whether a separate fact-finding hearing is "necessary and proportionate." The court and the parties should have in mind as part of its analysis both the overriding objective and the President's Guidance as set out in "The Road Ahead".[10]

14.15 The President's Guidance *Fact-finding hearing and domestic abuse in Private Law children law proceedings – Guidance for Judges and Magistrates* was published on 5 May 2022 and gave further directions on the necessity of a Finding of Fact Hearing to the judiciary.[11] 'Make Every Hearing Count' has become a mantra since.

> '*Make every hearing count.* Do not sanction short hearings or agree to insufficient preparation time for the first or other case management hearings on the basis that things can be "sorted out" next time. Seize the opportunity to probe. Remain "in control" throughout. Strive to achieve judicial continuity and take ownership of the case. Remember delay is inimical to child welfare.
>
> As the judge or magistrate, you have the relevant expertise and competence to analyse and determine the necessity for a fact-finding hearing, and if so, the extent of the hearing and the evidence that will be required. *The views of the parties, the CAFCASS officer or the advocates may be persuasive, but they are not determinative; interrogate their reasoning.*
>
> There is a time and a place to determine allegations of domestic abuse, but it may not be in your court. *Unless it will be relevant to, and necessary for, your decision regarding the welfare of the child, do not allow the court to be used to litigate such allegations.*'[12]

14.16 Points practitioners are exhorted to have in mind:

- Question whether contact per se is in issue or not. How does the adult relationship impact on the child's welfare?[13]

10 *Re H-N & Ors* (n 4), [37].

11 President's Guidance, *Fact-finding hearing and domestic abuse in Private Law children law proceedings – Guidance for Judges ad Magistrates* (judiciary.uk, 2022), https://www.judiciary.uk/guidance-and-resources/fact-finding-hearings-and-domestic-abuse-in-private-law-children-proceedings-guidance-for-judges-and-magistrates/.

12 President's Guidance (n 11), paras 1–3 (emphasis added).

13 President's Guidance (n 11), para 5.

- What does Form C1A say to you? Is there a response? Are you getting what you need from the form?
- Consider the definitions of PD12J, paras 2A and 3.
- Can you get more by asking for clarity in court or do you need more evidence?[14]
- What evidence do you need: what, when, where? What was the effect on the child and the parent?[15]

14.17 The guidance continues:

'a. the nature of the allegations and the extent to which those allegations are likely to be relevant to the making of a child arrangement order;

b. that the purpose of a fact finding is to allow assessment of the future risk to the child and the impact of any abuse on the child;

c. whether fact-finding is necessary or whether other evidence suffices; and,

d. whether fact-finding is proportionate.'[16]

PRACTICE NOTE

The bottom line is:

- The nature of the fact-find must be relevant to the welfare of the child: 'If you conclude that the allegations, however serious, would not be relevant to the decision, then no fact-finding hearing is required.'[17]
- The allegations, at their highest, must go to safeguarding in general or to particular circumstances which could not be mitigated by supervision of contact or some other measures.
- If it could be mitigated … why is a Finding of Fact Hearing required?[18]
- It is not an all or nothing question:
  - some allegations may be more obviously linked to welfare than others – can the less obvious ones be subsumed within those particulars rather than allocated a heading of their own?
  - looking at the allegations all together, then separately, are they determinative or supportive?

Do note that Family Justice Council guidance entitled *Family Justice Council Guidance on responding to a child's unexplained reluctance, resistance or refusal to spend time with a parent and allegations of alienating behaviour* is

14 President's Guidance (n 11), paras 7 and 8.
15 President's Guidance (n 11), para 11.
16 President's Guidance (n 11), para 12.
17 President's Guidance (n 11), para 16.
18 President's Guidance (n 11), paras 15–16.

also transferable to the issue of when a Finding of Fact Hearing is necessary despite the fact that the latter guidance primarily concerns alienating behaviours.[19] This guidance has been explored in **Chapter 8**.

14.18 Case management guidance is also given in the 2022 President's Guidance at paras 18–26. Again relevance, purpose and proportionality are fundamental to decision-making. Reinforcing what the Court of Appeal said in *Re H-N & Ors*, the 2022 Guidance states 'it is important for the court to have regard to the need for procedural *proportionality* at all times, both before and during any fact-finding process'.[20]

PRACTICE NOTE

Practice points the Court will have in mind (and so practitioners must do too):

- If third-party disclosure is ordered (police/GP) make it specific, make orders 'targeted and precise' and refuse fishing expeditions.
- Don't timetable without a completed witness template so as to manage party expectations.
- Expect questions directed at controlling questioning.
- Consider and address participation directions. Family Procedure Rules 2010 (SI 2010/2955) (FPR 2010), r 3A and PD3AA are mandatory considerations.
- Make clear in the order what participation steps are to apply going forwards. This is particularly important if the Court is going to have to organise them – such as screens in court and separate reserved waiting rooms.

14.19 In addition, the guidance emphasises the importance of gatekeeping and directions, for example asking whether a Mediation Information and Assessment Meeting (MIAM) has taken place prior to the First Hearing Dispute Resolution Appointment (FHDRA) and, most importantly, interrogating if a fact-finding hearing is required.

14.20 Questions may be raised about Children and Family Court Advisory and Support Service (CAFCASS) knowledge of the case and what it recommends. CAFCASS has previously expressed the view that there should be CAFCASS

19 Family Justice Council, *Family Justice Council Guidance on responding to a child's unexplained reluctance, resistance or refusal to spend time with a parent and allegations of alienating behaviour* (December 2024), https://www.judiciary.uk/wp-content/uploads/2024/12/Family-Justice-Council-Guidance-on-responding-to-allegations-of-alienating-behaviour-2024-1-1.pdf.

20 President's Guidance (n 11), para 36 (emphasis added).

involvement prior to the determination of whether or not a Finding of Fact Hearing is necessary. In *Re H-N & Ors*, CAFCASS told the Court that:

> '... early social work assessment could lead to a conclusion that a fact-finding hearing is not necessary, but that some other intervention would be more helpful. At present, it is rare for there to be any substantive Cafcass involvement prior to fact-finding.'

Contending that the current system is 'sub-optimal,' CAFCASS also suggested in the Court of Appeal that:

> 'the court should direct that Cafcass undertake an enhanced form of safeguarding assessment (including where appropriate meeting the child) prior to the case being listed for a second gatekeeping appointment, with any resulting listing decision being made on a more informed and child-centred basis.'[21]

PRACTICE NOTE

- The practitioner should be alert to any indication that CAFCASS has taken it upon itself to make determinations of key issues of fact that impact on either their contact recommendations or inform their view as to whether a fact-finding hearing is necessary.
- This is not uncommon in the author's experience and this must be challenged early on.
- CAFCASS advice that a fact-finding hearing is not necessary will weigh heavily with a court who is confronted with a long lead time to trial and provided with a way out through an influential CAFCASS recommendation (as they are) that more time spent on contentious litigation and the consequent delay caused is not in the interest of the children.
- The recent CAFCASS *Domestic Abuse Practice Policy* might be said to be rather bland on the need for fact-finding hearing but have it in mind because this will be what the CAFCASS officer has read:

> '36. When there are reports of domestic abuse, that are denied, practitioners must consider the necessity and relevance of a finding of fact hearing as outlined in judicial guidance, which is included within the Cafcass practice aid.
>
> 37. A finding of fact hearing will not be required in every case where domestic abuse is raised as a concern, nor should one be unnecessarily recommended. First and foremost, where there are concerns about domestic abuse and the safety of the child/ren and adults, there needs to be an effective assessment by the practitioner about the nature and impact of any abuse as described throughout this policy. Practitioners are required to consider multiple factors such as, whether there is any other evidence before the court, for example

21 *Re H-N & Ors* (n 4), [38].

> local authority information, criminal convictions and police reports and / or, acceptance of domestic abuse, the child's wishes and feelings and most importantly whether the finding of fact hearing is going to assist the court in conducting its welfare and safety evaluation.'[22]

HOW PRACTITIONERS SHOULD PREPARE FOR THIS

14.21 What really emerges from the guidance is the expectation that the advocates attending court are expected to know the case in detail so as to be able to answer the questions posed by the Court.

> PRACTICE NOTE
>
> The practitioner has to claim ownership of the case, probing and interrogating the papers.
>
> In practice that means being prepared to argue:
>
> - What is necessary in terms of litigation issues/what is a dispensable/optional extra?
> - What evidence is being relied on/challenged?
> - What can be agreed?
> - What disclosure is essential?
> - What questioning of witnesses is necessary, on what issues and how long it will take?
>
> It would also be wise to make allowances for time required for participation adjustments and, above all, come armed with the material cited in this chapter and a thorough knowledge of the papers and case law to argue against short-termism if that is not what justice for your client's case warrants.

14.22 How many advocates, in reality, are briefed or given the file with sufficient time and information to do justice to this onerous task when they may not be the trial advocate? Nonetheless, that is the task that must be done – for the client and for the practitioner's professional reputation.

CASE LAW LIBRARY

14.23 To assist, we set out some of the key case law that the practitioner needs to be familiar with in addition to the material above. It's not an exhaustive list and

22 CAFCASS, *Domestic Abuse Practice Policy* (January 2026), https://www.cafcass.gov.uk/domestic-abuse-practice-policy.

as soon as this has gone to print more authorities will be online. *The practitioner will need to keep abreast of guidance and precedent*, to check what still stands as good guidance or has been refined, rejected – but we provide these case examples as a good base to start from.

14.24 *F v G* must be read in full as it highlighted the importance of active case management, considering the necessity of a Finding of Fact Hearing at the earliest opportunity and considering paras 16 and 17 of PD12J at all procedural junctures.[23] The background is complex and would take too long to repeat here. The appeal judgment offers up salutary reminders about the respective roles of the judge as fact finder and the CAFCASS officer (who is not), the source evidence that the Court should scrutinise, the vital steps in assessing relationships between the respective parents and children that must be undertaken by CAFCASS and the attention it and the Court should give to options other than ceasing direct contact. CAFCASS and the lower court lost its way in managing the case. The litany of professional and case management failing is painful to read.

14.25 In *K v K*, the Court of Appeal considered the circumstances when it is necessary and proportionate for a Finding of Fact Hearing to take place, this time with a *particular emphasis on the primacy that should be given to allegations of coercive and controlling behaviour*.[24] *K v K* concerned a father's second appeal in relation to findings which had been made against him. The mother also made allegations that the father had raped her and that she had been subject to bullying and controlling behaviour by him. At a Finding of Fact Hearing that had been listed at the FHDRA, the judge made a finding of rape, verbal abuse *and* bullying and controlling behaviour.

14.26 The Court of Appeal, however, found that the finding of rape was unsafe because the judge had not looked at the matter in the round. Whilst some of the allegations were made out, the judge at first instance should have considered them in the context of the most serious allegations as this would be definitive as to contact going forward. *Re H-N & Ors*[25] was endorsed but *K v K* issued words of caution to practitioners and the judiciary that a Finding of Fact Hearing should only be listed when it is relevant to the child arrangements. The Court of Appeal chose this case to give 'general guidance on the proper approach to fact-finding hearings in private law family proceedings' post *Re H-N & Ors*. Some have openly said (including one of the authors of this book – Professor Jo Delahunty KC) that this was not the most appropriate fact-based case to be used for such guidance given that allegations of rape were involved.

23 *F v G* [2020] EWHC 2396 (Fam).
24 *K v K* [2022] EWCA Civ 468.
25 *Re H-N & Ors* (n 4).

PRACTICE NOTE

Two points for practitioners to note from *K v K*:

- Legal argument was limited given that, although the mother was represented by (two) junior counsel, the appellant father appeared in person and the child was not a party and hence, not represented.
- We now have 2024 guidance from the Family Justice Council entitled *Family Justice Council Guidance on responding to a child's unexplained reluctance, resistance or refusal to spend time with a parent and allegations of alienating behaviour* to consider (as approved by the President).

14.27 In *K v K* Sir Geoffrey Vos said:

> 'A fact-finding hearing is not free-standing litigation. It always takes place within proceedings to protect a child from abuse or regarding the child's future welfare. It is not allowed to become an opportunity for the parties to air their grievances. Nor is it a chance for parents to seek the court's validation of their perception of what went wrong in their relationship. If fact-finding is to be justified in the first place or continued thereafter, the court must be able to identify how any alleged abusive behaviour is, or may be, relevant to the determination of the issues between the parties as to the future arrangements for the children.
>
> At the risk of repeating what has been said at [37] in *Re H-N* and at [41] above, the main things that the court should consider in deciding whether to order a fact-finding hearing are: (a) the nature of the allegations and the extent to which those allegations are likely to be relevant to the making of a child arrangements order, (b) that the purpose of fact-finding is to allow assessment of the risk to the child and the impact of any abuse on the child, (c) whether fact-finding is necessary or whether other evidence suffices, and (d) whether fact-finding is proportionate.
>
> It seems that a misunderstanding of the court's role has developed. There is a perception that the Court of Appeal has somehow made it a requirement that in every case, in which allegations of domestic abuse are made, it is incumbent upon the court to undertake fact-finding, involving a detailed analysis of each specific allegation made. That is not the case. As *Re H-N* explained and we reiterate here, the duty on the court is limited to determining *only* those factual matters which are likely to be relevant to deciding whether to make a child arrangements order and, if so, in what terms.
>
> In *Re H-N* at [50]-[59], the court explained the correct approach where an allegation of coercive or controlling behaviour is made. The message in those paragraphs was plain. *Where coercive or controlling behaviour is alleged in this context, it is likely to be the primary matter requiring determination, providing that it is likely to be relevant to a live issue relating to a child's*

welfare. Re H-N at [56] made clear that the focus on coercive or controlling behaviour as the primary issue should make it generally unnecessary to determine other subsidiary date-specific factual allegations.

Re H-N at [53] included the following sentence which may inadvertently have been misunderstood. It read:

> "Where however an issue properly arises as to whether there has been a pattern of coercive and/or controlling abusive behaviour within a family, and the determination of that issue is likely to be relevant to the assessment of risk of future harm, a judge who fails expressly to consider the issue may be held on appeal to have fallen into error."

That sentence is a requirement to consider an overarching issue of coercive or controlling behaviour, where to do so is necessary for the determination of a dispute relating to the child's welfare. It is not a requirement for the court to determine every single subsidiary factual allegation that may also be raised. The court only decides individual factual allegations where it is strictly necessary to do so in addition to determining the wider issue of coercive or controlling behaviour when that itself is necessary.'[26]

14.28 We pause to reflect on what could be more serious in terms of partner abuse than rape since it is an extreme form of physical and emotionally coercive controlling behaviour. We suggest that not to have a Finding of Fact Hearing on such an allegation would be striking. In reality, the prevailing view in the profession is that *K v K* was used by the CA as a first opportunity to stem the flood of fact-finding hearings that had been listed since *Re H-N & Ors)*.

PRACTICE NOTE

Practice points going forwards:

- How rape, if proven, can properly be isolated from child protection and welfare issues is an important question and it must be subject to full and proper analysis.
- Use the CAFCASS *Domestic Abuse Practice Policy*[27] to your advantage. It considers the issue to be so significant the presumption of contact falls away. If rape is alleged then surely the only way for the Court to determine contact (in the absence of an admission to the assault or an acceptance there should be no/restricted/limited contact) is for the issue to be litigated?
- Read and apply Annex B of that same Guidance which identifies and analyses the impact of sexually harmful and abusive behaviours for children (dealt with in full in **Chapter 15**) This gives you a toolkit to frame the test of relevance and necessity. Use it.

26 *K v K* (n 24), [65]–[70] (emphasis added).
27 CAFCASS (n 22), para 28.

- Bear in mind the approach taken by Peter Jackson LJ in *Re L (Relocation: Second Appeal)* which we have addressed already in this chapter:

  > '… not all directive, assertive, stubborn, or selfish behaviour, will be "abuse" in the context of proceedings concerning the welfare of a child; much will turn on the intention of the perpetrator of the alleged abuse and on the harmful impact of the behaviour.'[28]

- When should you consider whether a Finding of Fact Hearing is necessary and proportionate? *As soon as possible.* This should also be given *ongoing consideration* throughout the case.
- Can you circumvent the necessity of a Finding of Fact Hearing by proceeding on unproven and disputed facts that are relevant to the welfare analysis? *Obviously not.* That is a basic rule yet one which is often overlooked in the Family Court, with an over-emphasis on issues of delay and court resources.
- Don't be afraid of appealing a decision on refusing to hold a fact-finding hearing that you think is wrong. Make sure you have a reasoned argument, then take the issue on. Failing to grapple with a wrong decision now will have consequences if a later fixture has to be vacated because it is later decided a fact-find hearing *is* required because the welfare implications become more obvious – delay and cost (emotional and financial) have to be faced up to. Be brave.

14.29 In *Re A and B (Children) (Summary Return: Non-Convention State)*, the mother appealed against the decision made by Poole J, asserting that the first instance court failed to apply guidance and PD12J and the judge was wrong not to conduct a Finding of Fact Hearing.[29] The Court of Appeal dismissed the appeal, with Moylan LJ reiterating:

> 'The observations in *Re H-N*, and indeed PD12J itself, make clear the established understanding that domestic abuse is "pernicious." They also make clear that this does not mean the court must undertake a finding of fact hearing in every case in which domestic abuse is alleged.
>
> The approach set out in *Re H-N* is consistent with that set out by Lord Wilson in *Re NY*, at [50], namely that, when the court is considering whether to make a summary order, "it will initially examine whether, in order sufficiently to identify what the child's welfare requires, it should, in the light of the practice direction, conduct an inquiry into the allegations and, if so, how extensive that inquiry should be."'[30]

28 *Re L (Relocation: Second Appeal)* (n 3).
29 *Re A and B (Children) (Summary Return: Non-Convention State)* [2022] EWCA Civ 1664.
30 *Re A and B (Children) (Summary Return: Non-Convention State)* (n 29), [69]–[70].

14.30 In *Re B (A Child) (Allegations of Domestic Abuse in Private Law Proceedings*) the mother appealed against a case management order which set out that her allegations of DA would not be determined or investigated at a final hearing.[31] The mother invited the Court to conduct a composite fact-finding/welfare hearing, which was refused by the first instance judge, leading to the mother appealing that decision which was also dismissed (by Peel J). The mother sought leave to appeal again, which was granted by Peter Jackson LJ. The appeal was allowed since the case turned on 'whether the allegations made by the mother and a third party are relevant to the issue between the parties and capable of having an impact on the final decision'.[32] The Court of Appeal reiterated the President's Guidance from May 2022 which said 'the fundamentals are relevance, purpose and proportionality'[33] and reminded us of the importance of full and proper analysis as required by PD12J.

14.31 In *Re A (A Child) (Findings of Fact)*, a mother appealed against a fact-finding judgment arising from allegations of DA.[34] The mother made 41 allegations, which were grouped under seven headings: stranding, physical abuse and threats, sexual abuse, controlling and coercive behaviour, emotional and psychological abuse, financial abuse, and abuse of the parties' child, S. The father denied all of these allegations, and the first instance judge only made findings on the stranding allegation. The mother pursued an appeal on two grounds: the judge had failed to consider the relevance of the finding of stranding to the other allegations; and there was a flawed approach to the other evidence and insufficient reasons for those findings. The appeal was allowed and remitted for rehearing.

14.32 Jackson LJ highlighted the potential outcomes that the court at first instance could have considered:

> 'In this case, the mother gave a detailed account of a consistent course of seriously abusive behaviour in two countries while the father denied everything. On the face of it, there were three main possibilities for the court to consider: that the mother was broadly telling the truth, that the father was broadly telling the truth, or that each was telling the truth about some things and lying about others, there being no room for an honest mistake. The judge's conclusion was the mother was lying about events in England and the father was lying about events in Pakistan, their credibility in effect running on geographical lines. On these facts that was in my view a truly surprising conclusion. *Perpetration of domestic abuse is an expression of an aspect of a person's character within a relationship and the fact that a person is capable of being seriously abusive in one way inevitably increases the likelihood of them having been abusive in other ways.* There is no indication that the judge acknowledged this. Instead, and despite her correct self-direction, she treated the various limbs of the mother's allegations as

31 *Re B (A Child) (Allegations of Domestic Abuse in Private Law Proceedings)* [2022] EWCA Civ 1439.
32 *Re B (A Child) (Allegations of Domestic Abuse in Private Law Proceedings)* (n 31).
33 President's Guidance (n 11), para 13.
34 *Re A (A Child) (Findings of Fact)* [2022] EWCA Civ 1652.

if they existed in unconnected compartments, so much so that I accept Mr Gration's submission about the stranding allegation and the finding about it being invisible elsewhere in the judgment.'[35]

14.33 In *Re A and B (Child) (Summary Return: Non-Convention State),* the mother and father married in 2007 and lived in Dubai.[36] After separating in 2018, the mother brought the children, A aged ten, and B aged eight to England for a two-week holiday. After arriving in England the mother decided to remain in the country. The father applied for the summary return of the children and the mother alleged that she had been subjected to abusive, coercive, and controlling behaviour. The judge at first instance, declined to order a Finding of Fact Hearing and ordered the summary return of the children. The mother appealed to the Court of Appeal against the return order and the appellate court dismissed the mother's appeal, endorsing *Re H-N & Ors* guidance on the application of PD12J.[37] Moylan LJ indicated that careful consideration must be given to whether it is necessary and proportionate to have a Finding of Fact Hearing.[38] The outcome was that the first instance judge had not erred in deciding that a Finding of Fact Hearing into the mother's allegations of DA against a father was not required before making a summary return order. The judge had referred to those allegations but concluded that a detailed investigation into them would not assist the Court in making decisions about the children's return.

14.34 *A v B (Appeal: Domestic Abuse)*, the appellant mother appealed a private law Finding of Fact judgment where the judge declined to make DA findings against the respondent father. The mother alleged that she had been subjected to sexual, physical, psychological and emotional abuse by the respondent father throughout their marriage as well as alleging that the father physically assaulted their son. The Court took a broad brush approach when examining whether there was a pattern of coercive and controlling behaviour. Poole J held:

> 'The allegations of sexual abuse needed to be considered in the context of all the evidence. As the Court of Appeal said in *Re H-N [2021] EWCA Civ 448* at [45], reducing the field of focus risks robbing the court of "a vantage point from which to view the quality of the alleged perpetrator's behaviour as a whole" and removing "consideration of whether there was a pattern of coercive and controlling behaviour from its assessment." Similarly, the narrow focus of the remaining grounds of this appeal must not obscure the fact that the Judge was considering the whole of the evidence and did not find patterns of coercive and controlling behaviour.'[39]

14.35 In *A v K (Appeal: Fact Finding: PD12J)*, the appellant mother challenged the decision of the first instance judge not to hold a Finding of Fact Hearing within

35 *Re A (A Child) (Findings of Fact)* (n 34), [42] (emphasis added).
36 *Re A and B (Children) (Summary Return: Non-Convention State)* (n 29).
37 *Re H-N & Ors* (n 4).
38 *Re A and B (Children) (Summary Return: Non-Convention State)* (n 29), [68].
39 *A v B (Appeal: Domestic Abuse)* [2023] EWHC 1499 (Fam), [29].

private child law proceedings.[40] At the initial hearing in September 2023, the mother and father made cross allegations of DA. The judge indicated that he did not intend to investigate the allegations of DA and determined that a Finding of Fact Hearing was not necessary to determine the welfare issues in the case. At the subsequent appeal Cobb J upheld the decision on appeal finding that the judgment was faithful to the above principles. Cobb J emphasised that, when deciding whether to hold a Finding of Fact Hearing, the Family Court is underpinned by FPR 2010, rr 1.2, requiring judges to deal with cases 'proportionate to the nature, importance and complexity of the issues' and 1.4(2)(c)(i), requiring judges to '[decide] promptly which issues need investigation and hearing and which do not'.[41]

14.36 In the same paragraph, Cobb J also outlined several points that the courts should consider when deciding whether to hold a Finding of Fact Hearing:

> 'i) Not every case requires a fact-finding hearing even where domestic abuse is alleged (*Re H-N and Others (Children) (Domestic Abuse: Finding of Fact Hearings)* at [8]);
>
> ii) It is important for judges to hold firm to the notion that "[e]very fact-finding hearing must produce something of importance for the welfare decision" (*Re H-D-H* at [21]);
>
> iii) There is a "need for advocates to focus on those issues which it is necessary to determine to dispose of the case, and for oral evidence and/or oral submissions to be cut down only to that which is necessary for the court to hear" (*Re B-B* at [6](iv));
>
> iv) "Decisions about the scope of fact-finding are core case management decisions with particular consequences for the length and cost of proceedings, the impact of the litigation on parties and others, and the allocation of court time" (*Re H-D-H [2021] EWCA Civ 1192* at [3]);
>
> v) The function of the family court judge in resolving issues of fact is different from that of the criminal court judge: see *Re R [2018] EWCA Civ 198* at [62] and *Re H-N and Others (Children) (Domestic Abuse: Finding of Fact Hearings)* at [66]-[74]. The Judge in this case was right not to be distracted by the submission on behalf of the mother that any decision about whether to hold a fact-finding hearing should await a charging decision from the CPS.'[42]

14.37 In *TRC v NS*, the mother appealed against a decision made by magistrates to vacate a Finding of Fact Hearing, who then went on to conclude that a Finding of Fact Hearing was no longer necessary.[43] In allowing the appeal, Lieven J held that PD12J was guidance rather than binding legal precedent and that following PD12J was not a formal 'tick box' exercise but instead: 'the duty on the court is

40 *A v K (Appeal: Fact Finding: PD12J)* [2024] EWHC 1981 (Fam).
41 *A v K (Appeal: Fact Finding: PD12J)* (n 40), [47].
42 *A v K (Appeal: Fact Finding: PD12J)* (n 40).
43 *TRC v NS* (n 9).

to consider whether a fact-find is necessary and proportionate and to have regards to PD12J and apply the relevant case law'.[44]

14.38 In seeking to distinguish Finding of Fact Hearings in private law from those in public law proceedings, Lieven J said:

> 'This case is a good example of why separate fact finds will often be neither necessary, nor indeed helpful in a private law dispute such as this. There is a very strong overlap here between the "facts" and the welfare analysis of what is in the children's best interests. The holding of separate fact finding hearings, and the concept of findings of fact being "binary" emerged from public law cases. In public law cases under Part IV of the Children Act 1989, it will often be necessary to make findings of fact before threshold is crossed, see (inter alia) *Re H (Minors) (Sexual Abuse) 1996 AC 563*. Threshold must be crossed before intervention by a public authority is lawful.
>
> However, in private law there are no "threshold" findings and it may well be that issues of the factual matrix and welfare interests are closely bound up, and best considered together. The jurisdictional basis for private law orders are the considerations under s.1 of the Children Act 1989, and the welfare checklist. This encompasses matters of fact, but also welfare issues. It is both difficult, and often unhelpful to try to compartmentalise these matters.
>
> In many private law cases with allegations of domestic abuse, where the court is focussing on the relevance of such allegations to the best interests of the children, it is much less clear that separating fact finding from welfare is a helpful way to proceed. The welfare checklist focuses the court in considering the case in a holistic manner. The neat categorisation of truth and untruth and hard binary facts, often sits uneasily with the reality of failed relationships. It may be more useful for a court to consider the evidence, including that of the Family Court Advisor, in a holistic way rather than trying to separate facts from welfare.'[45]

14.39 In *Re G & Anor (Children) (Return Order: Return to Ghana)*, Poole J allowed the father to return the two children G, aged 13 and H, aged seven to Ghana following the mother's relocation of the children to England.[46] The mother made allegations of DA against the father and sought a Finding of Fact Hearing. At the Pre-Trial Review (PTR) the Court refused to order a Finding of Fact Hearing, and the mother renewed her application at the start of the final hearing. The Court applied PD12J, *Re H-N & Ors*[47] and *K v K*[48] and the *Fact Finding Hearings and Domestic Abuse in Private Law Children Proceedings – Guidance for Judges and Magistrates*, from Macur LJ, dated 5 May 2022.[49]

44 *TRC v NS* (n 9), [36].
45 *TRC v NS* (n 9), [45]–[47].
46 *Re G & Anor (Children) (Return Order: Return to Ghana)* [2024] EWHC 1453 (Fam).
47 *Re H-N & Ors* (n 4).
48 *K v K* (n 24).
49 President's Guidance (n 11).

Additionally Poole J explained why a Finding of Fact Hearing was not required, referencing case law concerning the return of a child to a non-Hague Convention country and the relevant guidance on DA:

> 'In *Re A and B [2022] EWCA Civ 1664* Moylan LJ held that a "judge has a discretion when deciding the extent of any welfare inquiry including the extent to which allegations of domestic abuse require investigation and determination … As Lord Wilson said in *Re NY*, part of that exercise will include the court determining, in respect of all relevant matters, but in particular in respect of the matters set out in section 1(3) of the Children Act 1989 and any allegations of domestic abuse, whether, in order sufficiently to identify what the child's welfare requires, the court should conduct an inquiry into any or all of those matters and, if so, how extensive that inquiry should be.'[50]

PRACTICE NOTE

When considering the need for a Finding of Fact Hearing, consider the following:

- the intent and impact of the alleged act;
- the impact on any child (direct and indirect);
- the relevance to the welfare of child;
- proportionality; and
- necessity.

Allegations which are not pursued or are unproven must not carry forward into assessment and welfare decisions. They have a binary value of 0.

Practitioners should be careful about the implications of non-pursued allegations and bring the forensic consequences to the Court's attention. The 'stain of suspicion' (Jo Delahunty KC's words) must not be allowed to taint or impact on welfare decisions.

In the absence of a factual determination a practitioner should have the Court order record that the allegations are not being pursued for the given reasons, that the Court has NOT made a summary judgment on their credibility and set out the consequences of that decision.

14.40 In the recent decision of *ER v NT*, MacDonald J offers practitioners a useful summary of the legal principles which ought to be applied when considering necessity and proportionality of a Finding of Fact Hearing.[51] It strongly emphasises that the Court relies upon the Court of Appeal decisions in

50 *Re G & Anor (Children) (Return Order: Return to Ghana)* (n 46), [7].
51 *ER v NT* [2025] EWHC 2146 (Fam).

Re A (A Child)[52] and *Re H*[53] where the Court of Appeal characterises the approach set out in PD12J as obligatory. We can do no better than to direct practitioners to this judgment.

14.41 It is of particular note that MacDonald J specifically considered the decision of Lieven J in *TRC v NS*,[54] observing that it was not a binding decision and did not appear consistent with the Court of Appeal's approach in *Re A* and *Re H* (referred to at **14.40** above) and sought to distinguish between a Finding of Fact Hearing in private law proceedings as opposed to public law proceedings, observing that:

> '... I agree that it is not helpful to seek to draw a distinction between the nature of the fact finding exercise in private law proceedings and that in public law proceedings. The burden of proof in all family proceedings lies on the party seeking to prove the fact asserted and the applicable standard of proof is the balance of probabilities. If follows from these principles that an asserted fact is either proved or it is not proved to the requisite standard by the person on whom the burden rests. The purpose of fact-finding in a case about children is foundational, i.e. to provide a sufficient factual basis for the welfare decisions that fall to be made by reference to s.1 of the Children Act 1989. Whilst in some cases a separate finding of fact hearing may be necessary, in very many cases the fact finding process and the welfare evaluation based on the facts found can be encompassed in a single hearing. However, in circumstances where the findings of fact made by the court provide the foundation of the welfare evaluation, to conflate fact finding and welfare evaluation in private law proceedings as elements of a broadly defined "holistic" process seems to me to risk introducing confusion by depriving the parties of the legal and procedural certainty inherent in the well established civil law approach of finding the facts, applying the relevant law to the facts found and, thereby, arriving at a case specific answer.'[55]

14.42 Finally, the recent case of *Re A (Appeal: Findings of Fact)* is one which should be considered when deciding whether to appeal a Finding of Fact Hearing that did not go your way.[56] This case reaffirmed the high threshold for successful appeals: compelling evidence is required to demonstrate that the judge at first instance failed to consider all relevant information in their determination.

CONCLUDING REMARKS

14.43 Any decision regarding necessity and proportionality is a matter for the Court: it is a judicial decision that carries with it significance for the remainder

52 *Re A (A Child)* [2015] EWCA Civ 486.
53 *Re H* [2016] EWCA Civ 988.
54 *TRC v NS* (n 9).
55 *TRC v NS* (n 9), [59].
56 *Re A (Appeal: Findings of Fact)* [2025] EWHC 1279 (Fam).

of the proceedings. Such a decision will direct the trajectory for the remainder of the proceedings.

14.44 Key points have been highlighted throughout this section but the guiding light will remain: what is the point of the Finding of Fact Hearing? It does not and cannot represent an opportunity for parties to air their grievances against each other. If the allegations (if proven) are likely to interfere with the subsequent welfare decision, the Court should be leaning towards a Finding of Fact Hearing.

14.45 Inevitably, a Finding of Fact Hearing will introduce delay to the proceedings and is likely to result in the parties becoming more polarised: such a process is not conducive to positive co-parenting relations. However, whilst these factors are likely to be informative for the Court, they should not be determinative.

CHAPTER 15

Welfare Decisions in Domestic Abuse Cases

INTRODUCTION

15.01 Making welfare decisions in cases where domestic abuse (DA) is a feature – whether because of convictions, findings or admissions – is far from a straightforward process. The Family Court is equipped with the means to ensure that the welfare decisions it makes are founded on a solid assessment of risk. However, there remains a lack of knowledge, a lack of understanding and a lack of application of these important tools when the Court is making its welfare decisions. That has contributed to debate within the profession, and public campaigning by those who have experienced DA and been involved in Family Court proceedings, which questions whether the Family Court has fairly and properly deployed its arsenal of options to the best effect for children.

15.02 There has been much debate regarding how the Family Court uses the tools available to it brought about as a result of campaigning, as well as the high level of publicity generated by those who have experienced DA and been involved in Family Court proceedings.

15.03 One of the foundations of any welfare decision-making in the Family Court, which has attracted scrutiny for a number of years, is the presumption of parental involvement.

THE PRESUMPTION OF PARENTAL INVOLVEMENT

15.04 With the coming into force of the Children and Families Act 2014, the presumption of parental involvement became effective, inserting s 2A into the Children Act 1989:

> '(2A) A court, in the circumstances mentioned in subsection (4)(a) or (7), is as respects each parent within subsection (6)(a) to presume, unless the contrary is shown, that involvement of that parent in the life of the child concerned will further the child's welfare.'

15.05 Critics of the presumption of parental involvement assert that it has reinforced a pro-contact culture in the Family Court, leading practitioners and judges to minimise (or otherwise ignore) the impact of DA, instead prioritising the need for a child/children to spend time with an abusive parent. This culture can be traced back to the 1970s, with family policy, legal decision-making and professional practice in family proceedings being shaped by the strong assumption that children need contact with non-resident fathers for their emotional, psychological and developmental health.

15.06 In the Ministry of Justice report *Assessing Risk of Harm to Children and Parents in Private Law Children Cases* (the *Harm Report*) it was said that 'respondents felt that courts placed undue priority on ensuring contact with the non-resident parent, which resulted in systemic minimisation of allegations of domestic abuse'.[1] Indeed, the *Harm Report* ultimately concluded that the priority placed on ensuring contact between the child and both parents by the family justice system was one of the barriers to the Family Court addressing DA effectively. Instead, *all* factors that fall to be considered by the Family Court when determining the arrangements for a child/children once DA has been proven must be applied robustly to ensure that the arrangements are safe for both the child(ren) *and* the parent who has suffered DA.

15.07 Since the publication of the *Harm Report*, there have been calls to repeal Children Act 1989, s 2A. As the campaigning organisation Right to Equality identifies, 'decisions about contact should be made that are commensurate with the risks involved and with a full understanding of the nature, dynamics and effects of domestic abuse and the tactics of perpetrators'.[2] However, it has to be observed that in order to fully understand the nature, dynamics and effects of DA and the tactics of perpetrators, there must be a solid knowledge foundation amongst those deciding such cases, those assisting the Court in deciding such cases and those who are representing parties in such cases.

15.08 It is beyond the scope of this book to delve into the arguments for and against the continuation of the presumption of parental involvement. For the time being, it remains on the statute books. Irrespective of the competing arguments, those who are assisting the Court with making decisions about the arrangements for a child must not afford excessive weight to the presumption of parental involvement and must consider whether, in light of the established DA, the presumption has been displaced. This is an exercise which is often overlooked, and practitioners should be alive to the need to seek proper analysis of this issue and, if required, judicial determination. Practitioners will be alive to the legal principles which are applied in the Family Court when determining whether a child should spend time with their other parent. In the decision of *Re M (Children)*, Lady Justice Macur said (emphasis added):

> 'A child's continuing relationship with a non-residential parent is *highly desirable* and contact should not be denied *unless the child's welfare*

1 Ministry of Justice, *Assessing Risk of Harm to Children and Parents in Private Law Children Cases* (Final Report, 2023), para 8.

2 Right to Equality, *Ending the Presumption of Contact in Courts* (May 2024), https://righttoequality.org/wp-content/uploads/2024/05/Presumption-of-Contact-Report-14-May-2024-.pdf, p 43.

demands it. Domestic violence is not, in itself, a bar to direct contact, but *must be assessed in the circumstances as a whole.*'[3]

15.09 In *Re M (Children)*, the Court of Appeal was not seeking to give primacy to the presumption of parental involvement. The emphasised parts of Macur LJ's comment illustrate that contact is not essential but rather *'highly desirable'* and must be viewed in the context of the child's welfare as a whole. Additionally, DA *'must'* (note the Court of Appeal's use of the word 'must') be viewed in the context of the individual case.

15.10 In October 2025, the government announced its intention to repeal the presumption of parental involvement from the Children Act 1989 when Parliamentary time allows.[4] The Ministry of Justice (MOJ) review suggested that the Family Court takes 'a "no stone unturned" approach and [is] intrinsically geared towards fostering involvement for a child with both their parents after separation'. However, at the same time, 'evidence around judicial decision-making suggested that the presumption was not routinely referenced by judges and magistrates when they made decisions about contested child arrangements orders'. It was further suggested that practice and the resulting court decisions could leave children at risk of ongoing harm. Repealing the presumption of parental involvement will mean that the Family Court need no longer work from the starting point that parental involvement is in the child's best interests and will allow a proper, thorough and holistic assessment of each child's wellbeing on a case-by-case basis, according to the Domestic Abuse Commissioner, by prioritising this approach, decisions will be safer.[5]

15.11 The December 2025 (released 6 January 2026) reissue of the Children and Family Court Advisory and Support Service (CAFCASS) *Domestic Abuse Practice Policy* deals with this interregnum stage through its Annex A. It states:

> 'Until the repeal takes effect, Cafcass' position remains, as clearly set out in our Domestic Abuse Practice Policy and training, that the presumption falls away when a parent has caused harm or there is a risk of harm or further harm to the child. Cafcass practitioners must always proceed with their assessments using the primary principle of the Children Act 1989 which is that the safety and welfare of every child must remain paramount. This means adhering to:
>
> - The welfare checklist in section 1(3) of the Children Act 1989, which focuses on the individual needs and specific family circumstances of each child.

3 *Re M (Children)* [2013] EWCA Civ 1147, [14].

4 Ministry of Justice, *Review of the Presumption of Parental Involvement Final Report* (October 2025), https://assets.publishing.service.gov.uk/media/68f5f5c206e6515f7914c7e3/Review_of_the_Presumption_of_Parental_Involvement_Final_Report_.pdf.

5 Domestic Abuse Commissioner, 'Domestic Abuse Commissioner responds to the removal of the presumption of parental involvement' (October 2025), https://domesticabusecommissioner.uk/domestic-abuse-commissioner-responds-to-the-removal-of-the-presumption-of-parental-involvement/.

- The UN Convention of the Rights of the Child, especially in relation to the best interests of the child being the primary consideration (Article 3); preventing separation from family against their will except when authorities subject to judicial review determine that separation is necessary for the best interests of the child (Article 9); and the right of the child to be heard in matters affecting them (Article 12).
- Cafcass' Child Safeguarding Policy (as well as the domestic abuse practice policy) which sets out what practitioners must do when they are concerned about a child's welfare or safety.'[6]

PRACTICE DIRECTION 12J

15.12 It is important to acknowledge that, in cases where DA is found, proven or otherwise established, the presumption of contact falls away but contact between the child and a perpetrator *may* still be viable. It is a question of risk assessment and whether such a risk can be managed. When assessing such risks, it is important that the risks the Court concerns itself with are not simply the risks for the child. The risks for the *victim* of the DA must also be carefully evaluated, not just at the closing stages of a case, but throughout. The bullet points above from Annex A of the policy demonstrate issues CAFCASS will be directing itself towards in such a situation. Every case will turn on its facts.

15.13 The issue of contact between an alleged perpetrator of DA and a child will, almost always, be raised as a preliminary issue for the Court to resolve at the commencement of proceedings. Practice Direction 12J (PD12J) of the Family Procedure Rules 2010 (SI 2010/2955) (FPR 2010) provides practitioners and the Court with a framework within which to consider both interim arrangements for a child in cases where DA is *alleged* and substantive decisions in cases where DA is *established*. Of course, the Court is unlikely to make decisions relating to the arrangements for a child without some professional input. In the majority of cases, this input is likely to come from CAFCASS and, particularly at the outset of proceedings, such input is likely to be based upon limited (and contested) information.

PRACTICE NOTE

It is important that practitioners familiarise themselves with CAFCASS' own DA guidance, which will be discussed later in this chapter, as this is likely to inform the input they offer to the Court. This will also allow practitioners to check which formulation CAFCASS is applying in each case. A step they must take, given the evolution of the guidance in recent months, the most recent version being reissued December 2025 and published on 6 January 2026 as this text was going into final edit.

6 CAFCASS, *Domestic Abuse Practice Policy* (January 2026), https://www.cafcass.gov.uk/domestic-abuse-practice-policy.

Interim orders

15.14 At the outset of Children Act 1989 proceedings in which allegations of DA are raised, the Court is highly likely to be engaged with the issue of interim arrangements for the children. In many cases, this will be the priority for the parties – particularly the parent who is not currently spending time with the children. Decisions are usually informed by the information provided to the Court by CAFCASS in its preliminary letter to the Court.

15.15 There are, however, a number of factors which result in the Court having difficulty grasping this particular issue at a First Hearing Dispute Resolution Appointment (FHDRA). Some of these factors are, arguably, systemic issues focused more on getting cases through the court system quickly and efficiently than on the welfare of the children with whom the Court is concerned.

15.16 These include:

(a) In cases allocated to the magistrates' court (of which there are many), FHDRAs are routinely conducted by a legal adviser sitting without magistrates. The powers a legal adviser has in such circumstances can be identified by reference to Practice Direction 2C of the FPR 2010. In short, they are unable to resolve or otherwise determine disputed issues, one of which is usually interim contact.

(b) FHDRAs are typically given one hour of court time: an insufficient length to determine all disputed issues.

(c) The information before the Court on the welfare issues at this stage is routinely limited.

(d) Resources which may allow for safe arrangements for contact to take place (ie contact centres) are scarce and/or expensive, therefore placing them outside of the reach of the parties.

15.17 In addition to these practical issues, practitioners must have regard to para 25 of PD12J, which requires setting out in full:

> 'Where the court gives directions for a fact-finding hearing, or where disputed allegations of domestic abuse are otherwise undetermined, the court should not make an interim child arrangements order unless it is satisfied that it is in the best interests of the child to do so and that the order would not expose the child or the other parent to an unmanageable risk of harm (bearing in mind in particular the definition of "victim of domestic abuse" and the impact which domestic abuse against a parent can have on the emotional well-being of the child, the safety of the other parent and the need to protect against domestic abuse).'

PRACTICE NOTE

For the Court to be satisfied that it is in the best interests of the child to make an interim child arrangements order, the Court needs two things: information and time to evaluate that information in the context of the case. When preparing a case for court, practitioners should – objectively – consider what information is likely to assist the Court in determining whether it should make an interim child arrangements order and ensure that this information is placed before the Court in a timely manner. This information should have regard to what the Court should be considering – not simply what the parent seeks. For the best chance of a favourable outcome, the parent seeking an interim child arrangements order would be well advised to frame their aspirations in the context of the factors the Court must take into consideration. These factors are clearly set out in paras 26–27B of PD12J and should not be ignored. This is important reading for all practitioners and parents who are inviting the Court to make an interim child arrangements order.

Given the limited time often allocated to FHDRAs (as well as the limited powers available to legal advisers when sitting alone), dealing with contested issues relating to interim child arrangements is likely to be difficult. Parties may be keen to invite the Court to list a further hearing of sufficient length to determine interim arrangements: the success or otherwise of such an invitation is likely to be case-specific as well as court-specific (some courts will be more willing than others to list such a hearing). It is, however, important to understand – and to ensure that clients understand – the factors that the Court should take into consideration when making an interim welfare decision. Framing a case in accordance with such considerations, rather than avoiding them or minimising their importance and relevance, is likely to assist the Court in arriving at a decision.

Substantive arrangements for children

15.18 In addition to the guidance it gives to the Family Court in making interim child arrangements orders, Practice Direction12J sets out the factors the Court should take into consideration when determining whether to make a child arrangements order in all cases where DA has occurred.

15.19 The case of *Re H (A Child: Contact: Domestic Abuse)* involved an appeal to the Court of Appeal against a first instance decision which saw a child arrangements order being made against a background of DA.[7] The child arrangements order provided for the father to have no face-to-face contact with his three-year-old son for an indefinite period. The Court of Appeal endorsed the approach of MacDonald J in *D v E (Termination of Parental Responsibility)* with

7 *Re H (A Child: Contact: Domestic Abuse)* [2024] EWCA Civ 326.

regards to the general approach to be taken towards contact in cases where DA is a feature, setting out what MacDonald J said at paras [24]–[27]:

'Child Arrangements Order – Termination of Contact

Applications for a child arrangements order under s.8 of the Children Act 1989 require the court to apply the principles set out in s.1 of the 1989 Act. In this case, the order sought is that there be no contact between G and her father. Within this context, I in particular note and bear in mind that s.1(2A) of the Children Act 1989 provides as follows:

> "(2A) A court, in circumstances mentioned in subsection (4)(a) or (7), is as respects each parent within subsection (6)(a) to presume, unless the contrary is shown, that involvement of that parent in the life of the child concerned will further the child's welfare."

With respect to assessing whether the contrary is shown for the purposes of s.1(2A) of the Children Act 1989, I further bear in mind that the courts have, historically, held that it is almost always in the interest of a child whose parents are separated that he or she should have contact with the parent with whom he or she is not living. This principle, and the following further applicable principles can be drawn from the decisions of the Court of Appeal in *Re C (Direct Contact: Suspension)* [2011] 2 FLR 912 at [47], *Re W (Direct Contact)* [2013] 1 FLR 494 and *Re J-M (A Child)* [2014] EWCA Civ 434 at [25]:

> "i) The welfare of the child is paramount and the child's best interests must take precedence over any other consideration.
>
> ii) There is a positive obligation on the State and therefore on the judge to take measures to promote contact, grappling with all available alternatives and taking all necessary steps that can reasonably be demanded, before abandoning hope of achieving contact.
>
> iii) However, the positive obligation on the State, and therefore on the court, is not absolute. Whilst authorities must do their utmost to facilitate the co-operation and understanding of all concerned, any obligation to apply coercion in this area must be limited since the interests, as well as the rights and freedoms of all concerned must be taken into account and, more particularly, so must the best interests of the child.
>
> iv) Excessive weight should not be accorded to short term problems and the court should take a medium and long term view.
>
> v) Contact should be terminated only in exceptional circumstances where there are cogent reasons for doing so, as a last resort, when there is no alternative, and only if contact will be detrimental to the child's welfare.
>
> vi) The key question, and the question requiring stricter scrutiny, is whether the court has taken all necessary steps to facilitate contact as can reasonably be demanded in the circumstances of the particular case."

These principles must be read in light of FPR 2010 PD12J, entitled Child Arrangements and Contact Orders: Domestic Abuse and Harm, which provides as follows at paragraph [7]:

> "In proceedings relating to a child arrangements order, the court presumes that the involvement of a parent in a child's life will further the child's welfare, unless there is evidence to the contrary. The Court must in every case consider carefully whether the statutory presumption applies, having particular regard to any allegation or admission of harm by domestic abuse to the child or parent or any evidence indicating such harm or risk of harm."

The foregoing principles set out in PD12J are expressed by reference to domestic abuse. However, it is plain that this approach will apply, in proceedings relating to a child arrangements order, to all allegations or admissions of harm to the child or parent relevant to the question of contact or evidence indicating such harm or risk of harm. Within this context, I note that paragraphs 35 to 37 of PD12J enjoin the court, inter alia, to take the following factors into account when considering child arrangements in cases where the court is satisfied that such harm has occurred:

> "i) The court should ensure that any order for contact will not expose the child to an unmanageable risk of harm and will be in the best interests of the child.
>
> ii) The court should apply the individual matters in the welfare checklist set out in s.1(3) of the Children Act 1989 with reference to the harm that has occurred and any expert risk assessment obtained.
>
> iii) In particular, the court should consider any harm which the child, and the parent with whom the child is living, is at risk of suffering if a child arrangements order is made.
>
> iv) The court should make an order for contact only if it is satisfied that the physical and emotional safety of the child and the parent with whom the child is living can, as far as possible, be secured before, during and after contact.
>
> v) The court should consider, inter alia, whether the parent is motivated by a desire to promote the best interests of the child or is using the process to continue a form of abuse against the other parent and the capacity of the parents to appreciate the effect of past abuse and the potential for future abuse."'[8]

15.20 In endorsing the approach of MacDonald J in *D v E (Termination of Parental Responsibility)*, the Court of Appeal emphasised, at [46], that:

> '… the court must approach the fundamental welfare assessment that underlies every decision with full alertness both to the inherent value of the

8 *D v E (Termination of Parental Responsibility)* [2021] EWFC 37, [24]–[27].

parent-child relationship and to the significance of any harm that a contact order may entail for the child or for the parent with care. Where these considerations conflict, the court must identify the best solution for the child or, where there is no good solution, the least worst one.'[9]

PRACTICE NOTE

Practitioners should be alert to the approach taken by MacDonald J in *D v E (Termination of Parental Responsibility)* as well as the summary offered by Peter Jackson LJ in *Re H (A Child: Contact: Domestic Abuse)* and have this at the forefront of their minds when considering the guidance given in PD12J, which goes some way to directing those engaged in these cases towards the factors that are likely to assist the Court.

Paragraph 32

15.21 The guidance within PD12J begins with para 32 of PD12J which provides that:

> 'The court should take steps to obtain (or direct the parties or an Officer of Cafcass or a Welsh family proceedings officer to obtain) information about the facilities available locally (to include local domestic abuse support services) to assist any party or the child in cases where domestic abuse has occurred.'

15.22 In reality, this information is provided by CAFCASS and local authorities who are preparing reports pursuant to Children Act 1989, s 7 or s 37 (or guardians representing children). It is likely to be of assistance for such information to be freely available in family court so that information is readily available at each stage of the process. Unfortunately, such reports are usually only available many weeks after the determination of any domestically abusive behaviour. This issue will be returned to at para **15.23**.

Paragraph 33

15.23 The guidance continues at para 33:

> 'Following any determination of the nature and extent of domestic abuse, whether or not following a fact-finding hearing, the court must, if considering any form of contact or involvement of the parent in the child's life, consider:

9 *Re H (A Child: Contact: Domestic Abuse)* (n 7), [46].

(a) Whether it would be assisted by any social work, psychiatric, psychological or other assessment (including an expert safety and risk assessment) of any party or the child and if so (subject to any necessary consent) make directions for such assessment to be undertaken and for the filing of any consequent report.[10] Any such report should address the factors set out in paragraphs 36 and 37 below, unless the court directs otherwise;

(b) Whether any party should seek advice, treatment or other intervention as a precondition to any child arrangements order being made, and may (with the consent of that party) give directions for such attendance.'

15.24 It is worth highlighting the use of the word 'must' in the opening sentence of para 33: the Court *must* consider the need for further assessment and the outcome of such an assessment as part of its overall consideration. Again, the Court is likely to rely upon some form of social work assessment – whether that be prepared pursuant to Children Act 1989, s 7 or s 37, or as part and parcel of an FPR 2010, r 16.4 guardian role – in order to discharge its obligation under this paragraph. Practitioners (particularly those representing or otherwise assisting victims of DA) must be on the lookout for this.

Paragraph 34

15.25 Paragraph 34 provides some clarity surrounding the advice, treatment or other intervention referred to in para 33:

> 'Further or as an alternative to the advice, treatment or other intervention referred to in paragraph 33(b) above, the court may make an Activity Direction under section 11A and 11B Children Act 1989. Any intervention directed pursuant to this provision should be one commissioned and approved by Cafcass. It is acknowledged that acceptance of a domestic abuse intervention is subject to a suitability assessment by the service provider, and that completion of a domestic abuse intervention will take time in order to achieve the aim of risk-reduction for the long-term benefit of the child and the parent with whom the child is living.'

15.26 Whilst there is an acknowledgment that such intervention will take time, what is not clear from this paragraph is whether such time should be permitted before the Court is able to make final welfare decisions. This is particularly relevant in light of the statutory principle that delay is inimical to the child's welfare[11] and the current pressures upon the Family Court to resolve cases quickly and expeditiously.

10 Whilst this paragraph refers to 'whether the court would be assisted by [an expert report],' it is important to bear in mind that any such application must be considered 'necessary for the just resolution of the proceedings' and therefore, the wording of this paragraph does not imply a lower standard.

11 Children Act 1989, s 1(2).

Paragraphs 35–37

15.27 Not only do paras 35–37 guide those who are preparing reports for the Court, they allow practitioners to ensure that all relevant matters are covered and serve as a benchmark for the Court in considering the most appropriate welfare outcome.

15.28 Note that, within para 35, the language changes so that 'the court *should*' rather than '*must*':

> 'When deciding the issue of child arrangements the Court should ensure that any order for contact will not expose the child to an unmanageable risk of harm and will be in the best interests of the child.'

15.29 There are two aspects at play within para 35. Firstly, the Court *should* ensure that any order for contact will not expose the child to an unmanageable risk of harm. This issue will require a clear and unambiguous determination as to the nature and extent of DA experienced by the victim so that the impact of that DA can be properly explored. It is important to highlight that the impact of the DA cannot simply be confined to the parent who suffered it but extends to the child(ren) also.

15.30 Secondly, the court *should* consider whether any order for contact will be in the best interests of the child. The case law in this area may lead to the conclusion that contact is almost always in the child's best interests but care should be taken to consider the nature and extent of the proven DA so that the child's best interests are assessed in full possession of the facts.

15.31 Paragraph 36 goes on to offer some guidance as to the factors which the Court should take into consideration:

> '(1) In the light of-
>
> > (a) any findings of fact,
> >
> > (b) admissions; or
> >
> > (c) domestic abuse having otherwise been established,
> >
> > the court should apply the individual matters in the welfare checklist with reference to the domestic abuse which has occurred and any expert risk assessment obtained.
>
> (2) In particular, the court should in every case consider any harm-
>
> > (a) which the child as a victim of domestic abuse, and the parent with whom the child is living, has suffered as a consequence of that domestic abuse; and
> >
> > (b) which the child and the parent with whom the child is living is at risk of suffering, if a child arrangements order is made.
>
> (3) The court should make an order for contact only if it is satisfied-

(a) that the physical and emotional safety of the child and the parent with whom the child is living can, as far as possible, be secured before, during and after contact; and

(b) that the parent with whom the child is living will not be subjected to further domestic abuse by the other parent.'

15.32 Again, this is not mandatory and simply highlights the factors that the court *should* take into consideration, with para 37 providing further detail:

> 'In every case where a finding or admission of domestic abuse is made, or where domestic abuse is otherwise established, the court should consider the conduct of both parents towards each other and towards the child and the impact of the same. In particular, the court should consider –
>
> (a) the effect of the domestic abuse on the child and on the arrangements for where the child is living;
>
> (b) the effect of the domestic abuse on the child and its effect on the child's relationship with the parents;
>
> (c) whether the parent is motivated by a desire to promote the best interests of the child or is using the process to continue a form of domestic abuse against the other parent;
>
> (d) the likely behaviour during contact of the parent against whom findings are made and its effect on the child; and
>
> (e) the capacity of the parents to appreciate the effect of past domestic abuse and the potential for future domestic abuse.'

15.33 It is important that practitioners are familiar with the matters which ought to be considered in any welfare report placed before the Court in cases where DA has been established. Familiarity with these important parts of PD12J will enable practitioners and the judiciary to apply a benchmark to the welfare evaluations advanced by CAFCASS/CAFCASS Cymru/The National Youth Advisory Service (NYAS)/local authorities to ensure that all relevant matters are explored and evaluated, thereby testing the strength or otherwise of the recommendations advanced within them.

15.34 Contact between a child and parent who has perpetrated DA can take many forms, from the full parental role, including extended periods of overnight, unsupervised contact, through to indirect contact in the form of letters and gifts and, in some cases, no contact at all.

CAFCASS DOMESTIC ABUSE POLICY: AN OVERVIEW OF ITS EVOLUTION

15.35 In September of 2024, CAFCASS published a new *Domestic Abuse Practice Policy*, partly in response to the recommendations made within the

Harm Report, published in 2020.[12] The policy was then subject to review – and was republished – in January 2025. That reissue emphasised CAFCASS' statutory responsibilities in assessing harm and risk for children, reinforced the importance of the Family Court Adviser's independence and responsibility to assess and advise the court of the unique characteristics and vulnerability of the child. It also clarified when referral should be made to the local authority. January 2026 brought the publication of the next iteration of the policy to professional and public attention (dated 10 December 2025).

15.36 What does this latest formulation add? CAFCASS says it:

> 'emphasises the importance of engaging with other adults and professionals that know the child, strengthen[s] equality, diversity and inclusion considerations, further clari[fies] … language, update[s] on the presumption of parental involvement, emphasises analysis of post-separation abuse and action when experiencing intimidation from adults in proceedings, clarifie[s] evidence needed to consider perpetrator behaviour, [provides] additional guidance on identification and analysis of sexually harmful adult behaviour.'[13]

15.37 The policy is made up of 45 points that practitioners must consider in their assessments under headings: Domestic abuse practice policy; Child safeguarding; Public law; Private law; Investigation or conviction of domestic abuse offences, including sexual offences; Practice Direction 12J; Findings of fact; and Requirements derived from learning from practice and from victims of domestic abuse. The CAFCASS policies do not stand alone as a set of rules in the Family Court proceedings but they do set out what is expected as part of effective professional practice when making recommendations to the Court. Although not legally binding, this guidance does set out what factors CAFCASS – and therefore, the Court, practitioners and those who have cases before the Family Court – expect its Family Court advisers and guardians to take into consideration in their practice and their recommendations.

CAFCASS makes the practical effect of this policy clear

> 'Our policies do not stand alone as a set of rules. They set out what is expected as an integral part of effective professional practice in preparing advice for family court proceedings, and they must be applied in parallel with professional assessment and the balancing of information about what is known and understood in respect of the safety, welfare and best interests of children.'

15.38 With the Domestic Abuse Act 2021 (DAA 2021) and PD12J informing CAFCASS' policy, the protection of children from harm or further harm is the central and fundamental purpose of the policy. It is important to note that this policy is applicable to both public and private law proceedings. Practitioners

12 CAFCASS (n 6).
13 CAFCASS (n 6), p 11.

must familiarise themselves with the policy as it continues to evolve. Note the next update is due June 2026.

15.39 Key aspects of this policy which are likely to be of particular relevance to those who are advising and representing those who have experienced DA (including where care is likely to be required by those acting for parties in the Family Court) include:

(a) As the DAA 2021 recognises the child as a victim of DA (DAA 2021, s 3), CAFCASS officers must be specific in their reports about what has happened to the child. This draws on the Domestic Abuse Commissioner's report *Tell Nicole*: children 'want to be listened to, taken seriously, treated respectfully and to be believed when they share their experiences'.[14] This must include being specific about what the CAFCASS officer has been told has happened, what is already known, and the further risk of harm to them should they live with or spend time with a domestically abusive parent or carer. The latter assessment must include consideration of the impact of supervised contact and other forms of contact such as letters, telephone and video calls. This information must weigh heavily in any analysis, assessment and advice to the Court.

PRACTICE NOTE

The incorporation of the DAC material on the significance of a child wanting to be 'believed' is going to be an interesting scenario in terms of practice. In public law we have long since relinquished words that imply an allegation amounts to an established fact. Belief is subjective. The older the child, the more challenging their questioning of the professional may be 'do you believe me'/'you must believe me'. How will that challenge be negotiated, recorded and relayed to the Court (or indeed back to the child – either directly or indirectly). The CAFCASS officer cannot go beyond facts found or predict what may or may not be found.

(b) The child's experiences, views, wishes and feelings must be clearly set out. If they are too young or have additional needs, their perspective and the impact of harm that has already happened and/or the risk of further harm must still be clear to the Court, 'practitioners must be especially clear about harm or the risk of harm to them by listening to their primary carers and those who know them well' including other adults and professionals. In order to ensure the integrity of the child's experiences, views, wishes and feelings, care should be taken to ensure that this information is as objective as possible.

(c) Any analysis must include the impact on the parent(s) or carer(s) with parental responsibility and their capacity and safety if they are or it is

14 Report referred to at CAFCASS (n 6), n 2: DAC, *Tell Nicole "Our feelings matter" Children's views on the support they need after experiencing domestic abuse* (2025), https://domesticabusecommissioner.uk/wp-content/uploads/2025/04/dac_bcyp_tell-nicole_report_FINAL-DIGITAL-2.pdf.

proposed they are to manage family time with an adult who is or may be a risk to their child and to them. This information must weigh heavily in any analysis, assessment and advice to the Court.

(d) CAFCASS officers must provide a clear, unequivocal, evidence-informed and compelling rationale in their reports when recommending 'time with' or 'live with' arrangements with a parent when DA and harm has been shared with the practitioner by the child or by one or both parents.

PRACTICE NOTE

Care must be taken to ensure that such information accords with any findings which the Court has made. Additionally, whilst PD12J requires a proper analysis of risk before the Court makes a Child Arrangements Order, practitioners must remain alive to the case law insofar as parent-child contact is concerned.

(e) In long running or repeat proceedings, CAFCASS officers must reflect and take account of previous history and patterns of behaviour, reports of or known DA, safeguarding checks, previous findings of fact and criminal history, identifying any gaps or themes and including the reasons for proceedings (which might be used to further control and abuse victims). Further or additional police information which becomes available during proceedings must be scrutinised to inform assessment and new or additional reports to court.

(f) When adults describe DA, including coercive control, rape and similar criminal acts, and the child is living with, or spending time with, the parent who is or may have perpetrated these acts, practitioners must consider and describe in their reports to court how they assessed the harm or risk of further harm to a child and their main carer.[15] Where this assessment concludes that a child is at risk of harm, they report they are being harmed or they are known to have been harmed, *and* there is considered to be a *current* risk to the child of harm, then formal child protection procedures must be followed in the form of a referral to the local authority children's social care service where the child is living. If such a referral is made, then a Children Act 1989, s 16A risk assessment report should be made to the Court immediately, setting out the rationale for any urgent action that is required to protect the child(ren).

(g) In accordance with Children Act 1989, s 1(2A), the presumption of parental involvement in the life of a child is not absolute. The presumption falls away when the parent has caused harm or there is a risk of harm or further harm to the child

15 Those who are familiar with how the Family Court *should* be dealing with these cases will recognise that this exercise should have been undertaken if regard was had to PD12J.

PRACTICE NOTE

It is unclear whether those professionals who are undertaking assessment are able to displace this statutory presumption or whether this requires a judicial determination. Further, there is a distinction between parental involvement and contact. Any analysis by CAFCASS must consider this distinction. See the aforementioned Annex A to the reissued policy guidance as to how CAFCASS will interpret that balance.

(h) In considering recommendations for family time when the applicant or respondent has a conviction, or has been sentenced for an offence in relation to DA (including coercive control), violence or a sexual offence, practitioners must consider that the adult or adults concerned present a risk of significant harm to the child, connected children and the main carers. The advice to the Court should clearly set out an analysis of the risk of harm to the child and how this affects the advice regarding contact and/or live with arrangements, including any action that should be taken to protect the child(ren) and their main carer from harm or risk of further harm.[16]

PRACTICE NOTE

Now see para 28 of the reissued policy guidance and specifically Annex B. This represents an evolution in approach.

Annex B identifies that 'behaviour often reveals underlying attitudes and patterns that increase risk to children'.

- 'A history of violence or coercion in intimate relationships indicating a pattern of using power and control, which can extend to children.
- The minimisation or denial of offending behaviour suggesting a lack of accountability and poor motivation for change.
- Sexual entitlement or distorted beliefs about consent, for example beliefs such as "consent is negotiable" or "victims provoke".'

The victim's voice must be captured in their own words, with the impact of the abuse clearly reflected in recommendations, directly linking harm analysis to decisions about family time and safety planning.

15.40 Moving on to consider PD12J, CAFCASS highlights that, if a parent has a conviction for a sexual offence such as rape, the risk of harm to a child should they have contact with that parent is likely to be significant. Earlier in this chapter, we considered paras 35–37 of PD12J and noted that the wording of those paras was not mandatory but, rather, set out what should be taken into account by those

16 As stated earlier, this exercise should have been undertaken if regard was had to PD12J.

considering contact with children upon findings of DA. In contrast, CAFCASS' guidance makes it clear that the factors set out in paras 35–37 *must* be followed in order to evidence the risks to the child.

15.41 As part of CAFCASS' analysis, the guidance suggests that consideration should also be given to Practice Direction 12Q and an application for an order pursuant to Children Act 1989, s 91(14).

15.42 CAFCASS reminds its practitioners that they must not dismiss or minimise DA as 'historical' or as a one-off incident – whilst such a reminder should not be necessary, the fact that it is needed is indicative of some of the views in the family justice system regarding DA. CAFCASS explains that dismissing or minimising DA: 'reveals to victims a lack of understanding of the ongoing and long-term trauma of domestic abuse and perpetuates it. It may also increase the risk of harm or further harm to the adult or child victim'.[17]

PRACTICE NOTE

The relevance of 'historic', 'one-off' abuse. This is a key point. We know from case reports and anecdotal evidence of many a time when past DA has been minimised and said not to be a current risk factor because it was said to be an issue of the past, implying it has been resolved by time or a flash in the pan. Not so. It is a risk red flag.

Paragraph 35 of the reissued policy guidance is directly referable to the *Harm Report*. CAFCASS now acknowledges that

> 'Practitioners are required to be specific about and act upon the risk, behaviours and impact of post separation abuse. Domestic abuse does not stop because a relationship has ended. It is often a point of escalation in frequency and severity of risk that can include using the family proceedings to harm, coerce and control.'[18]

15.43 Furthermore, CAFCASS warns its practitioners that they should not reinterpret or reword what they are told about a person's experience of DA, including the impact of that DA. Now Annex B tells CAFCASS that the 'victim's voice *must* be captured in their own words' (the emphasis on must). Clearly recognising that using the person's own words and account of their experience *may not* accord with the Court's determination of matters, CAFCASS reminds those reading the policy that it is for the Court to consider disputed accounts and to determine the facts.

15.44 This policy is an important development in how DA is considered in the Family Court. Whilst it, in part at least, addresses some of the recommendations

17 CAFCASS (n 6), para 38.
18 CAFCASS (n 6), para 35.

from the *Harm Report*, the extent to which it will be implemented remains to be seen. The policy offers clear guidance in many respects; but the true impact of its implementation will depend on systemic change and education throughout the family justice system.

CHILD ARRANGEMENTS

15.45 Pursuant to Children Act 1989, s 8, the Court has the power to make an order regulating the arrangements for a child, whether those be living arrangements or the time the child should spend with the other parent. Prior to the coming into force of the Children and Families Act 2014, such an order was often two separate orders: a 'residence order' and a 'contact order'. Notwithstanding the passage of time, it is still common for terms such as 'residence' and 'contact' to be used interchangeably with 'child arrangements order'.

15.46 Earlier in this chapter, we discussed the factors the Court should take into consideration when determining whether to make a child arrangements order – those factors will not be repeated here *but see below*.

PRACTICE NOTE

Bear in mind that the Court must consider whether to make a Child Arrangements Order goes beyond what the *actual* arrangements for the child should be and focuses instead on the name to be given to each component of the order, further bearing in mind that the labelling can have a significant impact on how the parties involved respond to and feel about the order. Furthermore, should the Court make an order which provides for the child to live with both parents, or an order which provides for the child to live with one parent and spend time with the other? The making of a Child Arrangements Order which provides for the child to live with both parents – in the context of a domestically abusive relationship – can result in the perpetrator of DA gaining a sense of power and control which can, in turn, be used as a tool (whether literal or otherwise) to continue to perpetrate abuse. The Court must ensure that it takes care when making such an order and should not simply 'rubber stamp' it.

See *AZ v VX*, explored below.

15.47 It is important to appreciate that, in disputes between parents, and particularly when such disputes reach the final stages, both parents are highly likely to hold parental responsibility for the child, either because the parties were married, the father is named on the birth certificate or the Court has made (or is about to make) a parental responsibility order.

15.48 Importantly, however, Children Act 1989, s 13(2) enables a person who is named in a Child Arrangements Order as a person with whom the child lives to remove the child from the jurisdiction for up to a month without requiring the written consent of others who hold parental responsibility or an order from the Court. This is likely to be a factor which leads parents to preferring a 'shared care' Child Arrangements Order.

15.49 An important case for practitioners to be aware of is that of *AZ v BX (Child Arrangements Order: Appeal)*. In this appeal, Poole J considered the question of when to make a shared lives with order and to what extent a Child Arrangements Order should be defined. Whilst this case was not in the context of a domestically abusive relationship, the Court offers guidance as to the factors to be taken into account when deciding whether to make such an order. Poole J identified the following principles which would apply to a decision whether or not to make a shared lives with order:

> 'i) The choice of whether to make a shared lives with order or a lives with/spends time with order is not merely a question of labelling – it is likely to be relevant to the welfare of the subject children and must be made by applying the principles of CA 1989 s1. In some cases where, for example, an unmarried father does not have parental responsibility, a shared lives with order will result in him having parental responsibility whereas a lives with/spend time with order (the children living with the mother) will not. That is a material difference to take into account, although it did not apply in the present case. In every case the appropriate choice of order depends on a full evaluation of all the circumstances with the child's welfare being the court's paramount consideration.
>
> ii) The choice of the form of any lives with order should be considered alongside the division of time and any other parts of the proposed child arrangements order.
>
> iii) A shared lives with order may be suitable not only when there is to be an equal division of time with each parent but also when there is to be an unequal division of time.
>
> iv) It does not necessarily follow from the fact that the parents are antagonistic or unsupportive of each other that a shared lives with order will be unsuitable.'[19]

15.50 Whilst Poole J went on to extol the welfare advantages to each child of a shared lives with order in the case which he was presiding over, at [81], the advantages are likely to be analogous in the majority of cases:

> 'i) It would make it more difficult for either parent to regard themselves as being in control of contact or to seek to control contact – a problem that the Judge had specifically identified.
>
> ii) In particular, it would mitigate the effects of the Respondent's attempts to control contact which the Judge had noted from the ISW's evidence and had

19 *AZ v BX (Child Arrangements Order: Appeal)* [2024] EWHC 1528 (Fam), [77].

himself observed were not positive. Rather than ordering the Respondent to make sure the children spent time with the Appellant, a shared lives with order would set out arrangements for the division of time in the same terms for each parent, if not the same periods of time. It would thereby put the parents on an equal footing when seeking to make arrangements for the children.

iii) It would also put the parents on an equal footing with regard to holidays abroad including during school holidays when the children are going to spend equal time with each parent.

iv) A shared lives with order would signal to each parent that each was of value in the lives of the children, something the Judge had found each parent failed to appreciate.

v) It would also signal to the children that each parent has, in their capacity as parent, the same inherent importance in the children's lives.

vi) It would promote a sense of stability within the family: whatever the disagreements between the parents, the court had ordered that the children shall live with both of them.'[20]

Supervised contact

15.51 In cases where DA is established, it has not been uncommon for the Family Court to determine that a child should spend time with the perpetrator of DA, but that such time should be supervised in order to ensure that any risks that the child – or the victim – may face are mitigated and managed. However, rather than engage with the factors set out in paras 35, 36 and 37 of PD12J, the Family Court and those advising it often consider that the imposition of supervised contact is capable of mitigating any risks.

15.52 A relatively recent example of this approach can be seen in the decision of *Re M (Children: Contact in Prison)*.[21] In this case, the father was a police officer up until his conviction for the rape of the mother, for which he was serving a sentence of imprisonment. It was noted in the criminal court, at the point of sentencing (in June 2024) that the father had no insight into his offending behaviour. At first instance, Lieven J did not hear any oral evidence but made a Child Arrangements Order which included supervised contact, specifically, monthly telephone contact and direct, supervised contact three times a year as well as an order pursuant to Children Act 1989, s 91(14) lasting a year. Concluding that Lieven J had failed to take into account, or evaluate, a number of critical factors, the Court of Appeal allowed the appeal and set aside the Child Arrangements Order. Peter Jackson LJ, giving the lead judgment in the Court of Appeal, observed, at [21]:

20 *AZ v BX (Child Arrangements Order: Appeal)* (n 19), [81].
21 *Re M (Children: Contact in Prison)* [2024] EWCA Civ 1104.

'A decision about contact needed to take account of all these matters, and any other matters arising under the welfare checklist and PD12J. That did not happen, with the gravity of the Father's offending being overlooked, and priority given to a limited assessment of the children's wishes and the Judge's own perception of their need for contact. The appeal must therefore be allowed. The Guardian suggested that we might substitute an order for written contact only, but that would be to make the same mistake twice. It is unfortunate that the proceedings will be prolonged, but a decision about contact must now be retaken in the light of all the relevant factors. Until a final order can be made, contact will take place only in accordance with the Family Court's directions.'[22]

15.53 The assistance of family members or appropriate third parties is often called upon with this task (although this will require those who are seized with the supervision of contact understanding and appreciating the purposes of supervision, what they are protecting against and what their role is). However, in many cases, family members or third parties may not be available or appropriate to undertake this task and parties must look to the provision of professional supervision, whether that be in a contact centre or elsewhere. The use of professional supervision is not free or routinely provided by local authorities in private law cases; the issue which the Court is often faced with in such cases is who is going to pay for it?

15.54 When faced with this question, practitioners must have regard to the decision of Arbuthnot J in *Griffiths v Griffiths (Guidance on Contact Costs)*. This high-profile case concerned two Members of Parliament. Mrs Griffiths was a victim of DA at the hands of her former husband, which included rape, physical assault and controlling and coercive behaviour. The parties had a child, who was born in 2018. Prior to the Court embarking upon a Finding of Fact Hearing, it had directed that contact between the father and the child was to take place on a supervised basis in a contact centre with the costs shared equally between the parents.[23]

15.55 Following a Finding of Fact Hearing in which serious findings were made against the father, the Court made an order which provided for the father to have direct, supervised contact with the child, again, with the costs of that being shared between the parties. The mother sought permission to appeal, with Lieven J giving permission and stating that, 'the case raises issues of public importance as there is no case law on contact costs; and whether a victim of domestic abuse should contribute to the costs of maintaining the child's contact with the perpetrator of that abuse'. [24]

22 *Re M (Children: Contact in Prison)* (n 21), [21].
23 *Griffiths v Griffiths (Guidance on Contact Costs)* [2022] EWHC 113 (Fam).
24 *Griffiths v Griffiths (Guidance on Contact Costs)* (n 23), [33].

15.56 In her judgment, Arbuthnot J expressed caution at giving guidance on this issue which is too narrow and which might not cater for an extraordinary situation. Whilst the Court could not envisage a situation where a court would order a victim to share the costs of contact, it was acknowledged that it would be impossible to give guidance which would cater for every case. The following guidance was given at [131]–[132][25] and it should form part of every practitioner's toolkit:

- First, there must be a very strong presumption against a victim of DA paying for the contact of their child with the abuser.
- Second if, wholly exceptionally, the Court has to consider this, the matters it might want to take into account could include the following:
  - the welfare checklist including the age of the child;
  - the factors in PD12J;
  - the nature of the abuse proved or admitted, and the parties' conduct that the Court considers relevant;
  - the impact of the abuse on the caregiver with consideration as to whether any payment would give rise to financial control;
  - the extent of the relationship between the child and the abusive party;
  - the nature of the s 8 order;
  - the parties' financial resources;
  - the cost of the contact;
  - whether, if the contact is in the best interests of the child, it could take place without a sharing of the costs.

PRACTICE NOTE

It is crucial that practitioners remember this judicial guidance. It should only be in a wholly exceptional case that the Court requires a victim of DA to fund, wholly or in part, the costs associated with supervised contact. In cases where the Court is contemplating making such an order, practitioners should ensure that the guidance set out in *Griffiths v Griffiths (Guidance on Contact Costs)* is carefully and robustly applied; advocates should not hesitate to invite the Court to set out its reasons with care to ensure that this important guidance is adhered to. It is important to note that, although this guidance does not seek to trespass upon the Family Court's discretion, very strong language is used by Arbuthnot J in this judgment: there must be a *very strong* presumption against a victim of DA paying for the costs of contact between a child and the perpetrator of that DA *and* such a step would be *wholly exceptional*. With an ever-increasing dwindling of resources for parents, it is sadly increasingly common for parents to find themselves in a situation where the costs of funding professional supervision are prohibitive.[26]

25 *Griffiths v Griffiths (Guidance on Contact Costs)* (n 23), [131]–[132].

26 This is not simply limited to professionally supervised contact centres. Increasingly, independent social workers are offering to supervise contact which may allow for increased flexibility and duration of contact.

15.57 For some, strict adherence to the presumption of parental involvement, as well as the case law highlighting the importance for the child of having contact with both parents, may result in the Family Court considering making orders pursuant to Children Act 1989, s 11.

15.58 As mentioned previously, just because the Court has determined that one parent's contact with a child must be supervised, this does not necessarily require professional supervision. Supervision by family members or friends may allow for a degree of flexibility so as to ensure that the time the child spends with their parent is meaningful and positive. There is, however, a tendency to avoid the making of Child Arrangements Orders providing for *long-term* supervision.

15.59 Practitioners should note the decision of the Court of Appeal in *Re S (A Child)*. In this case, the Court of Appeal heard an appeal against an order that contact between the father and the child should be via indirect means only. The recommendation made by CAFCASS was that there should be direct contact but this should be supervised indefinitely, as a result of the father being assessed as posing a small risk of harm to the child. At [22] and [23], the Court of Appeal had this to say on the question of long-term supervised contact:

> 'As was accepted by Ms McGinty, there is no general proposition that there should be no direct contact if the welfare of the child in question requires that contact to be supervised over a long period of time. It is undoubtedly the case that, all other things being equal, unsupervised contact will be the goal for any child, allowing as it does for a more natural relationship between a child and an absent parent that that which is subject to supervision, no matter how benevolent or unobtrusive such supervision may be.
>
> There are and will be cases where long term supervision of contact is in the interests of a child – examples which immediately spring to mind are children placed in long term foster care by the courts but who continue to have supervised contact with their parents; or the increasingly common situation, where children are placed with family members following care proceedings and the natural parents continue to have contact supervised either by the local authority or family members. Both these examples relate to public law proceedings but have no less application to private law cases, particularly where there are child protection issues but there is no need of local authority involvement because the caring parent, as here, has proved that they are capable of protecting their child. The reality is that, with ever decreasing resources and the closure of contact centres, long term supervision will rarely be a realistic option in private law cases such as this; that does not mean however that in an appropriate case such a route should not be deployed as a means of allowing a child to continue to have a relationship with her absent parent.'[27]

27 *Re S (A Child)* [2015] EWCA Civ 689, [22]–[23].

PARENTAL RESPONSIBILITY

15.60 In the context of this book, the most relevant principle of parental responsibility can be found in Children Act 1989, s 2(7):

> 'Where more than one person has parental responsibility for a child, each of them may act alone and without the other (or others) in meeting that responsibility …'

15.61 The powers and responsibilities which come with parental responsibility are significant. Not only does the fact that a child is born within a relationship tie the parties to that relationship together in some form for a significant period of time, but the presence of parental responsibility also fortifies those ties. Parental responsibility is a significant matter of status, with McFarlane LJ (as he then was) stating in *Re W (Direct Contact)*:

> 'Whether or not a parent has parental responsibility is not simply a matter that achieves the ticking of a box on a form. It is a significant matter of status as between parent and child and, just as important, as between each of the parents. By stressing the "responsibility" which is so clearly given prominence in the Children Act 1989, section 3 and the likely circumstance that that responsibility is shared with the other parent, it is hoped that some parents may be encouraged more readily to engage with the difficulties that undoubtedly arise when contemplating post separation contact than may hitherto been the case.'[28]

15.62 The use – or misuse – of parental responsibility can be a powerful tool in the arsenal of a perpetrator of DA. It can be used to yield unspoken power and control. It can be used to frustrate arrangements for a child. It can be used to obtain information which may expose the child/children and/or the other parent to a continuing risk of harm. Whilst this tool can be deployed during the course of a parties' relationship, such deployment can often persist long after the relationship between the parties is over.

15.63 But how can such a power be curtailed? It is a question that may be on the lips of many victims of DA.

15.64 Where parental responsibility is conferred upon a father by virtue of being married to the mother pursuant to Children Act 1989, s 2, there is no provision for the termination of such parental responsibility. However, in cases where parental responsibility is conferred pursuant to Children Act 1989, s 4(1), the Court has the power to remove such parental responsibility (see Children Act 1989, s 4(2A)).

28 *Re W (Direct Contact)* [2013] 1 FLR 494, [80].

15.65 This anomaly, between married and unmarried fathers, has been considered, relatively recently, by the Court of Appeal in *Re A (Parental Responsibility)* where the mother sought to argue that the distinction between married and unmarried partners was incompatible with the European Convention on Human Rights (ECHR). The Court of Appeal – led by the current President of the Family Division – declined to declare that the current law was incompatible with the ECHR and concluded that:

> 'it is clear that the difference in the treatment of unmarried and married fathers is justified by the long-standing principle that married fathers (and mothers) should have irrevocable parental authority/responsibility for their children. Affording priority to the establishment and maintenance, of stable family life by commitment through marriage or civil partnership is what it is all about.'[29]

Restricting the use of parental responsibility

15.66 In the case of *Re T-D (Children: Specific Issue Order)*, the Court of Appeal considered whether the Family Court has the power to restrict the extent to which a parent may exercise their irrevocable parental responsibility by the use of orders made under Children Act 1989, s 8.[30] In the case of *Re A (Parental Responsibility)*, the President of the Family Division remarked:

> 'Irrespective of whether or not there is a statutory power to bring parental responsibility to an end, in every case the court may control and limit a parent's ability to exercise parental responsibility through the making of prohibited steps orders, and may enhance the ability of the other parent to exercise parental responsibility with respect to specific issues …
>
> Whilst a prohibited steps order and/or a specific issue order may normally be made to regulate one or more aspects of the exercise of parental responsibility, it is accepted that, where the facts of the case justify it, the court may make a combination of orders which have the effect of prohibiting a parent from taking any step in the exercise of his or her parental responsibility and clothing the other parent with the exclusive right to exercise parental responsibility without reference to any other person who holds parental responsibility.'[31]

15.67 During the course of the judgment in *Re T-D (Children: Specific Issue Order)*, the Court of Appeal surveyed a number of earlier decisions, beginning with the observations of Hale J (as she then was) in *Re M (Leave to Remove Child from Jurisdiction)*:

29 *Re A (Parental Responsibility)* [2023] EWCA Civ 689, [101].
30 *Re T-D (Children: Specific Issue Order)* [2024] EWCA Civ 793.
31 *Re T-D (Children: Specific Issue Order)* (n 30), [10].

'… the Children Act 1989 was designed to provide a range of orders for the court to use in disputes between parents and other private individuals which was much more flexible than in the past. In the past there had tended to be the rigid categories of custody and access, where s8 of the 1999 Act allows the court to make any one of a number of orders appropriate to promote the welfare of the child.'[32]

PRACTICE NOTE

Having set out the underpinnings of a wide discretion afforded to the Family Court, along with a menu of orders which are designed to be flexible, the Court of Appeal set out a number of subsequent decisions in which both the Court of Appeal and the Family Court used the menu of orders within Children Act 1989, s 8 to limit the extent to which parental responsibility can be exercised. The cases referred to by the Court of Appeal provide practitioners with an idea of the range of ways such orders can be utilised whilst also providing 'real world' examples of when such issues may arise. It is important to note that some of these examples do not necessarily feature cases in which DA has been a feature.

15.68 The summaries that follow are directly lifted from the judgment in *Re T-D (Children: Specific Issue Order),* from [35] onwards:

'Re H (A Child: Parental Responsibility) [2002] EWCA Civ 542 concerned a child who needed major ongoing medical care. It was an appeal from the refusal of parental responsibility to a father who had been denied contact by the court. Allowing the appeal to what it described as a very limited extent, this court substituted a parental responsibility order but accompanied it with a specific issue order giving the mother sole responsibility for all decisions relating to medical treatment, and a prohibited steps order preventing the father from attempting to locate her address. At [16], Thorpe LJ stated:

"The notion that he should involve himself profoundly with the consultants and other professionals treating L is completely inconsistent with his acknowledgment that in that area the mother has sole responsibility. There is simply no basis upon which he could justify an involvement with medical services equal to, or anywhere near approaching, the involvement of the mother."'[33]

15.69 In *Re P (Parental Dispute: Judicial Determination)*, the Court of Appeal was concerned with a schooling dispute concerning two children of divorced parents.

32 *Re M (Leave to Remove Child from Jurisdiction)* [1999] 2 FLR 334, [339].

33 *Re T-D (Children: Specific Issue Order)* (n 30), [35]; *Re H (A Child: Parental Responsibility)* [2002] EWCA Civ 542, [16].

'The judge's order had been that:

> "1 M shall go to [name] senior school with effect from September 2002.
>
> 2 In respect of both M and O future questions which may arise about either child's schooling, including O's senior school, shall be finally determined by the children's mother following consultation with their father, MP."

Allowing the father's appeal, and replacing the second paragraph with an order that, absent agreement, matters be determined by a judge, Thorpe LJ said this:

> "[6] Despite Mr McCarthy's valiant efforts, I am in no doubt at all that Mr Horowitz QC is entitled to succeed in his fundamental submission that the judge's design, however laudable, amounted to the plainest failure to adjudicate, coupled with a failure to address evidence material to that adjudication. This was, says Mr Horowitz, an abdication of judicial function and an unprincipled empowering of one parent to disempower the other.
>
> …
>
> [8] … Of course, it is important that judges use their power and influence to steer parents from unnecessary discord whenever they can. In that function they must have the broadest of discretions. A judge may adjourn a case, expressing the strong view that the parents should mediate or that they should seek professional help to enable them to resolve their differences. But in the end, the parents have a right to a judicial determination, and this was a case in which two highly intelligent parents had reached convinced positions that were most unlikely to shift through further discussion, negotiation or even mediation.
>
> …
>
> [11] … [T]he end result is an unprincipled order which cannot stand. Mr Horowitz is right to say that in situations such as this, where clarity is required, the final decision is the decision of the judge. It is not as a matter of principle open to a judge to abdicate that responsibility and simply appoint one of the parents with more or less absolute responsibility."'[34]

15.70 In *A v A (Shared Residence)*, the Court, after hearing the submissions of both parties in a dispute between professional parents, ordered that there would be equal shared residence. In *T-D (Children: Specific Issue Order)*, [118] of that judgment was specifically noted:

34 *Re T-D (Children: Specific Issue Order)* (n 30), [36]; *Re P (Parental Dispute: Judicial Determination)* [2002] EWCA Civ 1627, [6], [8], [11].

> 'At [118], Wall J emphasised that parents should not be seeking to interfere with one another in matters which are taking place when they do not have the care of their children.'[35]

15.71 In *Re P (Shared Residence Order)*, the Court of Appeal considered the position of a father whose child lived *almost* equally with him and the mother respectively. Neither parent had interfered, or attempted to interfere, with the other parent's care when the child was living with the other.

> 'The father's proposal for a shared residence order was refused by the judge but was granted on appeal. At [16] Thorpe LJ observed that:
>
> > "It is not a case in which there is any evidence of either parent having interfered, or having sought to interfere, with the exercise of responsibility and judgment of the parent in possession."
>
> While at [22] Wall LJ stated that:
>
> > "[F]irst, a shared residence order is most apt to describe what is actually happening on the ground; and, secondly, that good reasons are required if a shared residence order is not to be made. Such an order emphasises the fact that both parents are equal in the eyes of the law, and that they have equal duties and responsibilities as parents. The order can have the additional advantage of conveying the court's message that neither parent is in control and that the court expects parents to co-operate with each other for the benefit of their children."'[36]

15.72 From [39] onwards in *Re T-D (Children: Specific Issue Order)*, the Court of Appeal refers to a small number of cases in which the Court has prevented a parent from taking some or any steps to exercise their parental responsibility.

15.73 It is important for practitioners to be aware of these cases and, for this reason, they are set out as a reference tool:

> '*P v D [2014] EWHC 2355 (Fam)* concerned formerly married parents. The mother and children were living in hiding and the father was serving a lengthy prison sentence for extreme violence and rape of the mother. Baker J (as he then was) made a prohibited steps order prohibiting the father from taking any steps in the exercise of his parental responsibility, and a raft of other orders to protect the mother and children. He observed at [110] that:
>
> > "In some cases, it is necessary for the court to make a prohibited steps order restricting a parent from taking steps that he or she would normally

35 *Re T-D (Children: Specific Issue Order)* (n 30), [37]; *A v A (Shared Residence)* [2004] EWHC 142 (Fam), [118].

36 *Re T-D (Children: Specific Issue Order)* (n 30), [38]; *Re P (Shared Residence Order)* [2005] EWCA Civ 1639, [16].

be entitled to take in the exercise of parental responsibility. That power extends, in very exceptional cases, to making an order prohibiting a parent from taking any steps in the exercise of parental responsibility. Such orders could be made in very exceptional cases."[37]

H v A (No 1) [2015] EWFC 58 concerned formerly married parents. The mother applied to revoke the parental responsibility of the father who was serving a life sentence for driving a car into, and setting fire to, the family home when she and the children were present, and then, from prison, soliciting other inmates to murder her. MacDonald J held that parental responsibility acquired under section 2(1) of the Act could not be revoked, but he declared that the mother was under no obligation to inform or consult with the father in respect of the exercise of her parental responsibility, and that the father was prohibited from exercising any parental responsibility throughout the children's childhoods. In making the order, he stated:

"55. Finally, it is important to note that, however extreme or exceptional the facts of a particular case, a prohibited steps order is a statutory restriction on the exercise by a parent of their parental responsibility. Any such order made by the court must accordingly be based on objective evidence. There is a high responsibility on the court not to impose such a restriction without good cause and reasons for imposing a restriction must be given (see *Re C (Due Process) [2013] EWCA Civ 1412*). Specific consideration must be given to the duration of the prohibition (see *R (Casey) v Restormel Borough Council [2007] EWHC 2554 (Admin)* at [38]).

56. Within this context, and in circumstances where a prohibited steps order constitutes an interference with the Art 8 rights of both the parent against whom the order is made and the child who is the subject of the order, the making of, the terms of, and the duration of a prohibited steps order must be proportionate to the mischief that the order is designed to address."[38]

In *Re B and C (Children) (Change of Names: Parental Responsibility: Evidence) [2017] EWHC 3250 (Fam), [2018] 4 WLR 19* concerned children who had been retained in Iran by their father before being brought back to the UK by their mother. They were living at an undisclosed address because of the risk of re-abduction. Cobb J approved a change of names, and he made a prohibited steps order preventing the father from taking any steps in the exercise of any aspect of his parental responsibility and a specific issue order permitting the mother to make all decisions and give parental consent unilaterally and without reference to the father in all matters relating to the children's upbringing. In making the order he said:

37 *Re T-D (Children: Specific Issue Order)* (n 30), [39]; *P v D* [2014] EWHC 2355 (Fam), [110].
38 *Re T-D (Children: Specific Issue Order)* (n 30), [39]; *H v A (No 1)* [2015] EWHC 58 (Fam), [55]–[56].

> "42. … The mother seeks, by her applications, to disenfranchise the father in practice as a holder of responsibility for the children, and to create for the children wholly new identities which are deliberately to be secret from the father. Orders of this gravity should plainly only be made by a court if there is a solid and secure evidential and factual basis for doing so, and where the orders are palpably in the best interests of the children concerned."[39]

In the case of *His Highness Sheikh Mohammed Bin Rashid Al Maktoum v Her Royal Highness Princess Haya Bint Al Hussein [2021] EWHC 3480 (Fam), [2023] 1 FLR 12* concerned maximally oppressive behaviour by one parent towards the other, so that the children's lives were dominated by the consequence of their father's abusive actions. The mother was given sole responsibility for determining all issues relating to the children's medical care and schooling. Sir Andrew McFarlane P observed that the order was outside the norm, but that there was no dispute that the power to make it existed: [77, 80]. He noted at [94] that the mother could not contemplate sharing parental responsibility with the father, and concluded:

> "[95] The decision to afford the mother sole responsibility for these important matters is justified by the need to reduce the potential for continuing harm to the children. It is very much in their interests for the balance to be recalibrated and for their mother to feel that she now has enhanced autonomy as a parent and that this will be protected by a court order.'"[40]

PRACTICE NOTE

Drawing all of this together, a number of principles can be distilled:

(a) Orders that seek to limit the extent to which a parent can exercise their parental responsibility should only be made in exceptional cases.

(b) The making of such orders should be based on objective, solid, and secure evidence and have a factual basis which allows the Court to identify the concerning behaviour. The behaviour must be at the upper end of the scale and considered to be 'extreme'.

(c) The parent against whom such restrictions are sought should be minimally involved or absent in the life of the child.

(d) There is a high responsibility upon the Court not to impose such a restriction without good cause, with any orders being proportionate.

39 *Re T-D (Children: Specific Issue Order)* (n 30), [39]; *Re B and C (Children) (Change of Names: Parental Responsibility: Evidence)* [2017] EWHC 3250 (Fam); [2018] 4 WLR 19, [42].

40 *Re T-D (Children: Specific Issue Order)* (n 30), [39]; *His Highness Sheikh Mohammed Bin Rashid Al Maktoum v Her Royal Highness Princess Haya Bint Al Hussein* [2021] EWHC 3480 (Fam); [2023] 1 FLR 12, [95].

The Court should only make a general, wide-reaching order, if discrete orders will not suffice.

(e) The Court should be mindful to ensure that such orders are only be in place for as long as necessary.

(f) The Court must consider and apply the welfare checklist set out in Children Act 1989, s 1(3).

(g) In making such orders, the Court must give reasons for doing so.

15.74 Those who represent victims of DA and those who advise the Family Court should be alive to the ways in which parental responsibility can be misused by a perpetrator of DA. These can include:

(a) refusing to agree to changes of school or nursery provision;

(b) refusing to agree to a change of GP or dentist;

(c) refusing to agree to a change of address;

(d) refusing to agree to a change of/addition to the child's surname.

15.75 These are only examples. They are not exhaustive. Life may throw up situations whereby those with parental responsibility ought to be consulted or give consent. The flexible use of the Children Act 1989, as referred to by Hale J in *Re M (Leave to Remove Child from Jurisdiction)*, should ensure that practitioners are alive to the myriad of situations which may arise.[41] The Children Act 1989 can and should be used creatively in order to protect victims of DA, which by virtue of DAA 2021, s 3, now also includes children.

PRACTICE NOTE

Practitioners should be aware of some authorities which suggest that the inherent jurisdiction of the High Court provides a better remedy. In the case of *Re W (Children) (Education: Choice of School)*, Hale LJ (as she then was) observed at [5]:

> '... The family lawyers amongst us will know that the whole purpose of having specific issue orders is to decide the issue and not to give the right of exclusive decision making to one parent or another.'[42]

15.76 In overturning a decision in which the mother had been given the ability to make final decisions regarding the child's schooling, the Court of Appeal observed in *Re P (Parental Dispute: Judicial Determination)* that:

41 *Re M (Leave to Remove Child from Jurisdiction)* [1999] 2 FLR 334.
42 *Re W (Children) (Education: Choice of School)* [2002] EWCA Civ 1411, [5].

> '... it was not as a matter of principle open to a judge to abdicate that responsibility and simply appoint one of the parents with more or less absolute responsibility.'[43]

15.77 The use of the inherent jurisdiction to restrict the extent to which parental responsibility can be exercised was demonstrated in the case of *A London Borough v X* in which Theis J, having made the child a ward of court and relying upon the decision of Hale LJ in *Re W (Children) (Education: Choice of School)*, held that:

> '... orders restricting the exercise of parental responsibility under s.8 CA 1989 were not aimed at giving one parent the right of exclusive decision to one parent or the other.'[44]

15.78 Whilst the use of Children Act 1989, s 8 provides a mechanism through which the Family Court can limit the extent to which a parent can exercise parental responsibility, there are some circumstances which may call for the termination of parental responsibility. The Family Court has the power to restrict the exercise of parental responsibility in those cases where parental responsibility cannot be removed.

Terminating parental responsibility

15.79 In cases in which DA has been established, practitioners are often asked by those who have suffered DA whether the perpetrator's parental responsibility can be terminated. The simple answer is: yes, it can. That is, as long as the father acquired parental responsibility as an unmarried father. However, whilst the Family Court does have the power to remove parental responsibility from a parent (who has revocable parental responsibility – see earlier in this chapter on how the law operates in respect of irrevocable parental responsibility), it is a power that should be used sparingly.

15.80 Section 4(2A) and (3) of the Children Act 1989 provides the statutory basis for an application to terminate parental responsibility:

> '(2A) A person who has acquired parental responsibility under subsection (1) shall cease to have that responsibility only if the court so orders.
>
> (3) The court may make an order under subsection (2A) on the application—
>
> (a) of any person who has parental responsibility for the child; or
>
> (b) with the leave of the court, of the child himself,
>
> subject, in the case of parental responsibility acquired under subsection (1)(c), to section 12(4).'

43 *Re P (Parental Dispute: Judicial Determination)* [2002] EWCA Civ 1627, [11].
44 *A London Borough v X* [2019] 12 WLUK 450, [64(iv)].

15.81 The case which is often cited in cases where the Family Court is considering an application to terminate parental responsibility is *Re P (Terminating Parental Responsibility)*. In this case, the father had pleaded guilty to causing serious injuries to the child, who was only nine weeks old at the time. The injuries resulted in the child being permanently and profoundly disabled. The Court concluded that the father's continuing parental responsibility would undermine the child's best interests, with Singer J stating, at p 1052:

> 'I start from the proposition that parental responsibility – both wanting to have it and its exercise – is a laudable desire which is to be encouraged rather than rebuffed. So that I think one can postulate as a first principle that parental responsibility once obtained should not be terminated in the case of a non-marital father on less than solid grounds, with a presumption for continuance rather than for termination.
>
> The ability of a mother to make such an application therefore should not be allowed to become a weapon in the hands of the dissatisfied mother of the non-marital child: it should be used by the court as an appropriate step in the regulation of the child's life where the circumstances really do warrant it and not otherwise.
>
> I have been referred in outline to four authorities as to the circumstances in which a court will make an order for parental responsibility on application to it under s 4, notwithstanding maternal opposition and, more particularly, as to the criteria and considerations which are relevant. The authorities in question are: *Re H (Minors) (Local Authority: Parental Rights) (No 3) [1991] Fam 151, sub nom Re H (Illegitimate Children: Father: Parental Rights) (No 2) [1991] 1 FLR 214; Re C (Minors) (Parental Rights) [1992] 1 FLR 1, in the Court of Appeal, and Re G (A Minor) (Parental Responsibility Order) [1994] 1 FLR 504, also in the Court of Appeal; and, finally, a decision of Wilson J, Re P (A Minor) (Parental Responsibility Order) [1994] 1 FLR 578.*
>
> Such applications for parental responsibility orders are governed by the considerations set out in s 1(1) of the Children Act, namely that the child's welfare is the court's paramount consideration. I can see no reason why that principle should be departed from in considering the termination of a parental responsibility order or agreement.
>
> Key concepts to the consideration of the making of an order are evidence of attachment and a degree of commitment, the presumption being that, other things being equal, a parental responsibility order should be made rather than withheld in an appropriate case.'[45]

15.82 The guidance given by Singer J in *Re P (Terminating Parental Responsibility)* has stood the test of time. In the case of *CW v SG (Parental Responsibility Consequential Orders)*,[46] Baker J (as he then was) endorsed the

45 *Re P (Terminating Parental Responsibility)* [1995] 1 FLR 1048, p 1052.
46 *CW v SG (Parental Responsibility Consequential Orders)* [2013] EWHC 854 (Fam).

guidance given by Singer J which was subsequently endorsed by the Court of Appeal in the case of *Re D (Withdrawal of Parental Responsibility),* with Ryder LJ stating, at [13] and [14]:

> 'The paramountcy test is overarching and no one factor that the court might consider in a welfare analysis has any hypothetical priority. Accordingly, factors that may be said to have significance by analogy or on the facts of a particular case, for example, the factors that the court considers within the overarching question of welfare upon an application for a parental responsibility order (the degree of commitment which the father has shown to the child, the degree of attachment which exists between the father and the child and the reasons of the father for applying for the order) may be relevant on the facts of a particular case but are not to be taken to be a substitute test to be applied (see *Re M (Parental Responsibility Order) [2013] EWCA Civ 969, [2014] 1 FLR 339*, at paras [15] and [16]).
>
> An unmarried father does not benefit from a "presumption" as to the existence or continuance of parental responsibility. He obtains it in accordance with the statutory scheme and may lose it in the same way. In both circumstances it is the welfare of the child that creates the presumption, not the parenthood of the unmarried father. The concept of rival presumptions is not helpful, although I entirely accept that the fact of parenthood raises the welfare question, hence the right of a parent (with or without parental responsibility) to make an application under s 8 of the CA 1989 without permission (see s 10(4)(a) of the CA 1989). There is also ample case-law describing the imperative in favour of a continuing relationship between both parents and a child so that ordinarily a child's upbringing should be provided by both of his parents and where that is not in the child's interests by one of them with the child having the benefit of a meaningful relationship with both. A judge would not be criticised for identifying that, as a very weighty, relevant factor, the significance of the parenthood of an unmarried father should not be under estimated.'[47]

15.83 Practitioners may look to a recent case for the exercise of this power in practice – *Westcarr v Gogoa Lois Tape*.[48] Unsurprisingly it attracted significant media coverage because of the chilling facts placed before the Court. It involved a mother killed by a father. The decision embraced a change of name, s 91(4) and termination of parental responsibility. It reads as a very human, pragmatic judgment following arguments made on the type of detail we have exhorted practitioners to apply to their thinking, preparation and presentation. The decision reaffirms that the theme running throughout the authorities on the issue of termination of parental responsibility is the need for the Court to be guided by the welfare of the child.

47 *Re D (Withdrawal of Parental Responsibility)* [2014] EWCA Civ 315; [2015] 1 FLR 166, [13]–[14].
48 *Westcarr v Gogoa Lois Tape* [2025] EWFC 374.

CHILDREN ACT 1989, S 91(14)

15.84 In recent years, there has been a growing awareness of the harm that protracted and repeated proceedings can cause both to the children who are the subject of the proceedings but also the adults who are actively engaged in them. Furthermore, there has been growing awareness and acknowledgment that perpetrators of DA are able to use Children Act proceedings as a vehicle through which they are able to continue their abusive behaviours, only this time disguised by a veil of justification and legitimacy.

15.85 Since the coming into force of the Children Act 1989, there has been a statutory mechanism which allows the Court to filter applications brought under the Children Act 1989 so as to prevent, or control, the extent to which perpetrators of domestically abusive behaviour can use the family justice system as a tool in their arsenal to continue their abusive behaviours.

15.86 Prior to the coming into force of the DAA 2021, there was limited guidance offered in statute as to the application of Children Act 1989, s 91(14); instead practitioners and judges alike turned to case law. Now, having acknowledged the lengths to which perpetrators of DA will go, the law seeks to offer a meaningful and accessible remedy which the Family Court is able to deploy in order to protect both children and victims alike.

15.87 Such a development should bring a number of benefits:

(a) By ensuring that only meritorious applications proceed, the pressures upon the Family Court are likely to be lessened.

(b) Victims of DA are likely to be afforded a greater degree of protection from being brought to court needlessly, thereby limiting a perpetrator's ability to use court process as a means to continue abusive behaviour.

(c) The impact upon the children concerned is likely to be lessened, bringing with it less professional intervention in their lives.

Evolution

15.88 Section 91(14) of the Children Act 1989 provides:

> 'On disposing of any application for an order under this Act, the court may (whether or not it makes any other order in response to the application) order that no application for an order under this Act of any specified kind may be made with respect to the child concerned by any person named in the order without leave of the court.'

15.89 Even the most cursory consideration of s 91(14) reveals the limited extent to which the statute sought to offer guidance as to the extent and applicability of this particular aspect of the Children Act 1989; one may question whether, when drafting this legislation, the future significance of this was really appreciated. It was not until 1999 that assistance was given by the Court of Appeal in the case of *Re P (A Child)* in which Butler-Sloss LJ gave guidance at [41]:

> 'A number of guidelines may be drawn from the cases to which I have referred to above, and I am also indebted to Wall J for the helpful summary of propositions set out in Part III of this judgment. It is however important to remember that these are only guidelines intended to assist and not to replace the wording of the section …
>
> 1. Section 91(14) should be read in conjunction with section 1(1) CA 1989 which makes the welfare of the child the paramount consideration.
> 2. The power to restrict applications to the court is discretionary and in the exercise of its discretion the court must weigh in the balance all the relevant circumstances.
> 3. An important consideration is that to impose a restriction is a statutory intrusion into the right of a party to bring proceedings before the court and to be heard in matters affecting his/her child.
> 4. The power is therefore to be used with great care and sparingly, the exception and not the rule.
> 5. It is generally to be seen as a useful weapon of last resort in cases of repeated and unreasonable applications.
> 6. In suitable circumstances (and on clear evidence), a court may, impose the leave restriction in cases where the welfare of the child requires it, although there is no past history of making unreasonable applications.
> 7. In cases under paragraph 6 above, the court will need to be satisfied first that the facts go beyond the commonly encountered need for a time to settle to a regime ordered by the Court and the all too common situation where there is animosity between the adults in dispute or between the local authority and the family and secondly that there is a serious risk that, without the imposition of the restriction, the child or the primary carers will be subject to unacceptable strain.
> 8. A court may impose the restriction on making applications in the absence of a request from any of the parties, subject, of course, to the rules of natural justice such as an opportunity for the parties to be heard on the point.
> 9. A restriction may be imposed with or without limitation of time.
> 10. The degree of restriction should be proportionate to the harm it is intended to avoid. Therefore, the court imposing the restriction should carefully consider the extent of the restriction to be imposed and specify, where appropriate, the type of application to be restrained and the duration of the order.
> 11. It would be undesirable in other than the most exceptional cases to make the order ex parte.'[49]

49 *Re P (A Child)* [1999] EWCA Civ 1323, [41].

15.90 As we shall see later in this chapter, this guidance has remained in place for the quarter of a century since it was offered and, in some respects, has stood the test of time. Seeking to explain the purpose of an order made under s 91(14), at p 593, Butler-Sloss LJ described the order under s 91(14) as a 'partial restriction' on access to the Court in that:

> '... it does not allow him the right to an immediate inter parties hearing. It thereby protects the other parties and the child from being drawn into the proposed proceedings unless or until a court has ruled that the application should be allowed to proceed. On an application for leave, the applicant must persuade the judge that he has an arguable case with some chance of success. That is not a formidable hurdle to surmount. If the application is hopeless and refused the other parties and the child will have been protected from unnecessary involvement in the proposed proceedings and unwarranted investigations into the present circumstances of the child.'[50]

15.91 The Court of Appeal's offering in *Re P (A Child)* remains, in many respects, good law and represents a solid starting point for either the Court when considering whether to make such an order or an applicant inviting the Court to make such an order.

15.92 The *Harm Report* responded to *Re P (A Child)*, commenting upon Butler Sloss LJ's interpretation of the law. Cognisant that repeated and protracted litigation can be used as a vehicle through which domestically abusive behaviours can continue, the *Harm Report* noted:

> 'In relation to section 91(14), the panel notes that the provisions of the Children Act 1989 are non-prescriptive, but the sub-section has been interpreted in case-law from Re P [1999] to apply only in exceptional circumstances. In order to enable section 91(14) to protect children and adult victims more effectively from harm, the panel recommends that measures be included in the Domestic Abuse Bill to reverse the "exceptionality" requirement for a section 91(14) order laid down most clearly in Re P (Section 91(14) Guidelines) [1999]. These measures should amend, replace or supplement section 91(14) in an Article 6 compliant way to ensure that the following policy objectives are clearly and explicitly provided for in statute:
>
> - that section 91(14) orders may be made where it is in the best interests of the child to make such an order;
> - that section 91(14) orders may be made where the court concludes that the bringing or prolonging of proceedings constitutes domestic abuse against the other parent;
> - that it is not necessary to demonstrate repeated applications before the court could properly make such an order;

50 *Re P (A Child)* (n 49), p 593.

- that the court may make such an order of its own motion;
- that leave to apply for a child arrangements order following the imposition of a section 91(14) order should only be granted where the applicant provides evidence to show that circumstances since the imposition of the order have materially changed, and where the grant of leave would not create a risk of harm to the child or the other parent.'[51]

15.93 The '*Re P*', guidance was considered more recently by the Court of Appeal in *Re A (A Child) (Supervised Contact: s.91(14) Orders).* Whilst King LJ held that the *Re P* guidance 'ha[s] substantially withstood the test of time', it was placed in a more modern context at [34]–[36]:

> 'In the [22 years since *Re P* was decided] the forensic landscape has changed out of all recognition. Amongst the many advances is the advent of the smart phone and of social media in all its forms. Of particular relevance in this context is the almost universal use of email as a means of instant communication. Another development of relevance is that as a result of the withdrawal of legal aid in the majority of private law cases, a large proportion of parents are unrepresented and therefore do not have, as the judge described it in the present case, the "steadying influence" of legal advisors. One of the consequences of these changes which is seen not uncommonly in private law proceedings is that the other parties, and often the judge him or herself, can be (and often are) bombarded with emails from a parent, whether male or female, who is representing him or herself. Such behaviour may be the result of anxiety but in other cases, as in this case, it is part of a campaign of behaviour by one parent against the other which amounts to a deeply disturbing form of oppressive behaviour on their part.
>
> Regardless of the motivation, behaviour of this type, as exhibited by the mother in this case by way of an example, is deeply distressing to the parent who is the subject of such abuse and litigation at this level and is highly debilitating to each of the parties and to their children. All too often such communications are ill-considered and ill-judged with the consequence that every minor dispute or misunderstanding is met with an application to the judge. More importantly, the distress and anxiety caused to the other parent and to the children at the centre of such a raging dispute cannot be overestimated, nor can the damaging consequences where the focus of the litigation veers away from what, on any objective view, would and should be regarded as the real issues going to the welfare of the children concerned.'[52]

51 Ministry of Justice (n 2), p 178.

52 *Re A (A Child) (Supervised Contact) (Section 91(14) Children Act orders)* [2021] EWCA Civ 1749, [34]–[36].

PRACTICE NOTE

Note that the panel also recommended some ways in which the judiciary could continually identify and manage abusive applications in any case:

- There should be '[j]udicial continuity between prior and subsequent applications, and between section 91(14) orders and leave to apply applications'.
- The Court should treat 'further applications *cautiously* where there have previously been findings of domestic abuse'.
- As well as considering applications from parties, the Court should be 'actively considering whether to make a section 91(14) order of its own motion in such cases'.
- In addition to s 91(14) orders, the Court should consider on its own motion whether it is appropriate to make 'additional orders granting protection from continuing harassment or abuse (e.g. non-molestation and prohibited steps orders)'.
- The management of leave to apply applications should be exercised in a way 'to minimise their effect on the other parent and children'.[53]

As you will have noticed, whilst these appear to be appropriate procedural rules, their exercise and scope is somewhat vague.

15.94 The *Harm Report* readily recognised that the making of an order pursuant to s 91(14) would limit the extent to which a parent or other relevant individual could access the Court, and therefore had the potential to interfere with rights protected by ECHR, Art 6. However, such access was not completely prohibited, with s 91(14) acting as more of a filter. Therefore, reference to a s 91(14) order as a 'barring order' is perhaps a misnomer and fails to properly address the purpose of the Court making such an order.[54]

15.95 The *Harm Report* recommended a dilution of the 'exceptionality' test that *Re P (A Child)* had set out.[55] The 'exceptionality' test set out in *Re P* came from a time when society's understanding of DA was nowhere near as sophisticated as it is today; in 1999, there was limited, if any understanding of controlling and coercive behaviour and the thought of the Family Court being used as a vehicle to continue domestically abusive behaviours was inconceivable. Therefore, the dilution of this 'test' has to be viewed through the lens of what we now understand DA to be, together with the nuances and far-reaching nature of it.

53 Ministry of Justice (n 2), pp 178–179.
54 Ministry of Justice (n 2), p 128.
55 *Re P (A Child)* (n 49).

15.96 Following the publication of the *Harm Report*, the Court of Appeal was afforded the opportunity to consider the law relating to s 91(14) orders in *Re A (A Child) (Supervised Contact) (Section 91(14) Children Act orders)*.[56] In this case, the Court of Appeal sought to place the *Re P (A Child)* guidance in a modern context and was able to consider the amendments to s 91(14) only months after the coming into force of the DAA 2021.

15.97 Although the *Re P (A Child)* guidance has stood the test of time and received Court of Appeal endorsement on a number of occasions, the Court of Appeal observed that 'in those 22 years, the forensic landscape has changed out of all recognition'.[57]

15.98 The Court stated that these changes serve both as a reflection on the realities facing the family justice system today and a sign of appreciation for lawyers who work in this area. Another development of relevance noted by the Court is that, as a result of the withdrawal of legal aid in the majority of private law cases, a large proportion of parents are unrepresented and therefore do not have, as the judge described it in the present case, the 'steadying influence' of legal advisers.[58] Giving the lead judgment, King LJ provided useful guidance via a modern prism through which the *Re P (A Child)* guidance can be viewed and the sort of circumstances which may justify the greater use of s 91(14) orders are considered:

- Meritless applications (even if the number of applications has not been excessive) may justify the making of a s 91(14) order. This not only protects the child from the effects of repeated applications but also serves to prevent the use of litigation as a means of harassing or using the litigation as a continuation of DA.[59]
- Where a party's conduct has been inappropriate (eg, excessive emails during the course of proceedings or vindictive complaints to the police and social services).[60]
- Cases in which the proceedings have effectively been used by a party as a form of coercive control.[61]

15.99 Section 67 of the DAA 2021 also created a new s 91A in the Children Act 1989 which now enables the Court to make an order pursuant to s 91(14) of the Act if the Court is satisfied that the making of further applications would put either the child or a relevant individual at risk of harm:

> **'Section 91A Section 91(14) orders: further provision**
>
> (1) This section makes further provision about orders under section 91(14) (referred to in this section as "section 91(14) orders").

56 *Re A (A Child) (Supervised Contact) (Section 91(14) Children Act orders)* (n 52).
57 *Re P (A Child)* (n 49), [34].
58 *Re A (A Child) (Supervised Contact) (Section 91(14) Children Act orders)* (n 52), [22].
59 *Re A (A Child) (Supervised Contact) (Section 91(14) Children Act orders)* (n 52), [40].
60 *Re A (A Child) (Supervised Contact) (Section 91(14) Children Act orders)* (n 52), [39].
61 *Re A (A Child) (Supervised Contact) (Section 91(14) Children Act orders)* (n 52), [41].

(2) The circumstances in which the court may make a section 91(14) order include, among others, where the court is satisfied that the making of an application for an under this Act of a specified kind by any person who is to be named in the section 91(14) order would put—

(a) the child concerned, or

(b) another individual ("the relevant individual"),

at risk of harm.

(3) In the case of a child or other individual who has reached the age of eighteen, the reference in subsection (2) to "harm" is to be read as a reference to ill-treatment or the impairment of physical or mental health.

(4) Where a person who is named in a section 91(14) order applies for leave to make an application of a specified kind, the court must, in determining whether to grant leave, consider whether there has been a material change of circumstances since the order was made.

(5) A section 91(14) order may be made by the court—

(a) on an application made—

(i) by the relevant individual;

(ii) by or on behalf of the child concerned;

(iii) by any other person who is a party to the application being disposed of by the court;

(b) of its own motion.

(6) In this section, "the child concerned" means the child referred to in section 91(14).'

15.100 It should be noted that there is no reference in s 91A to the harm needing to be significant. Further, s 91A directs the Court to consider whether there has been a material change of circumstances when considering whether permission to make an application should be given. Prior to the coming into force of the DAA 2021, the only guidance available was to be found in case law. As recognised by King LJ in *Re A (A Child) (Supervised Contact) (Section 91(14) Children Act 1989)*, s 91A elevates some of the *Re P (A Child)* guidance to a statutory footing.[62]

15.102 The extent to which s 91A clarified the law will be assessed through its application in case law. Since its coming into force, its provisions have been considered in the following cases.

15.102 First to consider s 91A was Knowles J in *A Local Authority v F & Ors:*

'... s91A(2) provides that an order may be appropriate if the child is at risk of harm, harm being defined in accordance with section 31(9) of the

62 *Re A (A Child) (Supervised Contact) (Section 91(14) Children Act 1989)* (n 52).

Children Act 1989 to mean "the ill-treatment or the impairment of health or development including, for example, impairment suffered from seeing or hearing the ill-treatment of another." The risk that harm may arise to a child under the age of 18 unless the making of applications is restrained is not qualified by words such as "serious" or "significant" and neither is the degree of harm that a child may experience. I observe that, insofar as the risk that harm may arise to a child is concerned, section 91A(2) sits a little uneasily alongside guideline 7 of the *Re P* guidelines which states that there must be a "serious risk [Knowles J emphasis] that, without the imposition of the restriction, the child or primary carers will be subject to unacceptable strain". Correctly applied to a child's circumstances, section 91A(2) gives a court greater latitude to make section 91(14) orders than the *Re P* guidelines so. Thus, in coming to my decision in this case, I have applied the new statutory approach to harm set out in s91A(2) rather than guideline 7 of the Re P guidelines and, in so doing, I have adopted the ordinary civil standard of proof. That course is consistent with the modern approach of the Court of Appeal in *Re A* as outlined above.

I observe that section 91A(3) introduces a narrower definition of harm which applies to a child or other individual who has reached the age of 18, namely that harm is to be read as a reference to ill-treatment or to the impairment of physical or mental health. The explanatory notes to the Domestic Abuse Act 2021 provide that this narrower definition has been used because, in contrast, the definition in section 31(9) of the Children Act 1989 encompasses elements specific to a child, such as the impairment of development.'[63]

15.103 The next year Hayden J considered s 91A in *F v M:*

'The provisions within Section 91A are transformative. The section provides a powerful tool with which Judges can protect both children and the parent with whom they live, from corrosive, demoralising and controlling applications which have an insidious impact on their general welfare and wellbeing and cause real emotional harm. This amended provision strikes me as properly recognising the very significant toll protracted litigation can take on children and individuals who may already have been vulnerable, for a variety of reasons. It also dovetails with our enhanced understanding of the nature of controlling and coercive behaviour. When all other avenues are lost, too often the Court process becomes the only weapon available. Lawyers and Judges must be assiduous to identify when this occurs, in order to ensure that the Court is not manipulated into becoming a source of harm but a guarantee of protection.'[64]

15.104 Finally, HHJ Vincent considered s 91A in *Re A and B (No 3) (Domestic Abuse – no direct contact – s 91(14))*:

63 *A Local Authority v F & Ors* [2022] EWHC 127, [56]–[57].
64 *F v M* [2023] EWFC 5, [20].

'Drawing the statute, procedural rules and case law together, the approach to an application for a section 91(14) order can be summarised as follows:

a. If findings of domestic abuse are made, even if the victim did not apply for this relief, the court is now bound to consider whether or not to make a s91(14) order.

b. Whilst such an order is "the exception and not the rule," it does not follow that the case or its circumstances must somehow be adjudged to be "exceptional" before such an order could be made.

c. The court should bear in mind that such orders represent a protective filter – not a bar on applications – and that there is considerable scope for their use in appropriate cases.

d. Whether the court makes an order is a matter for the court's discretion. There are many and varied circumstances in which it may be appropriate to make such an order. These may include cases in which there have been multiple applications ("repeated and unreasonable"), but that is not a necessary prerequisite. They may also include cases in which the court considers that an application would put the child concerned, or another individual, at risk of harm (without the need to find the "risk" to be "serious" or the likely "harm" to be "significant" or "serious").

e. Subject to any inconsistency with the above, the *Re P* guidelines continue to apply.

f. If the court decides to make an order, it must consider:

   i. its duration, as to which, any term imposed should be proportionate to the harm the court is seeking to avoid, and in relation to which decision the court must explain its reasons;

   ii. whether the order should apply to all or only certain types of applications under the Children Act 1989;

   iii. whether service of any subsequent application for leave should be prohibited pending initial judicial determination of that application.

g. In all of this, the welfare of the child is paramount. That said, any interference with a parent's otherwise unfettered right of access to the court, including the duration of any such prohibition pending permission, must be proportionate to the harm the court is seeking to avoid.'[65]

PRACTICE POINT

Please note the really helpful suggestion to target and time the s 91(14) order specifically to the harm seeking to be prevented. Different types of risk to the child's stability/welfare may indicate the need for different time limits. Just because a s 91(14) order appears to be appropriate, the Court's thinking should not stop on a single application/timeline. An order prohibiting an application to change residence may justify a longer timeline than one directed to a review of contact for example.

65 *Re A and B (No 3) (Domestic Abuse – no direct contact – s91(14))* [2023] EWFC 192, [72].

The limitations of the law at this point

15.105 It has been observed that one of the difficulties with the original s 91(14) was the lack of any real guidance regarding the applicability and extent of s 91(14). With the advent of the DAA 2021, which sought to change the landscape in the way envisaged by the *Harm Report*, those difficulties are now ameliorated and practitioners, litigants and judges alike have extensive guidance.

15.106 Nonetheless, the deficiencies in the available guidance were highlighted by Cobb J (as he then was) in *Re P & N (Section 91(14): Application for Permission to Apply: Appeal)*, in which the Court observed that there was nothing in the Children Act 1989 or the FPR 2010 specifically prescribing how the Court should approach an application for permission to apply for a Children Act 1989 order following the imposition of a s 91(14) order.[66] The Court noted that a judge sitting in the Family Court generally enjoys a wide spectrum of procedure when determining applications under the Children Act 1989 *(Re B (Minors) (Contact)*[67]). The Court also concluded that Children Act 1989, s 1(1) and (3) do not apply to the application for permission to apply for an order, although the welfare of the child will be a relevant consideration.[68] The Court should, however, have some regard to the 'overriding objective' of family court process, and the obligations arising under FPR 2010, r 1 – in particular to deal with the application 'justly' and 'fairly', 'ensuring that the parties are on an equal footing' and 'saving expense'.

15.107 Sections 91(14) and 91A are now complemented by a Practice Direction within the FPR 2010; Practice Direction 12Q now provides the guidance which had been hitherto missing. Seeking to strike a balance between offering guidance without fettering the Court's discretion, Practice Direction 12Q should be a familiar guide to those working in this area of law.

Practice Direction 12Q – orders under Children Act 1989, s 91(14)

15.108 Practice Direction 12Q (PD12Q) of the FPR 2010 came into force in July 2022. This is an important Practice Direction for practitioners to be aware of and familiarise themselves with. The key principles set out in PD12Q do not seek to go behind or otherwise undermine the case law which has guided practitioners for a number of years; instead the guidance offered in the case law is to be considered in the light of Parliament's insertion of s 91A into the Children Act 1989.

66 *Re P & N (Section 91(14): Application for Permission to Apply: Appeal)* [2019] EWHC 421 (Fam).
67 *Re B (Minors) (Contact)* [1994] 2 FLR 1.
68 *Re B (Minors) (Contact)* (n 67), p 6: Butler Sloss LJ states: 'There is a spectrum of procedure for family cases from the ex parte application on minimal evidence to the full and detailed investigations on oral evidence which may be prolonged. Where on that spectrum a judge decides a particular application should be placed is a matter for his discretion.'

15.109 Whilst we encourage you to read the legislation itself, the main points are as follows. Firstly, PD12Q confirms the nature of s 91(14) orders, as argued in the *Harm Report*:[69] s 91(14) does not 'bar' a person from making applications to the Court, it prevents applications unless leave of the Court is obtained. In other words, s 91(14) allows the Court to *'filter'* applications it receives to best protect the *'interests of children'*.[70]

15.110 In recognition that each case is unique, PD12Q has allowed the Court the discretion to restrict an individual's ability to make court applications in 'many and varied ... circumstances'. In appropriate cases, a s 91(14) order would be made where a future application would put the child, or 'another individual', at a 'risk of harm'.[71] Paragraph 2.5 notes that 'another individual' is likely to be 'another person who has parental responsibility for the child and/or is living with or has contact with the child'; but, crucially, it is not limited to such individuals, leaving the scope of this term to judicial discretion.

15.111 Paragraph 2.3 builds upon the guidance in *Re P (A Child)*, the *Harm Report* and *Re A (A Child) (Supervised Contact) (Section 91(14) Children Act orders)* by setting out the types of cases where a s 91(14) order would be appropriate in more detail. Whilst the latter sources agreed that appropriate cases would include those where the individual's conduct had been inappropriate or abusive, and would not be restricted to cases where there was a history of repeated applications, para 2.3 of PD12Q lists these non-exhaustive circumstances:

- where the individual against which the s 91(14) application would apply has made 'repeated and unreasonable applications' to court;
- where 'a period of respite is needed following litigation';
- where 'a period of time is needed for certain actions to be taken for the protection of the child or other person';
- where the person's conduct merits an order to 'protect the welfare of the child directly, or indirectly due to damaging effects on a parent carer'. This conduct could include 'harassment, or other oppressive or distressing behaviour beyond or within the proceedings including via social media and e-mail, and via third parties'.[72]

15.112 Paragraph 2.4 further states that a s 91(14) order would be appropriate where a further court application by that individual is likely to be part of a pattern of 'coercive or controlling behaviour or other domestic abuse'.

15.113 It appears that the 'exceptionality' principle described by Butler Sloss LJ in *Re P (A Child)* no longer strictly applies to s 91(14) orders.[73] In fact, para 2.6

69 Ministry of Justice (n 2), p 128.
70 PD12Q, paras 2.1, 2.7.
71 PD12Q, para 2.2.
72 PD12Q, para 2.3.
73 *Re P (A Child)* (n 49), [41].

strongly encourages courts to consider s 91(14) orders in *any* proceedings where DA is *alleged* or *proven*, and para 2.7 states that 'there is considerable scope for their use in appropriate cases'.

15.114 Greater clarification was certainly given through PD12Q, but the judiciary's work isn't finished yet. At para 2.8 the Court is encouraged to 'consider case law for further guidance and relevant principles', suggesting that further guidance is to come.

Procedure

15.115 Several procedural points were confirmed or clarified. First, at para 3.1 it is confirmed that the Court may make a s 91(14) order of its own motion. If it does consider this at any point during proceedings, 'it should record this fact in an order, together with any related directions'. In addition to the Court, an application can be made by an individual, by or on behalf of the child(ren) involved or by 'another party to the application being disposed of'.[74] The application should adhere to FPR 2010, Part 18 procedural rules, be made on Form C2 or be made orally.[75]

15.116 Where an application is made, 'the court should also consider what opportunity for representations should be provided to the parties', relying on precedent for guidance and principles.[76]

15.117 As indicated in para 2, para 3.4 makes it clear that in cases featuring DA or a risk of harm which is alleged or proven, the judiciary should consider whether a s 91(14) order should be made very early on in proceedings. This consideration should encompass, 'whether any particular findings of fact will be needed to determine the section 91(14) application'. According to para 3.4 this order can only be made 'when disposing of another application under the Act', although the *application* can be made at any time.

15.118 Finally, if the Court decides to make a s 91(14) order, it must consider the following factors:

'a. the duration of the order (see section 4);

b. whether the order should cover all or only certain types of application under the 1989 Act;

c. whether service of any subsequent application for leave should be prohibited until the court has made an initial determination of the merits of such an application (see section 6). Such an order delaying service would help to ensure that the very harm or other protective function that the order is intended to address, is not undermined; and

74 PD12Q, para 3.2.
75 PD12Q, para 3.3.
76 PD12Q, para 3.5.

d. whether upon a subsequent application for leave, the court should make an initial determination of the merits of the application without an oral hearing (see section 6).'[77]

Duration

15.119 Sections 91(14) and 91A are silent on the duration of a s 91(14) order. The Court, therefore, has a discretion as to the appropriate duration of the order. Any time limit imposed should be proportionate to the harm it is seeking to avoid and the Court should explain its reasons for the duration ordered.

15.120 As indicated above, it is important for practitioners to note that orders pursuant to Children Act 1989, s 91(14) can attach to different orders for different durations: eg, an order pursuant to s 91(14) can be made in respect of applications for a 'lives with' order for five years and a 'spend time with' order for two years.

15.121 The decision of Harrison J in *Re A and T (Children) (Appeal: Duration of section 91(14) Order)* is a key read for practitioners.[78] In this decision, the Court – sitting on appeal – considered the current legal landscape with regards to not only the making of an order pursuant to s 91(14) but also factors to be taken into account when determining the appropriate duration of such an order.

Types of application

15.122 Sections 91(14) and 91A give a discretion to the Court as to the type of application that can be made under the 1989 Act subject to permission from the Court. If the Court decides to make a s 91(14) order, it should consider which types of application should be specified in the order, and explain its reasons.

Application for leave

15.123 An issue noted in *Re P & N (Section 91(14): Application for Permission to Apply: Appeal)*[79] was that there is nothing in the Children Act 1989 or the FPR 2010 prescribing how the Court should approach an application for permission to apply for a Children Act 1989 order following the imposition of a s 91(14) order.

15.124 PD12Q sets out more specific guidelines for this at Section 6. Firstly, the application should be made in accordance with the Part 18 procedure, subject to the following directions:[80] Form C2 must be used, which attaches both a draft of the application they seek to make and a witness statement which covers the

77 PD12Q para 3.6.
78 *Re A and T (Children) (Appeal: Duration on section 91(14) Order)* [2025] EWHC 3052 (Fam).
79 *Re P & N (Section 91(14): Application for Permission to Apply: Appeal)* (n 66).
80 PD12Q, para 6.1.

grounds for their application for leave and whether there has been a material change in circumstances since the s 91(14) order was made.[81] Although there does not have to have been a material change of circumstances, it is a factor the Court must consider.[82] A Section 7 report is not necessary since the order would only be to provide leave to make an application rather than determining if the direction itself would be appropriate.[83]

15.125 Generally, Part 18 rules on service apply. However, if the Court, when making the s 91(14) order, had decided that service would not take place until an initial determination of the merits of an application for leave had been made (in accordance with para 3(c) above), then service must wait until the Court directs for this to happen. If the Court makes an early determination without an oral hearing in line with its power under para 3(d), the applicant can request an oral hearing within seven days' notice of the Court's decision.[84] Should this request be made the Court must make directions for this hearing, including with regard to service (it can decide not to serve on the respondent).[85] This is particularly useful for practitioners to be aware of: serving unmeritorious applications prior to the determination of leave may amount to post-separation abuse and using court process as a tool in such malign conduct.

PRACTICE NOTE

A careful consideration and actioning of these guidelines is particularly important in the context of a case involving DA. The Court's attention should be drawn back to PD12J, and in particular para 37A, which provides:

> '37A.1 In every case where a finding of admission of domestic abuse is made, or where domestic abuse is otherwise established, the court should consider whether an order under section 91(14) of the Children Act 1989 would be appropriate, even if an application for such an order has not been made. Section 91(14) orders are available to protect a victim of domestic abuse where a further application would constitute or continue domestic abuse. A future application could be part of a pattern of coercive or controlling behaviour or other domestic abuse toward the victim, such that a section 91(14) order is merited due to the risk of harm to the child or other individual. The court should refer to Practice Direction 12Q for direction on section 91(14) applications and orders.'

By actively encouraging the Court to consider the making of a s 91(14) order in cases where DA is established, it is clear that Parliament intended for the courts and parties to give much greater consideration as to whether an order under s 91(14) is appropriate.

81 PD12Q, para 6.2.
82 PD12Q, para 6.4.
83 PD12Q, para 6.5.
84 PD12Q, para 6.6.
85 PD12Q, para 6.6.

Concluding remarks on s 91(14) orders

15.126 Following the aforementioned developments, and a growing awareness that litigation can be a form of DA or controlling and coercive behaviour, the threshold for the making of s 91(14) orders has been lowered, allowing for possible greater use from now onwards.

15.127 Perhaps the most encouraging development is that the Court now has a duty to consider making a s 91(14) order in all cases involving alleged or proven DA. Whilst falling short of being mandatory like other aspects of PD12J, it is nevertheless a step in the right direction.

PRACTICE NOTE

- Do not be afraid of an order pursuant to Children Act 1989, s 91(14).
- Ensure that any contemplation by the Court of such an order at an earlier hearing is properly recorded.
- Pursuant to para 2.6 of PD12Q, it is important to flag the potential need for an order pursuant to s 91(14) at the earliest opportunity.
- Ensure that the potential need for such an order is brought to the attention of any professional who is preparing a welfare report, whether that be pursuant to Children Act 1989, s 7 or s 37 or as part of a FPR 2010, r 16.4 guardian appointment.
- In your application make sure to address the practical considerations in PD12Q (para 3.6).

Ask yourself these questions when preparing an application for a s 91(14) order:

- Is it necessary for there to be a finding of fact?
- What is the extent of the harm relied upon? (s 91A(2)).
- Should CAFCASS/NYAS/etc be called upon to assist the Court in establishing the likely impact on the child or relevant person if the order was not made?

CONCLUDING REMARKS

15.128 In practice, the Family Court and those working within it do give particular consideration to PD12J at the earlier stages of proceedings but still approach the issue of DA in somewhat of a binary fashion in the later stages: would the alleged conduct, if proven, amount to a bar to contact between the child and the perpetrator? This rather simplistic approach perhaps indicates the point that many lessons are still to be learnt in the family justice system.

15.129 Welfare decisions in cases involving DA are not simple decisions. They require careful consideration – not only in respect of the child and the risk of further harm being occasioned to them, but also in respect of the victim. These careful decisions, whilst made by the Family Court, are informed by CAFCASS officers, social workers or other experts: it is vital that all of those involved in such decisions have a solid understanding as to the impact of DA on both the children and the victims involved with the inevitable consequence that the impact of DA must be considered as a part of any welfare evaluation.

15.130 The law provides practitioners and the Family Court with the tools required to deal with cases involving DA properly. We must not be afraid to use them.

Final Words

There are a few key points to pick up in closing. The first reaches back to the opening chapter which set out the history of the Family Court's approach to domestic abuse (DA). I now bring that up to date by reference to the speech given at the Association of Lawyers Conference (ALC) on 14 November 2025 by McFarlane P (who we now know will hand over the reins to his successor in April 2026). We, as he, also pay heed to the report of the Domestic Abuse Commissioner (DAC), *Everyday Business*, the first since its role was established by the Domestic Abuse Act 2021.[1] We have continued to be guided by our judiciary in cases handed down and by professional associations such as the Family Justice Council and CAFCASS. It will be interesting to see what the take of our incoming President of the Family Division will be and what they will do when their term begins in April 2026. The professional and personal agendas of the President direct (covertly or overtly) many a tectonic shift in priorities and focus. Family law does not stand still because the society it is designed to serve is an ever-changing community. Law and the practice of it must be capable of adaption if it is to offer effective protection for the vulnerable

My parting words address our welfare in the workplace as advocates because, I say openly, we are seriously impacted on by the work that we do for vulnerable parties and the struggles we face in an underfunded, often misunderstood, legal sector. My book, *We Set The Bar* will be published in April 2026.[2] It takes an unflinching look at the consequences of working within a shattered legal aid landscape whether we practice in crime or family or any of the other sectors that touch on injustice and pain. My co-author in this book, Ian, features in it as one of the people who have gifted me their narratives about their journey to, struggles at, and vision for Bar.

To those that read this book, take heed that it was written to share knowledge in a way not often seen in legal textbooks – it is a 'download' of decades of experience at the frontline of family law in court, written to share lessons learned rather than hold them close to increase our desirability in a competitive self-employed world. Being prepared to learn from one another and having a generous space to do it in is one the very best hallmarks of our profession. We lean into the camaraderie when feeling in need of support and advice – that is why I reached out and embraced colleagues who have relevant expertise that Ian and I do not – namely Michelle Heeley KC and Chloë Ashley; two principled and passionate practitioners in crime. So too, are Ian and I grateful to Anita Metha,

1 Domestic Abuse Commissioner, *Everyday Business, Addressing domestic abuse and continuing harm through a family court review and reporting mechanism* (October 2025), https://domesticabusecommissioner.uk/wp-content/uploads/2025/10/Everyday-Business-full-report-web.pdf.

2 J Delahunty KC, *We Set the Bar: Fighting for Equality, Empowerment and Change within the Legal Profession* (Bristol University Press, forthcoming, 2026), https://www.amazon.co.uk/We-Set-Bar-Empowerment-Profession/dp/1529221285; https://bristoluniversitypress.co.uk/we-set-the-bar.

a consummate professional specialising in complex financial family remedy and private law cases. Anita came in at the last minute to help us with the finance chapter when I faltered in confidence at the edit line.

Lastly, I pay my respect to Sir James Munby, former President of the Family Division who died, suddenly on 1 January 2026. He was a titan in family law. A man of moral clarity and compassion with intellectual vision and creative energy. He is already much missed. We will not see his like again and that is a huge loss to family law, our profession and the vulnerable families who come to us for assistance.

THE MCFARLANE ALC SPEECH

This was timely and apposite given the aim of this book and its contents. Our current President said that he had chosen to speak on this topic because getting DA 'right' in the Family Court has been a priority throughout his tenure as President. He flagged why that was so:

> 'The issue impacts on so very many of the cases that come before the court. A finding, or otherwise, of domestic abuse is likely to have a significant impact on the arrangements for the future safety and welfare of children and vulnerable parents. Yet, the forensic difficulties facing a court in engaging with and determining allegations of domestic abuse are complex. In terms of the court getting it "right", what is the test and who is to say? …'[3]

The President clearly sees Pathfinder courts as the way forward, being a 'far more appropriate and effective model for resolving disputes between separating parents, safely, in a less confrontational manner and with the voice of the child front and centre'.[4] His view is influenced by the courts' focus on the child, facilitated by the early provision of the Child Impact Report (CIR) prepared by CAFCASS, CAFCASS Cymru or a local authority. That, the President says, will enable the parties and the Court to look forward, 'through the lens of the child's own views and welfare needs'.[5] The President is clear that, 'addressing and engaging with any issues of domestic abuse is an integral part of the new model, and the CIR is expected to offer analysis and advice concerning domestic abuse, just as it does in relation to safeguarding more generally'.[6] The aim of the Pathfinder process (notably supported by the DAC) is that it is said to enable the Court and the parents to look to the future to become a problem-solvers – rather than looking backwards and 'picking over' highlights of the adults' dispute.

There are two issues which spring to mind when I read this. The first being – what quality assurance do we have in terms of the training of the authors of the CIR, given their report will be so fundamental to the future direction of family practice

3 Sir Andrew McFarlane, 'Domestic Abuse and the Family Court', Association of Lawyers for Children Annual Conference, 14 November 2025, https://www.judiciary.uk/speech-by-the-president-of-the-family-division-domestic-abuse-and-the-family-court/ .

4 Sir Andrew McFarlane (n 3).

5 Sir Andrew McFarlane (n 3).

6 Sir Andrew McFarlane (n 3).

fairness, and how much interview/investigation time have they been permitted to invest in the work required to make the CIR a document that provides the framework for future planning? I say that given that trust and confidence in the approach taken to DA by previous report authors is not at its highest. By way of example, too often it has been CAFCASS, through its appointed children's guardian, who has not enabled the child's experiences, wishes and feelings to be expressed in the child's own words and the impact of the DA and CCB on the adult victim and the child has been poorly appreciated – hence revised guidance published in October 2024, with CAFCASS saying the new policy was needed because 'errors in judgment persist, with terrible consequences for child and adult victims'. CAFCASS Chief Executive, Jacky Tiotto, stated that, as an organisation, it is 'intent on eliminating practice that isn't good enough'.[7]

In addition, too often it has been CAFCASS recommending or supporting 'expert' assessments in alleged alienation/CCB/DA cases in place of a Finding of Fact Hearing – often presenting the names of non-accredited 'specialists' to do the work that should be the province of the Court. I say this from personal and anecdotal experience over many years. How much damage has been done by the use of them in the past is unknown. I note the call made in October 2025 by the incoming Victims Commissioner, Claire Waxman, that a review be conducted of all cases in which unregulated psychologists have been used with potentially devastating consequences for the children and their parents brought within their reach of influence. We are hungry for statistical analysis of conduct and outcomes in the lower courts where the vast majority of these cases are heard.

We now see light on the horizon with the new CAFCASS *Domestic Abuse Practice Policy*, which actively, and positively, engages with both the caveats I posed above. There is now a express acknowledgment of the interplay between DA/CCB and alleged alienation. The relevance and seriousness of sexual abuse for both the adult victim and the child who is part of that adult dynamic is properly acknowledged. Previous (erroneous) minimisation of 'historic' abuse is now firmly addressed and the policy specifically says that non-accredited, non-regulated psychological 'experts' are to be avoided.

Looking forward to 2026, our current President, in his ALC speech, flagged the imminent publication of two documents in January: *President's Practice Guidance: Protective Orders under the Family Law Act 1996*; and the Family Justice Council, *Best Practice Guidance for Practitioners on making an application for a Protective Injunction*.[8] They have not yet been seen at the time of writing.

We are told the new President's Practice Guidance will entirely replace the 2023 guidance and that these materials will include two important new templates:

7 CAFCASS, *Domestic Abuse Practice Policy* (October 2024), https://www.cafcass.gov.uk/media/1943; Bureau of Investigative Journalism, 'Cafcass Issues New Rules to Protect Abuse Victims in Family Court System' (16 October 2024) https://www.thebureauinvestigates.com/stories/2024-10-16/cafcass-issues-new-rules-to-protect-abuse-victims-in-family-court-system.

8 Sir Andrew McFarlane (n 3).

- an example model witness statement in support of an application for protective injunction; and
- a model template injunction order (using plain, simple and non-legal language).

MacFarlane P heralded a way to tackle local variance under the current scheme in relation to 'without notice' hearings. His new guidance will remind courts that, when deciding whether it is 'just and convenient' to make an order without notice, the Court's approach must be informed by a modern understanding of DA, referring to the modern definition set out at Domestic Abuse Act 2021, s 1, with its specific reference to CCB and psychological, emotional or economic abuse. He announced 'a radical change' in that the new guidance must be followed in every court centre.

That has got to be helpful I suggest.

I hope that we, as a profession, and our judiciary, will learn from the October 2025 publication of the *Everyday Business* report from the DAC, Dame Nicole Jacobs, which addressed the issues of DA and continuing harm through a family court review and reporting mechanism.[9] The 'review and reporting mechanism' involved in-depth research, led by Professor Mandy Burton and Professor Rosemary Hunter KC (Hon), looking at a significant number of court files and observing court hearings at three dissimilar court centres across England and Wales. The report was also based upon the testimony of survivors who were identified by local DA support groups in the three court areas and who met the researchers in focus group sessions. The researchers found DA in 87 per cent of the closed files they reviewed and in 73 per cent of the live cases that they observed.

MacFarlane P said of its statistics:

> 'those figures are strikingly different to the national data for England produced by CAFCASS which put the average degree to which domestic abuse was alleged in private law children proceedings at 60 % of cases, and the more general working assumption that I have had that the issue is raised in two thirds of cases.'[10]

He also acknowledged the 'good number' of complaints by court users about:

> 'the very negative experience that they had each had in proceedings related to domestic abuse before the Family Court. The complaints recorded in the report are striking and of concern, in equal measure.'[11]

Dame Nicole Jacobs' overall conclusion was that, post the seminal *Harm Report*, there is 'a disturbing truth: that the level of change remains largely unfulfilled'.[12] The report found evidence of a continuing 'pro-contact culture' and a 'failure

9 Domestic Abuse Commissioner (n 1).
10 Sir Andrew McFarlane (n 3).
11 Sir Andrew McFarlane (n 3).
12 Domestic Abuse Commissioner (n 1).

to recognise abuse', which 'contributed to decisions that may have put children in harms way'.[13] A clear theme of the accounts given in the focus groups of those who alleged abuse was that they were dissuaded from raising allegations as, they were advised, it would have no sway over whether the alleged abuser would in the end be granted contact. The researchers also found evidence of an outdated understanding of DA amongst some legal professionals who saw physical violence and sexual abuse as more serious than CCB despite the latter often underpinning other more physical abuse.

I recognise that disquiet from the work I have done in court and outside it since 2021.

It is correct, as the current President said, that 'in terms of training, every single judge and magistrate who is authorised to sit in the Family Court was offered focused, and in terms of the judges extensive, training on domestic abuse and it remains a fixed element in every refresher course'.[14] That is as it must be. Magistrates undertake a significant volume of this work as do lower tribunal judges. But it is often towards those courts that most criticism is directed as to the adequacy of their understanding of this complex area of work and its outcomes – controversial though that may be it cannot be countered when the decision-making of these courts is the least visible of all judicial forums.

Back in 2021 we had evidence that supported Dame Jacobs' flag of concern regarding practice in the lower courts. In a survey of practitioners undertaken by the University of Sussex, very significant concerns were identified regarding the ability of Tier 1 judges to manage cases of DA fairly.[15] Lack of transparency bedevils a true understanding of the existence and scale of the problem. The cases are heard in private. Few accredited bloggers or journalists attend them. We have no library of decisions made by lower courts uploaded on any portal. There are very few appeals from lower courts for the many reasons that we identified in our submissions of behalf of our successful appellant client to the Court of Appeal in *Re T* back in 2021.[16] We argued that a better scrutiny of decisions was required and, in any event, frontline practitioner experience was (and is) that the appeal process is poorly placed to identify and correct errors. For litigants-in-person, navigating the appeal rules and time frames and identifying points of law presents real difficulties. Publicly funded parties are, usually, represented by relatively junior advocates given the low-level fees. The appeal process is inaccessible because public funding isn't available without counsel's opinion on appeal and that opinion is usually not capable of being secured without a transcript which, in itself, can rarely be obtained within the time frame for appeal

13 Domestic Abuse Commissioner (n 1).

14 Sir Andrew McFarlane (n 3).

15 University of Sussex, *Practice Direction 12J, What is the experience of lawyers working in private law children cases?* (11 February 2020), https://www.transparencyproject.org.uk/press/wp-content/uploads/FJQC-Sx-University-Report-of-Survey-FINAL-11th-feb-2020.pdf .

16 The legal team comprised myself, Chris Barnes, Adele Cameron-Douglas of 4PB chambers, instructed by Jenny Beck of Beck Fitzgerald in *Re H-N & Os (Children) (Domestic Abuse: Finding of Fact Hearings)* [2021] EWCA Civ 448.

and without cost. For privately funded parties, the appeal process is inaccessible because it carries a cost risk.

Appeals are not a window into the approach to cases in the lower courts, nor the lack of them a benchmark of success. I note that the President said, in his ALC speech:

> 'I have, in the ordinary course of my Presidential ramblings, visited a number of courts. At each, I have raised the report with the local district judges, who, with the magistrates, hear many of these cases. None of the judges I have met recognise the scenario described by those who have spoken of their experience of the Family Court to the DAC's team.'[17]

However, for my part I do not think we can be reassured by self-report and I stand by Dame Nicole Jacobs' research and analysis.

I note that Mc Farlane P told the ALC that 'as President, I welcome the publication of [the DAC] report'.[18] If it is his role, 'as President … to accept the research findings of [it] and redouble our efforts to ensure that all judges and magistrates have a full understanding of issues of domestic abuse and approach the cases by affording paramount consideration to the welfare of the child, through an holistic evaluation' then it is also our duty to do so to as a profession.[19]

Hurrah to that.

The DA family system is rightly now under scrutiny. We, as advocates, must take responsibility when we have failed to assist the process for clients as they were entitled to expect.

We, as lawyers, are not required to undertake accredited training before taking on this complex work, which can involve the most serious categories of abuse, such as anal and oral rape, and attempted strangulation. The FLBA/ Bar Council training on vulnerable witnesses is not compulsory – there is a good case for making it so.

AND SO – ARE WE NEARLY THERE YET? HAVE WE GOT THE DA FAMILY JUSTICE SYSTEM THE PUBLIC DESERVE AND THE PROFESSIONALS WORKING IN IT WANT?

No, but we have gone up a gear with the appointment of the DAC and the new President's guidance as well as that of CAFCASS, looks promising. I welcome the acknowledgment that DA is a scourge on society that must be tackled and not minimised.

As the President eloquently said:

> 'Domestic abuse, where it occurs, is likely to be the all-pervasive factor which takes over the life of the victim and all family members. Coercive

17 Sir Andrew McFarlane (n 3).
18 Sir Andrew McFarlane (n 3).
19 Sir Andrew McFarlane (n 3).

> and controlling behaviour, has many elements akin to grooming, may well involve 24 hour a day, 7 day a week, dictatorial domination of a victim, so as to sap any sense of autonomy or freedom from them. The psychological and emotional impact of such sustained abuse, is likely to have a longer and more profoundly negative impact on the victim than any but the most severe physical or even sexual abuse. Such physical or sexual abuse is but part of the overall coercive and controlling environment that totally surrounds the victim. Any child of the family unit who lives in that environment will be just as much a victim, and will be harmed. Domestic abuse is totally intolerable in the context of an intimate family relationship and is responsible for pervasive and damaging harm to children and adult victim.'[20]

The authors of this book unreservedly agree.

SIGNING OFF THIS BOOK: MY THANKS AND, FINALLY, REFLECTIONS ON HOW BETTER TO SURVIVE OUR COMPLEX WORKING WORLD

This book has had a long gestation, having been commissioned by our patient and skilled publisher, Kiran Goss, in 2021, when she first approached me to write it after learning of my work in *Re T* within *Re H-N & Ors* and the judicial and professional training I devised and delivered along with Jenny Beck KC (Hons) that followed.

As I've prefigured, the writing task was so daunting that it couldn't have been undertaken without morphing into a collective of skilled, dedicated and experienced colleagues at the Bar. Ian, Michelle and Chloë were pulled in and, last but not least, we added Katie Tooley, a young ambitious legal researcher aspiring to the Bar, to the team to help us through the final surge. And then Anita Mehta came through and delivered at my last minute request to cast her expert eye over the financial chapter.

The camaraderie and patience that has sustained us during the unrelenting graft required to write the text has been in sharp contrast to the drop in morale at the legally aided Family Bar seen in the same period.

Never has the divide between wealth and wellbeing at the Family Bar been so evident; whether in the barristers and solicitors who undertake the bulk of the DA work, dependent on legal aid or low rates of pay extracted from client savings or family loans to pay them (poorly) for complex and contentious work; or in the public that come to court, approaching those same lawyers with a mixture of hope and desperation, underpinned by deep distrust in the fairness of the court process.

We owe those lawyers credit and thanks for the work they do to help some of our most vulnerable members of our society survive a family justice system dependent on overburdened court staff and judges working hard to keep a broken-down system going after decades of underfunding.

20 Sir Andrew McFarlane (n 3).

For those that do invest in – and benefit from – well paid, privately funded litigation, another danger looms: that of litigation warfare not client welfare.

Too often, sitting as a Recorder, appearing as a silk, or being consulted by a junior, I am exposed to reams of correspondence filed with the Court purporting to be 'evidence' and where competing clients and firms argue about whose letters are culled if the judge properly insists on a 350-page bundle. Why? The content of the correspondence is not evidence. The correspondence is not written by a direct participant or witness. Even when written as a record of first report, the tone is often as lacking in balance as the contents. The veiled (and sometimes open) threats about conduct and costs set the bar too high to permit client climb down or civilised client mediation. Barristers can, regrettably, take on the mantle of their case. Competing draft orders exchanged (or rather fired) in email volleys after a hearing, deepen the path of attrition, wearing down patience and energy. Enough of this.

Every lawyer should be familiar with and apply Resolution's Codes of Good Conduct.[21] There is a specific one for correspondence. It is sad that it was needed, sadder still that it can sometimes seem to be guidance more honoured in the breach than the observance. Its tenets are not hard to understand. In order to comply with the Code, correspondence should be:

- constructive, informative and effective;
- without emotive or inflammatory language;
- easily understandable, without jargon or complicated language.

As Resolution says:

> 'The use of emotive and inflammatory language will antagonise the recipient and damage the relationship between the parties. This needs to be avoided, particularly when children are involved. Drafted well, correspondence can reduce conflict and help to achieve an early settlement. In extreme cases the court can deem the correspondence to be unreasonably hostile and inflammatory and amount to litigation misconduct, leading to costs penalties for your client, or you/your firm.'[22]

This is not a new issue. Over 30 years ago it was recognised as poor practice. In the case of *F v F*,[23] Holman J condemned the first letter written on behalf of the husband, which set the tone for all that followed in a highly adversarial case. He commended the initial letter written on behalf of the wife and quoted it in full in his judgment. I have relied on that principle in cases in which I have appeared or sat because with the clear professional codes we now have at our disposal there is no excuse for failure to engage with one's opponent with civility and respect when writing to them.

21 Resolution, *Good Practice Guide to Correspondence*, https://resolution.org.uk/good-practice-guides-and-guidance-notes/good-practice-guide-to-correspondence/.

22 Resolution (n 21), p 1.

23 *F v F* [1996] 1 FLR 833.

Rude, hostile or bullying behaviour is as inappropriate in court as it is in correspondence. September 2025 saw the publication of the Baroness Harriet Harman KC *Review on Bullying and Harassment at the Bar*.[24] As she said 'this was a moment of reckoning'.[25] Her key recommendations include mandatory anti-bullying and anti-harassment standards, policies and training that are consistent across the profession. The Bench is not immune from, nor above, critical scrutiny, and the conduct of some judges fell well below the standards to be expected from those who take a judicial oath to serve justly and fairly.

We set out the purpose of this book in its preface. We said it was designed to be a trigger point for learning, reflection and discussion, its core message being that 'we cannot be bystanders to poor practice'. That message goes to the heart of how to survive this contentious area of the law. We must hold our colleagues at the Bar, fellow solicitors and judges to account for conduct and practice that falls below the standards set by statute, rules, case law, guidance and codes of conduct.

All lawyers have a duty to assist the Court as well as to assist their client.

Private law is not an island within the family world.

The most important sentiment of the authors of this book, one that led them to collaborate and write it, is echoed in the closing words of the President in his ALC address:

> 'The criminal and family courts will continue to deal with the fall out where domestic abuse has occurred, but the message needs to be that this behaviour should not be tolerated by any person in society. It is harmful, it is dangerous, indeed, it can, tragically, be deadly, for both adult and children. It needs to stop.'[26]

Quite simply, we have to do better for more vulnerable children and parents.

We must be better trained, better read and more emotionally intelligent when taking on these complex cases.

We assist no one by making court litigation a war of attrition or crisis management. It has a toxic effect on parents and professionals alike that is poisonous not just in the courtroom but also infects private spaces. Well-prepared clients, whose expectations are acknowledged and managed is the key to a well-run and well-presented case. Good mannered case conduct aids resolution of issues outside of court and proportionate, child-focused litigation within it. Aspire to both. The judge will thank you for it.

Good luck.
JDKC
1 December 2025

24 Baroness Harriet Harman KC, *Independent Review of Bullying, Harassment and Sexual Harassment at the Bar* (Bar Council, September 2025), https://www.barcouncil.org.uk/static/8ae513e7-07e2-4b20-b49c1c8dbbfa1377/563cbd91-791f-4ce0-9aa12600331609c8/Report-master-file-6.pdf.

25 Bar Council, 'Independent review into bullying and harassment unveils "radical" reforms to tackle "unsustainable situation" at the Bar' (Press Release, 8 September 2025), https://www.barcouncil.org.uk/resource/independent-review-into-bullying-and-harassment-unveils-radical-reforms-to-tackle-unsustainable-situation-at-the-bar-press-release.html.

26 Sir Andrew McFarlane (n 2).

IN MEMORIAM: SIR JAMES MUNBY 1948–2026

Former President of the Family Division (2013–2018); a Lord Justice of Appeal (2009–2013), Privy Councillor and Chair of the Law Commission (2009–2012).

We learned yesterday of the untimely death of Sir James on New Year's Day, aged 77. The outpouring of grief at that news was striking but totally befitting the titan at the Bar and Bench that James was. In rereading these chapters today I was struck by how many times his decisions are mentioned within its pages and how they have stood the test of time. His colossal intellect was matched by his curiosity about human nature and (counterintuitively one might say) his lack of moral judgment concerning its flaws. He was a humane and kind person who never lost sight of the people impacted upon by his decisions. He had a moral clarity and compass that was rare. He was prepared to speak out about injustice and would not stand by to permit it to happen when seized of the chance to make change. To me he was a mentor, friend and champion of 25 years' standing. I cannot yet contemplate the reality of not being able to plunder the richness of his intellect and compassion, and I am not the only one to feel his loss keenly. James' influence on law, legal practice and its vulnerable, reluctant participants was profound. He will be missed.

Bibliography

Advisory Board on Family Law: Children Act Sub-Committee, *A Report to the Lord Chancellor on the Question of Parental Contact in Cases where there is Domestic Violence* (HMSO, 2000)

The Advocate's Gateway https://www.theadvocatesgateway.org

'Alienating Behaviour' (Courts and Tribunals Judiciary) https://www.judiciary.uk/related-offices-and-bodies/advisory-bodies/family-justice-council/resources-and-guidance/parental-alienation/

Al-Othman, Hannah, 'Dangerously outdated': high court overturns ruling implying domestic violence would not affect children' (*The Guardian*, 28 October 2025) https://www.theguardian.com/law/2025/oct/28/dangerously-outdated-high-court-overturns-ruling-implying-domestic-violence-would-not-affect-children

Association of Lawyers for Children, *Comments and response to the Family Justice Council's draft guidance entitled 'Covert Recordings in Family Law Proceedings Concerning Children*' (12 December 2022) https://www.alc.org.uk/uploads/images/FJC-Covert-recordings-ALC-response-2.pdf

Attorney General Guidelines on Disclosure 2013 (Gov.uk, 2013) https://www.gov.uk/government/publications/attorney-generals-guidelines-on-disclosure-2013

Bar Council, 'Independent review into bullying and harassment unveils "radical" reforms to tackle "unsustainable situation" at the Bar' (Press Release, 8 September 2025), https://www.barcouncil.org.uk/resource/independent-review-into-bullying-and-harassment-unveils-radical-reforms-to-tackle-unsustainable-situation-at-the-bar-press-release.html

Baroness Harriet Harman KC, *Independent Review of Bullying, Harassment and Sexual Harassment at the Bar* (Bar Council, September 2025), https://www.barcouncil.org.uk/static/8ae513e7-07e2-4b20-b49c1c8dbbfa1377/563cbd91-791f-4ce0-9aa12600331609c8/Report-master-file-6.pdf

British Psychological Society, *Psychologists as Expert Witnesses in the family courts in England and Wales: Standards, competencies and expectations* (May 2022) https://www.judiciary.uk/wp-content/uploads/2022/05/Psychologists-as-Expert-Witness-in-family-courts-in-England-and-Wales-standards-competencies-and-expectations-.pdf

Bureau of Investigative Journalism, 'Cafcass Issues New Rules to Protect Abuse Victims in Family Court System' (16 October 2024) https://www.thebureauinvestigates.com/stories/2024-10-16/cafcass-issues-new-rules-to-protect-abuse-victims-in-family-court-system

CAFCASS, *Child Impact Assessment Framework (CIAF)* https://www.cafcass.gov.uk/professionals/our-resources-professionals/child-impact-assessment-framework-ciaf

CAFCASS, *Domestic Abuse Practice Policy* (January 2026), https://www.cafcass.gov.uk/domesticabuse-practice-policy.

CAFCASS, *Understanding why a child does not want to spent family time with a parent: A guide to assessment* (August 2025) https://www.cafcass.gov.uk/sites/default/files/2025-07/Understanding%20why%20a%20child%20does%20not%20want%20to%20spend%20family%20time%20with%20a%20parent.pdf

Callaghan J E M, Alexander J H, Sixsmith J and Fellin L C, 'Beyond "witnessing" Children's Experiences of Coercive Control in Domestic Violence and Abuse' (2018) 33(10) Journal of Interpersonal Violence 1551–81

Courts and Tribunals Judiciary, *President's Guidance on Allocation and Gatekeeping for Proceedings under Part II of the Children Act 1989 (Private Law)* (judicary.uk, 2014) https://www.judiciary.uk/wp-content/uploads/2013/02/private-law-allocation-and-gatekeeping-guidance.pdf.

Courts and Tribunals Judiciary, *Schedule to the Allocation and Gatekeeping Guidance* (judicary.uk, 2014) https://www.justice.gov.uk/documents/schedule-to-allocation-and-gatekeeping-guidance.pdf

Crown Prosecution Service, 'Offences against the Person, incorporating the Charging Standard' (last updated October 2024) https://www.cps.gov.uk/legal-guidance/offences-against-person-incorporating-charging-standard

Department of Health, *Secure Futures for Women: Making a Difference* (London, 2002)

Devaney J, 'Research Review: The Impact of DA on Children' (2015) 12 Irish Probation Journal 79–94

'Domestic Abuse Act 2021: Overarching Factsheet' (Gov.uk) https://www.gov.uk/government/publications/domestic-abuse-bill-2020-factsheets/domestic-abuse-bill-2020-overarching-factsheet

Domestic Abuse Commissioner, 'Domestic Abuse Commissioner responds to the removal of the presumption of parental involvement' (October 2025), https://domesticabusecommissioner.uk/domestic-abuse-commissioner-responds-to-the-removal-of-the-presumption-of-parental-involvement/

Domestic Abuse Commissioner, *Everyday Business* (October 2025) https://www.gov.uk/government/publications/everyday-business-addressing-domestic-abuse-in-the-family-court/everyday-business-addressing-domestic-abuse-and-continuing-harm-through-a-family-court-review-and-reporting-mechanism

'Domestic abuse in England and Wales: year ending March 2018' (Office for National Statistics, 2018) https://www.ons.gov.uk/peoplepopulationandcommunity/crimeandjustice/bulletins/domesticabuseinenglandandwales/yearendingmarch2018

Doughty J, Maxwell N and Slater T, *Review of Research and Case Law on Parental Alienation* (April 2018) https://gov.wales/sites/default/files/publications/2018-05/review-of-research-and-case-law-on-parental-alienation.pdf

'Family Court Statistics Quarterly: January to March 2025' (Gov.uk, June 2025) https://www.gov.uk/government/statistics/family-court-statistics-quarterly-january-to-march-2025/family-court-statistics-quarterly-january-to-march-2025#domestic-violence-remedy-orders

Family Justice Council, *Draft Covert Recordings in Family Law Proceedings Concerning Children: Family Justice Council Guidance* https://www.nagalro.com/_userfiles/pages/files/covert_recording_guidance_for_consultation_final_91122.pdf

Family Justice Council, *Family Justice Council Guidance on Covert Recordings in Family Law proceedings concerning children* (May 2025) https://www.judiciary.uk/wp-content/uploads/2025/05/Covert-recordings-in-Family-Law-proceedings-concerning-children-Family-Justice-Council-Guidance.pdf

Family Justice Council, *Family Justice Council Guidance on Neurodiversity in the Family Justice System for Practitioners* (January 2025) https://www.judiciary.uk/wp-content/uploads/2025/01/Family-Justice-Council-Guidance-on-Neurodiversity-in-the-Family-Justice-System-for-Practitioners.pdf

Family Justice Council, *Family Justice Council Guidance on responding to a child's unexplained reluctance, resistance or refusal to spend time with a parent and allegations of alienating behaviour* (December 2024) https://www.judiciary.uk/wp-content/uploads/2024/12/Family-Justice-Council-Guidance-on-responding-to-allegations-of-alienating-behaviour-2024-1-1.pdf

Family Justice Council, *Interim Guidance in relation to expert witnesses in cases where there are allegations of alienating behaviours – conflicts of interest* (May 2022) https://www.judiciary.uk/wp-content/uploads/2022/05/FJC-interim-Guidance-use-of-experts-in-cases-with-allegations-of-alienating-behaviours.pdf

Family Justice Council Consultation, *Draft guidance on Responding to allegations of alienating behaviour* (August 2023)

Family Law Bar Association, *The Role of the Qualified Legal Representative in Family Court Proceedings* (July 2023) https://www.alc.org.uk/uploads/images/QLR_doc_v3.pdf

Fricker, HHJ, 'Molestation and Harassment after Patel v Patel' [1988] Fam Law 395

Gardner R, 'Recent trends in divorce and custody litigation' (1985) 29(2) Academy Forum 3–7

'Gaslight (1944 Film)' (Wikipedia) https://en.wikipedia.org/wiki/Gaslight_(1944_film)

Herring J, *Domestic Abuse and Human Rights* (Cambridge University Press, 2021)

Hester M, 'Who does what to whom? Gender and domestic violence perpetrators in English police records' (2013) 10 European Journal of Criminology 623–37

Holt S, Buckley H and Whelan S, 'The impact of exposure to domestic violence on children and young people: A review of the literature' (2008) 32 Child Abuse and Neglect 797–810

Home Office, *Controlling or Coercive Behaviour: Statutory Guidance Framework* (Home Office, 5 April 2023) https://assets.publishing.service.gov.uk/media/642d3f9e7de82b00123l364d/Controlling_or_Coercive_Behaviour_Statutory_Guidance_-_final.pdf

Home Office, *Domestic Abuse – Statutory Guidance* (July 2022) https://assets.publishing.service.gov.uk/media/62c6df068fa8f54e855dfe31/Domestic_Abuse_Act_2021_Statutory_Guidance.pdf

Information Commissioner's Office, 'Step 4: Access Necessity and Proportionality' https://ico.org.uk/for-organisations/uk-gdpr-guidance-and-resources/childrens-information/childrens-code-guidance-and-resources/dpia-tools/online-retail/step-4-assess-necessity-and-proportionality/

Jones, P, 'DA victim characteristics, England and Wales: year ending March 2023' (Office for National Statistics, 24 November 2023) https://www.ons.gov.uk/peoplepopulationandcommunity/crimeandjustice/articles/domesticabusevictimcharacteristicsenglandandwales/yearendingmarch2023

Judicial College, *Equal Treatment Bench Book* (July 2024, updated May 2025)

Judiciary of England and Wales, *President's Memorandum: Witness Statements* (2021) https://www.judiciary.uk/wp-content/uploads/2022/07/PFD-memo-on-witness-statements-12112021.pdf

Law Commission, *Family Law, Domestic Violence and Occupation of the Family Home* (Law Com No 207, 1992)

London Safeguarding Children Procedures, 'Safeguarding Children Affected by DA and Violence' (2016) https://www.londonsafeguardingchildrenprocedures.co.uk/sg_ch_dom_abuse.html

Lucy R, 'Domestic Abuse Act 2021 – What does it mean for Family Courts and the people using them?' (*Transparency Project*, May 2021) http://www.transparencyproject.org.uk/domestic-abuse-act-2021-what-does-it-mean-for-family-courts-and-the-people-using-them/?fbclid=IwAR0rcNRMjwva-1ytqt7iCwfLCKdPiaDwRpDzi4GCPIBVcE98OlOpa7R7Xms

McLeod D, *Coercive Control: Impacts on Children and Young People in the Family Environment* (Research in Practice, 2018) https://www.researchinpractice.org.uk/media/ybkc4pea/coercive_control_impacts_on_children_and_young_people_in_the_family_environment_literature_review_2018.pdfhttps://www.researchinpractice.org.uk/media/ybkc4pea/coercive_control_impacts_on_children_and_young_people_in_the_family_environment_literature_review_2018.pdf

Ministry of Justice, *Assessing Risk of Harm to Children and Parents in Private Law Children Cases* (Final Report, 2023)

Ministry of Justice, *DA and Private Law Children Cases: A Literature Review* (Ministry of Justice Analytical Series, 2020)

Ministry of Justice, 'Government action to protect children from abusive parents' (Press release, 22 October 2025) https://www.gov.uk/government/news/government-action-to-protect-children-from-abusive-parents

Ministry of Justice, *Review of the Presumption of Parental Involvement Final Report* (October 2025), https://assets.publishing.service.gov.uk/media/68f5f5c206e6515f7914c7e3/Review_of_the_Presumption_of_Parental_Involvement_Final_Report_.pdf

Ministry of Justice, *Statutory Guidance: Qualified Legal Representative appointed by the court* (updated June 2024) https://assets.publishing.service.gov.uk/media/665ef0d98f90ef31c23ebdb0/Qualified_legal_representative_appointed_by_the_Court_Statutory_guidance.pdf

Ministry of Justice, 'Thousands of children protected from abuse under victim reforms' (gov.uk 20 October 2025) https://www.gov.uk/government/news/thousands-of-children-protected-from-abuse-under-victim-reforms

Mullender A, *Tackling Domestic Violence: Providing Support for Children Who Have Witnessed Domestic Violence* (London: Home Office, 2005)

Myhill A, 'Measuring domestic violence: context is everything' (2017) 1(1) Journal of Gender-Based Violence 33–44

President of the Family Division, *Fact-finding hearing and domestic abuse in private law children law proceedings – Guidance for Judges and Magistrates* (2022) https://www.judiciary.uk/guidance-and-resources/fact-finding-hearings-and-domestic-abuse-in-private-law-children-proceedings-guidance-for-judges-and-magistrates/

President of the Family Division, *Family Court Duration of Ex Parte (Without Notice) Orders,* Practice Guidance (January 2017)

President of the Family Division, *Practice Guidance: Non Molestation Injunctions under the Family Law Act 1996* (July 2023) https://www.judiciary.uk/wp-content/uploads/2023/07/Practice-Guidance-Non-Molestation-Injunctions.pdf

President of the Family Division, *President's Memorandum: Experts in the Family Court* (October 2021) https://www.judiciary.uk/wp-content/uploads/2021/10/PFD-Memo-Experts.pdf

Resolution, *Domestic Abuse in Financial Remedy Proceedings* (Resolution, 2024) https://resolution.org.uk/wp-content/uploads/2024/10/Resolution_DAFRP_Report_ONLINE.pdf

Resolution, *Good Practice Guide to Correspondence*, https://resolution.org.uk/good-practice-guides-and-guidance-notes/good-practice-guide-to-correspondence/

Resolution, *Good Practice Guide to Working with Litigants in Person* (2024) https://resolution.org.uk/wp-content/uploads/2024/10/GPG2024_WorkingWithLitigantsInPerson_Sept2024_24-09-24.pdf

Right to Equality, 'Ending the Presumption of Contact in Courts' (May 2024), https://righttoequality.org/wp-content/uploads/2024/05/Presumption-of-Contact-Report-14-May-2024-.pdfhttps://righttoequality.org/wp-content/uploads/2024/05/Presumption-of-Contact-Report-14-May-2024-.pdf

Secretary of State for the Home Department, *Transforming the Response to DA: Consultation Response and Draft Bill* (Cm 15, ISBN 978-1-5286-0923-4, 2019)

Senior Coroner for Birmingham and Solihull, *Regulation 28 Report to Prevent Future Deaths* (Coroner's Report, 2022)

Sir Andrew McFarlane, President of the Family Division, 'A View from The President's Chambers' (November 2022) https://www.judiciary.uk/guidance-and-resources/a-view-from-the-presidents-chambers-november-2022/

Sir Andrew McFarlane, President of the Family Division, 'A View from The President's Chambers: July 2023' (2023) https://www.judiciary.uk/guidance-andresources/a-view-from-the-presidents-chambers-july-2023/

Sir Andrew McFarlane, President of the Family Division, 'Domestic Abuse and the Family Court', Association of Lawyers for Children Annual Conference, 14 November 2025, https://www.judiciary.uk/speech-by-the-president-of-thefamily-division-domestic-abuse-and-the-family-court/

Sir Andrew McFarlane, President of the Family Division, *The Family Court and COVID 19: The Road Ahead*, https://www.judiciary.uk/wp-content/uploads/2020/06/The-Road-Ahead_FINAL.pdf

Smith L, *Children Experiencing Inter-Parental Coercive Control* (The Institute for Research and Innovation in Social Services (IRISS), 2018) https://www.iriss.org.uk/sites/default/files/2018-04/iriss-esss-outline-children-experiencing-interparental-coercive-control-2018-3-19.pdf

Stanley N, *Children Experiencing Domestic Violence: A Research Review* (Research in Practice, 2011) https://www.researchinpractice.org.uk/media/zssp0cum/children_experiencing_domestic_violence_signpost_summary.pdf

Stark E, *Coercive Control: How Men Entrap Women in Personal Life* (2nd edn, New York: Oxford University Press, 2023)

Strickland P, *Labour Policy on Domestic Violence – 1999-2010* (House of Commons Library Standard Note SN/HA/3989, 2012) https://researchbriefings.files.parliament.uk/documents/SN03989/SN03989.pdf

Sturge C and Glaser D, 'Contact and domestic violence – the experts' court report' (2000) 30 Family Law 615–29

Transparency Project, *Parents Recording Social Workers – A Guidance Note for Parents and Professionals* (2015) https://www.transparencyproject.org.uk/press/wp-content/uploads/2016/05/Whymightparentswanttorecordmeetingsv2jan16.pdf

University of Sussex, *Practice Direction 12J, What is the experience of lawyers working in private law children cases?* (11 February 2020), https://www.transparencyproject.org.uk/press/wp-content/uploads/FJQC-Sx-University-Report-of-Survey-FINAL-11th-feb-2020.pdfhttps://www.transparencyproject.org.uk/press/wp-content/uploads/FJQC-Sx-University-Report-of-Survey-FINAL-11th-feb-2020.pdf .

Victims Commissioner, 'Domestic abuse victims are being failed by the criminal justice system at every stage' (22 January 2025) https://victimscommissioner.org.uk/news/domestic-abuse-victims-are-being-failed-by-the-criminal-justice-system-at-every-stage/

Wallerstein J S and Kelly J B, 'The effects of parental divorce: Experiences of the child in later latency' (1976) 46(2) American Journal of Orthopsychiatry 256–69 https://doi.org/10.1111/j.1939-0025.1976.tb00926.x

'What is Domestic Abuse?' (United Nations) https://www.un.org/en/coronavirus/what-is-domestic-abuse

Index

[All references are to paragraph numbers.]